LOIS WEBER IN EARLY HOLLYWOOD

The publisher gratefully acknowledges the generous support of the Ahmanson Foundation Humanities Endowment Fund of the University of California Press Foundation.

Lois Weber in Early Hollywood

SHELLEY STAMP

UNIVERSITY OF CALIFORNIA PRESS

University of California Press, one of the most distinguished university presses in the United States, enriches lives around the world by advancing scholarship in the humanities, social sciences, and natural sciences. Its activities are supported by the UC Press Foundation and by philanthropic contributions from individuals and institutions. For more information, visit www.ucpress.edu.

University of California Press
Oakland, California

Library of Congress Cataloging-in-Publication Data

Stamp, Shelley, 1963– author.
  Lois Weber in early Hollywood / Shelley Stamp.
    pages cm
  Includes bibliographical references and index.
  ISBN 978–0-520–24152–7 (cloth : alk. paper)
  ISBN 978–0-520–28446–3 (pbk. : alk. paper)
  ISBN 978–0-520–96008–4 (ebook)
    1. Weber, Lois, 1879–1939. 2. Weber, Lois, 1879–1939—Criticism and interpretation. 3. Motion picture producers and directors—Biography. 4. Women motion picture producers and directors—United States. 5. Women in the motion picture industry—United States. 6. Silent films—History. I. Title.
  PN1998.3.W4S73 2015
  791.4302′3309—dc23
[B]
                                                        2014031384

24 23 22 21 20 19 18 17 16 15
10 9 8 7 6 5 4 3 2 1

Contents

Acknowledgments

Cari Beauchamp once said that those of us studying women film pioneers nurture attachments to "dead girlfriends." Lois Weber has certainly served that role in my life these past many years. But I have also been thankful countless times for a network of living friends and colleagues who helped so much, in so many different ways, during the long process of writing this book.

Little could have been achieved without funding, and I am grateful for generous support from the National Endowment for the Humanities, the Academy of Motion Picture Arts and Sciences, and the University of California President's Research Fellowship in the Humanities. The University of California, Santa Cruz, also provided funding through the Arts Research Institute, the Committee on Research, and the Arts Dean's Excellence Fund.

Many archivists and librarians aided my quest to find extant prints of Weber's films and other materials related to her career. Pride of place must go to Madeline Matz, now retired from the Library of Congress, Motion Picture, Broadcasting and Recorded Sound Division. Madeline's knowledge and passion for early women filmmakers has fueled many projects over the years, and I was very fortunate to benefit from her guidance early on. Thanks also to Madeline's colleagues Rosemary Hanes, Christel Schmidt, Kim Tomadjoglou, and George Willeman. Close behind Madeline is Barbara Hall, former Head of Special Collections at the Margaret Herrick Library at the Academy of Motion Picture Arts and Sciences. Barb is a researcher's dream: unfailingly generous, widely knowledgeable, and eager to publicize the rich resources of her collections. She and Val Almendarez shared their encyclopedic knowledge of other LA-area resources as well. Barb's predecessor at the Herrick, Scott Curtis, helped introduce me to the library's Weber materials. Also extremely helpful were Jan-Christopher Horak, Mark Quigley, and Jim

Friedman at the UCLA Film and Television Archive; Elif Rongen-Kaynakçi at EYE, the Nederlands Filmmuseum; Bryony Dixon and Nina Harding at the British Film Institute; Fumiko Tsuneishi at the National Film Center in Tokyo; Virginia Callanan at the New Zealand Film Archive; and Annette Melville at the National Film Preservation Foundation in the U.S. Mariann Lewinsky Sträuli, my comrade-in-arms for the Weber retrospective at Il Cinema Ritrovato, deserves tremendous credit for her help unearthing extant prints in European archives. Staff at the New York Public Library for the Performing Arts, and in the Rare Books and Manuscripts Division of the New York Public Library, were also very helpful, as were librarians at the Los Angeles Public Library, the state censorship archives in Pennsylvania, and Ned Comstock at USC's Cinematic Arts Library. John Canning of the Allegheny City Society helped fill in the picture of Weber's early years there.

Among the many generous colleagues who read or discussed this research with me, I am particularly grateful to Mark Lynn Anderson, Mark Garrett Cooper, Charlie Keil, Judith Mayne, Anne Morey, Gaylyn Studlar, and Jane Gaines, cheerleader-in-chief. Many others provided feedback and encouragement along the way: Ally Acker, Kay Armatage, Constance Balides, Jennifer Bean, Cari Beauchamp, Caetlin Benson-Allott, Martin Berger, Vicki Callahan, Liz Clarke, Monica Dall'Asta, Leslie Midkiff DeBauche, Mary Desjardins, Victoria Duckett, Annette Förster, Christine Gledhill, Hilary Hallett, Amelie Hastie, Maggie Hennefeld, Laura Horak, Jennifer Horne, Antonia Lant, Michele Leigh, Denise McKenna, April Miller, Christie Milliken, Charles Musser, Diane Negra, Jennifer Lynn Peterson, Lauren Rabinovitz, Laura Isabel Serna, Amy Shore, Art Simon, Dan Streible, Drake Stutesman, Yvonne Tasker, Kristen Anderson Wagner, Haidee Wasson, Kerrie Welsh, Mark Williams, Tami Williams, Kristen Whissel, and Paul Young. I am especially indebted to Eric Smoodin for his early faith in the project.

One of the unforeseen benefits of working on this project so long is that many people came to know I was interested in Weber and sent me items they came across in their own research or helped me get access to far-flung materials. Thanks especially to Richard Abel, Diana Anselmo-Sequeira, Rob Byrne, Scott Curtis, William M. Drew, Kathryn Fuller-Seeley, Lee Grieveson, Mark Johnson, Hiroshi Komatsu, Richard Koszarski, Luci Marzola, Sawako Ogawa, Jessica Rosner, Eric Schaefer, Scott Simmon, Pamela Skewes-Cox, Marilyn Slater, Hank Soboleski, Greg Waller, Marc Wannamaker, and especially Martin F. Norden, who was unstintingly generous in sharing his many Weber-related finds. Peter Gantz, Weber's stepson, and Rick Snaman, her second cousin, were both exceptionally generous in sharing invaluable information about her family tree.

Help from research assistants made this massive undertaking much more manageable. Sirida Srisombati provided extraordinarily proficient and enthusiastic research in both Santa Cruz and Los Angeles at the outset of the project. Logan Walker stepped in later on with his characteristic quiet efficiency, organizing and digitizing my research collection with great skill and care. Dave Gurney proved an able ally in Chicago, and Eric Hoyt was my enterprising surrogate in LA.

Scholarly gatherings helped launch and sustain this work, particularly the 1999 conference Gender and Silent Cinema, coordinated by Eva Warth and Annette Förster in Utrecht; the conference Women and the Silent Screen, which Amelie Hastie and I organized at UC-Santa Cruz in 2001; and subsequent meetings in Montréal, Guadalajara, Stockholm, Bologna, and Melbourne, as well as the Doing Women's Film and Television History conferences in England. Colleagues at these groundbreaking events provided indispensable sounding boards, methodological models, research tips, and inspiration.

I must also thank a group of truly remarkable colleagues and students in the Film and Digital Media Department at UC–Santa Cruz for providing such a warm and supportive working environment. At or with the University of California Press, Mary Francis, Kim Hogeland, Bradley Depew, Rachel Berchten, and Steven Baker have been incredibly dedicated and helpful.

Friends in Santa Cruz distracted me at just the right moments. Elizabeth Abrams, Gabriela Arredondo, Noriko Aso, Jennifer González, Miriam Greenberg, Kirsten Silva Gruesz, Cat Ramírez, and Alice Yang are an inspiring group of academic women and fellow moms whom I am proud to call my friends. Lots more fun was had with my other mom comrades— Cherie Barkey, Chesa Caparas, Sumita Jaggar, Ashley Spencer, Marie Stephen, Tam Welch, Maureen Wyland, and so many others.

By helping take care of my kids, Lado Adlakha contributed as much to this book as any archivist or fellow scholar. Her energy and creativity allowed me valuable hours to work, though, quite honestly, there were times when I would much rather have taken a nap. My parents, Arlene and Bob Stamp, always curious about my findings, bought old copies of Motion Picture for me one rainy afternoon when they found Weber featured in several issues.

Beto Byram came into my life just as I began to embark on this project and has supported it unfailingly ever since. Sean, Evan, and Clare joined us somewhere in the middle. What love and joy—and noise—they've brought to my time outside the archive.

Figure 1. Lois Weber at her typewriter. Courtesy of Bison Archives.

Introduction

Portrait of a Filmmaker

Consider this portrait of Lois Weber, early Hollywood's preeminent female filmmaker. Sitting outdoors at her typewriter, shoulders draped in a shawl, Weber appears hard at work on one of her screenplays. The sharp focus of her attention, the intense concentration etched on her face, renders the image immediately compelling. Hands poised above the keyboard as if in midstroke, eyes fixed on the page before her, Weber seems gripped by creative energy. Quotidian details of her writing practice are evident all around her—pens and pencils overflowing from their container, leather satchel lying nearby, books and papers close at hand, ready for quick consultation. What is she writing? One of her films or a script that might never have been completed or shot? Perhaps she is at work on one of the novels or plays she aspired to write, projects for which no other traces survive. What were her writing habits? Did she write daily or only in short bursts during preproduction? Did she often write outdoors? The image, in fact, grounds Weber's creative labor in the solitary act of writing, rather than her more collaborative—and better-known—work directing and acting. Here, the photograph commands us to believe, is where her films come to life. Above all, the portrait is compelling for the way it makes visible the work of one of early Hollywood's leading filmmakers, equally fascinating because it seems to capture the ever-elusive, mental labor of screenwriting, and because it foregrounds the contributions women made to early Hollywood, working behind the scenes sitting at their typewriters, wielding megaphones, directing players, and running studios.[1]

Yet the promise this photograph seems to offer is subverted by a series of other, lesser-known views apparently taken during the same photo session in 1926. In an alternate pose, Weber is shown with a younger woman sitting at the typewriter, possibly an assistant or secretary. Weber might be

Figure 2. An alternate vision of the female filmmaker. Courtesy of Bison Archives.

dictating letters or script changes. In this second portrait Weber's authority is clear, for she stands above the other woman, overseeing her activities, but her creativity is less evocatively rendered. Indeed, the whole scene now seems forcibly staged—Weber's slightly outturned ankle, the shawl cast over her shoulders, the table placed in the garden. It now looks like nothing more than a contrived fantasy of California living where one might work outdoors year-round, or of trailblazing Hollywood where women could pursue novel occupations. Assumptions we have built around the first image no longer hold. Is it Weber's own satchel and desk in the photo, her own typewriter, her own backyard? Is she, in fact, writing anything at all or simply posed behind the machine? Weber, after all, did not actually write at a typewriter, preferring to hold a pencil and pad on her knee. Two additional portraits, also evidently taken that same day, make increasingly obvious the effort undertaken—on both sides of the camera—to stage women's contributions to early moviemaking. They highlight the performative dimension of women's work in an industry dominated, even then, by the idea that women belonged in front of the camera, not behind or beside it.

Figure 3. Two additional poses at the same scene. Courtesy of Corbis Images.

The challenge of discerning what these images, any images, have to say about Lois Weber encapsulates the larger challenge of tracing a history of women's contributions to the fledgling motion picture industry. Discovering that a seemingly privileged glimpse of Weber's creativity is staged in no way discounts the reality of her career as a director, screenwriter, and performer. It simply reminds us of how hard this work is to see or trace. It reminds us of how views of female filmmakers, in particular, are often clouded by ideas of glamour and stardom, how the importance of being seen always figures in their working life. It reminds us of what little documentation exists outside this sphere of performative labor, how bound we are as historians to look at the public persona of our subjects, especially if they are women. It captures the challenges of narrating the career of an artist who left behind no papers, no diaries, no memoir, and whose professional life must be reconstructed entirely through ephemeral traces, many of them staged for publicity purposes, as these photos evidently were. And, finally, the pull these photographs exert testifies to the strength of our own libidinal investments as historians, so eager for evidence of women's contributions to early moviemaking that we willfully misread a contrived portrait as a genuine vestige of creative enterprise.

Lois Weber is a notorious blind spot in American film history. Among early Hollywood's most renowned filmmakers, considered one of the era's "three great minds" alongside D. W. Griffith and Cecil B. DeMille, her career has been marginalized or ignored in almost every study of silent cinema and Hollywood history, while her contemporaries have long enjoyed privileged positions as "fathers" of American film. Of all the women active in the first decades of moviemaking, Weber produced the most sustained and substantial body of work. She spent more than twenty-five years in the industry, writing and directing more than forty features and more than one hundred shorts. Weber's career, in fact, mirrors the development of Hollywood itself. After getting her start in New York working with Edwin S. Porter at the Rex Motion Picture Company, she arrived in Los Angeles in 1913, just as film production began to coalesce there in and around the city. After Rex was absorbed into the powerful Universal Film Manufacturing Company, Weber began working within the emergent studio system, serving as mayor of the sprawling new Universal City complex and soon thereafter becoming the studio's top director and the first woman inducted into the Motion Picture Directors' Association. An early advocate for the craft of screenwriting and a proponent of trained actors in films, she was among the first directors associated with quality feature filmmaking in the mid-1910s. Weber left Universal to form Lois Weber Productions in 1917, among the vanguard of directors striking out on their own in the postwar years. If initially lucrative distribution contracts with First National and Paramount signaled the promise of independent production and a recognition of the artistry of individual filmmakers, this illusion was short-lived. Lois Weber Productions ultimately fell victim to increased vertical integration as a few powerful studios consolidated control of the movie business. Struggling to find work in the late 1920s and early 1930s, Weber encountered challenges faced by women in a profession that was becoming ever more "masculinized." Where her feminine decorum had once served to enhance the industry's cultural capital, by the Jazz Age it had become a liability. Still, Weber weathered the transition to sound production in the late twenties, making a final feature in 1934 and remaining active after most of her generation had stopped working.

Weber's career thus maps the arc of American cinema's evolution from a series of companies scattered throughout the country churning out thousands of one- and two-reel shorts each week, to a massive, capitalized industry based in Hollywood and controlled by a few names still dominant in today's media landscape. Her career also maps the shift from an era when women's participation in moviemaking was valued, even eagerly sought, by an industry vested in improving its reputation, to a period when women's creative contributions were marginalized, derided, and ultimately largely forgotten.

Even within this narrative Weber's career stands out. At a time when many remained wary of cinema's cultural impact, she made hugely successful and wildly controversial films on key issues of her day. Weber's engagement with Progressive politics set her apart from contemporaries like Griffith and DeMille who sought to legitimate the new art by aligning it with highbrow culture, leaning on literary, historical, and biblical adaptations to lend cinema some legitimacy. Taking an opposite tack, Weber viewed motion pictures as "living newspapers" capable of engaging popular audiences in debates about the most deeply provocative subjects. She wrote and directed narrative features advocating abolition of capital punishment and legalization of birth control, while drawing links between urban poverty and women's wage equity. She also found script ideas in less sensational, though equally compelling, questions surrounding religious hypocrisy, undervalued educators and clergy, gossip mongering, celebrity culture, and consumer capitalism. Weber's work consistently grappled with the profound changes in women's lives, and consequently in male-female relationships, that unsettled Americans at the beginning of the twentieth century. She recognized that her films might intervene in contemporary debates, not only through on-screen stories depicting social problems like poverty, criminality, and addiction, but also by featuring female characters in complex leading parts that resisted two-dimensional stereotypes like "ingénue," "flapper," or "wife." As her career progressed, Weber became increasingly conscious of Hollywood's role in constructing and circulating popular images of women, and she became all the more determined not only to write better parts for women on screen but to speak out against Hollywood's narrowing imagination of gender norms.

If Weber understood cinema's social impact as a "voiceless language," she also recognized its visual impact as a storytelling medium. Collaborating with a host of pioneering cinematographers including Dal Clawson and Arthur C. Miller, Weber experimented with dissolves and superimpositions, matte shots and choreographed camera movements, sophisticated lighting techniques, and location shooting both indoors and out, producing some of the more subtle cinematic effects of her era. From her Rex days onward, critics noted the fine visual storytelling Weber employed in her films. Although she often spoke of screenwriting as her primary enterprise—the arena where she laid out themes, patterns, and characters—her films demonstrate a remarkable attention to visual detail and a notable ability to visualize interior psychology. A talented performer in her own right, Weber also mentored actresses such as Mary MacLaren, Mildred Harris, Claire Windsor and Billie Dove, directing them in mature parts she wrote especially for them. Throughout her career she paid particular attention to both the craft of acting, often underappreciated in the medium's formative years, and the limited roles that women were frequently asked to play onscreen.

Renowned for her films, Weber also became one of the first celebrity filmmakers, famous in a way that virtually no other director was at the time. Weber's relationship with her husband, Phillips Smalley, was a central facet of this publicity early on. The couple's working partnership was often featured as a model for ideals of companionate marriage emerging in American culture; at the same time, their collaborative endeavors became a way of packaging Weber's image as a professional woman working in an industry principally conceived as masculine. Her reputation as a filmmaker renowned for producing quality films on subjects of social and historical import, unquestionably associated with respectability, was fostered as much through publicity materials focused on her status as a married, middle-class woman as it was on the films themselves. Toward the end of her career, however, Weber was increasingly isolated as Hollywood's "only" female filmmaker, a designation that marginalized her work and consigned her to the lowly rank of a "woman's filmmaker." As she had used her feminine "respectability" to bolster popular perceptions of the film industry early in her career, Weber became more vocal in later years about the difficulties of working in a business that was becoming hostile to female directors and unremittingly narrow in its vision of women on screen. Weber's gender, always central to her public persona, became a growing liability toward the end of her working life.

Lois Weber in Early Hollywood thus uses the filmmaker's career as the nexus for a larger investigation of nascent Hollywood—its institutional structures, its celebrity culture, its evolving visual grammar, and its ever more dominant role in American daily life. By tracing the career of the silent era's most prominent female filmmaker, the study also seeks to broaden our understanding of the extraordinary role that women played in shaping early film culture, a story just now beginning to be told.[2] Examining how Weber's films navigated Progressive politics and changing gender roles, and how censorship controversies and celebrity culture complicated discourses around women's labor in the early industry, the study ultimately demonstrates how female filmmakers who once served Hollywood's bid for respectability were written out of that industry's history early on.

Chapter 1 examines Weber's early career, demonstrating how the shorts she made at Rex interrogate gender norms, marital tropes, and, most reflexively, the circulation of mass-produced images of women in popular media. Read against Weber's evolving public persona as a married, middle-class, professional woman, Weber's shorts demonstrate the contradictory position she enjoyed in the early movie business—at once an emblem of respectability useful in the industry's bid for cultural cachet and a potent agent of cultural and political change. Weber also used her growing celebrity to draw attention to the evolving craft of screenwriting, calling for greater complexity and variation in movie plots and more nuanced characterization. In doing so, she shifted attention away from the roles she played onscreen toward her work as a screenwriter and director. Moving to Bosworth, Inc., in 1914, Weber took advantage of early opportunities for feature filmmaking by writing and directing a series of films notable not only for the way they engage contemporary notions of "quality" filmmaking but also for the way they foreground her distinctly feminine mode of authorship, epitomized by the handwritten signature "Yours Sincerely, Lois Weber," inscribed at the outset of *Hypocrites* (1915), the film that established Weber's reputation as one of the leading filmmakers of her day.

Chapter 2 investigates the period of Weber's greatest renown, when as the top director at Universal she demonstrated cinema's capacity to engage topical issues for popular audiences. In *Shoes* (1916) Weber examined urban poverty and women's wage equity, fostering viewers' empathy with an impoverished heroine in a way that traditional reform tracts could not. But Weber's penchant for provocative subjects also drew the attention of the gatekeepers of culture. Dogged by censorship battles, her birth control films, *Where Are My Children?* (1916) and *The Hand That Rocks the Cradle* (1917), demonstrate the challenges cinema posed to the country's shifting media terrain. Weber's image as a respectable married woman helped to temper the controversies that swirled around her social-problem films, even as media profiles of her working relationship with her husband furnished templates for both companionate marriage and new relations between men and women in the workplace.

After her success at Universal, Weber formed her own independent company, Lois Weber Productions, the focus of Chapter 3. At her own studio Weber moved away from the social-problem films that had made her famous, opting instead for more intimate films on domesticity and sexuality. Weber sought to challenge popular "sex comedies" with more nuanced studies of marriage and consumer culture told from a woman's point of view. Yet her evolving image as a "star maker" for young actresses began to obscure her accomplishments as a screenwriter and director, not to mention the labor and talent of performers she mentored. Under such a rubric women's aspirations in Hollywood were reduced solely to looking beautiful and being famous. Weber's network of relationships with female peers inside and outside the industry, as well as feminist clubwomen throughout the country, was undercut by the idea that her work as director and screenwriter might simply be reduced to the task of turning other women into stars. Increasingly pigeonholed as Hollywood's "only" female director during these years, Weber was celebrated for her ability to cater to female moviegoers, who now dominated at the box office, while she was simultaneously marginalized for producing "women's pictures." Such limited perceptions of her work effectively blunted the sharp critique of heterosexual marriage and consumer capitalism at the heart of her mature films.

Chapter 4 looks at Weber's later career, demonstrating not only that she remained active throughout the 1920s but that she actively resisted what was happening to women such as herself who had pioneered creative roles in the industry, and to a newer generation of female performers now reduced to playing nothing more than decorative accessories on screen. Persistently vocal about both the difficulties she faced as a female filmmaker and the limited roles offered to women on-screen, Weber wrote and directed a series of films that complicated perceptions of the "flapper," that dominant icon of Jazz Age femininity. Although she continued to play a highly visible role in the industry, including an instrumental position in the early days of the Academy of Motion Picture Arts and Sciences, Weber became more marginalized as Hollywood began to chronicle its own history. Before her career was even over, Weber was effectively written out of the story.

In the end, then, this is a study as much about Weber's public persona as it is about her films. It is as much about Weber's legacy as it is about her career. Her films cannot be considered in isolation from her evolving celebrity, for both are essential to understanding women's place in early Hollywood. Nor can her career be considered without reference to her legacy of marginalization in dominant histories of American filmmaking. In fact, these two elements of Weber's history are interrelated. Understanding her career in relation to the evolving discourse on women's work in early Hollywood helps explain her subsequent absence from histories of American filmmaking. If the image of Weber at her typewriter ultimately tells us little about her working life, save its performative dimension, perhaps the portrait remains compelling for the way it mirrors the historian's own enterprise—sitting alone at her keyboard, deep in concentration, surrounded by files and papers, a bag at her side, creating a "story" of her own. A story not of loss and forgetting, but of possibility.

1 Creating a Signature

Weber's 1915 feature *Hypocrites*, the film that secured her place among the foremost filmmakers of her generation, opens with a still photograph showing her elegantly dressed, posed against a chaise lounge, eyes cast sideways out of frame. A handwritten signature across the corner proclaims, "Yours Sincerely, Lois Weber." Although viewers would have been accustomed to seeing favorite screen personalities introduced in opening vignettes, it was unusual to see a filmmaker so visibly embodied in her own production. A title card has already announced that *Hypocrites* was "written and produced by Lois Weber." By adding her photograph and the trace of her signature across the screen, Weber asserts full authorial control over *Hypocrites*. And she does so in a manner that is distinctly feminine and distinctly bourgeois. Certainly this brief prologue tells us just how far Weber had come after a few short years in the motion picture business, evolving from an unknown actress working behind the scenes, writing and directing her productions, to a filmmaker of commanding authority whose personal signature guaranteed quality cinema. But the prologue also tells us a great deal about how Weber negotiated the terrain of feminine propriety, how keenly aware she was of the need to embody and visualize her femininity within and around her own work. Indeed, Weber evolved a highly public persona in the early years of her career, quite unique for a filmmaker in this era. She used this persona to demonstrate a distinctly feminine mode of authorship and artistry in the new art form.

Weber entered the movie business at a time of significant transformation, her early career fueled by developments of the transitional era, some of the most far-reaching in U.S. film history. Single-reel films, which had dominated the market since late 1908, were being replaced with longer offerings of two, three, and even four reels, signaling the growth of more intricate storytelling and more nuanced demands on audience attention, and paving ground for feature-length titles. As films grew in complexity, scenario writing became a more valued and better understood component of filmmaking, and acting for the screen a more nuanced art. Independent production companies, such as Rex and later Universal, became viable alternatives to the powerful Motion Picture Patents Company (known as the Trust), which had attempted to monopolize film production and distribution. Los Angeles became the center of U.S. film production, and enormous new facilities like Universal City showcased the evolution of moviemaking there, while also signaling a growing standardization of film production in factory-like studio settings. An energetic and vocal trade press helped stabilize and solidify the industry throughout this period, while also providing an increasingly sophisticated discourse on aesthetic aspects of moviemaking. Cinematography, performance style, and storytelling were evaluated with considerable nuance during these years. New fan magazines and regular newspaper coverage of films and filmgoing culture put movies and movie stars at the forefront of the nation's cultural imagination. Industry leaders made a concerted effort to woo middle-class patrons, and motion pictures became, for the first time, the preferred recreation for most Americans.[1]

Even as Weber's career flourished in the burgeoning movie business, her work sometimes challenged dominant filmmaking norms emerging at the time. Working at Rex with founder Edwin S. Porter and her husband, Phillips Smalley, Weber honed a collaborative, artisanal mode of production that she would retain throughout most of her career, long after it had fallen out of favor, replaced by the highly rationalized, highly stratified Hollywood studio model. Even in the early 1910s Weber's approach to filmmaking remained out of step with a general drive toward greater standardization and formula. Weber also embraced her growing celebrity as a female filmmaker, assuming leadership roles first at Rex and then as mayor of Universal City, and speaking out for "better" pictures and quality scenarios. Publicity at the time attempted to position her as a matronly embodiment of refinement behind the scenes—and subsequent historians have also aligned her with this cause—but a closer look at her comments on screenwriting and, especially, at her films reveals a much more radical approach to filmmaking than simple feminine uplift. What emerges is a body of work at Rex and Bosworth in which complex, well-developed, often unconventional female characters dominate, and in which institutions like marriage and the family are interrogated. In Weber's case, the reality of a feminine hand, so desired in the industry at the time, was a near–wholesale rejection of popular female screen types. As Weber's own celebrity grew, she evidently became all the more aware of cinema's role in circulating, reformulating, and challenging feminine norms.

"MY LIFE WORK"

Details about Weber's early life are difficult to verify and come mainly from interviews and profiles published later in her career, but two distinct themes emerge from her recollections.[2] She grew up in a household that valued creativity and the arts; yet her early forays into professional life were marked by a persistent struggle against social expectations for "respectable" young women of her generation. Weber's passion for creative work and her determined efforts to challenge restrictive gender norms would inform her entire career, so it is not surprising that she stressed these elements of her upbringing when talking about it later in life.

Florence Lois Weber was born in Allegheny, Pennsylvania, in 1879, the middle daughter of George and Tillie Weber. Her older sister, Bessie, had been born two years earlier; their younger sister, Ethel, with whom Weber would remain especially close, joined them eight years later. Weber spoke with tremendous fondness about her father, an upholsterer and decorator who had worked on the Pittsburgh Opera House. "We were great pals," she said, recounting his talent for telling "fascinating fairy stories," his penchant for waking her up early to see the sunrise, and his obvious pride once she began writing stories of her own. When he finished his work on the opera house, "mine was the first opinion he wanted," she recalled with evident delight. To him she credited her artistic temperament and her talent for writing stories. "I don't remember when I did not write," she said. "Certainly I've written and published stories ever since I could spell at all." As a young girl Weber also had a flare for the dramatic, performing ballads at church and reciting historical narratives at school, often with significant embellishment. "I never studied," she explained, "but crammed at the 11th hour and dramatized the recitations of others. I was terribly impatient of book learning."[3]

Musical training was also an integral part of Weber's childhood, and at age sixteen she was already working as a concert pianist, sometimes touring with famed mandolinist Valentine Abt. She often told interviewers a story of how she had been startled one night when a piano key fell apart as she was playing. "The incident broke my nerve," she confessed. "When that key came off in my hand, a certain phase of my development came to an end."[4] After a brief stint back in Pittsburgh teaching kindergarten, Weber left again for New York City, eager for a career in light opera and armed with the address of a singing teacher given to her by a family friend. Her father did not approve, worried that the opera might lead her into the theater world he considered unsavory. But off she went nonetheless. "I was very green," she recognized later. "New York seemed a very large place to me."[5] Setting up camp at the YWCA on 124th Street, she discovered that her singing teacher had left town for the summer. Without much in the way of savings and with only one good dress to her name, Weber lived a meager existence before finding a post as an accompanist at a girls' school, taking a room across the street with two friends from the Y. She took up voice lessons in the fall when her teacher returned, moving to a boardinghouse in Greenwich Village where she received free room and board in exchange for playing piano for other tenants. Her sister Ethel visited and was apparently very impressed.

But after the girls' father fell ill, Weber was called back home to help support Ethel's schooling—crying "tears of ice" all the way, she remembered.[6] She offered to sing again in her church choir, but because she had appeared on stage, the deacons would not allow it. It is clear that, though for years associated with respectability and bourgeois refinement in her motion picture publicity, Weber's early independence and her dogged commitment to work on stage challenged reigning assumptions about what refined young ladies ought to do with their time. "If you have chosen a worldly career, don't pretend to be religious," her grandmother advised her, warning her against becoming a "hypocrite."[7] Weber's break came when an uncle who was a theater producer in Chicago helped get her into musical theater. He alone among her relatives supported her creative ambitions, and she recalled him telling her that folks "out West" were more "broad-minded" about careers for women—an impression that surely must have stuck. With her uncle's help Weber joined the Zig Zag Company and toured with them through Pennsylvania and New England for six months. "It does not require much effort of the imagination," one writer later declared, "to see the earnest, ambitious little concert singer of twenty-five years ago in the magnificently poised, vibrantly magnetic Lois Weber of today."[8]

To "atone" for her disreputable life in the theater, Weber explained, she spent much of her spare time engaged in missionary work, providing entertainment in prisons, hospitals, and military barracks, including penitentiaries on New York's famed Blackwell's Island, and working with impoverished women in the city's urban tenement districts. She was determined, it would seem, to challenge her grandmother's assumptions about the incompatibility of entertainment and religion. As a seventeen-year-old in

Pittsburgh Weber had joined a "church army" group that toured the city's red-light district with a small street organ and a hymnal—"a terrible experience for a young girl," she later recognized.[9] These encounters left a lasting impression on the filmmaker, for she later described how cinema, with its mass appeal, allowed her to overcome the limitations of working one-on-one with individuals, many of whom, she recalled, "spoke strange tongues." By contrast, cinema's "voiceless language" was a "blessing," a medium that allowed her to "preach to my heart's content."[10]

When work with the Zig Zag Company dried up, Weber joined a touring production of the popular melodrama *Why Girls Leave Home* in Holyoke, Massachusetts. There she met stage manager Phillips Smalley. As Smalley later recalled, he asked her to marry him the very next day, and they wed just three weeks later at her uncle's home in Chicago, though records indicate as many as three or four months elapsed between when the couple met and when they married.[11] Still, it was a hasty courtship. Weber was twenty-four at the time. Smalley, fourteen years her senior, had, according to one observer, "a certain well-built erectness of bearing; six foot in height; direct, brown eyes; sleek, black hair; his accent is slightly English, and his manner is the extreme of courtesy."[12] Several years later the couple had a daughter, Phoebe, who died in infancy, their only child, though Weber never spoke publicly about the episode.

Unlikely to find work together on the stage, Weber and Smalley initially decided to pursue separate engagements, and Weber soon found work singing at the New York Hippodrome. But after being advised by the actress Ellen Terry, a friend of Smalley's mother, never to separate from her husband, she declined the appointment and then, by her own recollection, spent two years on the road with him, writing scenarios in hotel rooms while he appeared on stage and waiting for her own opportunity.[13] Like many other women of her generation, she "first became interested in pictures through writing scenarios," as she put it. When she began to sell these stories, with but few connections in the business, Weber was delighted and "surprised . . . no little bit. Not that I doubted their meriting production," she confessed, "but I imagined they had to be introduced to the scenario editor by some person with influence. I was wrong, and the check I received testified to the illusion under which I had labored."[14]

To hear her describe it, Weber's start in the motion picture business was almost accidental. "To keep my mind off the horror of our first separation," she explained, "I went out to the Gaumont Talking Pictures. I wrote the story for my first picture, besides directing it and playing the lead. When Mr. Smalley returned . . . he joined me and we co-directed and played leads in a long list of films."[15] What is striking about this memory, apart from the offhanded way Weber characterizes her beginnings, is the fact that it was Weber, not Smalley, who initiated work in the movies, then still considered somewhat tawdry employment for theater folk; that she aimed to combine writing, directing, and acting from the start, not entirely uncommon for the time but still remarkable for its ambitious reach; and that Smalley followed *her* into the business, assisting Weber's far-reaching ambition from the outset. Indeed, Weber was forever grateful for the support her husband had shown in leaving his stage career to join her in the "movies," by all accounts a risky venture at the time. "My husband, who had a great deal of faith in me, left a splendid position on the dramatic stage, to act in [my scenarios]," she later recalled.[16] Dissatisfied with the material they were given to work with, Weber recounted her frustration with hastily thrown-together scripts containing weak characterizations and thin plots, "insipid in conception and pathetic in sentiment"—material that, even then, did not live up to her ideas about the medium's potential. "No amount of clever acting can redeem a character poorly drawn, or a play that is hopelessly deficient in plot and execution," she pronounced in retrospect. "So I began to write scenarios around the personalities of Mr. Smalley and myself. It was not such a difficult matter for one with my experience in legitimate and motion picture drama to improve on the scenarios of that period."[17]

Recollecting her time at Gaumont, Weber described an easy transition from writing to performing and directing, her tendency to take the lead evident early on: "I wrote, or rather devised, the story as we went along. There was no technique, no settled method or procedure, and no one had had much experience. . . . My principal task was to synchronize the plot with the words and music of the record. As I knew more about stories, or thought I did, than anyone there, I took charge of the directing. I played in the picture too, of course."[18] Weber's capacity for leadership and her desire to be fully engaged at all levels of production are obvious even in these earliest forays into motion picture work: she "knew more" than anyone else, "took charge" of directing, and "of course" acted in the productions as well. Her stage experience as a pianist and singer also seems to have served her well at Gaumont, where she made Chronophone films with synchronized sound-on-disk technology.[19] Alice Guy Blaché, also directing at American Gaumont during these years, later remembered only that Weber "recorded several songs" for the Chronophone. Weber's account, however, suggests that her responsibilities were far wider ranging. Curiously, Weber makes no mention of Guy Blaché. But the seasoned filmmaker, who had been directing for more than a decade at this point and was only a few years older than Weber, would likely have made a strong impression on the new-comer. As Guy Blaché remembered it, rather dismissively, Weber "watched me direct . . . and doubtless thought it was not difficult."[20]

In the end it was Guy Blaché's husband, Herbert Blaché, then in charge at American Gaumont, whom Weber remembered. He gave her "every encouragement," she recalled. "I was fortunate in being associated with broad-minded men. Both Mr. Smalley and Mr. Blaché listened to my suggestions." Recounting how the trio worked "in perfect harmony," she explained, "We brought our individual talents into an effective combination . . . [making] many original and successful photoplays."[21] Writing, performing, and directing, she was able to employ her gift for storytelling, her love of performance, and her ability to visualize entire imaginary worlds. After having been hampered by restrictive notions about careers that women ought or ought not to pursue, Weber must have been relieved to find such fulfilling work at Gaumont. "I grew up in the business when everybody was so busy learning their particular branch of the new industry," she later explained, "that no one had time to notice whether or not a woman was gaining a foothold."[22] However she got there, Weber had discovered her true calling. "In moving pictures I have found my life work," she pronounced in 1914. "I find at once an outlet for my emotions and my ideals."[23]

THE SMALLEYS AT REX

It was at the Rex Motion Picture Company that Weber and Smalley first became recognized as filmmakers of the first order. They joined the company in the fall of 1910, shortly after it had been formed by Edwin S. Porter and his partners, Joseph Engel, a theater owner, and William Swanson, a well-connected independent distributor and exhibitor. Porter, at this stage in his career, was considered "the dean of all producers," a man whose innovations had helped transform motion picture storytelling throughout the previous decade.[24] Like many who had worked for companies affiliated with the powerful Trust—Porter spent his early career at Edison—he branched out on his own as opportunities for independent production improved with the ever-accelerating demand for films. In fact, during the first year Rex was in business, the number of films made outside the Trust by independent companies tripled. They had numbered a mere twenty titles in September 1910 when Porter formed Rex, but jumped to sixty releases the following year. Starting modestly, Rex began with one studio in a rented floor atop a six-story building in New York. By early 1912, a little over one year later, the company occupied that entire building, now equipped with two complete studios and a third in preparation. Each studio was assigned its own producer and its own stock company of performers. Vast collections of props and scenery supported the outfit's productions.[25]

Weber and Smalley began work on Rex's second film, which was actually the first to be released: *A Heroine of '76*, the story of an innkeeper's daughter (played by Weber) who discovers a plot to assassinate George Washington and dies saving his life. With twenty films completed by February 1911, Rex began a weekly release schedule with a considerable backlog of titles, allowing it to release fifty-six films its first year. Within a year Rex had tripled in size, and in January 1912 the company began releasing two films per week.[26] "We worked very, very hard," Weber recalled of her time at Rex. "I wrote the scenarios, Mr. Smalley selected the types, assisted in directing, and we both acted." Indeed, Weber began writing one scenario per week shortly after the couple joined the company and continued this prodigious output for at least another three years. It is difficult to verify the exact number of films the couple made during this period, but one account suggested that by early 1914 Weber had already completed more than two hundred pictures.[27]

Beginning with *A Heroine of '76*, Rex titles were immediately celebrated for their artistic achievements, furnishing exhibitors with "quality of the dependable, consistent variety."[28] Rex films offered "the finest possible photographic technique, allied with a clear, convincing dramatic story, perfectly acted," according to *Moving Picture World*. Strongly written and carefully constructed narratives focused on a few well-defined characters marked Rex releases, not large-scale action and spectacle, demonstrating that it was "not necessary to out-Pathé or out-Selig" in order to succeed in the film business.[29] Writing in 1911 about "the civilizing value of the photoplay," Hanford C. Judson singled out Weber and Smalley's *Where the Shamrock Grows*, noting the "civilizing force" and simple "human dignity" evident in a strongly acted love story featuring a humble blacksmith and a lady of "the Hall."[30] Acting and scenario writing especially improved throughout the company's first year, *Moving Picture World* claimed—areas of Weber's distinct expertise.[31] Trade commentators also praised innovative lighting and silhouette effects in many Rex productions and the overall quality of tinting and toning in their releases.[32] Describing another early Weber film, *On the Brink* (1911), as "simply beautiful," *Motography* declared: "Any licensed manufacturer who is overweeningly proud of his photography had better go and see these smooth, clear, steady beautifully tinted pictures, and then decide to take a back seat until he can do as well.

Figure 4. Weber as featured in early publicity for the Rex
Motion Picture Company. Author's collection.

Rex has shown Americans that *de luxe* photography is not a secret of the
foreign makers."[33]

Arguments about "quality" filmmaking in the early 1910s raised the
specter of cinema's uplift and an appeal to "refined" (middle-class) audiences,
a cause invariably championed by industry trade papers. In Rex releases,
trade critics saw the promise of an evolving medium. It was presumed

(correctly or incorrectly), for instance, that bourgeois audiences brought little taste for action-adventure, slapstick comedy, or visual spectacle to the cinema, preferring instead tasteful dramas based on subtle human interaction, and that they might appreciate fine cinematography and color. Here, trade critics insisted, lay cinema's future. Values praised in these early Rex productions are those Weber would continue to emulate throughout her career. The company's emphasis on drama over action, for instance, was a philosophy Weber and Smalley would maintain in their filmmaking long after Porter's departure from Rex. Smalley echoed these sentiments in a 1914 interview, stressing the couple's interest in "smaller casts, closer focus" over action and spectacle.[34] The emphasis placed on character, story development, and cinematography at Rex meant that the company's titles did not always keep pace with other formal developments, as filmmakers began to explore closer camera positions and accelerated editing in the transitional era. Well into the early 1910s, Charlie Keil finds, Rex continued to rely on long-shot framings, along with a less verisimilar performance style suitable to such full-body views. Indeed, Rex was singled out as one of the few production outfits that had not pursued the "craze" for closer camera positions, with *Moving Picture World* twice praising the company's efforts to maintain "the full figure on the screen."[35] According to Keil's statistics, cutting rates were also considerably below the norm for these years, and well below those employed in Biograph releases.[36] Closer camera positions and more rapid editing are the formal innovations most associated with this transitional period, but Rex films demonstrated an alternate conception of sophisticated, quality filmmaking.

If Porter's taste for well-crafted narratives, skilled performances, and expert cinematography influenced Weber and Smalley, so too did his production methods. Although the quality of Rex releases was widely recognized within the industry, Porter's approach to filmmaking was not, as Charles Musser points out. Porter preferred a collaborative mode of production, popular in early motion picture days when he got his start, but increasingly out of step with an industry looking to streamline shooting methods in the early 1910s.[37] Porter also favored an artisanal approach that stood out against the move toward efficiency and rationalization in U.S. filmmaking. His habit of remaining involved at all levels of production from script writing to directing to developing the negatives and tinting the prints was a practice Weber would emulate throughout her career even as it pushed against the increasingly rigid dictates of studio filmmaking. The "devotedness, tenacity and application" that *Moving Picture World* noted in Porter's approach would be echoed in later accounts of Weber supervising every detail of her own productions.[38]

Also notable was Porter's support for husband-and-wife filmmaking teams. After working successfully with Weber and Smalley for several months, Porter hired actress Marion Leonard and her husband, Stanner E. V. Taylor, to produce a series of vehicles for Leonard, evidently favoring a collaborative, egalitarian model of production not much in evidence beyond outfits like Solax, where Herbert and Alice Guy Blaché worked together on her productions.[39] According to Musser, Porter produced the Weber and Smalley films, while Taylor produced the Leonard titles. Clearly influenced by Porter's methods, Weber and her husband would continue to work under the joint signature of "The Smalleys" long into the 1910s when few others were working that way. Conditions at Rex offered the couple a unique combination of collaboration and independence: encouraged to work together on joint projects with a consistent team of performers and technical personnel, they were also apparently free to pursue whatever projects interested them without interference from others in the company. The uniqueness of this arrangement was recognized in a 1926 profile of the director which noted that during these early years "Miss Weber and her husband were as independent as any famous stars are today. . . . In her long and varied motion picture career, she has practically never worked under the direction of anyone but herself."[40]

Porter also played a crucial role in supporting women. Long after Weber and Leonard had left Rex, Porter continued to work with women in positions of equality, as Musser points out. His alliance with Mary Pickford on her early features, including *Tess of the Storm Country* (1914), particularly echoed his collaborations with Weber, for that film was adapted from a woman's novel, centered on a strong female character, and designed to appeal largely to female moviegoers.[41] "I shall never forget Edwin Porter," Weber later told a reporter. "He is the most artistic person I have ever met. I miss him to this day, for there was never anything that couldn't be done when he was with us. Mr. Porter would always find a way."[42] Calling Porter one of the "greatest masters of motion picture technique today," Smalley also noted his influence on their own productions: "I am sure those who understand his methods can recognize in our work touches that come from him."[43]

Despite Porter's close association with early Rex releases and his evident influence on collaborators like Weber and Smalley, he did not remain focused on Rex for long. Throughout 1912, the company's second year in business, Porter frequently became involved with outside ventures. In May of that year he played an instrumental role in the formation of the Universal Film Manufacturing Company, an alliance spearheaded by Carl Laemmle that brought Rex under the Universal banner with several other independents, among them Bison, Powers, and IMP (the Independent Moving Picture Company), in defiance of the Trust. Alongside the Universal merger, Porter's attention was also drawn to feature film production. In July of 1912 he formed a partnership with Adolph Zukor and Daniel Frohman to purchase American distribution rights to Sarah Bernhardt's *Queen Elizabeth,* an association that eventually led to the formation of the Famous Players Company, designed to support high-profile feature releases.[44] With Porter's attention frequently focused elsewhere, Weber and Smalley were increasingly left in charge of day-to-day operations at Rex. When Leonard and Taylor, the company's other primary producing couple, left in July 1912, Weber and Smalley solidified their stature as Rex's primary filmmaking team.[45]

Porter formally severed his ties with Rex in October 1912, announcing his decision to devote his energies to Famous Players full-time and thereby free himself from "the weekly release routine" in the hope of making "bigger and better productions unhampered by time limitations."[46] His investment in producing fewer films of higher quality over a longer period of time must surely have been appealing to Weber and Smalley as well, for they had been making one title per week for nearly two years with little rest. In fact, in the months prior to Porter's official departure the couple took an extended vacation in New York's Catskill Mountains, purportedly because Weber had been working too hard and needed rejuvenation. Upon returning to New York City in October 1912, they did not immediately resume production at Rex. Possibly uncertain about the company's future in the wake of Porter's departure and the Universal merger, they were also likely scouting opportunities of the sort Porter had himself found outside Rex. Several publicity items focusing on the couple appeared in the trades that month, suggesting that, swayed by Porter's move to Famous Players, they may have been eager to promote their own talents to other fledgling feature outfits, perhaps eager themselves to break out of Rex's weekly release schedule. *Moving Picture World* announced that Weber and Smalley were "ready to resume" work in a manner that implied the two were seeking new ventures; and *Photoplay* profiled both of them in its "Player's Personalities" column that same month.[47] Although the couple still marketed themselves as a team and were still often referred to as "The Smalleys," Weber emerged in press accounts as the driving force behind their productions. Her work as a gifted scenario writer and director was singled out in the *Moving Picture World* report, for instance; and she alone was the focus of an in-depth half-page profile in that paper the following week. Entitled "Lois Weber on Scripts," the piece drew singular attention to her writing and producing talents, quoting her authoritative views on the subject.

These profiles marked a decisive shift for Weber, who had previously been promoted only as a "leading lady" of the Rex stock company, without reference to the writing and directing roles she took on behind the scenes. Weber's picture, for instance, had been featured in *Moving Picture World* in April 1911, just as several companies began to promote their stable of performers.[48] Such publicity was typical, for it was often female players who carried the banner for their companies. "Sending pictures of beautiful women to the press was a time-honored way for the newer production companies to get some publicity," as Eileen Bowser points out.[49] By late 1912, however, Weber had begun to shift this attention away from her role as performer toward her other creative talents as writer and director, always conscious as well of crafting a reputation associated with high-minded productions.

Despite the intensity of the couple's promotional efforts in late 1912, they did not ultimately result in a contract with another outfit. So after their sojourn in the Catskills, Weber and Smalley rejoined Rex, but they did so with a higher profile, greater creative control, and a new studio environment. Now in charge of the Rex brand, early in 1913 they moved west to begin production at the new Universal City facilities then under construction on the outskirts of Los Angeles. "When Mr. Porter left to go to the Famous Players," Weber later recounted, "he was nice enough to tell Mr. Laemmle that he left the Rex in capable hands, meaning Mr. Smalley and myself."[50]

Shortly after the Universal merger that previous summer, the company had purchased a large tract of land east of Los Angeles and had begun constructing state-of-the-art production facilities, part of a general move westward during these years as U.S. film production increasingly clustered around Los Angeles.[51] Rex's facilities were considerably enhanced by the move to Universal City. Not only were Weber and Smalley given an elaborate suite of offices and dressing rooms, but the company could now rely on the extended services at Universal, which included facilities for set construction, miniature modeling, costume design, and editing—not to mention an entire department devoted to publicity.[52] Even so, the small-scale production methods Weber and Smalley had refined while working in New York were still supported at Universal City, despite the studio's grandeur. Perhaps because they themselves worked at all levels of the filmmaking process (writing, performing, directing, editing), they were able to retain many of the earlier methods associated with "craft" filmmaking, while also taking advantage of the extensive facilities available on the Universal lot. Southern California also afforded ample opportunities for location shooting, and the couple frequently took actors and crew outside Universal City to shoot scenes in Laguna Beach and Riverside and as far north as Monterey.[53]

Even within Universal City, Weber and Smalley continued to run Rex like a small repertory company, releasing two films per week on Thursdays and Sundays and working with a consistent group of performers and with their main camera operator, Dal Clawson. In early 1913 when the couple first arrived at Universal City the studio was "was very strong on teams," according to I. G. Edmonds. "Groups developed almost into stock companies with the same director, actor, actress, and supporting cast." Alongside Weber and Smalley were several other successful male-female production teams, including Francis Ford and Grace Cunard, Pauline Bush and William Dowlan, Dorothy Phillips and William Stowell, Rosemary Theby and Hobart Henley, and Robert Z. Leonard and Ella Hall.[54] Among these teams, Weber and Smalley quickly became "the mainstay of the producing force."[55]

Weber spoke of how, working with a consistent group of actors, she tailored her scenarios for individual types in her company.[56] Sixteen-year-old Ella Hall worked frequently with the couple during this period, after having worked at Biograph and Bison. She credited Weber with giving her a deeper understanding of acting, saying that without the director's guidance "I really don't think I should be where I am today."[57] Husband-and-wife team Rupert Julian and Elsie Jane Wilson also joined the company in the fall of 1913, after having worked on the stage. Julian began playing male leads in many of Weber and Smalley's productions shortly thereafter and would be cast in the role of Antonio in Weber's first feature, *The Merchant of Venice*, early the following year. Like several others who worked with the couple in these early days, both Julian and Wilson would themselves later go on to directing.[58]

After they returned to Rex, Weber and Smalley were increasingly identified as individual artists responsible for the brand. If Rex releases had been praised for their quality from the start, it was now understood that Weber and Smalley stood behind this artistry. Universal promoted the couple's return to the studio with trade notices and ads announcing that "the Rex has 'come back'" and "Lois Weber and Phillips Smalley Are Again with the Rex" in pictures "written, directed and acted by themselves."[59] Critics also took notice. Beginning with the release of *His Sister* in February 1913, the couple was mentioned by name much more consistently in reviews, with one writer noting their "characteristic style" and another reporting that their work had been "attracting attention." So identified were they with its Rex brand that Universal sometimes referred to the company as "Rex (Smalley)" and trade commentators described films "made by the Smalleys" or "The Smalley-Weber Company."[60] If brands like Rex were an important marketing tool for the fledgling Universal Film Manufacturing Company, especially prior to the full bloom of the star system, as Mark Garrett Cooper stresses, then Weber and Smalley's personal association with the brand pushed at the limits of these strategies.[61] Even so, characterizing individual filmmakers as expressive artists aided the industry's larger bid to elevate its cultural stature, as Charlie Keil reminds us.[62] Weber and Smalley, with their pedigreed reputations already in the works, were tailor-made for such publicity.

Even as the Smalleys' imprimatur became increasingly identifiable, Weber's scenarios were singled out for praise. Indeed, she was usually given primary credit for the success of Smalley productions even in these early years. This began to happen relatively early in the couple's tenure at Rex; publicity for the late 1911 film *The Martyr*, for instance, described it as having been "written and acted by Miss Lois Weber."[63] Few other titles released then by any company were identified as the work of an individual writer or producer. Rex's "reputation for novel, out-of-the-ordinary stories containing a vital 'punch,'" could be directly traced to Weber, one newspaper item suggested, calling her "one of the most gifted scenario writers in the field."[64] She had become "famous through filmdom for her ability to inject psychological power into her writings," another observer reported, and was famed, according to one more, for her "fertile brain."[65] By 1914 *Moving Picture World* would declare, "Something substantial is always to be expected from the pen of Lois Weber."[66]

Growing recognition of Weber's authorial signature at Rex had much to do with the new respect accorded scenario writers during these years. With the industry's drive toward greater standardization in the single-reel format and increasing rationalization of filmmaking in studio hierarchies, scenario writing became an important cornerstone of production, as Janet Staiger has demonstrated.[67] By 1911 many manufacturers had established scenario departments with a staff of writers and editors. This marked a clear break from earlier years when filmmakers would have crafted (or improvised) scenarios, then shot and directed the action themselves. The following year U.S. copyright law officially recognized film scenarios as distinctly authored works.[68] The demand for scenarios allowed many women like Weber to enter motion picture work during these years, often transitioning smoothly from acting to writing, as did contemporaries like Gene Gauntier and Jeanie Macpherson. To hear Gauntier talk, it is as if the secretarial role of jotting down ideas on paper for the group, casually foisted upon women, quickly evolved, without anyone really noticing, into an extremely valuable and

Figure 5. Weber at her writing desk. Courtesy of the Martin S. Quigley Collection, Georgetown University Library.

respected craft, though Weber's own narrative suggests a more calculated effort to garner creative control.[69] By the 1920s virtually all of the top-drawer screenwriters were women, including Macpherson, June Mathis, Frances Marion, and Anita Loos. Estimates suggest that half of all scripts written in the silent era were by women, a percentage much higher than in any other period in history.[70]

Throughout her career Weber presented writing, not performing or direct-ing, as her formative creative experience, evident in her recollections of writing and storytelling as a child, and in the way she often framed her acting and direct-ing work through her writing. Even as Weber assumed greater control as a director at Rex, it was her scenarios that signaled the couple's artistic signature, as we have seen. Indeed, both she and Smalley continued to consider Weber's scenarios the central act of authorship in their collaborative productions. Her husband referred to their codirected films as "Mrs. Smalley's pictures," indicat-ing the overriding influence of her artistic vision.[71] It was certainly not uncom-mon in this era to assign sole authorial status to the scenario writer, as Charlie Keil has pointed out, but in Weber's case it seems as much the privileging of one form of labor over another as it was a recognition of her creative dominance on projects in which she also costarred and codirected with Smalley.[72] For Weber, writing remained paramount. "I cannot be happy to direct someone else's story. That would be only half a creation," she later explained.[73] It is clear that Weber saw *writing* as her primary artistic endeavor during these years—and that the work that came afterward in casting, set decorating, location scouting, acting, directing, and editing was all done to ensure the integrity of her initial creative concept. Of all these tasks, writing was the one she pursued on her own.

Weber's screenwriting also defined much of her public persona during the Rex years, for she used her growing reputation to speak in published interviews about her goals for the industry. Here she articulated a highly activist role for scenario writers. Resisting the trend toward standardization, Weber bristled against formulaic plots that relied too heavily on happy end-ings or climatic sequences improbably engineered through murders, thefts, suicides, and elopements. "Don't let us all cut out after the same pattern," she cried.[74] Instead, she presented herself as a strong advocate of "artistic" pictures unwilling to bend to commercial demands, particularly calls from theater managers to provide happy endings. "The ending should not inter-fere with the artistic features of the play," she insisted. "If it is necessary to bring tears to the eyes of the public, in the last act and the last scene, in order to carry the artistic idea and the dramatic force of the production, do it by all means!"she advised other writers.[75] She also spoke out against artificially plotted stories, making the case, instead, for "the value of simple themes in pictures"—well-told stories "moved simply and with dignity."[76] Rather than leaning too heavily on plot devices, Weber said, she drew stories from her own life experiences and incidents she read about in the press, rejecting highly fabricated photoplay storylines.[77] Along with Anita Loos, Weber was also an early proponent of intertitles, advocating that they be employed to furnish not just expository information but also more poetic musings.[78]

Weber's strong advocacy for scenario writers did more than draw attention to this newly identified craft, giving the profession weight and depth; she also articulated a forceful view of quality motion pictures. The best prospects for quality productions resided with screenwriters, Weber seemed to insist. Throughout this discourse Weber positioned herself in opposition to many other forces within the industry: exhibitors who demanded easy material for their viewers, directors and studios who changed writers' material, and poorly attuned audiences. "The person who applauds loudest at an entertainment is not necessarily the best judge of its merits," she claimed. In fact, she added, "few people of superior minds lean toward noise." If manufacturers and exhibitors listened only to "the rabble," quality pictures would never get made, she said, betraying a marked class bias.[79] "Too often, I am obliged to sacrifice some effect, artistic or dramatic, to make the picture end happily," she said,[80] bristling against studio restrictions, a precursor to the kinds of censorship she would face later in her career. It is one of the few indications we have that circumstances at Rex were anything short of an extremely satisfying, if exhausting, creative experience.

Weber's efforts to professionalize screenwriting were not always recognized within the industry, however. Torey Liepa reports that when a group of photoplaywrights dined together at Henderson's Restaurant on Coney Island in August 1912, at perhaps their first professional gathering, women were barred from the event. Incensed, Weber wrote a letter of protest to Epes Winthrop Sargent at *Moving Picture World,* author of that paper's column "The Photoplaywright" and one of the evening's organizers. Apologetic and effusive in his praise for Weber, whom he called "a high-degree playwright" and later a "writer of strength and versatility," Sargent promised to invite "the ladies" to subsequent meetings. Although Liepa found that the group did meet again at various New York–area restaurants, it is not clear whether Weber attended.[81] When the Photoplay Authors' League formed in early 1914, however, Weber was prominent among its founding members, which also included Loos and D. W. Griffith.[82]

Celebrated for her ability to craft quality scenarios, Weber also began to receive notice for her talents as a director. As early as June 1913 certain films, including *Suspense,* billed as "a picture by Lois Webber [sic]," were identified in the trades with her individual signature.[83] Even Smalley proudly admitted that it was his wife, not he, who "personally supervised" all of their pictures from conception to completion.[84] "She is as much the director and even more the constructor of Rex pictures than I," he told one interviewer; to another he said, "I want to give as much credit as possible for the pictures we make to Mrs. Smalley."[85] Anyone who doubts that

Weber's authorial voice began to emerge from her husband's during these early years need only look to films Smalley was directing independently for the Crystal brand at this same time, mostly comedies staring Pearl White and Chester Barnett. Without Weber's voice, the scripts were one-dimensional and repetitive. Without Weber's input, the staging and compositions were minimal and, apart from providing legibility, did not serve the storytelling particularly well. Press accounts usually failed to mention the name of the director behind the action.

Weber herself stressed her own command of the couple's productions. "I had only one copy of the story," she recalled, "and everyone had to run to me to find out what it was all about. Mr. Smalley got my idea. He painted the scenery, played the leading role and helped direct the cameraman."[86] Leading a reporter through Universal City in early 1914, Smalley discovered Weber in the editing room. The reporter pronounced himself

> agreeably astonished to find Miss Lois Weber in the costume she wore when I left her earlier that day. Clustered round her was a huge pile of what seemed to me to be interminable miles of snake-like film. . . . If anyone imagines that the life of a director is one of ease, one should drop in some evening after the usual working day is done, and see these men [and women] busily going over yard after yard of film with the expert assemblers, instructing, suggesting and giving information relative to how their films should be pasted together. Many nights in the week these men [and women] are engaged there until midnight.[87]

Another visitor to Universal around the same time found Weber at the center of activity, beset by queries from all manner of personnel. "Every face lights up with a smile as she passes through the rambling quarters of the company . . . always a hand is laid confidingly on her shoulder when one approaches to speak to her."[88]

The respect Weber commanded on the Universal lot is evident in her appointment to the post of mayor of Universal City in September 1913. Weber had run for the position on an all-female, suffragist ticket earlier that spring, shortly after California granted women the right to vote, well before most other states in the nation.[89] "Hurrah for Lois Weber and woman's suffrage!" *Motography* declared.[90] Weber, along with running mates Ethel Grandin for prosecuting attorney and Laura Oakley for chief of police, attracted national press attention, and not a little ridicule. Reports, predictably, lampooned the feminist ticket, with the *Los Angeles Examiner* noting that Universal City's "scenic beauty" had been "perturbed" by "vociferous election speeches, soap box oratory and woman suffragist campaigning."[91] Weber initially lost the election to studio manager A.M.

Kennedy, but took over as mayor when he left the studio later that summer. "There is but one woman mayor in the world," the *New York Telegraph* announced, making Universal City "the only bona fide woman's sphere on the map, where women do all the bossing, and where mere man is just tolerated—that's all, just tolerated." Noting the community's female chief of police, the paper took delight in imagining costumes a female police force might don: "caps, blouses, short skirts, and black silk stockings with thirteen gold buttons down the side," it speculated.[92] For her part, Weber used the office to articulate her vision of quality cinema, masking the radical dimensions of this stance in a more conventional role associated with middle-class female reformers. "Cleanliness in municipal rule and cleanliness in picture making will be the basis of my endeavors," she declared, strongly echoing conservative suffragist rhetoric at the time. Female candidates and a woman's electorate could "clean up" corrupt political machines and introduce progressive social reforms, they proclaimed.[93] Echoing such rhetoric, Weber suggested that female leadership at the studio (and behind the camera) could bolster the fledgling "better films" movement run by clubwomen across the country. Later in life, she would quip, "Why, all the President of the United States has to be is a good housekeeper."[94]

In October 1913, shortly after she became mayor, Weber was the subject of a lengthy profile in *Universal Weekly*, a publication distributed to Universal's exhibitors and exchanges throughout the country.[95] Here too Weber's commitment to quality, socially responsible filmmaking was stressed over and against any feminist ardor that might have been suggested by her suffragist electioneering. Under the heading "A Rare Combination of Beauty, Genius and Kindness," the article stressed Weber's talents as a screenwriter and director alongside her philanthropic role in Los Angeles, her background in "church army" work, and her experience as a stage actress and concert pianist—all traits associated with bourgeois feminine refinement that Universal was presumably quite happy to have as its public face in 1913.[96] Weber's mayoral post was only one of many high-profile missions she began undertaking after the couple's move west. Branching out into the larger Los Angeles community, she began to fashion herself as a spokesperson for the industry, addressing the Woman's City Club of Los Angeles in September 1913; her speech, "The Making of Picture Plays That Will Have an Influence for Good on the Public Mind," received considerable publicity in local newspapers.[97] Here Weber aligned herself with the drive toward quality motion pictures and a particularly middle-class concern with commercial recreation activities. But in tackling the question of films that might "influence" the "public mind," Weber also indicated her early interest in films of social conscience. Clearly she was aware not only of cinema's budding role in popular culture but also of the importance of her own profile as activist bourgeois clubwoman. Weber here modeled a class- and gender-specific approach to cinema, embodying from within the industry a respectable, bourgeois femininity that exhibitors sought in their patrons and, more than that, the type of women whom the industry sought to impress because they were the medium's most vocal critics.

A national profile began to emerge for Weber in the fall of 1913, then, well before most other filmmakers or screenwriters had achieved any kind of notoriety. Featured in Gertrude Price's nationally syndicated newspaper column as "director of the Rex company" in September 1913, she was celebrated as "one of the very few women in the business."[98] Price, as Richard Abel has documented, consistently focused on powerful female figures in the early movie business—Alice Guy Blaché and Nell Shipman had also been recently featured in Price's column.[99] Price was part of a network of female journalists who wrote consistently about women's work in early Hollywood, helping fashion what Hilary Hallett calls "women-made women" for their female readers.[100] In Price's hands Weber was presented as someone who cared deeply about the industry, was an expert in her field, and whose artistic ambitions often bristled against the commercial demands of the medium. A similar piece in the *Nashville Democrat* also noted Weber's unique status as "one of the very few women directors" in the business.[101] By March of the following year, Bertha Smith profiled Weber as an "Interesting Westerner" in *Sunset* magazine, the filmmaker's femininity and commitment to cinema's uplift stressed in equal measure with the respect she commanded at Universal.[102] So while the novelty of Weber's position was invariably noted throughout this early publicity, she used her standing as a woman director to ground her claims for quality filmmaking and to embody a creative role for women behind the scenes other than that of performer. Female filmmakers like Weber, these profiles insisted, brought a distinct vision to filmmaking and a distinct mode of working in the industry.

Weber's work in motion pictures challenged reigning assumptions about suitable occupations for young women of her generation, but Weber found in the fledgling industry a platform for her creative impulses and her Progressive sensibilities. Despite initial attempts to frame her only as a "picture personality," Weber cultivated a voluble public persona. She argued for quality filmmaking based on character development and nuanced storytelling; she was instrumental in the professionalization of screenwriting; she fought hard to ensure female leadership in the industry, whether as part of the newly formed Photoplay Author's League or as mayor of Universal

City; and she used her growing renown to build bridges to women's organizations. She persuaded clubwomen that women working behind the scenes in Hollywood could steer the cinema toward "uplift," while also demonstrating to Hollywood that female leadership was as essential to its success as its feminine constituency in communities around the country. As Smalley would later remind a reporter, his wife had "fought every step of the way, and fought hard," to attain her position in the industry.[103]

A FEMININE HAND

If Weber was positioned as a signal feminine voice within the film industry, a voice of uplift and propriety, how might this persona be manifest in her film work? Looking closely at her early films, it becomes clear that however much Weber's feminine hand might have been associated with refinement, the subjects she took on at Rex demonstrate a radical approach, particularly to gender, that challenged notions of genteel uplift and the matronly persona with which she was so often associated. Indeed, the viewpoint Weber brought to her scripts, her performances, and her direction at Rex often produced sophisticated critiques of bourgeois institutions and gender norms. So we must look again at the screenwriting methods she espoused in interviews. When Weber disparaged happy endings in favor of more complicated plots, she was not simply rejecting filmmaking formulas; she was calling for a wholesale rethinking of tropes surrounding heterosexual romance that, even then, governed cinematic narratives. When she advocated nuanced character development over action and spectacle, she was not simply rejecting a penchant for sensationalism; she was demanding that we rethink roles typically assigned to men and women on screen. This undercurrent of Weber's comments may not be immediately discernable from her interviews, but it emerges clearly in an examination of the work itself.

Weber's Rex scripts are concerned almost exclusively with central female protagonists who frequently lead quite unconventional lives, roles that Weber herself usually played on screen. After starring as the innkeeper's daughter who thwarts George Washington's assassination in Rex's first offering, *A Heroine of '76*, she played an opium addict in *The Dragon's Breath* (1913); a single mother who works to support a child and her younger sister in *Woman's Burden* (1914); a woman on trial for murder in *The Final Pardon* (1912); a "human spider" who "causes good men to commit terrible crimes" in *The Spider and Her Web* (1914); and in *On Suspicion* (1914) a bride who jumps from a speeding car where she has been handcuffed to a detective hired by her father to prevent her from eloping with her fiancé.[104] In other plots, Weber tackled heterodox gender roles more directly, showing how women living outside rigid feminine norms could be persecuted or ostracized. *The Greater Christian* (1912) tells the story of "the sufferings of a woman who led an unconventional life, and was spurned by her pious friends," according to Rex publicity.[105] Rejecting her previous life as a "sport" and her "sporty friends," the heroine joins the Salvation Army, reforms her life, and becomes a governess. When a local minister proposes marriage, she feels compelled to reveal the truth about her past. Instead of accepting her, he exposes her to her employers and rejects her. In several other plots, heroines become the targets of malicious gossip and scandal, victims of restrictive ideas about feminine propriety. In *His Sister* (1913), Weber played a young woman whose engagement to a local minister is nearly derailed by a "trio of female scandal mongers" who spread unseemly rumors about her male living companion, a man who turns out to be her brother.[106] Weber and Smalley played Lois and Phil in *The Power of Thought* (1912), two lovers threatened when an interloper spreads rumors of Lois's infidelity. Believing her sweetheart has died in a dual defending her honor, Lois dies "a martyr to cruel imagination," leaving Phil to find her body.[107] Weber again took the role of a woman victimized by gossip in *Troubled Waters* (1913), playing a sailor's wife who teaches knitting in hopes of surprising her husband with some extra income, only to find that a local gossip arouses her husband's jealousy with unfounded accusations.[108]

Male-female relationships also stood at the heart of many of Weber's scripts, with she and Smalley assuming lead roles in virtually all of these productions. While romance would have been a common trope in other contemporary screen stories, Weber's Rex films demonstrate a repeated fascination with heterosexual alliances that transgress racial, class, or moral boundaries and with stories that focus on marital discord, rather than courtship and romance. Male volatility, jealousy, and even domestic violence figure in many of these scenarios. These are not, then, simple tales of uplift and highbrow culture. Weber evidently had a more complex understanding of cinema's audience in mind. The wife of an abusive miner in *Through Strife* (1913) attracts the attention of a young suitor but, respecting her wedding vows, refuses to leave. Misunderstanding their relationship, the husband shoots the would-be lover and drags his wife back to their cabin, where he intends to kill her. The lover, though injured, manages to intervene, stabbing the husband to death in an ensuing struggle.[109] In *His Brand* (1913), a film that contained "too much brutality" according to *Moving Picture World,* a husband brands his wife with an "S" after becoming jealous of her sophisticated male friend.

Unbeknownst to him, the brand also marks his unborn son, a fact discovered only when the boy is fifteen and wildly afraid to brand cattle.[110] A colonel and his estranged wife are the subjects of *In the Blood* (1913). To escape her husband's violent temper, the woman finds company with a young lieutenant but becomes embroiled in scandal after he commits suicide. Banished, she watches from afar as her husband tries unsuccessfully to raise their daughter, then connives a ruse to get the girl away from him. She does a good job of raising the girl in the end, and when the husband visits and recognizes how wrong he has been, the family is reunited.[111]

As *Through Strife* illustrates, courtships that do figure in Weber scripts are often relationships that transgress the boundaries of adultery, even sometimes of race and class. In *The Pursuit of Hate* (1914), Weber plays a woman who falls in love with a married man who has abandoned his wife. When the wife tracks down the adulterous couple, Weber's character convinces her to leave them alone, saying, "If you hate him, you will be glad he left you and if you love him you will sacrifice yourself for his happiness and leave him alone."[112] Romance crosses both marital and racial lines in *Civilized and Savage* (1913), in which Weber plays an exoticized "native" woman who nurses a white man back to health after his own wife has abandoned him, then falls in love with him.[113] Siding with its heroine, the title seems to provide an ironic commentary on who among the characters might be considered "civilized" and who "savage." In *The Troubadour's Triumph* (1912), set in Elizabethan England, a young woman about to wed a knight falls in love with a humble troubadour, learning only in the end that he is in fact a nobleman.[114] Transgressive female sexuality figures in several other plots as well. In *The King Can Do No Wrong* (1913), Smalley plays a soldier who watches as his wife (Weber) and their daughter fall prey to the attentions of a king and his son.[115] *Fallen Angel* (1913) depicts "the regeneration of a woman living unwedded with a man of means," according to Universal publicity.[116]

Artistic characters—painters, singers, actors, and poets—figure frequently in Weber's Rex scripts, often representing lifestyles that fall outside the parameters of bourgeois domesticity. Errant masculinity, particularly in the form philandering husbands, is often colored by an artistic personality in these scenarios. In *James Lee's Wife* (1913), Weber's adaptation of Robert Browning's poem, the director plays an artist's wife living in the south of France who discovers that her husband, played by Smalley, has fallen for a young "peasant girl," whom he is painting. After first contemplating suicide, the wife finds solace in religion, with her faith ultimately setting an example for her husband. Realizing his mistake, the painter makes amends in the end, kneeling beside his wife to pray.[117] In *Lost Illusions* (1911), a young woman infatuated with a local painter nearly destroys her own marriage in pursuit of him, before finding out that he too is also married—another example of Weber's tendency to use artistic characters as a means of figuring complexities in bourgeois family life.[118] In another instance, 1913's two-reel film *Shadows of Life*, released just before *James Lee's Wife*, Weber takes an opposite tact and offers the artistic life as an escape from a stultifying marriage. Still favoring a feminine perspective, Weber shifts the focus from the philandering artist's wife to that of a married woman attracted to a sensitive artistic mate. Here Weber plays a woman whose husband, played by Rupert Julian, has married her only for her money. Disgusted with their hollow life, she becomes attracted to a wandering musician, played by Smalley. Her husband, in the midst of an affair with another woman, played by Cleo Madison, tries to kill his wife by staging a riding accident. When she is crippled instead, the musician rescues her and prays for her daily.[119] With the narrative unable to imagine either a happy reconciliation for the original couple, or an extramarital alliance between the woman and the musician, her death in the end provides the only means of closure.

In *Fine Feathers* (1912), explored in more depth later in this chapter, Weber provides yet another view of this same subject, that of the young artist's model attracted to her employer—the perspective missing from *James Lee's Wife*. By eliminating any suggestion that the artist in *Fine Feathers* is married, Weber provides fewer complications for the plot and a less morally ambiguous role for her heroine, his model. But in doing so, she also shifts the terms of inquiry, for whereas marriage had served in her other scenarios as the foil for artistic liaisons (good and bad), in *Fine Feathers* marriage is collapsed onto artistic flirtation in a manner that asks us to question the very institution itself.

In *From Death to Life* (1911) the "artist" portrayed is actually a scientist in ancient Greece intent on turning flesh to stone. If the film offers a cautionary tale about scientific experimentation, especially the temptation to control life and death, it also furnishes a lesson about the dangers of ignoring a feminine point of view, here associated with compassion, humanity, and respect for the powers of creation. In the opening scene Aratus (Smalley) banishes his wife (Weber) from his lab, where he is perfecting a potion to freeze flesh. Stop-action camera work shows how he turns a live fish and a rabbit to stone, even freezing a calla lily brought to him by his wife. Aratus remains blind to the inhumane consequences of his experimentation until his wife inadvertently falls into a bath of his solution and is turned to stone herself. He worships her statue, now frozen on a pedestal, until it become clear that the effects of his potion are temporary and she comes slowly back to life, her husband now chastened in his quest to control life.

So few of these films survive that it is difficult to gauge their visual impact, though reviews consistently praised the films' sets, locations, and cinematography. It is clear from written descriptions that Weber's screenplays sought to convey interior psychological states on screen in a manner highly innovative and unusual for its time. In *Angels Unaware* (1912), for instance, a husband and wife decide to separate and divorce, but agree to keep up appearances while his parents visit. During the visit the husband's father asks them about their courtship, prompting fond memories from each. *Moving Picture World* described a "mirror of their souls," in which "they see a vision . . . a vivid vision of the happy day of their courting and the tender truth of their troth."[120] Many such titles, as *Angels Unaware* shows, had spiritual components. In *The Haunted Bride* (1913) Weber plays an affluent young woman who has spurned her tutor's affections to marry another man, only to be plagued by constant visions of the rejected tutor on the verge of suicide.[121] In *The Triumph of Mind* (1914) a woman whose husband has been falsely accused of murder consults a psychic, played by Weber, who visits the true killer. Describing the visions she has had of him committing the crime, the psychic then encourages the murderer to imagine the hangman's noose, eventually prompting him to confess.[122]

While it is not clear how exactly such "visions" might have been rendered on screen, whether through double-exposure, matte shots, or parallel editing, Weber evidently sought to convey interior psychology through cinematic, rather than performative, means. In *The Rosary* (1913), an adaptation of a popular song about undying love, a man's memories of his beloved are framed within a circular rosary pendant in a series of matte shots that echo the song's lyrics:

> The hours I spent with thee, dear heart
> Are as a string of pearls to me.
> I count them over, ev'ry one apart,
> My rosary, my rosary.

Double-exposure work was particularly notable in *The Bargain* (1912), a film that could "take its place with any film d'art that has been produced," according to *Moving Picture World*.[123] A young woman, played by Weber, deserts her impoverished fiancé and marries a wealthy man in order to satisfy her mother's social ambitions. The husband turns out to be "a drunkard and a brute," while the woman's sister lives happily, if humbly, married to the suitor she had rejected.[124] A final shot of the unhappy woman abandoned in her beautiful home is overlaid with the image of a birdcage. "By this trick of photography," the *World* notes, "the moral of the story is told without words in one of the cleverest and strongest ways imaginable."[125] Helping with such technical experiments would likely have been Dal Clawson, a Universal cinematographer who worked with the couple during their Rex years and who joined them later at Bosworth, returning with them to Universal, then eventually working at Lois Weber Productions. The couple credited Clawson with the early effectiveness of their photographic techniques.[126]

Increasingly complex film narratives in this period, as Charlie Keil has demonstrated, often devoted more attention to developing characters' emotions and inner psychology; this was particularly true of "quality" dramatic productions aimed at highbrow audiences, such as the Rex films. Closer camera positions and more nuanced performance style aided such portrayals, but Keil emphasizes that because acting styles were so much in flux during these years, other means of conveying interior psychology were often favored. Characters' "visions"—memories, fantasies, fears—were frequently presented as a means of developing their personalities and their motivations.[127] Weber favored this method a great deal, and appears to have done so more with double-exposures than with editing or dissolves. Since Rex productions retained relatively long camera positions even into the early teens, it is even more understandable that Weber would have resorted to using visions, since her camera operators were less prone to experiment with closer framings.

Tom Gunning's influential argument that D.W. Griffith's films from this same period demonstrate a textual address to middle-class viewers that complements the industry's wider bid to increase middle-class patronage might also be applied to Weber and Smalley's work at Rex, but in a slightly different fashion.[128] If Griffith primarily used editing to convey interior psychology, Weber and Smalley explore a range of other cinematic devices, such as double-exposure, to convey character's thoughts and emotions. While the initial aim of such techniques might be similar, the final effect is quite different. In Weber's case, the arsenal of cinematic techniques used to address middle-class audiences furnishes not Victorian morality and anti-feminism, as it does so often with Griffith, but rather a critique of the very institutions upon which cinema's imagined bourgeois viewers depend: heterosexual marriage, feminine propriety, and class privilege.

Weber's view of cinema's potential impact during these years is perhaps best seen in the film *Eyes That See Not* (1912), the story of a selfish, wealthy woman who is transformed through her work for social justice. A mill owner's wife, she is confronted in her home by the leader of the mill workers' union, who shows her the shocking conditions under which he and his family live. Reformed, she donates her jewelry to feed impoverished workers and their families.[129] The title *Eyes That See Not* evokes the willful blindness of privileged characters like the mill owner's wife, but also the physical and structural barriers between classes, between industry and society, between workplaces and domestic spaces, that prevent her from recognizing the inequity that supports her lavish lifestyle. The title also plants the idea that cinema itself might be a particularly privileged visual instrument, capable of simultaneously visualizing *and* breaking down economic and class barriers. This was an early indication, perhaps, of the power Weber believed was vested in movies and moviegoers alike.

If Weber's Rex scripts illustrate her interest in developing complex, unconventional, and varied female characters and in complicating male-female relationships and institutions like marriage, three of her films stand out for their uniquely reflexive examination of female representation. *Fine Feathers, A Japanese Idyll* (1912), and *Suspense* (1913) interrogate the reproduction, circulation, and commercialization of female imagery in painting, photography, and cinema, respectively. Evidence we might glean from Weber's other scripts of her interest in representations of women is corroborated quite directly by these three surviving prints.

In *Fine Feathers* Weber plays Mira, a young woman who begins work as a cleaning woman for an artist, Vaughn (Smalley), after he rescues her from a life of poverty and abuse in her father's shoemaking shop. When Vaughn returns home to his studio late one evening and glimpses Mira sitting in the moonlight, he decides to paint her portrait—a portrait that eventually secures his fame. The two develop a romantic relationship that falters when Vaughn initially refuses to marry her, but he appears to relent in the end, sparing Mira a life alone with her violent father.

Working within a familiar melodramatic terrain, *Fine Feathers* introduces themes of urban poverty, economic and sexual exploitation, and victimization as a means of contributing rather pointed commentary on the plight of women in traditional workplace and familial relationships. Exploited by her abusive father, Mira is understandably attracted to the seeming glamour and sophistication of the world of artists and wealthy patrons in which Vaughn circulates. But she, and we, learn of a parallel form of exploitation there, based first upon Vaughn's commodification of her image in his award-winning paintings, then later upon his sexual exploitation of her economic dependency. What appears to be a fairly simple, even clichéd, story—impoverished young woman falls in love with an exploitive

Figure 6. In *Fine Feathers* (1912) Vaughn (Smalley) paints two portraits of Mira (Weber), showing her transformation from maid to companion and ensuring his own fame. Frame enlargements.

artist-employer—becomes a vehicle for a much broader interrogation of marriage, heterosexuality, and class, a critique that emerges as much through the film's visual systems—its use of space, composition, sight lines, and gesture—as through its narrative trajectory.

Fine Feathers revolves quite self-consciously around the manufacture and marketing of a woman's image. The painter Vaughn translates his private vision of Mira—caught unaware in his studio at night, disheveled and (presumably) sweaty from work, glistening in the moonlight—into a life-size painting on exhibit in public. In making available to others a scene that only he has been fortunate to witness, Vaughn asserts his privileged, proprietary role over Mira, while turning her into an object of exchange for other men. But Mira herself also intervenes in the production of her portrait. Alone while cleaning Vaughn's studio, she becomes curious about the painting and pulls back a curtain to reveal it, only to be disappointed to see that Vaughn has painted her in ragged clothes. Imagining another kind of image for herself, Mira tries on a beautiful robe lying nearby and fantasizes about wearing it in a portrait. When Vaughn returns with the good news that his work has been selected for an exhibition, he catches her modeling the dress in front of the mirror, then decides to paint her this way as well, creating a second, matching portrait for the show entitled "Fine Feathers," a reference to the performance of gentility she enacts. Mira's second, "Fine Feathers" portrait foregrounds her own performance much more than the first, both her performance of class mobility and her exhibitionist desire to sit for the portrait. The sight lines captured in the composition when Vaughn returns home register all of the dynamics of their relationship: Mira's self-adoration in the mirror is "caught" by Vaughn's gaze over the width of the frame; it is his view that structures the scene, his gaze we are encouraged to trace across the screen, and his gaze that is ultimately captured in the finished painting.

If at first the second canvas might seem to indicate Mira's growing influence over the circulation of her image, in fact the portrait's continued replication only reinforces her commodification by suggesting that her likeness is infinitely reproducible. Shots of Mira standing in front of the two life-size portraits at the art exhibition emphasize this point further by drawing attention to the multiplication of her image within the frame. Moreover, in painting her portraits and circulating them publicly, Vaughn assumes control of her image, fashioning her as an object of fascination and lust for other men. The film's narrative structure underscores the degree to which Vaughn's success is derived from the two paintings of Mira, since scenes of his first being accepted for the exhibition and then winning the competition are intercut with the scene when he first decides to paint her portrait, then the scene when he decides to paint the second, matching portrait of her in "fine feathers."

Vaughn's economic exploitation of Mira's image is bound up in his subsequent sexual exploitation of her as well, a point the film makes clear when he buys her a dress to celebrate the success of his art show. The dress, and its association with masquerade, lays bare the linked economic and sexual exploitation at the core of Vaughn's interest in Mira. It marks the shift in their relationship from employer/employee and artist/model to lovers, for in the next scene we see Mira wearing the dress as the couple prepares to entertain Vaughn's patron Beyer (Charles DeForrest), assuming the mantle of the bourgeois housewife even though the couple has not married. Mira's romance with Vaughn is also articulated by her movement through his apartment. As she evolves from maid to model to lover, Mira penetrates deeper into his living quarters, moving from his public teaching studio to the smaller private painting studio adjacent, then from his front parlor to (we presume) his bedroom, with the lateral trajectory of her movement mirroring the circulation of her portrait in the art world. The exchange of her image, in other words, is matched by the very real (sexual) effects on her body.

That this shift in the couple's relationship pivots on the dress is an ironic reversal of the earlier episode in which Mira had fantasized a more glamorous self-image by donning a costume in Vaughn's studio, the "fine feathers" in which he will ultimately paint her. Then she had been playing with class masquerade, showing how malleable social boundaries might be; here she is masquerading as married, a fact that outrages Vaughn's patron Beyer when he discovers she is not wearing a wedding band. Humiliated by Beyer's questions, Mira asks Vaughn to marry her and thereby "legitimate" their sexual liaison. When he refuses to do so, she leaves, casting off the dress and, in doing so, rejecting both her role as surrogate spouse and the artificially highbrow persona Vaughn has created for her through costume and paint. Such a masquerade, the film suggests, has necessitated the erasure of Mira's class and ethnicity. Indeed, the "fine feathers" she had longed for are false: one cannot simply pretend to be an elegant lady in order to transcend one's class and ethnic background any more than one can perform a semblance of marital propriety to mask a carnal relationship.

Mira's only other option would be to marry Beyer, who has fallen in love with her through Vaughn's portrait. Aghast when he discovers that Vaughn has not married and therefore "legitimated" Mira, Beyer offers to "educate" her on his own. Much older and wealthier than the other two characters, Beyer, as his name suggests, merely reinforces the idea that Mira can be bought and sold as a commodity, much like Vaughn's paintings, for the older man offers her only financial security and one-sided adoration based on Vaughn's idealized rendering. Mira is pinned between two men, then, both of whom take advantage of her for different reasons and in different ways, an entrapment that is further complicated when details of her family life are revealed in the film's final scene. With the emphasis placed on propriety in marriage, instead of romance, attention falls on the nature of the contract between Mira and Vaughn, rather than on any love they might feel for each other. In fact, marriage, or its masquerade here, is presented as nothing more than the evolution of Mira's role from cleaning obligations in the backroom to hostessing obligations in the front room and (unspoken) sexual obligations in the bedroom. All of this is accomplished with a quick change of costume, we are told, an act that only enhances the trope of masquerade.

The ending, in which Vaughn discovers that he loves Mira only after she has left, and after he has witnessed her being attacked by her abusive alcoholic father, does not cover over the obvious contradiction here: in marrying Vaughn, she only trades one form of exploitation for another (albeit lesser) one. On the one hand, *Fine Feathers* promotes a fairly conservative message: a couple cannot pretend to be married when this is not the case; a woman risks being morally "ruined" if she engages in marital "privileges" without benefit of clergy. On the other hand, the film appears rather cynical about marriage, presenting it quite unabashedly as a contract between a man and a woman in which the latter agrees to sexual activity in exchange for financial security, surrendering her independence to become the man's property, circulating in society at his will. This, the film suggests, is only a slightly better arrangement than living with one's abusive father.

Released just six months after *Fine Feathers*, *A Japanese Idyll* offers a similarly self-conscious meditation on the reproduction and commodification of the female image, on male and female desire, and on the use of voyeurism and exhibitionism to control diegetic space. In this case, the context is photography rather than painting, but again the story foregrounds a struggle for control over the circulation of a woman's portrait. Set in Japan, the film depicts Cherry Blossom's efforts to wrest herself from a marriage to an older man in order to escape with the beau she has secretly been meeting in her back garden. A wealthy merchant falls in love with Cherry Blossom after glimpsing a portrait that has been secretly taken of her by a Western photographer and circulated on commercial postcards. The merchant proposes the idea of marriage to her parents, who are delighted. Unbeknownst to them, Cherry Blossom has overheard the plan, for she has been courting her lover on the porch just outside the room, separated only by a shoji. Eager to get rid of the merchant, Cherry Blossom scares him away upon their first meeting by wearing Western clothing borrowed from her American friend and making "ugly" faces, thereby freeing herself to elope with her sweetheart in the end.

Photography and desire are foregrounded from the outset. Scenes of the wealthy merchant gazing adoringly at Cherry Blossom's postcard are intercut with those of her meeting her sweetheart in the garden at night, creating a juxtaposition that clearly poses the merchant's idealization of her image, frozen apart from time and space, against the reality of her own desire. It poses an Orientalist exoticization of Cherry Blossom dependent on isolating and commercializing her image, against her own agency. Yet all three men—the Western photographer, the infatuated merchant, and Cherry Blossom's lover—are linked in their voyeuristic relation to her. Both the photographer and the suitor watch her, unseen, from identical vantage points in her garden, then the merchant falls in love with a photo taken from this same view. So even as the film ostensibly distinguishes between each man's interest—pure commercialism on the part of the photographer, blind passion on the merchant's part, and "true" love on the suitor's part—in fact each man objectifies Cherry Blossom in a similar manner. By capturing, then marketing, her image, the photographer commodifies an experience both he and her lover have already had.

By setting the story in Japan, the film makes a further commentary on the racial dynamics of this situation. The Western photographer exoticizes Cherry Blossom and freezes her image, ironically marketing this very por-

Figure 7. Cherry Blossom's image circulates among male hands on a commercial postcard in *A Japanese Idyll* (1912). Frame enlargement.

trait of racial exoticism back to a Japanese man. It is not until the merchant sees her outside her exoticized Orientalism—when she dons Western dress and makes unflattering faces—that he can shed his infatuation. With a white woman in "yellow face" playing Cherry Blossom, the film engages a further level of masquerade. There is nothing at all "real" about the eroticized, Orientalized female image that circulates.

In a film about secrecy, exhibitionism, and voyeurism, both diegetic space and screen space become especially significant. Three adjacent spaces at Cherry Blossom's home are delineated: the exterior garden where she meets her lover, the interior room where the family gathers to meet guests, including the wealthy merchant, and the rear porch that straddles these two realms, separated from the house only by a shoji. Cherry Blossom is the only character who navigates all three sites. Her lover never enters the house; her parents never step outside to the garden; and the merchant remains indoors. This gives Cherry Blossom an element of control that other characters lack. The thin shoji that separates indoors from outdoors becomes a crucial prop that she employs to control space: early in the film she uses it to conceal her secret love trysts from her parents, at one point even canoodling with her sweetheart while the parents broker a deal with the merchant just on the other side of the screen. Later she sneaks through the screen to escape outside and meet her lover for their planned elopement.

Ironically, Cherry Blossom's savvy navigation of these spaces also makes her the most vulnerable to being watched unseen, for ultimately, *A Japanese Idyll* is about relative hierarchies of seeing and knowledge. Cherry Blossom is objectified, without her knowing, by both the photographer who snaps her picture unaware and the merchant who falls madly in love with the image. In both cases, seeing without being seen oneself confers a certain amount of power on the voyeur. But Cherry Blossom succeeds in reversing this dynamic, first by taking charge of her own representation in such a manner that she scares off her would-be husband; then by successfully concealing her love affair from her parents and thereby allowing herself to elope in the end. In both cases she is able to control who sees what, when. Although the ending does not deliver as radical a critique of marriage and domesticity as seen in *Fine Feathers*, *A Japanese Idyll* pursues an even more self-conscious exploration of the particularly cinematic representations of femininity through its use of racialized performance and diegetic screens and its elaborate play on seeing and being seen.

If *Fine Feathers* and *A Japanese Idyll* demonstrate Weber's self-conscious exploration of the circulation of female imagery in painting and photography, *Suspense*, her best-known Rex film, takes on *cinematic* figurations of femininity, reworking one of the era's most pervasive celluloid tropes—the last-minute rescue drama perfected by D.W. Griffith at Biograph. Drawing on a rich intertext, *Suspense* assumes viewers' familiarity with Griffith's formula: a young mother and her infant are isolated in a "lonely villa" far from town where they face a male intruder penetrating the farthest reaches of domestic space. The film's generic title condenses Griffith's well-worn plotline to its elemental component—suspense—in order to investigate how tension is created in and around domestic environments and female victims. Innovative and unaccustomed camera positions significantly complicate the visual syntax of last-minute rescues, best known for their clear delineation of spatial and temporal topographies. One might even suggest that the unusual camera angles so often noted in *Suspense* become a means of destabilizing the logic enforced by parallel editing, skewing the strict binarism that had come to characterize so many race-to-the-rescue films. If Griffith's rescues employ dazzling intercutting, the epitome of a "narrator system" Gunning sees evolving in this transitional era, *Suspense* demonstrates the storytelling potential of composition, evoking a narrator's presence in a manner wholly different from Griffith's.[130] *Suspense* does not have nearly

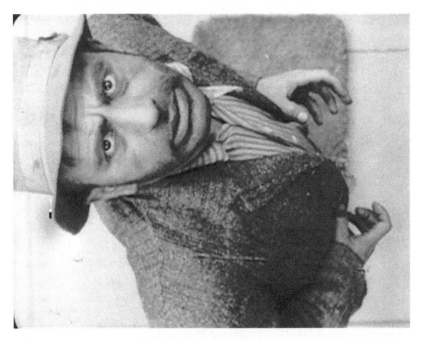

Figure 8. A mother's point of view of the intruder entering her "lonely villa" in *Suspense* (1913). Frame enlargement.

the shot count of a Biograph rescue, as Keil has documented, yet he notes how strikingly original the film remains. Its overhead and extreme high-angle compositions, its triangulated matte shots, and its use of moving camera work and diegetic mirrors, all place *Suspense* well beyond filmmaking norms at the time; in fact, Keil deems it "one of the most stylistically outré films of the transitional period."[131] That Weber should demonstrate such virtuosity through and against her main rival's celebrated formula, while playing the distressed heroine herself, suggests that she embraced the potential of her own cinematic authorship to craft alternate visions of femininity onscreen.

Fine Feathers, A Japanese Idyll, and *Suspense* testify to the evolving visual and narrative sophistication of Weber's work, developments that were echoed in the increasing length of her films, for her tenure at Rex coincided with a rapid evolution of multireel films in the United States. Universal brands were, proportionately, among the most active producers of multireel titles in the early teens, comprising fully one-third of the studio's output by late 1914. In fact, the number of three- and four-reel films released by Universal that year was exceeded only by companies devoted exclusively to feature film production.[132] Weber and Smalley began making two-reel films early in the spring of 1913, likely influenced by outfits pioneering the multireel trend in the United States, among them Porter's own Famous Players. In April alone they released two two-reel pictures, playing the leads in both films: *Until Death,* about a woman's love for two brothers, and *The Dragon's Breath,* about the wife of a college professor who unwittingly becomes addicted to opium after she cares for their Chinese servant.[133] *Moving Picture World* applauded this move, noting that the couple was "giving much attention to two-reel subjects, and with much success."[134] Several other two-reel pictures followed that year, including *Fallen Angel* in July and *Shadows of Life* and *Thumb Print* in October.[135] The couple's first three-reel production, the historical drama *The King Can Do No Wrong,* was released in June, with Weber and Smalley once again playing lead roles.[136] Their second three-reel picture, *A Jew's Christmas,* released for the holiday season in 1913, was promoted heavily by Universal and drew considerable attention. A contemporary story of prejudice and family reconciliation, Weber's script tackles a broad social issue through the lens of one family's tragedy, a model she would continue to exploit in her later social problem films. Her venture into longer, more complex narratives allowed Weber to explore more substantial social themes and to craft stories with plot arcs spread over a number of years.

A Jew's Christmas centers on Weber's character, Leah, the daughter of a conservative rabbi, played by Smalley. When Leah falls in love with the floorwalker in a department store where she works, her father ejects her from their home because her beloved is not Jewish. Leah chooses to marry the man anyway and does not see her family for years. After Leah's husband is disabled in an accident and can no longer work, the couple find themselves living in a tenement with their young daughter, making flowers to earn a living. Unbeknownst to all, Leah's parents live next door, and her father strikes up a friendship with the little girl, unaware that she is his granddaughter. When the girl mentions that she's never had a Christmas tree, the old rabbi buys her one, then discovers the truth about her identity. Forced to abandon his religious prejudices, he welcomes Leah back into the family. As *Moving Picture World* declared, "The ties of blood overbear the pride and prejudice of religion." Although the film's theme is religious intolerance, a theme to which Weber's scripts would frequently return, here the rabbi's prejudice, rather than anti-Semitism, is central. It is the Jew who must recognize the humanity of Gentiles, not the other way around. It is he who must accept Christian traditions, not they his. The message is inclusiveness, tolerance, and mutual respect, but the work must be done by Jews, not

"'GET FROM MY HOUSE,' HE SAID"

Figure 9. The rabbi (Smalley, *center*) orders his daughter Leah (Weber, *left*) out of the house in *A Jew's Christmas* (1913). Author's collection.

Gentiles. Universal was evidently sufficiently concerned about the subject to screen a print of *A Jew's Christmas* for a group of New York rabbis. *Moving Picture World* reported that the clergymen "were pleased with the story, with its treatment and with the fidelity with which the producers had followed Jewish ceremonies and customs, but were inclined to look with disfavor on the title." Although the paper's reviewers surmised that Jewish audiences might take offense at the film, they characterized it as "educational in its scope," presumably referring to its effect upon non-Jewish viewers.[137]

After seeing what Weber and Smalley had accomplished with the three-reel production of *A Jew's Christmas,* Carl Laemmle gave them their first opportunity to make a feature film, an adaptation of Shakespeare's *Merchant of Venice.* It would be the most ambitious project the studio had ever attempted.[138] The couple began production on the film in December 1913, three years into their tenure at Rex, just as another early Universal feature, the sensational *Traffic in Souls,* was at the height of its popularity.

With *The Merchant of Venice* Weber became the first woman in America to direct a feature film. Although she had adapted two Robert Browning poems for her Rex shorts, *The Light Woman* and *James Lee's Wife*, she had never attempted such an ambitious literary adaptation. In fact, *The Merchant of Venice* was relatively unique in Weber's screenwriting career. With the exception of her adaptation of the opera *The Dumb Girl of Portici* two years later, never again did she adapt Shakespeare or other highbrow literary sources, preferring instead scenarios adapted from newspaper stories or popular fiction. Why, then, might *The Merchant of Venice* have appealed to Weber as a source for her feature debut? Certainly she and Smalley were not the first to bring the play to the screen. Vitagraph, famed for its one-reel Shakespeare offerings, had released a version in 1908, and Thanhouser had produced a well-received two-reel version in 1912.[139] It is possible to surmise that the play appealed to Weber, if not for its novelty, then for more particular reasons: the pivotal role of Portia, which she would play herself, allowed Weber to continue her interest in female-centered narratives, even while dabbling in literary classics not always associated with such prominent female leads. Portia is a particularly active heroine, disguising herself as a man to serve as an attorney during the climactic trial sequence, and ultimately freeing her husband's friend from his onerous contract with Shylock. Portia's plea that morality ought to triumph over the letter of the law would likely also have appealed to Weber, as would the play's treatment of bigotry. Although it is not certain how much control Weber and Smalley had over choosing material for their first feature, it is safe to assume, given the degree of freedom they already enjoyed at Universal, that they had considerable say in the matter. *The Merchant of Venice*, then, offered Weber a means of working on a big-budget feature production, while also continuing thematic and narrative preoccupations of her earlier work.

By the time Weber and Smalley took on *The Merchant of Venice*, Shakespearian adaptations were not new to the screen. In the five years prior, some thirty-six American Shakespeare films had been released, with many more titles imported from overseas. As William Uricchio and Roberta Pearson point out, Shakespeare was associated with highbrow culture generally, and screen adaptations were embraced with particular enthusiasm by the film community as educational and uplifting.[140] By the early 1910s, however, even though filmmakers were exploring the new possibilities of multireel productions, fewer adaptations of Shakespeare were being made. *The Merchant of Venice*, for instance, was the only American Shakespearian film released in 1914. By the next year, no adaptations were made at all.[141]

Figure 10. Weber *(left)* played Portia and Smalley *(right)* played Shylock in her first feature film, *The Merchant of Venice* (1914). Author's collection.

Adapting Elizabethan drama for the silent screen presented scenario writers with a considerable challenge, arguably even more so in complex multireel films, since so much "action" is conveyed only through spoken dialogue. Weber tackled the problem by staging events that are only recounted by characters in the play's verse, thereby considerably reworking the drama.[142] Her script also radically condensed the play into some forty minutes, though this was longer than many earlier Shakespearean films. Such condensation enhanced the play, according to *Moving Picture World's* Hanford C. Judson, who felt that within the "narrower compass of four reels," comparisons between different elements of the play were brought into greater relief; he pointed in particular to the way Weber's adaptation highlighted comparisons between Portia's love story and Jessica's affair, and praised the "wisdom" of Weber's use of "quick strokes" to sketch in supplemental scenes. Judson, however, was less optimistic about what happened to characterization in the screen adaptation, and was concerned particularly that the subtle interplay between Shylock's outward actions and his thoughtful speeches was lost, even while commending Smalley's performance in the role.[143]

Weber and Smalley based much of the look of their production on existing material, in particular a 1909 edition of the play illustrated by Sir James

Dromgole Linton (1840–1916), a preeminent Victorian artist and past president of the Royal Institute of Painters in Watercolour.[144] Many of the costume designs bear strong resemblance to those illustrated in Linton's volume, though Linton's settings and stagings themselves do not appear to have been replicated in the Rex production. Weber and Smalley's production of *The Merchant of Venice* seems to have conformed to the broad outlines of other screen adaptations of the early teens, which, according to Uricchio and Pearson, tended to rely on key scenes and phrases already familiar to viewers in condensed versions of plays circulating in other media. Films further emphasized visual spectacle through elaborate costumes and stagings, often basing visual compositions on painterly renditions of the story.[145]

Universal promoted *The Merchant of Venice* as a "Special Release" outside its regular program. That meant that exhibitors would have to pay extra to show *The Merchant of Venice*, but the company assured theater owners that such an offering would "draw new patrons to your house," which would, as a result, "gain a prestige it never enjoyed before." Touting the film's "sumptuous settings, wonderful costumes, beautiful photography" and the "tremendous expense" of its production, Universal offered a special line of promotional materials designed to convey a similar message to theater patrons: colored lithograph six-sheets, window cards, and various smaller posters.[146] Smalley himself traveled to New York to promote the film, attending a screening at Universal with members of the trade press, and claiming that the film represented the best work he and Weber had done for the screen.[147] Though united in their praise of Weber's screen adaptation, contemporary commentators worried nonetheless about the suitability of presenting Elizabethan drama to cinemagoers, with both *Moving Picture World* and *Variety* expressing concern for the "average spectator."[148] The latter was concerned that without explanatory titles such viewers might find the complex plot "a little mystifying," though Judson praised Weber's adaptation for its ability to cater to "average" viewers by concentrating on Portia's love story, while he still declared its utmost value to "the thoughtful mind." One hears in trade discourse echoes of a broader uncertainty about cinema's future and its audience, so much in flux in early 1914. Could the cinema move toward such sophisticated material in such a "scholarly and dignified production," as Judson called it, while still pleasing its core audience? Commentators were emphatic in embracing the complex possibilities of cinematic narration, while they were also clearly leery about the medium's current social audience. They noted a tension between their faith in the medium's aesthetic sophistication and the realities of contemporary moviegoers.

The Merchant of Venice was itself also a problematic text. In one of her first brushes with censorship and controversy, issues that would dog Weber throughout the following years, *The Merchant of Venice* encountered trouble with the Chicago Board of Censors when a prominent rabbi in that city objected to the portrayal of Shylock. "More than any other book, more than any other influence in the history of the world," he argued, Shakespeare's play was "responsible for the creation of a world-wide prejudice against the Jew." After hosting a private screening for prominent Jewish community leaders at City Hall and inviting their commentary, the Chicago Board elected to pass the picture.[149] Although no particular mention was made of *A Jew's Christmas* in this controversy, one can imagine that the portrayal of Jewish intolerance of Christianity in that earlier Weber film would have added fuel to the critique of *The Merchant of Venice*.

Despite the praise Weber and Smalley received for *The Merchant of Venice* and the success of other early Universal features such as *Traffic in Souls*, Laemmle remained skeptical of a film program based entirely on such titles and lambasted the trend in the house organ *Universal Weekly* and in fliers sent to individual exhibitors. His argument was mainly economic: Universal could supply a week's worth of varied programming for a little more than double what many feature outfits were charging for one day's rental of a feature. "The heart and soul, lungs and liver, backbone and stamina, brains and brawn of the moving picture business is THE SCIENTIFICALLY BALANCED PROGRAM," Laemmle wrote. "The exhibitor who is building for the future ought to see by now that every time he indulges in so-called 'features' he is spending his money for fluff that will never get him anywhere or anything."[150] Rather than selling individual film titles, the company marketed "The Universal Program," guaranteeing exhibitors four-reel programs with daily changes for $105 per week. Programs generally consisted of a two-reel drama, a one-reel comedy, and a one-reel "general interest" subject that might contain an educational title, a drama, or a cartoon. Universal charged more than any other studio for its weekly program, save those producing feature films.[151]

Even following the success of *The Merchant of Venice*, then, Weber and Smalley continued to produce one- and two-reel shorts for Universal, making occasional three-reelers like *Helping Mother* (1914). But they did not return to feature productions. In fact, Anthony Slide speculates, with good reason, that the couple ultimately left Universal in August 1914 in search of improved opportunities for feature filmmaking.[152] When they were not selected to produce Universal's four-reel adaptation of Clara Louise Burnham's Christian Science novel, *The Opened Shutters*, a script that Weber had penned and a project likely very close to her heart, they seized an opportunity to leave Universal and join the upstart feature company Bosworth, Inc.[153]

But the three years Weber and Smalley had spent at Rex and Universal proved an invaluable education. They fostered a collaborative mode of production they would maintain for many years, sharing directing, producing, and editing chores, even as Weber assumed a more dominant role in the partnership. They operated a kind of repertory company, working with a consistent troupe of performers, several of whom would later direct films themselves. Weber honed her screenwriting craft to great acclaim, later remarking that the "hard apprenticeship" of writing one scenario a week had proved "an excellent mental exercise" that sharpened her writing talents immeasurably.[154] Screenwriting also facilitated Weber's move into directing, as she began to assume greater creative control of her projects. As mayor of Universal City, Weber certainly took on an increasingly prominent role at the studio, but she also became the face of feminine uplift in Hollywood, and a face of modern femininity more generally. Her public comments on the industry, and on screenwriting in particular, suggest, however, that she was much more than the matronly do-gooder some thought her to be at the time—a role into which subsequent historians have willingly cast her as well. The films Weber and Smalley produced at Rex, while continually noted for their exceptional cinematography, well-crafted staging, nuanced performances, and original narratives, were also advancing quite radical critiques of gender roles, patriarchal institutions, and even mass culture itself. They are evidence of the commanding role that Weber envisioned for the medium, and its viewers, just as cinema began to assume its role as the nation's premiere commercial entertainment.

"YOURS SINCERELY, LOIS WEBER"

Weber and Smalley joined Bosworth, Inc., on August 1, 1914, signing a lucrative contract that guaranteed them a salary of $500 per week, plus a percentage of the profits generated by their productions. One report suggested Weber's salary would amount to $50,000 a year.[155] Likely more important than the financial terms of the agreement was the fact that Bosworth offered an opportunity to focus on feature films, rather than the one- and two-reel productions still at the heart of the Universal program. In fact, with the exception of *The Traitor*, the couple's first production at

Bosworth, all films Weber and Smalley made at the company were four-and five-reel features. Multireel films allowed Weber to create more complex narratives with more fully developed characters and themes. In doing so, she showcased her authorial signature more than ever—a signature distinctly feminized.

Bosworth, Inc., had been formed a year earlier by Hobart Bosworth, a former stage actor and director who began working in motion pictures in 1909, starting first with Selig in Chicago. After writing, directing, and acting for various companies, he formed his own organization in August 1913, initially designed to produce adaptations of Jack London novels. London had sold Bosworth rights to all his existing and future work. Bosworth's first production, an adaptation of London's *The Sea Wolf* released in 1913, was the first seven-reel feature produced in the United States. Made on a budget of $9,000, the film grossed $4 million, allowing Bosworth to set up his own studio. Bosworth's partner in the venture was oil millionaire and Los Angeles financier Frank Garbutt, a man who believed cinema superior to the stage in its ability to convey real action and its democratic guarantee of an identical experience for all paying customers. Garbutt's daughter Melodie served as the company's secretary.[156] Bosworth was explicitly formed, then, to focus on the production of quality features. Trade ads proclaimed the company's interest in "powerful stories with unusual possibilities for screen visualization" that would "uphold the highest standard possible."[157]

With this goal in mind Hobart Bosworth, along with Jesse L. Lasky of the Lasky Company and Adolph Zukor of Famous Players, had also been instrumental in the formation of Paramount Pictures in May 1914. Declaring their "desire for the uplift of the industry and the further prestige of the feature film," the three men founded Paramount with the aim of centralizing, streamlining, and ultimately increasing distribution of feature films nationwide.[158] Bringing together local distributors from different regions, Paramount was able to guarantee production companies higher advances than they would have received through individual states' rights contracts—usually in the neighborhood of $20,000—thereby encouraging more ambitious film productions. Paramount also paid for the cost of film prints and trade advertising. The company quickly established a reputation for itself based on quality releases.[159] Bluntly referring to the associates as "high-brows," *Moving Picture World* professed the alliance "the greatest feature program every conceived."[160] As Rob King points out, Paramount was incredibly successful at "leveraging cultural capital into industrial might" with a business model that foretold the rise of vertical integration a decade later.[161]

Weber and Smalley signed with Bosworth just two weeks after the formation of Paramount was announced, suggesting their keen interest in the company's objectives. Shortly after their arrival, Paramount commenced a national advertising campaign, beginning with a two-page spread in the *Saturday Evening Post*, followed by full-page ads in subsequent editions of the *Post* and other mass monthlies.[162] Paramount assured exhibitors these ads would reach not only those patrons who already frequented "the better grade of motion picture shows," but also those who did not and might be convinced that they could see the equivalent of a "two dollar show" for as little as a dime.[163] Stressing the "cultured" audiences Paramount pictures were imagined to attract, ads featured patrons attending theaters in top hats and furs, driven there in chauffeured automobiles.[164] Showcased in omnibus Paramount advertisements, Weber's Bosworth productions were advertised alongside some of the most prestigious pictures of the day, including Mary Pickford's *Mistress Nell* (1915) and Cecil B. DeMille's *The Girl of the Golden West* (1915).

King describes 1914 as a "threshold" year for the film industry: feature films were on the rise—production increased over 500 percent that year alone—and new distributors were created to handle multireel productions, while elaborate "picture palaces" were constructed to showcase quality features for upscale audiences. Paramount was at the forefront of this evolution.[165] Signaling this trend in the fall of that year, *Moving Picture World*'s Louis Reeves Harrison announced that "demand for strong features" was "far outrunning supply."[166] By the new year, his colleague W. Stephen Bush noted a sea change in the industry, with power shifting away from "cheap men with cheap ideas" and into the hands of "men who strike at the highest possible aims in quality of plot and acting and photography," men committed to "the high class motion picture." Audiences were more appreciative than ever, he said, of such productions.[167] Weber was one of those men.

Signing Weber and Smalley to Bosworth was "about the first move" Garbutt made after the formation of Paramount, one report concluded.[168] If the two filmmakers were eager to be affiliated with a company producing quality features, Bosworth and Paramount were equally interested in promoting this ideal through the couple. From the beginning of their association with Bosworth, Weber and Smalley were marketed as movie personalities. Details of Smalley's background, often outrageously embroidered, were frequently cited: his pedigree dating back to Lafayette; his training at Oxford, in Sir Henry Irving's dressing room, and on stage with Mrs. Fiske; his education as a lawyer at Harvard; and his supposed friendship with the king of England all featured prominently in Bosworth press coverage.[169]

Weber, considered the company's "principal director," was cast as a leading filmmaker of her generation, "second only to D. W. Griffith."[170] Essential to all of these promotions was the vision of a married bourgeois couple working together on all aspects of their productions. "Rarely, if ever has it been given to one couple to combine the unusual talents and remarkable qualifications" represented in the two.[171] Banner ads for the Paramount lineup that had previously stressed Lasky's association with theater legend David Belasco, Famous Players' association with noted Broadway producers the Frohman brothers, and Bosworth's Jack London franchise now promoted Bosworth's association with Weber and Smalley. Not only were they singled out, but they were also allied with top feature filmmaking outfits and the uppermost echelons of the theater world.[172] Rarified company indeed.

Bosworth, in the midst of constructing a vast new studio complex, offered Weber and Smalley ideal conditions for feature filmmaking. Located on North Occidental Boulevard in the Wilshire neighborhood of Los Angeles, the new Bosworth studio was among the best production facilities on the West Coast, according to *Moving Picture World*. It included a sixty foot–by–ninety foot glassed-in stage equipped with a lighting system for year-round shooting, adjoining dressing rooms with full showers, a large property room, a carpentry shop, and a lab capable of processing 20,000 feet of film per day.[173] The following spring the studio was expanded even further to include a 2,500-square-foot addition to its glass-covered main stage, more dressing rooms, and a new scene dock with two new large paint frames for backdrop—a renovation that effectively doubled the property's floor space.[174] In accordance with the company's stated policy to present pictures "with unusual faithfulness to detail," Bosworth productions also often traveled to far-off locations to ensure realism.[175] All of this must have appealed tremendously to Weber and Smalley.

In addition to Hobart Bosworth, whom the couple evidently admired, and his wife, Adele Farrington, whom they had already directed at Rex, Weber and Smalley soon found themselves in the company of other notables from the theater world. After a trip to New York in November 1914, Garbutt signed several famed stage personalities, including James K. Hackett, Dustin Farnum (who would later star in *Captain Courtesy*), and Macklyn Arbuckle (whom Weber would later direct in *It's No Laughing Matter*). Garbutt also signed stage comedienne Elsie Janis. Janis, who wrote most of her own material, had never appeared in films, but soon relocated to Los Angeles with plans to star in two pictures she had written herself.[176] Weber and Smalley would later direct one of these projects, *Betty in Search of a Thrill*. Garbutt's main achievement was signing noted theater producer

Oliver Morosco, with whom he formed the Oliver Morosco Photoplay Company, a move one observer declared to be "further indication of the remarkable development of the feature film," one that "attaches greater prestige to Bosworth, Inc."[177] Morosco's stage properties would now become available for films. Weber and Smalley, who had often stressed the importance of theatrically trained actors and directors in the cinema, now found themselves in ideal company. Dal Clawson, their cinematographer from Rex, also joined the couple at Bosworth, where his innovations in cinematography served Weber's ambitious program of features.

A young Frances Marion also arrived at Bosworth in the fall of 1914 when Weber was in production on her first film, *The Traitor*. Marion remembered "a tall woman with classical features" who "seemed to glide rather than walk, her head held high and tilted slightly backward."[178] After assuring Weber that she preferred to work "on the dark side of the camera," rather than as an actress, Marion served as Weber's assistant, doing "whatever needed doing," according to biographer Cari Beauchamp. This included writing press releases, cutting film, assisting with set decoration and continuity, and even serving as stunt double on *Captain Courtesy*. Out of this experience the two women became lifelong friends; the aspiring screenwriter developed a "deep respect" for Weber's abilities and a "fierce loyalty" to her mentor, Beauchamp reports.[179]

At Bosworth the couple's working methods appear to have begun to vary. At times they worked together as they had at Universal, with Weber writing original scenarios and both of them acting on screen together and collaborating on the direction and production, even as Weber's authorship became more pronounced. Yet, in addition to codirecting and costarring in films written by Weber, such as *Sunshine Molly* and *False Colours*, the couple also directed separately (Weber on *It's No Laughing Matter* and Smalley on *Betty in Search of a Thrill*)—projects in which neither appeared on screen. Weber also directed *Captain Courtesy*, though neither she nor Smalley appeared in the film and she was not credited with adapting the novel for the screen.

False Colours, a five-reel feature released in December 1914, afforded Weber a chance to demonstrate her full potential. Rooted in themes and techniques she had been exploring in her Rex shorts, the film's expanded length, along with additional resources available to her at Bosworth, allowed Weber to craft a more complex script enhanced by complicated visual effects using superimpositions and character doubles. Set in the theater world, *False Colours* uses a backstage setting to explore the performative dimensions of femininity and role-playing in heterosexual relationships. While considering ideas of performance, impersonation, and substitution in its diegetic story, the film also explores these issues at a cinematic level through dual casting and double exposure. It is an ambitious production, an indication of how constrained Weber had been by the Universal program.

Smalley plays famed stage actor Lloyd Phillips, who gives up the profession after his beloved wife dies in childbirth.[180] He rejects the daughter born that night, leaving Dixie (Dixie Carr) to be raised by his housekeeper, Mrs. Hughes (Adele Farrington). Hughes squanders money intended for Dixie's education on her unscrupulous son Bert (Courtenay Foote), so Dixie flees the household and becomes a successful actress in her own right. Meanwhile, Mrs. Hughes's son Bert has married Flo Moore (Weber), the daughter of a wardrobe mistress devoted to Phillips's career (also played by Weber). Bert and Mrs. Hughes convince Flo to pose as Dixie when her father, hearing of his daughter's stage success, finally comes looking for her. Thinking she is his daughter, Phillips soon becomes fond of Flo, but when the ruse is revealed, Flo flees home to her mother in disgrace. Flo and Phillips are finally reconciled when Mrs. Moore, near death, asks Flo to take him the scrapbooks she has lovingly compiled throughout his career. Admitting their love for one another, Flo and Phillips are able to marry after the nefarious Bert Hughes dies in a botched robbery attempt. Although Flo had been originally cast as Phillips's daughter Dixie, a part she resisted, she now steps happily into the role of his wife. Dixie, too, is reconciled with her father in the end.

Phillips's growing affection for Flo is crystallized during two scenes in which her image is superimposed over photos of his dead wife. Early in the film Phillips's enduring love for his departed wife is evoked as he imagines her presence in ghostly, superimposed images. These compositions place Phillips in the same frame as his (spectral) wife, emphasizing his imagined relation with her through sight lines within the frame. Toward the end of the film, Flo literally takes over as the object of Phillips's "screen" fantasy. In the climactic moment, Phillips is pining over a photo of his deceased wife when Flo's image is suddenly superimposed over the other woman's, Flo's profile matching the wife's exactly. Flo then turns her head to face forward and smile at Phillips, seeming to bring the photo and his preserved fantasy to life. Double-exposure condenses in one image the overlay of past and present, death and life, mother and (imagined) daughter, former wife and present lover. The fact that Weber herself plays this role, that Weber herself turns to look directly into the camera, serves only to remind us of her authorial hand.

But this overlay is complicated still further. By falling in love with Phillips, Flo does more than assume the place of his deceased wife; she also

Figure 11. Weber used superimposition and dual casting to explore issues of gender performativity in *False Colours* (1914). Frame enlargement.

mirrors her own mother's long-held secret attraction to the actor, a fact only reinforced by having Weber play both roles. Overlaid diegetic and extradiegetic elements of performance and doubling in *False Colours* are almost too intricate to map. Weber, the off-screen writer and director, plays a woman (Flo) who is impersonating another woman (Dixie), who is herself a noted actress. While standing in for Dixie, Flo plays out her mother's infatuation with Phillips, at the same time as she takes the place of his deceased wife. Simultaneously Flo, Dixie, Mrs. Moore, and the late Mrs. Phillips (virtually all of the female characters in the story), *and* the film's author, Weber very self-consciously inhabits multiple roles both in front of and behind the camera.

Some indication of Weber's working methods as a director can be gleaned from two significant differences between Weber's original script and the finished film. First, scenes in which Phillips recalls his dead wife are not contained in the script. This suggests that Weber may have felt no need to document in writing the complex visual effects that were increasingly common in her films, as they were so integral to her artistic conception from the outset. These visual effects may also have been significantly elaborated on the set in collaboration with cinematographer Dal Clawson. Second, the written screenplay follows a more linear version of the story, which, on screen, jumps back and forth between action in the city (where Phillips's daughter Dixie is appearing on stage and living with his wardrobe mistress, Mrs. Moore), the country (where Bert and Mrs. Hughes live with Flo), and the island (where Phillips lives as a recluse). Weber apparently reworked her scripts considerably in the editing room, embroidering more intricate narratives with juxtapositions, comparisons, and foreshadowing.

If *False Colours* is emblematic of the pivot Weber made from her Rex shorts to more complex features at Bosworth, continuing her fascination with artistic personalities, heterosexual couplings, gender performance, and innovative camera work, *Sunshine Molly,* her last Bosworth production, signaled a shift in Weber's scripts toward more contemporary social issues and a greater emphasis on realism. Set amidst the roughneck world of California's oil boom, *Sunshine Molly* was shot on location in the La Brea oil fields and includes some spectacular cinematography, beginning with a nearly 360-degree tilting and panning shot around the oil field that ends with a long shot of Sunshine Molly herself standing with her suitcase on the side of the road, having just landed at the oil field. In addition to the sweeping panoramas afforded in this location shooting, Weber's staff created a miniature reproduction of the setting at the Bosworth studio, where they were able to stage the destruction of the oil field in an explosion and subsequent fire—a visual effect one reviewer called "exceptional and most unusual."[181]

Against this horizon, *Sunshine Molly* explores the issue of sexual harassment and sexual violence in the workplace.[182] After arriving at the oil field in the film's opening scene, Molly (Weber) finds work in a boardinghouse where she prepares and serves meals to men who work on the rigs. The film is focused less, in the end, on men toiling in the oil fields than on the less publicized but equally essential labor of women behind the scenes, feeding and caring for these workers. One of only a few women there, and confined largely to the boardinghouse, Molly nonetheless commands the men's attention. Staging in these early scenes emphasizes her prominence, placing her in the center of the frame serving meals in the dining hall or summoning workers inside for a meal, surrounded by men who frame her movements and whose eyes always seem on her. We see how the dining hall's architecture allows Molly to become an object of fascination, for it simultaneously puts her on display serving food to the men and hides the women's labor in the kitchen—they emerge only to deliver meals. Capable in all of her tasks, generous with her assistance to others, and always charming, Molly is "one of those adamant types upon which

Figure 12. In her last Bosworth production, *Sunshine Molly* (1915), Weber turned her attention to sexual harassment and sexual violence in the workplace. Author's collection.

the morality of our nation depends," Margaret I. MacDonald concluded in her review for *Moving Picture World*.[183]

Bull (Smalley), "a hard character whose opinion of women in general is not high," according to the film's publicity herald, "attempts to become familiar on short acquaintance," whereupon Molly promptly smashes a plate over his head and refuses all contact.[184] Shunned by the other men after his advance on Molly, Bull nurtures a growing fascination with her, coming to appreciate her dedication to others. Although she remains wary of him, their bond deepens when she asks him to help her care for "Old Pete" (Herbert Standing), an elderly oil worker. Through Molly, Bull learns the transformative value of selflessly helping others. Late in the film we discover, through a flashback, that Molly had arrived at the oil field just after having been released from prison, where she had served time for stabbing a man who raped her. This late revelation explains her violent reaction to Bull's early acts of physical aggression and her exceptional acts of kindness toward others. After Bull is blinded in a work accident, Molly nurses him back to health, and through this they fall in love. Torn by his attraction to her, Bull writes Molly a note saying, "Let someone else wait on me for I can't keep my hands off you and I'd rather die than lose your friendship again." Sitting down on the bed beside him, Molly then says, "I reckon it don't matter if a man puts his hands on his wife." The two embrace in the final shot.

What begins as a story about a feisty young woman who refuses to tolerate being pinched and leered at by roughnecks turns into a more complicated tale, once we learn that Molly has been the victim of a far more serious sexual assault, one for which she, not her assailant, has served jail time. Reviewers were coy about the film's sexual situations, describing how Bull "tries to force his love on Molly" and how Molly had been imprisoned for attacking a man who "tried to get fresh."[185] But the violence of these scenes is clear in the film itself; Molly is a victim of rape who forcibly resists Bull's sexual harassment and attempted assault. Indeed, the flashback structure does more than withhold crucial information about Molly's past; when that information is finally revealed, it is done so through Molly's own point of view. We come to understand her attitude precisely at the moment when we are invited to share her position of victimization. The nonlinear, flashback structure also places Molly's prior experience of sexual assault in closer proximity to Bull's attack, demanding that viewers compare the two episodes. The perpetrator of the rape was the boss's son at the factory where Molly worked, a man who targeted his father's employees under the guise of workplace surveillance. At the oil field, Molly, one of only two young women, is easily singled out for attention. The film is careful to show how her labor in cooking and caring for the men is effaced, and how sexualized she becomes in the performative arena of food service, echoing the situation in the factory where her boss's son eyed women at work in order to identify potential targets for his sexual violence.

Given *Sunshine Molly's* emphasis on the structural conditions of sexual assault in heterosocial workplaces, and its insistence on the repeated incidence of such attacks, the film's concluding scenes are troubling. Not only do they seem to present Molly's change of heart too abruptly, but Bull's violent sexuality is not entirely erased. Molly's quip about how marriage will allow him to put "his hands on his wife" echoes Bull's earlier vow to keep "my hands off" her following his attempted assault, which in turn echoes the euphemistic language used to describe Molly's rapist, who "wouldn't keep his hands off" her. In fact, just prior to this scene an older man tells Molly, "Bull ain't so bad, I used to pinch pretty girls myself when I was young," casting sexual violence as a boyish prank. The demands of narrative resolution—here achieved through the formation of a heterosexual couple in marriage—seem forced in *Sunshine Molly* and are ultimately unable to settle the pressures revealed between men and women in the workplace.

False Colours and *Sunshine Molly* stand at opposite ends of Weber's tenure at Bosworth, demonstrating the different ways in which she exploited new opportunities and resources available to her in feature filmmaking. If *False Colours* shows how she was able to develop the thematic preoccupations and formal experimentation of her Rex films to their fullest, *Sunshine Molly,* her last Bosworth release, provides an indication of the work she would produce when she returned to Universal later that year to embark on a series of enormously successful films on contemporary social issues. But Weber's most ambitious and notable Bosworth production, by far, was *Hypocrites,* the film that established her artistic reputation and defined her as one of the premiere filmmakers of her generation. Produced and released almost exactly coincident with D.W. Griffith's *The Birth of a Nation* (1915), *Hypocrites,* like its counterpart, asserts a complex argument about cinema's artistic potential. If Griffith sought cinema's legitimacy in a historical epic, a re-imagining of the Civil War to mark its fiftieth anniversary, Weber took a different tack, exploring the theme of religious hypocrisy through historical allegory.

In *Hypocrites* Courtney Foote plays a minister disturbed by the hypocrisies of his ever-so-modern congregation. Falling asleep after church one Sunday, the clergyman dreams he is a medieval monk named Gabriel who leads his parishioners up a steep mountain, then carves a controversial statue of "Naked Truth," which comes to life. "Since my people will not come to you," he says to Truth, "come to my people," taking her back into contemporary settings to visit his modern-day parishioners. There she holds a mirror of truth up to their activities, revealing hypocrisies in their views on childrearing, sexuality, politics, and the like. As one reviewer put it, "Miss Weber does not hesitate to flay hypocrisy in every form."[186] Striking visual effects convey these visits, as Naked Truth appears superimposed over these scenes, matte shots showing what she reveals in her mirror. At the end of the film the clergyman is discovered, dead, still seated at the altar, clutching a newspaper he had seized from one of the members of his choir. It features an item on Adolphe Faugeron's 1914 painting *La Verité,* a vision of truth as a naked woman that had scandalized Paris the previous year, the apparent inspiration for the minister's dream. His parishioners, ever hypocritical and still blind to their own moral failings, are mortified to find him with the nude image.

Hypocrites was widely recognized for its demonstration of cinema's potential as a serious art form. Describing the film as "quite remarkable from every angle of the picture art," *Variety* decreed that "no one else has attempted as much or has gone as far." Weber had achieved "a new revelation

Figure 13. The Naked Truth wields her mirror in *Hypocrites* (1915), the film that established Weber's reputation as a leading filmmaker of her time. Frame enlargement.

of the artistic possibilities of the photo-play," one critic declared. *Hypocrites,* another noted, "takes its place among the most exceptional films." Observing that it was "unjust" to consider the film merely a "strong pictorial drama," another writer even insisted, "It is a production to be compared favorably with the most powerful modern productions of the stage." The *Los Angeles Times* proclaimed *Hypocrites* "without a doubt one of the biggest and most outspoken, yet artistic productions yet seen on a local screen." When the film was revived the following year for a run at the Strand, the *New York Times* noted how well it held up, suggesting it was "superior to the majority that have followed in the two years since it was made."[187]

Even as it received praise for its artistic ambitions, *Hypocrites* also attracted considerable attention for its depiction of female nudity. Inspired by Faugeron's painting, Weber elected to allegorize truth as a naked woman, casting Margaret Edwards to play the part, though choosing to clothe the actress in a flesh-toned leotard. Even cloaked in such ideals, conceptualized in this way, Naked Truth elicited considerable sniggering from the press. Incensed by these responses, Weber sent a telegram to the *New York Mail,* writing, "I want to take exception to your statement that 'The Hypocrites' was produced to attract by reason of the nude woman." Instead, she wrote, "I hoped that the picture would act as a moral force. The nude woman is too delicately carried through to act otherwise."[188]

Likely because of Weber's decision to incorporate female nudity—or, more properly, the *suggestion* of female nudity—*Hypocrites*' release was considerably delayed. The production was apparently finished and copyrighted by the end of September 1914, so it was likely the first feature Weber completed at Bosworth. Some trade papers reviewed it in early

October, but the general release appears to have been held up by deliberations at the National Board of Censorship and negotiations with the New York district attorney's office. As a result, *Hypocrites* did not have its official premiere until January 1915. After a private showing at Roxy Rothafel's showcase Strand Theater, the film began an indefinite run at New York's Longacre Theater, a grand "legitimate" playhouse on West 48th Street just off Broadway, where it played to capacity crowds in afternoon and evening screenings. A live chorus, enlarged orchestra, and Wurlitzer organ accompanied screenings, with ticket prices ranging from twenty-five cents to one dollar. Reviewed by regular dramatic critics in all of the city's daily newspapers, *Hypocrites* received considerable attention and drew large audiences, especially for the higher-priced seats. One report boasted that the theater took in $5,000 in box office receipts for a single week's run.[189] After attending the show, *Moving Picture World*'s Hanford C. Judson reported an attentive and appreciative audience, predicting the film was destined "to enjoy a long and emphatic popularity."[190] Following a run of several weeks at the Longacre, *Hypocrites* moved to additional theaters in New York City and began playing across the country. Paramount exchanges, which normally required exhibitors to commit to an entire year's worth of programming, sold *Hypocrites* on an individual basis, encouraging bookings at legitimate theaters rather than regular movie houses.[191] In many cases *Hypocrites* marked the first occasion that motion pictures were shown in these venues, and such screenings often maintained the aura of the initial Broadway performances with lecturers on stage and orchestral or choral accompaniment. The first film ever shown at Philadelphia's Globe Theater, for instance, *Hypocrites* was accompanied there by a chorus, and scenic tableaus were presented before and after the picture. When it opened at Atlanta's Lyric Theater, marking "the advent of pictures" there, a critic announced, "Plenty of good pictures have been in Atlanta before, but none that can excel this last offering."[192]

Even with the imprimatur of New York's cultural and religious elite, *Hypocrites* enjoyed what one observer called a "stormy voyage" across the country.[193] Weber's use of female nudity continued to cause alarm, no matter how "highbrow" the context. The National Board of Review would ultimately ban all depictions of female nudity on screen in early 1917, likely as a result of the controversy ignited by *Hypocrites;* but in the meantime Weber's film tested regulatory agencies across the country at a time of patchwork regulation during which the National Board of Censorship often found itself at odds with local police and district attorneys, as well as competing municipal and state censorship agencies. Ohio's Board of Censors banned the film outright, as did several cities, including major markets like Chicago and Minneapolis. In other cities, such as Nashville, censors reviewed, but ultimately passed the film. In San Jose, California, the mayor and police chief tried to prevent screenings by seizing prints of the film, but a jury trial established that the film did not contravene the city's moral code, and showings were later permitted. Complaints were filed with the commissioner of public safety in Tacoma, Washington, in an attempt to prevent screenings in that city, but the film was viewed by the police captain and allowed to be exhibited.[194] After Boston's mayor called the film "indecent and sacrilegious," plans were apparently considered to drape Margaret Edwards's frame in a gown "of sufficiently classical style as to meet the requirements of the fastidious Bostonians," though it is doubtful that any such plans materialized.[195] Bosworth, which had encountered trouble with regulators over Hobart Bosworth's adaptation of the temperance drama *John Barleycorn* the previous summer, protested any attempts to censor *Hypocrites*, taking out trade ads denouncing the Ohio Board of Censors and calling on exhibitors to unite against "the evils of 'legalized censorship.'"[196]

In spite of continuing censorship battles, *Hypocrites* was a marked success in many parts of the country, playing extended runs and return engagements in cities such as Denver, Detroit, Dallas, Philadelphia, and San Francisco, where that city's *Chronicle* newspaper noted, "It has been some time since San Franciscans have displayed so much interest in a photoplay."[197] At Pearce's Tudor Theater on Canal Street in New Orleans the film broke box office records, despite the stiff twenty-five-cent admission price. When *Hypocrites* opened in Los Angeles, crowds gathered at the seven-hundred-seat Quinn's Superba, filling six shows daily for several weeks with sky-high ticket prices of twenty-five, thirty-five, and fifty cents. The struggle with regulators over whether the film could be shown in that city had received front-page coverage in LA's dailies. So popular was the film that Bosworth had to print a second run of posters and publicity materials in the spring of 1915. Paramount records indicate that in the end *Hypocrites* was an astonishing success: made at a cost of $18,000, the film ultimately netted some $133,000 from domestic and foreign sales.[198] Even as *Hypocrites* helped establish a market for ambitious feature films with high-art aspirations, it also succeeded in cementing Weber's reputation as a filmmaker. "After seeing *Hypocrites*," *Variety* proclaimed, "you can't forget the name of Lois Weber." As a result of the production, another observer noted, Weber had "attracted more attention to herself as a writer of scenarios than ... any other author during the past season." Profiles even began to suggest that she "ranked as second among American photoplay directors," bettered only by Griffith, and that she was "a great photoplay writer" and "a photo-play writer of consequence."[199]

If *Hypocrites* secured Weber's authorial signature, it is also one of her most sustained meditations on her own enterprise. As Paul D. Young points out, the film "embraces its own constructedness, the better to elevate the filmmaker to the status of an artist." *Hypocrites*, Young argues, is ulti-mately less about hypocrisy in modern society than "the possibility of imbuing the feature film with a poetic form of visuality." Weber's allusion to a Robert Browning poem at the outset of the film—her portrait dissolves directly into the quotation "What does the world, told a truth, but lie the more"—promises less an *adaptation* of the poem, Young suggests, than a text of comparable artistic complexity and merit.[200] *Hypocrites*, in the van-guard of allegorical "multiple diegesis films" common in the early feature period, as Moya Luckett notes, ultimately mounts an argument about cin-ema itself—about the possibilities of "a vision unbound by time."[201] While the film's allegorical construction draws attention to Weber's authorial hand, her use of such an overtly cinematic figure as the mirror of truth also signals the uniquely cinematic aspects of this "vision." Explicitly compar-ing her own enterprise to that of Naked Truth, Weber told an interviewer, "I merely held up the mirror of truth that humanity might see itself."[202]

Weber's distinctly feminine authorial "signature" was also embodied in *Sunshine Molly*, as the film opens on an image of a large book inscribed with the title "Sunshine Molly by Lois Weber." At the bottom edge of the frame a pair of female hands opens the cover to reveal the first page, inscribed "Book One," then turns to another page, where the story begins: "It was a great day for Oilfield when Sunshine Molly came looking for work." The hand turns the page again, cueing a cut to the first image of the film, the spectacular overhead panning shot that reveals Molly (Weber herself, of course) standing in the oil field, bag in hand. Intertitles continue this theme throughout the film with the feminine hand turning pages of a book to reveal titles or to cue new scenes. At each reel change book pages are shown indicating "End of Book One" and "Book Two," as the female hand again turns the pages. Noting the innovative page-turning intertitles, one reviewer took the opportunity to draw attention to Weber's authorship. *Sunshine Molly* "is attributed to Mr. Smalley," the reviewer noted, "but since he and his wife, Lois Weber, worked in the film, and knowing her handiwork so well, somehow I say it is the work of 'The Smalleys'"; the review went on to refer only to Weber when praising other elements of the film with great enthusiasm.[203]

Yet Weber's authorial inscription is even more nuanced than this com-ment allows. In *Hypocrites* Weber's photograph and signed dedication, vis-

Figure 14. Weber's intricate signification of authorship in
Sunshine Molly (1915). Frame enlargement.

ible only at the outset of the film, serve to ground a feminine authorial
presence otherwise evident in the text only through its allegorical construction and its reflexive use of "life's mirror." In *Sunshine Molly*, Weber's
self-inscription, woven throughout the film, is, if anything, more complex,
for it is associated with the script/book, hand-written as if by Weber herself; with the unfolding of the visual narrative, cued by the female page-
turner; with the spectacular command of optical space that this "hand"
facilitates; and with the very embodiment of the spirited heroine, Molly, the
kind of woman, as Margaret I. MacDonald put it, upon which "our nation
depends." More still, the film's narrative construction, in which crucial
information is withheld from viewers until the final reel, signals a narra-
tor/filmmaker/page-turner with nothing short of omniscient control.
Weber's authorship, which she secures through writing the original story,
embodying the heroine herself, then "summoning" the images as the film's
director, is total and complete.

After finishing production on *Sunshine Molly* in February 1915, Weber
and Smalley took a short vacation, then announced they would seek work
elsewhere, severing their association with Bosworth, Inc., after only seven
months at the company. Hobart Bosworth, who had been suffering "an attack
of nervous trouble," took a leave from the company around the same time,
though it is unclear how significantly Bosworth's absence affected Weber and
Smalley, who tended to work on their own productions independent of those

Bosworth was making. Press reports also suggested the pair were unhappy at Bosworth, yet it is not clear why. Were they dissatisfied directing projects like *Captain Courtesy* and *Betty in Search of a Thrill*—films they neither wrote nor starred in themselves? Did the absence of Hobart Bosworth, who had originally drawn them to the company, change the dynamics there? Anthony Slide even speculates that under Paramount's auspices Adolph Zukor began "interfering in the freedom of control in script preparation that Lois Weber took as her right." If true, this would certainly have rankled the director. Or were finances a cause of the couple's dissatisfaction? Four months after leaving Bosworth, they sued Garbutt, alleging failure to pay royalties.[204] Seizing an opportunity to leave, Weber and Smalley met with Carl Laemmle in April 1915 when he was in Los Angeles for a celebration marking the grand opening of Universal City. Laemmle agreed to re-sign the couple and, in doing so, committed to increased production of feature films, a form now thoroughly associated with Weber. During the couple's time at Bosworth, Weber had directed six features, including *Hypocrites*, one of the most ambitious motion pictures ever produced in the United States. More than this, she had fashioned a clear authorial presence in her films, using the celebrity persona Bosworth had erected for her to assert a compelling vision of cinematic authorship. By the time she re-signed with Laemmle, Weber's creative signature had been so indelibly established that one writer declared, "There is no man in the industry who is a greater writer than this woman at Universal City."[205]

2   "Life's Mirror"

Progressive Films for a Progressive Era

When Weber's headline-grabbing film on birth control and abortion, *Where Are My Children?* was released in 1916, just as Margaret Sanger's crusade to legalize contraception reached its peak, journalist Ernestine Black insisted that no filmmaking concern in the country would dare tackle that subject "with any other director than Mrs. Smalley." Only Weber, Black claimed, could approach the topic from an "intellectual standpoint" *and* "make a commercial success" of the enterprise.[1] At the height of her renown, Weber, still cloaked in the bourgeois propriety of "Mrs. Smalley," took on the Progressive Era's most vexing questions, placing popular cinema at the forefront of the nation's cultural landscape.

During her interval at Bosworth Weber had emerged as one of the leading filmmakers of her generation, her name now regularly mentioned alongside that of other Hollywood heavyweights—men such as Griffith, DeMille, and Thomas Ince. *Hypocrites*, Universal publicity declared, was "one of the masterpieces of the films" and had "almost over night" made Weber "a national figure." By the following year, *Universal Weekly* deemed Weber the "Greatest Woman Director in the World" without too much hyperbole—and with little mention of Smalley. There were even those, the paper reported, "who declare that the word 'woman' should be dropped from the title, to make it really fit her."[2] In recognition of her stature Weber became the first and only woman admitted to the Motion Picture Director's Association.[3] Noting "the genius she has displayed in the making of some of the most attractive and widely-discussed photoplays" in recent years, the association agreed by unanimous vote to set aside its exclusionary membership policy and admit Weber to its ranks in 1916.[4] Poised as this exception, the "greatest (woman) director," used her stature to mentor other women on the Universal lot and to speak forcefully for the value of female voices within the industry. With her renown growing, Weber also emerged as something of a celebrity, profiled not only in movie magazines but also in mass-circulation monthlies, her working partnership with Smalley an object of particular fascination. Their marital relationship overlaying their professional collaboration, Weber and Smalley provided models for both new ideals of companionate marriage and new heterosocial work environments, even as these paradigms were strained by Weber's growing dominance.

Soon after her return to Universal Weber embarked on an ambitious series of social problem films. Striking a more didactic tone than she had in her Bosworth features, Weber tackled such topics as poverty, drug addiction, contraception, and capital punishment just as they were emerging in newspaper headlines of the day. Not surprisingly, films on these contentious issues, even bolstered by Weber's bourgeois feminine pedigree, incurred intense scrutiny from censors. Chafing against any regulation of motion pictures, which she felt limited their capacity to engage in critical contemporary debates, Weber joined a host of voices insisting that filmmakers be guaranteed artistic freedom. In this regard, she staked out an ambitious claim for what mature cinema might look like: not the highbrow literary, biblical, and historical adaptations favored by her contemporaries Griffith and DeMille, but an activist cinema that could engage its viewers in substantial political and social issues of the moment. But as an analysis of these films proves, both the specular position that Weber's work offered moviegoers and cinema's own role in public debates was more complicated than she might have allowed.

LIFE AT UNIVERSAL CITY

Weber and Smalley returned to "the U" at a particularly auspicious moment. Universal City had staged its official opening just one month earlier; the Motion Picture Trust had been dissolved, guaranteeing greater freedom for independents like Universal; and the studio was making good money with a solid roster of stars, especially when compared to outfits such as Famous Players and Lasky that were struggling to produce features. Universal had the most expansive facilities and the largest body of employees, and produced more films than any of its competitors.[5] "This is a superb organization," Smalley remarked shortly after the couple's arrival, "and the facilities we find here are greater and better than we have found anywhere else in this country."[6] Completion of Universal City, at a cost estimated at $1 million, not only made it the largest film studio in the country but also definitively marked Los Angeles as the nation's film production center. Reporters who

Figure 15. Universal trumpeted Weber and Smalley's return to the studio in 1915. Advertisement in *Moving Picture World*, April 3, 1915.

visited the newly completed plant remarked on its sprawling size, the prevailing flavor of unreality, and the community dynamic fostered among its labor force. Amenities included a vast three-hundred–by–sixty-five-foot outdoor stage on which at least a dozen productions could be shot simultaneously, and another, smaller, two-hundred-foot stage, both equipped with electricity. Universal City also maintained standing sets for outdoor street scenes and a backlot for location shooting, massive prop and costume shops, film-processing labs and cutting rooms, restaurants and canteens, a zoo, horse corrals, and many other services, including a hospital and post office. Some fifteen hundred people were employed there.[7] "It seemed as if almost every human activity was being carried on somewhere in the grounds of Universal City," one visitor reported.[8]

This large facility was by 1916 releasing fifty-four reels each week, including two features and numerous shorts and serial episodes, making Universal the top producer in the industry. The company's heavy release schedule generated 250 separate products a year.[9] Universal relied heavily on serials and continued to release one- and two-reel shorts well into the teens, long after other studios had started to abandon the practice. Even in the mid-teens Laemmle maintained his resistance to feature films, promoting instead his "scientifically balanced" program of shorts. In fact, at least nine of Weber and Smalley's earlier Rex shorts were rereleased after the couple returned to the studio to concentrate on feature production. "The entire routine of the studio was geared to inexpensive mass production of mainly action-oriented movies," according to Richard Koszarski. "'Quality' films were generally left to the competition to supply."[10] But Universal was also beginning to introduce feature brands, some of which were released on the general program and others of which were distributed as specials or on a states' rights basis. Weber's films played key roles in articulating these brands. As Mark Garrett Cooper notes in his survey of the company's books, Universal entrusted Weber with quality features more than it did any other director during these years.[11] Two of the first features she completed after returning to the studio, *Scandal* (1916) and *Jewel* (1915), were released as Broadway Universal Features on the regular program. Later her social-problem films became staples of the Bluebird brand, introduced in late 1915 through a series of ads in the *Saturday Evening Post* appealing to middlebrow audiences with restrained artistry.[12] Although several other directors also released through Bluebird, including Rex Ingram, Otis Turner, Robert Leonard, and Rupert Julian, Weber was the filmmaker perhaps most associated with the brand, responsible for "some of the most pleasing of the Bluebird productions," according to *Moving Picture World*'s Margaret I. MacDonald.[13] After she left Universal and Ida May Park began directing for the brand, the *World* remembered that Weber had been "a great factor in promptly establishing Bluebirds," noting that there had always been a female filmmaker attached to the brand.[14]

Indeed, by the time Weber rejoined Universal, women were fast becoming prominent in the studio's creative workforce. Alongside Park, Grace Cunard, Cleo Madison, Ruth Stonehouse, Elsie Jane Wilson, Ruth Ann Baldwin, and Lule Warrenton were all directing at Universal in the mid-teens, making the studio's roster of female filmmakers unparalleled within the industry. By Cooper's count, the studio released some 170 titles directed by women between 1912 and 1919, a good measure of them by Weber herself, of course, but she was not alone. He notes that women filmmakers were more concentrated in the studio's feature brands, like Bluebird, and although most still continued to make shorts, female filmmakers usually made dramatic shorts, rather than comedies. (Cunard, of course, was the exception, directing episodic serials exclusively.)[15] Weber's stature on the lot and her association with quality features likely helped fuel creative ambitions in other women, and it is reasonable to assume that she may have actively mentored those around her. Madison, Wilson, and Warrenton, for instance, had all earlier worked as performers under Weber's direction before they began to direct themselves. Screenwriter Jeanie Macpherson also got her start acting in several early Weber productions. Wilson, for one, specifically mentioned her acting work with Weber when later discussing her directing career.[16] As one contemporary observer put it, Weber's esteemed place in the industry "opens up vistas for other women."[17]

Women may also have benefited from Universal's tremendous need for product during these years, along with Laemmle's preference for hiring lesser-known talent, rather than paying inflated salaries to established directors and stars, Koszarski speculates. But even he admits that there were other low-cost outfits that did not rely on female labor to such an extent.[18] It was the family-style camaraderie at Universal that fostered an acceptance of female directors, actress Ruth Clifford remembered: "When the women directed the films, the other directors, the men, were very cooperative. And the actors didn't resent it at all because a woman was directing. They took direction just the same as if it were a man directing. Everyone cooperated."[19] Indeed, Cooper argues that the "work-as-play" and "co-workers-as-family" ethos fostered at Universal City actively facilitated the careers of so many female filmmakers there in the 1910s. Universal City, he suggests, was designed and built to allow women and men to work in close collaboration, in stark contrast to other contemporary work spaces, such as office buildings, that scrupulously segregated the sexes.[20] Indeed, it was fitting, reporter Frances Denton noted, that a city that had "given women such perfect business equality with men, should be named Universal."[21]

As Weber emerged as the dominant member of "The Smalleys," she articulated a strong vision of the director's role in filmmaking and, in turn, the artist's role in society, elevating the director to a central creative position in filmmaking, while simultaneously elevating cinema to a status on par with that of other, more established art forms. Although she continued to speak with great pride about her scenario writing, Weber's work as a director began to take precedence in her thoughts. "A real director should be absolute," she said. "He [sic] alone knows the effects he wants to produce, and he alone should have authority in the arrangement, cutting, titling or anything else which it may be found necessary to do to the finished product. . . . We ought to realize that the work of a picture director, worthy of the name, is creative."[22] Discussing her craft, Weber stressed the level of training and study required for the job. Admitting that "there may be some truth in the opinion that a good director, like other artists, is born and not made," she allowed that certain innate talents were required for the job: an "infinite capacity for detail, an apparent sixth sense that intuitively recoils from the inartistic, and the faculty to visualize, from the artificial workings of the studios, how a play will appear on the screen" were, Weber said, necessary for any director and not capable of being learned. "But," she insisted, "given all the natural talent in the world, one must develop it by persistent study, or complete failure will result."[23] Evidence that Weber came to view directing as her chief occupation can also be seen in the way she sharply curtailed her acting roles after she returned to Universal, starring in only five of the sixteen features she produced there over the next two years. She also occasionally directed screenplays written by other women—*John Needham's Double* by Olga Printzlau and *Even as You and I* by Maude Grange.

With so many women active as directors at Universal, and more still in the industry at large, Weber and others began to consider the particular qualifications of female filmmakers. "I like to direct," Weber proclaimed, "because I believe a woman, more or less intuitively, brings out many of the emotions that are rarely expressed on the screen. I may miss what some of the men get, but I will get other effects that they never thought of."[24] Like Alice Guy Blaché before her, Weber not only made a clear case for female filmmakers but also insisted that women were actually *better suited* to directing than men. In her 1914 article, "Woman's Place in Photoplay Production," Guy Blaché had argued that women's "authority on the emotions" gave them an advantage when directing performers. Women's accustomed attention to detail, moreover, allowed them to employ props, costumes, and settings to tell cinematic stories more subtly and effectively. The intimacy of cinema, Guy Blaché maintained, was especially suited to women—an especially potent argument in the 1910s as camera positions grew closer, performance styles attended more to facial nuance, and continuity editing aimed to situate spectators in the scene.[25] Following in Weber's footsteps at Universal, Ida May Park would also make a similar case for female filmmakers. Confessing that she had at first resisted directing because it "seemed so utterly unsuited to a woman," Park maintained that "a woman can bring to this work splendid enthusiasm and imagination, a natural love of detail and a knowledge of characters. All of these are supposedly feminine traits, and yet they are all necessary to the successful director."[26]

Those who visited Weber on the set during these years described a filmmaker with "inexhaustible vitality, a clear, active mind and the determination of a woman accustomed to dealing with men and beating them at their own game."[27] Watching her direct a pivotal scene, one observer reported, "She stood on a tree-stump, in a silk shirtwaist and a smart skirt and chic tan boots; her commands were few, incisive and very direct."[28] Weber described how she usually directed without her scenario in hand, explaining that "I keep most of it in my head and direct without the manuscript."[29] The central figure on any set—"quite the most engaged person I have ever seen," one reporter noted—"she was wanted here, there and everywhere. Smalley came to her for advice upon every question that presented itself."[30] After observing Weber attend to all manner of questions as they toured her set, another reporter remarked, "I came away greatly impressed with the executive ability of this interesting woman."[31] Many mentioned her energy and her willingness to take on every aspect of the production process—"busy from early morning until late at night," working "48 hours on a stretch, with a sandwich in one hand and manuscript in the other."[32] Carl Laemmle later remembered, "Miss Weber is the only woman I have ever known who could work until two in the morning and be fresh and ready for another day's work at six."[33] She was also an exacting filmmaker, according to another observer: "There are times when everything has to be changed over and over before Miss Weber is satisfied."[34] Weber herself confessed: "I hate all limitation, all hampering, when I am directing. I am like a mad thing. My husband says the frown is never off my brow."[35]

At Universal, Weber directed a stock company of performers said to be "peculiarly adapted for her particular work."[36] Some she had worked with previously, like Rupert Julian at Rex and Adele Farrington, Hobart Bosworth's wife, who had followed Weber to Universal. Others included Marie Walcamp, Maude George, Juan de la Cruz, Betty Schade, Evelyn Selbie, Harry De More, Priscilla Dean, Charles Mailes, Ben Wilson, and Willis Marks. Working regularly with a company of actors evidently fostered a collaborative atmosphere, for actress Laura Sawyer reported that Weber was always willing to listen to suggestions from her players.[37] Weber also began adding trained stage actors to this group, notably Tyrone Power, first cast in *John Needham's Double* (1916), where he played two leading characters with the aid of double-exposure work, a performance highly commended at the time, a counter to "skeptics who deny the possibility for adroit characterization in a motion picture performance," Lynde Denig suggested.[38] Noting that she had been criticized for "deserting my colors" when she hired stage performers, Weber defended the practice, saying it "raises the class, both of the screen actors and of the audience which go to see them," allowing picturegoers to see "something besides fluffy-haired girls and handsome boys of no ability."[39] Now that Weber was squarely focused on feature film production, her scripts grew increasingly complex and demanded more subtle and sustained performances from actors.

As her scripts evolved, Weber also continued to explore cinema's visual dimensions, paying particular attention to cinematography and mise-en-scène. "A director cannot afford to slight a detail of the groupings, the acting, the lighting—anything," she said, "for upon the details depends the atmosphere so necessary to bring an audience *en rapport* with the play on the screen." Weber talked about how important it was that audiences "'feel' that they are in the plot, and undergoing the emotional suspense of the characters as the story develops."[40] Weber's interest in cinema's ability to convey interior psychology, evident early on in her work at Rex, entered a new phase when she returned to Universal. Working there with key cinematographers, including Allen Siegler and Dal Clawson (who had followed the couple first from Rex to Bosworth and now accompanied them back to Universal), Weber created cinematic effects designed to convey allegorical figures and intense psychological experiences.[41] Continuing to experiment with the use of double exposure, Weber used the technique to showcase Power's performance in *John Needham's Double*. The cinematography performed by Siegler and Stephen S. Norton in that film was the best "ever staged before any camera in America," *Variety* declared.[42] In *Even as You and I* (1916), allegorical figures of Lust, Drink, and Self-Pity threaten an artist and his wife as they compete with Truth, Honor, Love, and Beauty—"spectacular effects" rendered through double and triple exposure, according to *Variety*.[43] Double-exposure work also allowed Weber to portray the hand of poverty hovering over her heroine in *Shoes*, a loathsome figure of "Scandal" that haunts characters in that film (reportedly created through as many as fourteen simultaneous exposures), and the "eye of God" looking down upon characters in the film of the same name. If Weber took pride in cinema's ability to speak to a broader public than other art forms could, to render complex ideas and topics in popular modes, she relied on visual techniques—*uniquely cinematic* techniques—such as these.

Weber's directorial acumen was put to the test soon after her return to Universal when she was assigned to direct one of the most elaborate ventures ever undertaken by the studio: the screen debut of renowned Russian dancer Anna Pavlova in an adaptation of Auber's 1828 opera, *The Dumb Girl of Portici*, a project imagined on a grand scale from its earliest conception. Even though the film was not entirely successful and it represented a creative avenue that Weber did not continue to pursue at Universal, the fact that Laemmle—and Pavlova—entrusted Weber with the adaptation is a clear indication of her stature on the lot. *Moving Picture World*'s Lynde Denig would ultimately declare it "the most artistically ambitious" film in the studio's history, "a magnificent production that cannot be judged fairly by ordinary motion picture standards."[44] Hyperbolic language abounded in descriptions of the project. Before filming was even completed, *Universal Weekly* proclaimed it "a masterpiece, overshadowing even the famous *Birth of a Nation*."[45] Writing in the *Chicago Tribune*, Kitty Kelly declared, "*Cabiria* stood for spectacle, *The Birth of a Nation* for emotional thrill, *Carmen* for individual force, *The Dumb Girl of Portici* for artistic force."[46]

Bringing Pavlova to the screen was a striking coup for Universal, on par with the much-heralded motion picture debut of soprano Geraldine Farrar in DeMille's adaptation of *Carmen* the previous year.[47] One of the leading international artists of her generation, Pavlova had turned down prior offers to appear before the camera, but Laemmle apparently wooed the dancer by showing her the impressive production facilities available at Universal City and allowing her to choose the property in which she would make her screen debut.[48] Remembering that "ever since I was old enough to know what the stage meant, I have been possessed of a desire to play the role of Fenella," Pavlova requested that she star in a screen adaptation *The Dumb Girl of Portici*. An opera set in seventeenth-century Italy about a young peasant woman's tragic involvement in a tax revolt, Auber's work had rarely been staged, because mute Fenella was an unusually demanding role to play and few singing stars had been willing to take it on.[49] Surely, however, it was an inspired property to adapt for a dancer's first appearance on the silent screen, and Weber took on the exacting task of crafting the scenario.

Pavlova was reportedly paid $50,000 for her work on the project, a salary that was high not only by motion picture standards but by those of dance as well. She would have had to work nearly a year on stage to earn a comparable sum.[50] By her own admission, Pavlova was "not over-anxious to go into pictures" and was nervous about appearing on screen. Prior to filming, she bought a camera and had friends film her in various poses. But Smalley

Figure 16. Weber *(right)* directing Anna Pavlova *(left)* as Fenella in *The Dumb Girl of Portici* (1916), Universal's most ambitious production to date. Courtesy of Bison Archives.

remained confident: "When the picture is released," he declared, "we are going to introduce a new Pavlowa [*sic*] to the world—a Pavlowa who is equally good an actress as she is a dancer."[51] In deference to her touring schedule, the production began filming in Chicago in July 1915 on the grounds of the abandoned amusement park Sans Souci, which was adjacent to the open-air Midway Gardens Auditorium, where Pavlova and her company were giving daily dance performances. During the five-week shoot, Pavlova and her dancers, some forty-seven in all, shuttled back and forth between the two venues, with Pavlova often able to work with Weber and Smalley only for three to five hours a day. Pavlova then completed another five weeks of filming in Los Angeles, shooting location scenes on the beach, and interiors and backlot locations at Universal City. The final budget for the production was estimated at $300,000.[52]

In keeping with the hyperbolic tenor that greeted reports of its production, *The Dumb Girl of Portici* was premiered on a grand scale. Three thousand people attended the film's initial screening in Los Angeles at Clune's

Auditorium, including the mayor and other officials, where Weber and Smalley were roundly applauded for their work.[53] At the Chicago premiere, attended by Pavlova and Laemmle, applause broke out several times in recognition of "the sheer magnificence of the scenes and the well-drilled armies of supernumeraries."[54] Initially eleven reels long when it premiered in Chicago, the film was cut to nine reels for its general release.[55] Even with these changes, the film was poorly received. Although the scope of the production, its visual splendor in re-creating seventeenth-century Italy, and its cinematography were praised, most reviewers considered the film too long, overburdened with explanatory intertitles, and not an especially worthy showcase for Pavlova's talents. "Only at rare intervals . . . ," the *New York Times* reported, "does the screen reflect her great art."[56] *Variety* quipped that the dancer was "not quite camera broken" and failed to take full advantage of facial expressions in her performance, as most experienced motion picture players would have.[57] But the production remained an extraordinary triumph for Weber, proof that she could undertake even the most ambitious subject matter. "For a director to take the tremendous task of making an eight-reel scenario from an opera in eight weeks, with such a famous woman as Pavlova in the leading role, is something which requires expert ability," one writer observed, "and for a women to have accomplished it increases the enormity of the task."[58] If anyone had doubted after *Hypocrites* that Weber was a director of the first order, *The Dumb Girl of Portici*, marshalling all of the resources available at Universal City, made this fact abundantly clear.

A COUPLE AT WORK

As Weber's renown grew, so too did her celebrity. Central to any profile of Weber during these years was her relationship with Smalley, at once a professional partnership and a marital bond. Initially billed as "The Smalleys, collaborators in authorship and direction," the couple's creative alliance had been intertwined with their marriage from the very beginning of their fame.[59] Many pieces celebrated their "marital resolve," their "bride and groom determination" to work in the same field, forging an artistic alliance that represented "one of the most illuminating examples of marital happiness." Their equanimity and companionability were usually played up in such profiles: they were seen as "congenial co-workers" with Smalley described as Weber's "co-director, husband—and *chum*."[60]

As a particularly striking example of such synchronicity, consider publicity that Bosworth issued for the couple when they joined the company in

Figure 17. Bosworth promoted Weber and Smalley's pedigree when they joined the company in 1914.

1914 to produce upscale feature films. Images of Weber and Smalley in profile face one another in the ad, as if the two were gazing fondly into one another's eyes. Little cartoon figurations highlighting (sometimes apocryphal) details of their past lives and career achievements frame the page. In a pictorial, even cinematic, narrative showing their professional rise alongside their emergence as a couple, romantic union serves as an explicit metaphor for the logical melding of their interests. In fact, their wedding is presented as a significant event in Weber's *professional* evolution, poised between her triumphant stage performance and her celebrated feature-length project *Hypocrites*. Promoting nothing in particular, save its own highbrow reputation, Bosworth, Inc., trafficked in the couple's status—not

Figure 18. Weber and Smalley "conferring on a manuscript." Courtesy of the Academy of Motion Picture Arts and Sciences.

simply the exaggerated pedigree claimed in the cartoon captions but, more significantly, their standing as a solid, bourgeois couple.[61] Their marriage did as much to promote the company's highbrow reputation, it seems, as did the films they were to produce.

Bosworth's figuration of the couple's artistic synchronicity was certainly not unique, for publicity photos often pictured the pair side by side in analogous poses, the visual parallelism seeming to echo Weber's own description of how the pair labored "brain to brain, shoulder to shoulder in all our endeavors."[62] A portrait of Weber and Smalley "conferring on a manuscript" depicted the two posed intimately together, their bodies literally intertwined as they worked.[63] With domestic furnishings visible in the soft-focus background, Weber rests her elbow on Smalley's thigh as she holds a script in her lap. Such figurations offered marriage as an appropriate template for working partnerships between men and women, while simultaneously proposing egalitarian collaboration as a new blueprint for modern romance. Films produced by such a solidly respectable couple, however controversial their subject matter, could surely be grounded only in the finest bourgeois virtues, these images seemed to suggest.

The degree to which Weber's marriage underscored her reputation for respectability is most notable in celebrity items structured around a visit to her Los Angeles home, "personal" profiles that situated her as a married woman and as the denizen of well-appointed, but not too lavish, middle-class surroundings. Interviews staged in stars' homes became familiar conceits in celebrity writing of the mid-1910s, as star culture became increasingly focused on personal lives and living spaces. Fame in early Hollywood was built as much on audience knowledge of a star's on-screen roles as it was on familiarity with her *off*-screen, "private" life, as Richard deCordova has shown.[64] Romances, marriages, divorces, childhoods, and children all became targets of increased curiosity, as did dwellings, kitchens, closets, and dressing tables. This was a fan culture that, Kathryn Fuller argues, increasingly tailored its appeal to women by catering to "feminine" interests in romance, beauty, decorating, and family life, rather than by elaborating the technical and scientific details that had colored much of the earliest film publicity.[65] If the circulation of biographical tidbits shifted the fan's gaze toward an invisible, extratextual realm hidden from the screen, as Gaylyn Studlar stresses, we should not lose sight of the degree to which this other scene assumed its own visuality.[66] In her reading of Alice Guy-Blaché's memoirs, Amelie Hastie suggests that celebrity portraits often take on a cinematic quality in which visual symbolism and narrative juxtaposition play key signifying roles.[67] Thus even as "visits" to celebrity homes gave early motion picture fans vicarious, voyeuristic access to stars' hidden lives, furnishing imaginary entry into an unseen, off-screen world, they also blurred boundaries between this realm and the screen by fictionalizing domestic spaces and staging events and conversations for their readers.

One might suspect in the case of such a professionally accomplished woman that portraits of Weber's home life would be used to "domesticate" her, to sketch her within the lines of a more conventionalized femininity designed to temper her stature within the industry. Certainly some profiles served this function, anxiously assuring readers that the filmmaker "loves her work as she loves her home" and that she had "not sacrificed her home life for her public career."[68] Yet the interplay between Weber's creative endeavors and her personal affairs was not always so clearly defined, especially given her professional collaboration with Smalley.

Weber's name and her marital status, for instance, were belabored in virtually every publicity item, each of which offered some version of the statement "in private life Miss Weber is Mrs. Phillips Smalley."[69] Domestic architecture, in one case, was even employed to delineate boundaries between these facets of Weber's persona: "In her home," readers learned, "this writer-actress-director lays aside the sternness of the 'firing line,' drops her professional name and becomes Mrs. Phillips Smalley, wife of one of the best-known actor-directors in California."[70] But in another iteration of this same arrangement—"in private life Miss Weber is Mrs. Phillips Smalley, and her talented husband is associated with her in all her productions"—the boundaries failed to hold, for the couple's marriage appears to sustain their working partnership.[71] Certainly the most interesting twist on this recital described Weber's position as wife and homemaker as a masterful performance. In "A Perpetual Leading Lady," *Sunset* magazine's portrait of the director, Weber's "lead" slipped between starring roles on screen, positions of creative control behind the camera, and her convincing performance as devoted wife. "The part of Mrs. Phillips Smalley," author Bertha Smith noted, "is not the least picturesque role of Lois Weber."[72] Trivial though they may seem, deliberations over a woman's name were not without significance in the early years of Hollywood when many women juggled their own fame in relation to their status within a celebrity couple. Mark Lynn Anderson has demonstrated, for instance, that actress and director Dorothy Davenport played a vital role in domesticating her husband, matinee idol Wallace Reid, after a series of scandals. By changing her professional name first to Dorothy Davenport Reid, then to Mrs. Wallace Reid, she posthumously recovered her husband's wayward image in the guise of a man beloved by a wife who remained devoted even in death.[73]

While glimpses of her private life anchored Weber in a domestic setting, they also provided an opportunity to showcase her labor. Boundaries between the home and the workplace were complicated still further when interviews conducted in her residence invariably led Weber to discussions of her working methods, given that she spent so much of her time writing screenplays at home. Considering the invisibility of much of her labor as screenwriter and director, this was all the more significant. The books that lay within easy reach on her desk, the light streaming in her windows, her preference for writing in pencil on yellow pads propped on her knee—all these details became crucial to the filmmaker's persona. One such profile focused on her "exceptional" mahogany desk: "a gift from my husband," Weber noted, an explanation that simultaneously inscribes her writing within domesticity and marriage even as it hints at something altogether different—a husband's value and support of his wife's chosen profession.[74]

Images of the couple also stressed this integration of domesticity and motion picture work. In a photo-essay titled "The Smalleys" published in *Photoplay* magazine, Weber is posed sitting at her desk with pencil in hand and a writing pad on her knee, deep in concentration. Smalley, seated in a comfortable chair on the other side of a dividing screen, reads a book or per-haps a film script. It is a portrait of the couple comfortably and companion-ably working at home, their familial bond underscoring their creative part-nership. Although they are not physically intertwined, as they are in the portrait showing them "conferring on a manuscript," the balanced composi-tion reinforces a sense that the two are engaged in corresponding, comple-mentary activities that together support their combined creative endeavor as "The Smalleys." And here again, household space is framed as work space, not as a sanctified domestic realm set apart from studio labor.[75]

Visits to the couple's home also provided Weber with an appropriate forum for her views on uplifting the cinema. Exemplary in this regard is a 1915 *Movie Pictorial* feature on Weber and Smalley structured around a visit to their bungalow on Sierra Bonita Avenue.[76] Reporter Richard Willis narrated his encounter from the moment he "duly pressed the little button by the door of the bungalow and was accorded the welcome," to the point when he left the couple standing "in the doorway of their cheery home with the subdued lights behind them." Between these moments the couple, mainly Weber, discussed the progress of motion pictures, including the ill effects of recent melodramatic serials, ideal film lengths, literary adapta-tions, and stage performers, all the while surrounded by the couple's mod-est, tastefully decorated interiors. Here we see that in Weber's case high-brow filmmaking was associated, above all else, with bourgeois domesticity, in striking contrast to a contemporary like DeMille who, as Sumiko Higashi has demonstrated, was linked to improved motion picture standards and "famous players" chiefly through his *professional* background and his family's pedigree in the theater, not through details of his personal lifestyle.[77] Speaking with Willis in her living room, Weber embodied the persona most cherished by the film industry during these years—the tem-perate, educated, married, middle-class woman looking for refined enter-tainment for her family. In this case, Weber was especially notable, for she demonstrated that such women might also be found behind the scenes in the film industry.

In this regard Weber and Smalley differed from other celebrity couples in early Hollywood. What distinguished their collaboration from those of more famous duos just a few years later, such as Davenport and Reid or Mary Pickford and Douglas Fairbanks, was how closely Weber and Smalley's film-making accomplishments were overlaid with their marriage and how solidly the couple was associated with bourgeois values rather than Hollywood glam-our. In contrast to Pickford and Fairbanks, whose marriage was presented as a fairy tale romance played out in the imaginarily unified realm of "Pickfair,"

The Smalleys

The Smalleys in their Los Angeles home and at its gates. Mrs. Smalley—Lois Webber—is one of the very few women directors, and unquestionably the most successful. Phillips Smalley is equally known as actor and director. Mrs. Smalley's best-known picture is "The Hypocrites," which has caused a deal of discussion all over the country. Its director has the masculine force combined with feminine sympathies and intuition which seem the peculiarly combined gifts of women of genius.

Figure 19. Weber and Smalley at work, at home, pictured in *Photoplay,* 1915.

Weber and Smalley were cast as a married couple of long standing (not starry-eyed lovers) and solid citizens of the middle class (rather than denizens of that new fantasyland called Hollywood).[78] Whereas these other celebrity couples had met in Hollywood after having already achieved some measure of fame, Weber and Smalley's narrative stressed that they had been married outside the industry and entered motion picture work together. In perhaps the most striking contrast, fan magazines dwelt on the "majesty" of Pickfair, and the "royalty" of its inhabitants, as Christina Lane has shown, while items on Weber and Smalley emphasized the well-ordered hominess of their quintessential California bungalow. Unlike so many other early star profiles, which played up lavish Hollywood lifestyles, portraits of Weber's life at home did not celebrate the extravagance of her surroundings. Rather, it was precisely the ordinariness of the couple's "beautiful little vine-covered flower garden bungalow," their "charming house in Hollywood," and their "modest little bungalow" that was cherished.[79] Targeted almost exclusively at middle-class home owners and associated with a romanticized view of California living, bungalows were by far the most prevalent housing innovation of the 1910s. Pictured in such a residence, Weber and Smalley were pointedly identified with middlebrow taste and quite explicitly set apart from the grand Hollywood mansions then being erected by the industry's luminaries.

Portraits of Weber at home, then, refused much of the accustomed function of celebrity profiles: rather than domesticating a notable professional woman, they blurred boundaries between work life and home life; rather than reinserting Lois Weber under the banner of "Mrs. Phillips Smalley," they furnished an alternate model of a nonhierarchical marriage based on common creative interests and mutual support; and rather than spinning tales of otherworldly glamour akin to that found on the screen, visits with Weber and Smalley at home insisted, rather forcefully, on the couple's commonplace tastes and habits. Such profiles marshaled Weber's matronly persona in the service of the more general project of uplifting the cinema, while at the same time creating not only a legitimate place for women in the industry, but a privileged one.

It is clear that Weber's relationship with Smalley stood at the heart of the filmmaker's persona during key early years of her fame: a matronly stature enhanced her claims to cinematic respectability, and her marriage, far from competing with her filmmaking interests, was cast as their emotional and creative center. In a mutually reinforcing scenario, Weber and Smalley's unusual male-female business partnership was tempered through less threatening matrimonial imagery at the same time that the couple's personal interactions, modeled on the workplace, offered a fresh portrait of gender equality in marriage. Yet, however forward-looking, the overlaid metaphors surrounding Weber and Smalley's collaborative labor could not always mask the fundamental reorientation of gender roles that their partnership implied. Indeed, a closer look at portraits of the couple's relationship reveals a less celebratory tenor, an undercurrent of tension indicating something of the stress placed on tropes of their "bride and groom determination" as Weber became increasingly recognized as the dominant creative force within their partnership.

Fan magazines, eager to provide readers with a glimpse into the inner workings of the couple's relationship, were fond of staging conversations between them in which each modestly deferred to the other. In a vignette sketched for *Photoplay* readers, Smalley was depicted approaching Weber on the set with a proposed script change to which she readily agreed:

"You're right," said the wife.

"Say, 'as usual,'" ordered the husband.

"I won't," she answered with customary wifely obedience, and added in the manner of a side-show lecturer: "Here you see the only theatrical couple in captivity married thirteen years and still in love with each other."[80]

What is so remarkable about this exchange is not only the way that Weber and Smalley cloak their creative rivalry within an apparently healthy matrimonial tussle, but also the degree of self-consciousness each brings to the enterprise: Weber, narrating the episode, appears fully cognizant of their performance "on screen" as husband and wife. Employing zoo imagery to characterize the lens of media scrutiny, she knowingly plays up the exoticism of the working couple on display, all but acknowledging the presence of curious fan magazine onlookers. Perhaps more significant, in serving as side-show lecturer, Weber takes decisive directorial control away from her husband, who had presumed to give her direction in the first place.

Similarly self-conscious jockeying for power surfaces in a *Los Angeles Times* writer's account of his trip to Universal City in 1916 in which Smalley appears to be even less certain about the exact nature of the couple's partnership and his status within it. When Weber and her husband are introduced as "Mr. and Mrs. Smalley," Smalley jokingly offers a correction, insisting that the two be referred to as "Mrs. Smalley and husband," a change that reorders the implied hierarchy of their union, asserting Weber's dominance in the professional sphere while still holding her under the rubric of his name and their marriage.[81]

These humorous little incidents, however staged or manufactured they may be, perform two functions simultaneously. By offering behind-the-scenes glimpses of Weber and Smalley together in seemingly typical spousal moments, they intertwine the couple's off-screen bond with their working partnership all the more decisively, thereby normalizing the uncommon sight of men and women functioning together as equals not only in marriage but, even more profoundly, in the workplace. At the same time, however, each episode points to the remarkable destabilization of gender roles that this egalitarian arrangement poses, evident especially in the ongoing power struggle enacted in each circumstance. Obviously these scenes yield no access to the pair's "true" coexistence. However, such attempts to imagine their interactions, to evoke their simultaneous status as co-workers and spouses, necessarily reveal cracks in the fiction of their harmonious union and the mutually reinforcing metaphors of marriage and collaboration. Ideas of romantic companionability could not erase professional rivalry, any more than ideas about egalitarian working conditions could stand for the significant changes that parity might have introduced into their marriage.

It is no coincidence that Smalley's stature stood at the core of these jokes. In fact, the scope of his involvement in the couple's creative projects has been a source of uncertainty for film historians. Reviews from the time do not shed much light on the matter; indeed many seem concerned to distinguish each partner's contribution, to resurrect individual identities blurred under the joint signature of "The Smalleys." One writer, adopting a conservatively gendered assessment of the pair's division of labor, suggested that "to Mrs. Smalley is given the credit for the delicacy of the picture, the pictorial artistry, but her husband is said to be responsible for the big mob scenes and bolder masculine workmanship."[82]

After 1916, however, Weber's contribution was usually elevated above her husband's, sometimes in spite of their equal billing. Smalley's marginalization figures acutely in a *Los Angeles Times* cartoon depicting the goings-on at Universal City that year.[83] Under the heading "The Center of the Stage," Weber dominates the image in a way that identifies her as the studio's chief asset. Beneath her the caption reads, "Lois Weber, Wonderful Lois, her note book always filled with clever ideas." Smalley, drawn much smaller, stands noticeably in her shadow. As Smalley's eyes remain fixed upon his wife, Weber looks outward, meeting the reader's gaze, reinforcing the notion that she is the central object of attention, not her husband.

Indeed, scrutinizing depictions of the celebrity couple further, one finds their "bride and groom determination" increasingly precarious. Even as the mirrored compositions so frequently used to depict Weber and Smalley emphasize their egalitarian bond, the highly stylized symmetry points

Figure 20. Weber dominates the Universal City landscape in this 1916 cartoon from the *Los Angeles Times*.

quite strongly to the manufacture of this harmonious duo. Turning again to the rhyming layout of Bosworth's 1914 advertisement, we see that while it trumpets the couple's synchronous achievements on stage and screen, it also literally creates their partnership by pasting their two separate images together. In lieu of portraying the pair within the same frame, the ad juxtaposes solo portraits of husband and wife as if to create an effect of the couple gazing into one another's eyes. An engaging effect it would certainly be, but for the fact that the couple's sight lines do not match. This image of their synchronicity has been literally pasted together, we realize, much as we are forced to recognize how much the fiction of bourgeois marital happiness has been marshaled to prop up their image of cultural sophistication.

Similarly misaligned sight lines fracture the intimacy of other portraits as well. The photo discussed earlier of the couple "conferring on a manuscript" would seem the quintessential encapsulation of their collaboration. Yet, once again, the choreography of their interaction belies its naturalness. While Weber faces forward, her eyes cast downward reading the script, Smalley appears in three-quarters view, his back very nearly to the camera. His unfocused gaze lingers somewhere just beyond the frame, engaged neither with Weber nor with the material on which they are supposedly "conferring." In a half-controlling, half-protective stance he appears to hover over her; yet he remains isolated from the task she is undertaking. Although the composition emphasizes a symmetrical, and therefore egalitarian, placement within the frame, suggesting an intertwining of their two bodies and minds on one single project, it also communicates how composed the portrait is and how disengaged the two are from each other.

Smalley's marginalization in their endeavors is also readily suggested by the *Photoplay* portrait of the couple at work in their Hollywood home. Although the rhyming composition again seems to stress their complementary activities, Smalley is confined to the far right of the frame, contained within a much smaller portion of the image and in a much darker corner of the room. Weber, by contrast, is nearly centered within the frame, bathed by light from the window behind her and surrounded by empty, unrestricting space. Another portrait of their supposed companionability, it unwittingly points to the fissures in this very image.

Photos of Weber and Smalley with Anna Pavlova on the set of *The Dumb Girl of Portici* in 1916 betray still further contradictions in depictions of the couple's working relationship, even as they accompany a *Motion Picture Magazine* story on the project.[84] In one image Smalley stands to the right of the frame beside a camera embossed with "The Smalleys" on its side, while Weber stands to the left holding a script. At first glance the arrangement might seem to reinforce traditional ideas about the gendered division of labor on the couple's productions, with Weber handling script details while Smalley assumes the task of commandeering and shooting the action. But other facets of the composition belie this interpretation: Weber confers with Pavlova in an animated manner, meeting the other woman's gaze. Smalley, isolated on the other side of the frame, appears removed from the directing process, and, again, his unfocused gaze does not rest on anyone or anything in the frame.

A second photo, overlaid on top of the first in the same profile, shows a closer view of the lively interaction between Weber and her star. The juxtaposition only underscores how Smalley is displaced by the dialogue between the women, how theirs remains the true collaboration, outpacing any interaction between "The Smalleys," who are pictured conferring in a small image in the left-hand corner. Weber herself frequently mentioned her friendships and collaboration with female writers and performers who worked on her productions. Here we see more clearly how those alliances might vie with her partnership with Smalley. Perhaps most significantly, Weber's association with Pavlova, a woman of comparable fame and artistic stature, refused the maternal and matrimonial tropes that had been used to

LOIS, THE WIZARD 43

THE SMALLEYS AND
PAVLOWA CAUGHT IN
INFORMAL SNAPSHOTS
IN AND AROUND
THE STUDIO

actors
who seem
to be pecu-
liarly adapted for her
particular work. Most
of her pictures have
been based on morality
—in fact, I think she
was one of the very first
to produce this type of
picture. In every pic-
ture of hers there is a
hidden and appealing
sermon. Her pictures
not only interest and
amuse, but also genuinely help her audiences.
Her company includes such sterling actors as
Edna Maison, Rupert Julian, Wadsworth Harris, Douglas Gerrard, Betty Schade, John Holt,
Hart Hoxie, William Wolbert, Laura Oakley,
and many others, all of whom have won

Figure 21. Weber's collaboration with Anna Pavlova
marginalizes Smalley in this 1916 profile for *Motion
Picture Magazine*.

soften her working relationships in other celebrity portraits. Collaborating
with the dancer on a high-profile project, Weber could be cast neither as an
adoring "mother" nurturing another woman's careers, as she so often
was, nor as a faithful "wife" toiling alongside her husband in the family
business. Instead, she risked a much more politicized interpretation of the

relationship, one echoed in the text accompanying the photos. According to *Motion Picture*, Weber's working methods amounted to nothing short of "suffraget [*sic*] propaganda," because she so often favored screen stories with central female roles, adapted from properties written by women, that she herself directed.[85]

Ultimately, these illustrations, staged in some collaboration among fan magazines, studio publicity, and savvy stars, surely offer us no greater access into the couple's "real" interactions than do the dialogue scenes examined earlier. On the contrary, they allow us to see just how fabricated the couple's image was. Once we read this artifice back into written narratives of the couple's "bride and groom determination," we see the labor involved in creating a portrait of the congenial couple, a process so often disrupted by jokes (usually put in Smalley's mouth) that call attention to the fundamental destabilization of gendered professional and familial roles that the couple's partnership represented. Indeed, the fiction was not sustainable. When Weber and Smalley were featured in a *Photoplay* spread on Hollywood marriages in the summer of 1917, a caption beneath separate photos of the two described them, rather baldly, as "Phillips Smalley and his talented wife, Lois Weber, whose directorial fame has eclipsed his."[86] Smalley is shown in profile, his eyes are downcast, his mood somber, as he appears to focus on something unseen beyond the frame. Weber, by contrast, looks directly into the camera, smiling. Cut out from the original background, her portrait is repasted slightly on top of Smalley's, accentuating an inequity already stated so unequivocally in the photo caption.

If Weber's private life structured her evolving star persona in the mid-1910s, it did so in a contradictory fashion. Without a doubt, her reputation for high-minded feature filmmaking traded on her celebrity image as married, middle-class matron at a time when the industry was eager to present someone so upstanding, so righteous, so ladylike as its public face—someone whose behind-the-scenes persona mirrored that of the industry's idealized female clientele. Similarly, depictions of Weber's creative endeavors with husband Phillips Smalley provided mutually reinforcing metaphors that furnished new means of framing gendered roles at home and in the workplace. Yet the weight placed upon these combined analogies strained the marital imagery, revealing gaps in what had first been presented as the consummate model of professional and personal collaboration between equals. Ironically, rather than displacing her creative accomplishments, the emphasis placed on Weber's marital status ended up foregrounding her *husband's* marginalization. What ultimately suffered was not the ideal of female professional accomplishment, but the ideal of marital equality. Thus, the fiction of "The Smalleys" did not serve to erase Weber's filmmaking accomplishments under her husband's signature, as one might expect; rather, it served to preserve a fiction of egalitarian relations between men and women that her success ultimately challenged.

CINEMA OF SOCIAL UPLIFT

Weber's status as a married, middle-class woman also figured prominently in her reputation as a filmmaker. Though important in establishing her standing as a first-rate director, *The Dumb Girl of Portici* did not ultimately signal the path Weber's career would take at Universal, for she became best known for the social-problem films she wrote and directed on issues including poverty, contraception, addiction, and capital punishment. With a series of films released in quick succession in 1916 and 1917, many of them extremely popular with audiences but controversial as well, Weber cemented her reputation as a director of the first order and, more important, pioneered a mode of Progressive filmmaking that ran counter to the industry-wide trend toward uplift during these years. Through this body of work she articulated a vision of activist, engaged cinema ready to assume its place alongside other forms of mass media.

A profile of Weber at the height of her Universal career celebrated her ability to "set forth in a dignified and dramatic manner some of the complex questions which are challenging intelligent thinkers the world over."[87] Although she would later distance herself from what she called the "heavy dinners" she produced at Universal, Weber was, for a time, at the forefront of Progressive filmmaking in America, foremost among a host of filmmakers who sought to use cinema as a kind of living newspaper, capable of bringing discussions of complicated cultural questions to life.[88] For Weber, this project involved not simply elevating cinema's cultural cachet during an era of expanding popularity, but also uplifting its audience, speaking to them in a "voiceless language" capable of engaging some of the era's most deep-seated social problems. "I'll tell you what I'd like to be," she said, "and that is, the editorial page of the Universal Company. My close study of the editorial page has taught me that it speaks with stentorian tones and that its effect is far reaching upon thousands of readers. I feel that like them, I can, in this motion picture field, also deliver a message to the world in the plays we have in contemplation that will receive a ready and cheerful response from the better element of the big general public."[89] She viewed cinema as a populist medium, equivalent to other art forms in scope and complexity, but able to reach an audience they could not: unlike literature and drama,

she said, motion pictures are capable of erasing "boundary lines of ignorance and poverty." With cinema, "intellectual reservations of centuries are
thrown open to millions of new settlers."[90]

Weber's vision of cinema placed it squarely at the heart of Progressive
thought. As Moya Luckett argues, "Progressivism structured multiple ways
of seeing," emblematized in its "signature professions—social work and
investigative journalism"—which promised commanding views of the era's
social ills. Offering their own commanding views, motion pictures thus
become for Luckett the "emblematic entertainment" of this era, something
Weber herself surely grasped.[91] Noting that her scenarios were drawn from
newspaper reports and sociological case studies, Weber emphasized her
films' connections to topics of the day, downplaying her own manipulation
of cinematic devices designed to orchestrate viewers' attention. "I pin my
faith to that story which is a slice out of real life," Weber said, advocating
"the picture which carries with it an idea and affords a basis for the argument of questions concerned with the real life of the people who go to see
it."[92] Profiles frequently cited her penchant for drawing screenplay ideas
from current events. Indeed, Weber developed scenarios from some of the
most sensational news stories of the day. A journalistic exposé of opium trafficking in San Francisco's Chinatown became the basis for *Hop, the Devil's
Brew* (1916); a much-publicized capital punishment trial provided the inspiration for *The People vs. John Doe* (1916); Jane Addams's sociological study
of prostitution among urban working-class women fueled Weber's script for
Shoes (1916); and Margaret Sanger's storied crusade to legalize contraception was loosely dramatized in both *Where Are My Children?* and *The Hand
That Rocks the Cradle* (1917), with Weber herself playing the lead in the
latter picture. For Weber, the use of such "true-to-life" sources had less to do
with realism than with social intervention: she believed cinema, like any
good newspaper's editorial page, could provoke discussion about issues of
fundamental importance to the nation. "Lois Weber," one contemporary
commentary noted, "can deal successfully with subjects which other directors would not dare to touch for fear of condemnation."[93]

Weber's social-problem films thus differed from many other "problem
plays" of the era, which often sought to reform working-class moviegoers
with solemn sermons on temperance, sexuality, and hygiene. Nor did
Weber seek to bring "uplifting" bourgeois fare to the screen, as those in the
Better Films Movement advocated.[94] Instead, Weber's work was aimed at
middle-class audiences, the "better element" that she targeted, not simply
to recruit them into particular Progressive causes (though that was certainly one of her goals) but also to suggest a broader congruence between

film viewing and reformist sensibilities; to suggest, in other words, that cinema might aspire to much grander aims than commercial recreation for the masses, that it might compel its audiences to act outside theater walls to reform their own lives and their own communities. In this, Weber's conception of sophisticated cinema for middle-class audiences also diverged sharply from that of contemporaries such as Griffith and DeMille who relied on screen adaptations of well-known bourgeois literary, dramatic, and historical materials to garner respect for the fledgling medium.[95] Weber, by contrast, sought to engage moviegoers directly in activist reform, relying on intertext of an altogether different sort.

Alongside her films on such newsworthy topics as struggles to legalize contraception or to abolish the death penalty, Weber also tackled a host of other issues in her Universal work, focusing more obliquely on moral and psychological quandaries faced by individuals. "The day is past," she said, "when the public asked only for the little simple romance or poorly spun yarn on the screen. They want new ideas—big serious, broad-minded themes. They want educational pictures—they want pictures with sermons, pictures which stimulate the soul as well as appeal to the heart and the senses."[96] In *Scandal* and again in *Saving the Family Name* (1916) Weber took on the poisonous effects of gossip, exploring its particular effects on women. In the first film, Weber and Smalley play co-workers, Daisy and William, whom others suspect to be having an affair. William's marriage is ruined as a result of the relentless gossip, and Daisy is ironically forced into marrying a man she does not love in order to protect her reputation. The film makes a compelling argument that overweening propriety, expressed in the film through erroneous accusations and malicious gossip, actually undermines marriage, rather than upholding it. Praising Weber's handling of the material, one reviewer suggested, "The average moving picture director would have hopelessly botched this subject."[97] *Saving the Family Name* approached the topic from another angle, offering the story of a chorus girl tainted by a sexual scandal when her wealthy fiancé commits suicide after his family disapproves of their union.[98]

Moral challenges facing individuals also clearly interested the filmmaker. *Wanted—A Home* (1916), written by Weber but directed by Smalley while Weber was in New York, tells the story of a young homeless woman (played by Mary MacLaren) whose desperation causes her to fall into bad company. Reviewer Margaret I. MacDonald found "interesting" the heroine's "manner of seizing without complaint the only available path open to her on each occasion."[99] In *The Eye of God* (1916), a prisoner awaiting execution comes to recognize "the eye of God" watching over him as he almost allows another

Figure 22. Weber and Smalley play co-workers whose lives are nearly ruined when they are falsely accused of having an affair, in *Scandal* (1916). Frame enlargement.

man to die for the crime. A bored, wealthy playboy in *The Mysterious Mrs. M* (1917) reforms his life when he believes a fortune-teller's prophecy that he is about to die. The whole thing turns out to be a stunt orchestrated by his friends, but the lesson is a lasting one. In *Even as You and I* Weber took a broadly allegorical approach, not unlike her experiment in *Hypocrites,* showing how the devil sends Lust, Drink, and Self-Pity to undermine the humble life of a sculptor and his wife.[100] Considered in its entirety, Weber's output at Universal cannot be fully accommodated under the rubric of "social-problem films," as these brief synopses attest. Perhaps the best contemporary summation of her signature put it this way: "Most of her pictures have been based on morality—in fact, I think she was one of the very first to produce this type of picture. In every picture of hers there is a hidden and appealing sermon. Her pictures not only interest and amuse, but also genuinely help her audiences."[101]

For her first significant "issue" film at Universal, *Hop, the Devil's Brew,* Weber adapted a series of *Saturday Evening Post* articles by San Francisco writer Rufus Steele on that city's opium trade. One of several films on drug trafficking released during these years, *Hop, the Devil's Brew* reflected growing concern about and regulation of opium smuggling in the United States, for which San Francisco, with its large Chinatown, was perceived to be the main port of entry. The federal Opium Exclusion Act of 1909 had prohibited the importation and sale of opium; and authorities in San Francisco and the state of California had also enacted a slate of recent laws designed to curtail the opium trade perceived to be spreading from the city's Chinese community into its white population.[102] Much of this history was summarized for viewers in the film's opening titles. Shot on location in San Francisco, *Hop, the Devil's Brew* made extensive use of settings there that, according to local newspapers, included "raids on opium 'joints' in Chinatown and numerous hazardous encounters along the water front and throughout the underworld of this city."[103] Adding authenticity to the film's treatment of the subject, publicity also touted the involvement of actual customs inspectors and U.S. Treasury officials in the production, though this cannot be verified. Universal even made the highly doubtful claim that real opium had been used in several scenes.[104] *Hop, the Devil's Brew* was deemed the "most authentic" of the narcotics films by *Moving Picture World*, which added "no highly colored newspaper story ever gave the reader so complete an idea of how opium smugglers operate and how government inspectors work to check them."[105] This, one presumes, is exactly the sort of comparison Weber hoped for. As "living newspapers," her films furnished viewers with a complete picture of troubling social problems like drug trafficking. But also essential for Weber, alongside such realistic detail, was a personal narrative capable of stirring emotional investment and personal identification amongst her viewers.

Setting the fight to curtail illegal drug trafficking against a personal tragedy of addiction, Weber built her narrative around the story of a customs official who learns that his own wife is an opium addict, a strategy she would use again in *Where Are My Children?* later that year. Here male spheres of law, public policy, and policing are bound to the private and familial in the same way that social complexities of eugenics and family planning would be cast in relation to the domestic tragedy of a childless marriage in *Where Are My Children?* In both films white, middle-class protagonists furnish the entry point for viewers. In *Hop* Smalley plays the customs inspector, Ward Jansen, who returns from a six-month expedition to China to find that his wife, Lydia (Weber), has become addicted to smoking opium after the death of their infant child left her despondent. Hiding her drug habit under cover of bourgeois normalcy, Lydia is blackmailed by the couple's cunning maid, Jane (Marie Walcamp), whose fiancé, Con Leech

(Juan de la Cruz), aids the opium smuggling network from his position as a stevedore on the docks. Ward does not at first suspect his wife's addiction, attributing her strange behavior solely to grief. But when he cracks down on the narcotics trade and leads a raid on a Chinatown opium den, he finds his wife hiding there among the addicts. Lydia's father, Bill Waters (Charles Hammond), a respected city councilman leading the opium ring in secret, commits suicide when he discovers that his actions have contributed to his daughter's opium habit. Lydia is rehabilitated in the end and reunited with Ward.[106] So interesting and dramatic was the narrative, according to the *New York Dramatic Mirror*, that "one scarcely realizes until the picture is ended that a sermon has been preached."[107]

With Ward Jansen at the center of the drama, *Hop, the Devil's Brew* encourages viewers to identify with white, masculine forces of law and order against Orientalized villains and the feminized specter of addiction and weakness. A print of the film does not survive, so it is difficult to assess its visual strategies, but it appears that Ward's authority as customs inspector is associated with an optical and physical command over the city's geography, particularly its hidden recesses of drug trafficking and addiction. What Ward *fails* to see at first also seems crucial to the film's approach. Intercutting between different threads of the story—smugglers and customs inspectors on the docks, addicts in opium dens, Lydia's secret humiliation at home—permits viewers to recognize the true scope of opium's reach long before Ward himself does. The film encourages an emotional identification with the depths of Lydia's grief and subsequent addiction, while simultaneously framing that individual narrative within a comprehensive social view. This balance would lie at the heart of many of Weber's social-problem pictures, demonstrating her belief in cinema's unique ability to encourage intimate identification with profound social consequences.

Despite *Variety*'s assessment that *Hop, the Devil's Brew* lacked the "gruesome" exploitation of earlier offerings on the subject, and despite the extremely positive reviews it received, the film faced trouble with censorship boards in both Chicago and Pennsylvania.[108] Weber was angered by the censorship of a work she considered a "harmless but enlightening" treatment of the growing drug problem. Cuts requested in the film, she said, "stamped [censors] as either grossly inconsistent or defective."[109] To her astonishment the Pennsylvania Board of Censors allowed several scenes of opium smoking to remain in the release print, while deleting a close-up of the dead baby's shoes intended to accentuate Lydia's grief. "I do not know whether babies' shoes are obscene or merely immoral," she quipped.[110] What Weber did not say, but might be inferred, is that the effectiveness of her treatment of social problems could potentially be gauged by the degree of censors' concern.

Weber's examination of another polemical issue—capital punishment—in *The People vs. John Doe* once again drew upon contemporary news stories, resulting in what the *New York Times* would call "the most effective propaganda in film form ever seen."[111] Capital punishment became the focus of sustained attention and debate in the Progressive Era as increased discussion of how environmental factors contributed to criminal behavior led many Progressives to advocate abolition of the death penalty. The state, they argued, had no right to execute a person in order to punish a crime for which society itself was at least partly responsible. Those in favor of abolishing state executions included Thomas Mott Osborne, influential prison reformer and warden of Sing Sing prison in New York, who declared that capital punishment had "a seriously brutalizing effect upon the community at large." Former president Theodore Roosevelt was among those in the opposite camp, hoping to retain the death penalty; putting criminals to death further ennobled a manly society, he argued. But Roosevelt's views did not prevail. With the abolitionist movement stronger than it had been in nearly fifty years, nine states abandoned executions in the years leading up to the First World War and twenty-seven others modified mandatory death penalty laws permitting the option of life imprisonment.[112]

To make a case against capital punishment, Weber's script focused on the plight of an innocent man sentenced to die for a murder he did not commit. John Doe (Harry De More), an uneducated, out-of-work farmhand with a pregnant wife (Evelyn Selbie) and children to support, is hired by a wealthy farmer just days before the man and his sister are murdered. A detective eager for reward money (Charles Mailes) captures Doe and his "half-wit" brother-in-law and forces a confession using "inhumane third degree methods." Both men are convicted of murder and sentenced to die. Suspecting their innocence, a female attorney (Leah Baird) gets the detective to admit he forced the confession, then helps track down the real killer. With the attorney's help Doe's execution is stayed in the final moments of the film just as he is about to be electrocuted.[113] More than any of Weber's Universal social-problem films, *The People vs. John Doe* features an activist female protagonist leading the charge for social justice. Certainly women figure at the heart of all of the issues Weber considers—as both victims and agents of change—but here the attorney provides the clearest screen surrogate for female viewers ready to take up a cause outside the theater.

Originally called "The Celebrated Stielow Case," Weber's script was based on one of several highly publicized death penalty cases at the time.[114]

Figure 23. Mrs. Doe (Evelyn Selbie) visits her husband (Harry De More) in prison shortly after he has received a stay of execution, in *The People vs. John Doe* (1916). Author's collection.

Like the eponymous Doe, Charles Stielow was an uneducated farmhand sentenced to die for a murder many believed he did not commit. Attorney Grace Humiston had been instrumental in efforts to free him, along with noted suffrage activist Inez Milholland Boissevain, and was Weber's likely model for the lawyer in the film. While preparing the script, Weber had also consulted with Sophie Irene Loeb, a reporter for the *New York Evening World* who had chronicled Stielow's ordeal.[115] Weber plainly intended her film to intervene in Stielow's ongoing legal battle, as well as the growing opposition to debates about capital punishment that his case helped to fuel. However, all references to Stielow were ultimately eliminated from the film, and the title character's name was changed to a pointed "John Doe" at the behest of the National Board of Censorship, which screened a print several weeks prior to its release.[116] Universal would later claim the change had been made to permit the film "greater scope than the one immediate murder mystery which inspired it."[117] Sure of the film's topical appeal, whatever the central character's name, Universal rushed the film into release in late December 1916, less than a week after New York governor Charles S.

Whitman commuted Stielow's death sentence, delaying the release of its highly anticipated adaptation of *20,000 Leagues under the Sea*.[118] Trade notices advertising the film's availability on a states' rights basis prominently featured clippings from newspapers around the country with Stielow's name clearly visible.[119] Without ever mentioning Stielow directly, Universal succeeded in making the film's connection to his case plain for all to see. The story had "evidently been inspired by the Stielow case," Margaret I. MacDonald concluded in her *Moving Picture World* review. The *New York Dramatic Mirror* agreed: anyone who had followed the man's trial would have no trouble recognizing the film's source material.[120]

Leaders of the movement to abolish capital punishment seized upon the film to advocate their cause. *The People vs. John Doe* premiered in New York at a free Sunday-morning screening sponsored by the Humanitarian Cult, an organization instrumental in the fight to commute Stielow's death sentence. Misha Appelbaum, the group's leader, addressed movie audiences at screenings throughout the film's two-week run in New York, providing what MacDonald deemed "an impressive address on the abolishment of capital punishment."[121] Death penalty opponents also screened the film for Pennsylvania legislators at a hearing to abolish capital punishment in that state early the following year.[122] Indeed, many in the film industry considered Weber's film a splendid example of the far-reaching potential of activist cinema. *The People vs. John Doe* would "do more to make people THINK about capital punishment than all the pamphlets and speeches that could be prepared in a year's time," *Wid's* proclaimed, predicting that the film would help to "abolish capital punishment in every State in the Union."[123]

Much of the film's effectiveness lay in its realist aesthetic. Weber cast relative unknowns in the leading roles, preferring "types" over familiar screen personalities. The tactic worked, for virtually all reviewers praised the naturalistic performances that resulted. They played their parts so well, one reviewer claimed, that "one seems to be viewing a drab slice of life rather than the miming of a group of players before a camera."[124] The work of the principals was "quite beyond ordinary praise for its strength and sincerity," Grace Kingsley wrote in the *Los Angeles Times*.[125] Weber also relied heavily on location shooting, which contributed greatly to the film's realism. "The studio was dispensed with almost altogether," one reviewer raved, "and real places were used as backgrounds for many of the scenes."[126]

Also key to the film's effectiveness, ironically, was the decision to change the central character's name to John Doe. By selecting a name that is hardly a name at all, but a pseudonym given to unidentified corpses in the morgue, Weber actually drew attention to the elision of Stielow from its narrative, arguably forging even clearer parallels to the famous case. Yet at the same time, the pseudonym also universalized the story, suggesting that *any* man might find himself unjustly accused of murder and facing execution. Less clear is the effect that the generic name had on issues of ethnicity and immigration prominent in the actual Stielow case and played up in the film's early publicity. Universal had initially described the central character, then still "Stielow," as "a slow-witted honest-appearing foreigner, comprehending little of what is said to him in English," who possessed "dog-like honesty, though in a clumsy and lumbering sort of way."[127] Although the character's ethnicity was eventually masked by the Anglo pseudonym "John Doe," it would seem that Harry De More's performance in the lead role still clearly marked the character's ethnic difference.

However, the film's focus on the plight of an innocent man, a common enough strategy among death penalty opponents at the time, actually negates some of the force of its argument.[128] Audiences are asked to question abusive interrogation tactics and the ritual of putting citizens to death, but only in so far as they affect the lives of "innocent" members of society. Nowhere does the film suggest, for instance, that murderers be spared execution. Nor does the film appear to embrace the widely held Progressive view that social factors (such as poverty, inadequate education, and poor health care) contributed to criminal behavior. Like Weber's other 1916 films on controversial topics—*Shoes* and *Where Are My Children?*—*The People vs. John Doe* cloaks its radical critique—the death penalty is inhumane—in a conservative appeal surrounding an innocent man falsely accused. *Shoes*, in a similar vein, invites moviegoers to endorse women's wage equity through an appeal to traditional notions of feminine sexual purity and the dangers (physical and sexual) of women's presence in the workforce. In *Where Are My Children?* moviegoers are invited to embrace legal contraception through a racist and classist appeal to eugenics and a story about the perils of unchecked sexuality.

The ideological stance Weber adopts in *The People vs. John Doe* becomes even more evident when framed against her approach to a similar subject earlier that year in *The Eye of God*, a film narrated by a prisoner on death row awaiting execution. More an exploration of the psychology of guilt than the social consequences of coerced confessions and capital punishment, *The Eye of God* presents no argument against the death penalty and, in fact, seems to endorse it. Writing his confession as he prepares to die, the prisoner tells how the "eye of God" watched him as he almost let another man be executed for a murder he himself had committed. "At last he confesses and accepts the punishment for his deed," one reviewer surmises.[129] In the film's final moments the prisoner is strapped into the electric chair in a scene *Variety* found "rather too gruesome."[130]

Even acknowledging the complexity or even contradictory nature of Weber's politics, it must be admitted that she did not shy away from such subjects, considering them essential to cinema's ascendance as a mature art form. She tackled not only provocative subjects like contraception, capital punishment, and drug trafficking, but also more nuanced and subtle topics like guilt, morality, and propriety. Tied though these issues often were to sensational news stories of the day, Weber's scripts remained attentive to narratives of individual suffering and loss. As Ernestine Black wrote in her 1916 profile of the director, Weber fought "to give intellectual athleticism a place on the screen." She maintained "a specific creed, an erect and full grown idea about the place and power of the moving picture, and the marvel of it is that she has been able to keep her creed and commercial success moving in the same set!"[131]

SHOES AND THE SOCIOLOGICAL IMPULSE

With *Shoes* Weber tackled one of the Progressive Era's most pronounced social phenomena—the influx of young, single women into the paid labor force. Weber's interest in the fate of underpaid retail clerks echoed many sociological studies of the era that investigated the "problem" of young female wage earners, often raising questions about desires unleashed by commercial recreation culture and the consumer economy, particularly in the context of urban communities where young women lived and worked, often outside the immediate supervision of their families. "Shopgirls," such as the heroine in *Shoes*, were privileged in these studies, for their labor bridged the industrial and commercial spheres. In her 1911 report on such employees, Louise De Koven Bowen lamented how long working hours with few breaks at retail work sites often made it "difficult for girls to withstand the temptations which press hard upon them, and which lead to a moral as well as a physical breakdown. This is doubly true in department stores," she said, "where girls work surrounded by, and selling, the luxuries which they all crave for a wage compensation inadequate for a life of decency and respectability."[132] Reading *Shoes* against this reform discourse, it becomes clear that while the film does reproduce many of the same anxieties around female labor, consumer culture, and sexuality, it also engages structures of identification that are absent from most sociological studies and, indeed, are unique to cinema. While reinforcing much of the cautionary tenor of reform tracts, *Shoes* also allowed its targeted middle-class viewers (women in particular) access to the aspirations and longings of the "working girls" under scrutiny. Thus, rather than simply reflecting the pre-occupations of current reformers, *Shoes* actually demonstrates cinema's distinctive role in Progressive debates, its intertext producing a complex conversation about the role cinema might play in Progressive society.

The film focuses on Eva Meyer (Mary MacLaren), a five-and-dime store clerk whose meager five-dollar-a-week salary must support her mother and father, along with three younger sisters, supplemented only by the limited income her mother (Mae Witting) earns by taking in laundry. Her father (Harry Griffith) is unable, and the film suggests, unwilling, to find work to support his family, so his eldest daughter must shoulder their financial burden alone. Standing on her feet all day at the store, Eva quickly wears out the soles of her boots, and though she begs her mother for money to buy a new pair she has spotted in a display window, Mrs. Meyer cannot spare the extra money from an already-strained family budget. After catching cold walking in the rain with her deteriorating footwear, and again being refused money to purchase new shoes, Eva finally accepts an invitation from a persistent male flatterer who has pursued her at work, agreeing to meet him one evening at a cabaret. When she arrives home the following day wearing new boots, the implication is clear, and Eva falls weeping into her mother's lap, only to learn, too late, that her father has at last found a job to support his family.

Shoes engages quite self-consciously with contemporary sociological discourse at its outset, opening with a prologue associating Weber's directorial vision with that of famed reformer Jane Addams. A still close-up of a young woman's face is the first image we see, a woman later recognizable as the film's heroine, Eva Meyer. Her image then dissolves to the cover of Addams's well-known 1914 book on prostitution and white slavery, *A New Conscience and an Ancient Evil.*[133] Images of two pages from Addams's book follow, allowing viewers to read her account of a young woman who "succumbed to temptation" and "sold herself for a new pair of shoes." Rather than creating a suggestion that Eva is reading Addams's book, perhaps through an eye-line match, the dissolve between her face and the book's contents instead implies that the film's portrayal of her experience is lifted from its pages, for her face hovers over the book in the dissolve's slow superimposition. From the beginning, then, *Shoes* evokes cinema's capacity to visualize sociological observations made by Addams in her fieldwork and to transport her findings to the eyes of moviegoers across the country. In doing so, the prologue also suggests an analogy between Addams's settlement work and Lois Weber's Progressive filmmaking efforts, between the sociologist's gaze and that of the filmmaker.

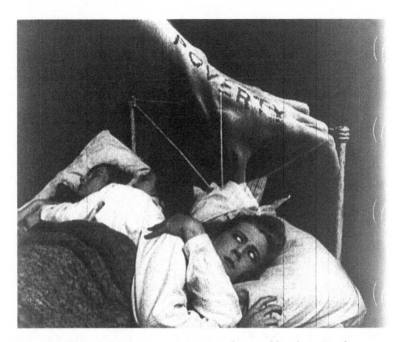

Figure 24. Eva Meyer (Mary MacLaren) is haunted by the grip of poverty, in *Shoes* (1916). Frame enlargement.

Although never acknowledged within the text of *Shoes* itself, there was a second, equally significant source for Weber's script, a short story published in *Collier's* magazine that dramatized the incident reported by Addams.[134] The *Collier's* story, also called "Shoes," provided a measurable backbone to Weber's scenario; yet the film itself points only to Addams's case history as its source, foregrounding an alliance between Progressive filmmaking and contemporary social work while eliding an equal basis in fiction. These two axes of the story are nonetheless crucial to understanding the film's strategies, for its address fluctuates between an imagined identification with a reformer's gaze from outside diegetic space—a gaze associated with not only Addams but Weber herself—and an identification with the heroine's own fears, desires, and emotions fostered through narrative and cinematic tropes. Even as Weber explicitly aligned her filmmaking eye with Addams's sociological observations, *Shoes* engages specifically cinematic modes of identification that counteract and complicate this address by focusing on psychological interiority and subjective experience. Viewers are invited to empathize with Eva's plight through a host of cinematic devices that visualize her imaginative longings, articulate the imbalances of power in her household, and invite us to share her experiences of exhausting labor and humiliating poverty—an address that challenges the film's initial claims of sociological authenticity.

Interviewed during the making of *Shoes*, Weber explicitly aligned her filmmaking methods with reform work by describing her background as "church army" missionary. Recounting her work with young women in particular, she said, "I know them and their problems, and not a few of my stories have been suggested by incidents recalled from those early experiences." In fact, Eva's character in *Shoes*, Weber claimed, had been "drawn directly from a life filled with the keenest sort of drama and pathos."[135] By occulting her script's genealogy in Jane Addams's mission and pointing instead toward its origins in her own lived experience and her own recollections, Weber fashioned a particular vision of the filmmaker as social worker, literally substituting her own gaze for Addams's fieldwork. Moreover, by emphasizing her evangelical history, and indeed posing filmmaking as the logical corollary of missionary work, Weber couched her output within a moral, rather than a political, framework, claiming that motion pictures allowed her to "preach to my heart's content."[136]

Reviews of *Shoes* also drew connections between the film's authentic re-creation of urban working-class life and its Progressive message. The fact that Weber was known to be "particular about the correctness of details" was a fact that Universal chose to emphasize in its publicity for the film.[137] *Shoes* was "made with all the skill and attention to detail which we have learned to expect from Lois Weber," the studio claimed, noting that the entire contents of a five-and-dime store had been transported to the studio for the retail scenes, that sets in the Meyer household had been equipped with furniture "specially bought from just such people as the Meyers were," and that corned beef and cabbage had been cooked on a functioning stove during scenes in the family's apartment.[138] Although the studio's emphasis on realism seems designed to side-step the more politicized question of women's wage equity, reviewers at the time stressed these connections, with Margaret I. MacDonald describing it as a "sociological study" that "rings true" and "reminds one of turning the pages of one of life's unhappiest chapters." The *Los Angeles Examiner* praised "its exact portraiture of the appalling currency of poverty," while *Variety* declared *Shoes* to be "a vision of life as it actually is, and devoid of all theatricalism." In her enthusiastic endorsement of *Shoes* for the *Chicago Herald*, Louella Parsons linked its message to "societies and organizations that are working night and day for the establishment of a minimum wage scale for women," connecting this aim, once again, to Addams's work.[139]

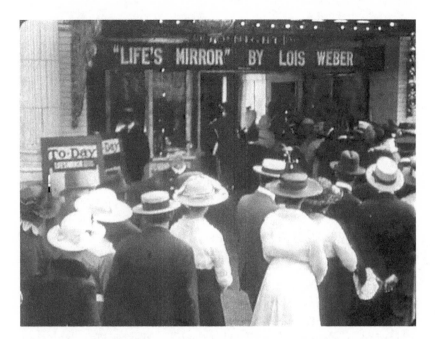

Figure 25. Patrons flock to see the film "Life's Mirror" directed by a certain "Lois Weber," in *Idle Wives* (1916). Frame enlargement.

Weber's most direct commentary on the intervention that cinema might perform in a progressive society is contained in her astonishingly reflexive film, *Idle Wives,* released in late 1916, less than two months after *Shoes.* Indeed, the film demonstrates a phenomenon that Weber herself did not acknowledge in interviews or profiles: the suasive power of cinematic spectatorship and its unique patterns of identification. Characters in *Idle Wives,* dissatisfied with their lives, attend a movie entitled "Life's Mirror" (pointedly directed by one "Lois Weber") in which they see visions of what their lives might become, should they choose a wrong path.[140] Mary MacLaren (the star of *Shoes*) plays a wayward shopgirl "stepping out" with her boyfriend against her parents' wishes; she watches her on-screen surrogate conceive a child and retire shamefully to a home for unwed mothers. Weber and Smalley take on the roles of an estranged married couple who watch as the wife's on-screen counterpart (Maude George) leaves her uncaring husband to return to her beloved occupation as a settlement worker. A third story shows a working family whose members learn the perils of living beyond their means. These three narratives—centered on a sexually compromised salesclerk, an idealistic social worker, and an impoverished family aspiring to more than they can afford—all refer unmistakably to the plot lines of *Shoes* and thus encourage us to read the earlier film as emblematic of Weber's larger cinematic project. Doubly inscribed within the diegesis, Weber appears as both social worker and filmmaker, drawing particular attention to the commonality she sees between these two roles.

With *Idle Wives* it becomes clear that the social components of moviegoing, together with the unique spectral aspects of film viewing, set cinema apart from other activist media, such as newspaper editorials, with which Weber often sought to compare it. Still, "Life's Mirror," the imaginary film within *Idle Wives,* indicates something of both Weber's aspirations and their inevitable complications, for what characters watch on screen are not their actual lives, but visions of future catastrophe, visions that ultimately produce a positive change in their lives. William D. Routt notes the similarities between Weber's self-inscription in *Idle Wives* and the figure of "Naked Truth" in *Hypocrites.* "There can be no doubt," Routt writes of the earlier film, "that this naked woman with a mirror is also on some level a figuration of the cinema—or, at least, of the cinema as Lois Weber intends it."[141] Certainly one must also see the figure of Naked Truth as Weber's allegorical inscription of herself. What the filmmaker wields in both cases is not a mirror per se, but a revelatory instrument, capable of reforming human behavior: an idealized view of cinema, for certain, but one from which Weber did not shy away. In fact, *Shoes* attempts a strategy even more daring than what is portrayed in *Idle Wives.* In the latter film, diegetic viewers simply watch their screen counterparts with the aim of reforming their own errant ways; in *Shoes,* viewers are invited to share the psychological interiority of a working-class retail clerk, and at other moments they are asked to step beyond her personal experience to observe the wider social and economic arena in which she operates. With *Shoes* Weber is addressing viewers she believes can become active agents of change in Progressive society.

Thus, three levels of intertext become crucial to understanding the mode of address *Shoes* engages: the intertextual reading the film itself invites, right at its outset, by invoking Jane Addams's work; the intertextuality Weber herself insisted upon in interviews, which encourage viewers (at least those in the "better elements" of society) to read the film as an editorial statement, or a sermon, on social problems; and the intertext suggested by Weber's own films. *Idle Wives,* in particular, demonstrates a phenomenon the filmmaker was herself reluctant to acknowledge in interviews—the wholly visual, and uniquely cinematic, structures of identification that film viewing engages.

While much of the rhetoric surrounding *Shoes,* and much of the way Weber's persona was framed in popular discourse, sought to align the film with Progressive reform work, suggesting there was little difference between reform efforts on screen and those circulating in other media, in fact, the tensions at work in *Shoes* highlight the *complexities* of cinema's engagement with reform discourse. The way the film mobilizes our identification with a character's psychological interiority, even as it invites us at other moments to step outside that experience and view the situation from a more detached vantage of sociological observation, points instead to the unique role that cinema might play in cultural debates surrounding issues like women's wage equity.

Particularly important in this economy of identification is the film's emphasis on female desire, focused in this case on a pair of button-up boots that condense many of heroine Eva Meyer's aspirations and longings. Standing on her feet all day in the five-and-dime store without adequate break periods or relief, Eva quickly wears out the thin soles of her boots. But her substandard wages do not permit her to replace the footwear, making them the most visible index of her exploitative working conditions. In its early sequences the film cuts between shots of Eva on the job and shots of her mother at home washing and ironing the laundry she takes in, making it clear that Eva labors behind the shop counter just as surely as her mother does as a laundress, while underscoring the distinction between such traditional, home-based modes of women's work and newer modes based in the consumer economy. Studies of department store employees in the 1910s also contributed to the perception of retail work as labor, for they found evidence that standing for periods of up to fourteen hours a day caused significant physical strain, and many reformers pushed for health and safety requirements such as seating and adequate breaks.[142] Progressives also called for a "living wage" for women working in the retail sphere, reporting that few could survive on their earnings. In its 1918 study of female wage earners, the Consumer's League of New York found that most women employed in factory work, clerical work, dressmaking, and retail work earned between seven and twelve dollars per week, significantly below a "living wage." Reporting that only a small proportion of the women used their wages as disposable income, that most were self-supporting, and that virtually all others contributed portions of their income to support their families, the organization asked, "Does this look like pin money?"[143] The Women's Trade Union League of Chicago produced similar findings, noting that between 25 and 30 percent of the women employed in that city's department stores could not support themselves on their income.[144]

In *Shoes* Eva works in a well-stocked five-and-dime store located in a district full of outlets selling similar goods, so that she is surrounded by merchandise not only on the job but also as she travels to and from work, even though she herself is not able to participate in the consumer economy that her labor supports. "The department store girl is much more subject to temptation" than other female wage earners, Louise De Koven Bowen reported in her 1911 study of these workers, since she is "constantly surrounded by the articles which are so dear to the feminine heart. She sees passing and repassing all day women who are gorgeously arrayed in the very kind of clothes which she naturally covets."[145] Shopgirls therefore occupied a unique position in the world of women's work, comparable to neither factory laborers nor domestics, nor even clerical workers, since their workplace was also a public venue where there was likely to be more confusion between their roles as workers and their aspirations as consumers.

This disparity is forcefully underscored in the film's opening scenes, which situate shopgirls at the intersection of wage labor and consumption beginning with the very first shot, where a lateral tracking movement follows the women as they line up to receive their pay. Filing through the mid-ground of the image, framed between a cashier handing out money in the background and the goods that line the store's counters and shelves in the foreground, the employees' movements emphasize the regimentation of the retail work space and their visual similarity to the goods on display. The fact that we see the women getting paid before we see them working underscores the importance of wages as the end product of their labor and the subsequent circulation of that income in the consumer economy.

Leaving the store after work, Eva and her friend Lil (Jessie Arnold) stop to chat on the street, framed against the store's display window in that liminal moment between work and leisure time, between labor and consumption. As she walks through the streets of the shopping district on her way home, Eva stops to admire a pair of boots in a storefront window, in a scene that suggests how readily her employment as a salesclerk complicates her role as potential consumer. A close-up provides us with a glimpse of the objects of her longing: boots that seem to be suspended in the air, detached from any body or any particular physical need. Her hand hovers over the glass, as if to fondle the new boots, but unable to do so because the window that displays the items also prevents them from being touched, in a mode of presentation that at once facilitates and frustrates Eva's desire. Here Eva's longing is rendered not through a conventional optical point-of-view shot that would underscore our identification with her gaze, but through a match-on-action cut as her hand moves toward the boots in close-up, so that her gesture is continued across the two images, her hand serving as synecdoche for her desire. Rather than emphasizing her gaze, this strategy draws attention to the transparent barrier between her and the merchandise on display, a vivid symbol of her paradoxical position in the consumer economy—surrounded by goods, drawn by an impulse to be fashionable, but able to afford little of what she sees. Since we do not yet know that Eva's own shoes are deteriorating badly, a fact not revealed until the following scene, the emphasis here falls solely upon Eva's desire for the boots as stylish commodities. Even though the narrative will later stress Eva's obvious need for new footwear, here the shoes are first identified only as items of fashion. Cinematic strategies, like the match-on-action cut, enhance film viewers' identification with Eva's longing in this sequence, demonstrating as much for us as for her the desirability of the boots. Yet, as the scene develops, we are invited to situate our understanding of Eva's desire within a broader framework of sociological observation, one that hinges (cinematically) on viewers seeing what Eva fails to see and (culturally) on understanding her social position in the consumer economy.

Thus, even as this early sequence links Eva's roles as wage earner and consumer, inviting us to share her interest in the new shoes, it also inscribes her desire within another economy we are invited to observe from a distance, a sexual economy that she will initially reject then ultimately embrace. As Eva and Lil pause in front of the window to admire the boots, Lil's friend Charlie (William V. Mong) emerges from the shop and stops to watch the two women before engaging them in flirtatious conversation. Even in the moment of consumption, then, the young women are themselves desired objects. Following a triangulated composition with Charlie positioned between the two women, a close-up signals his interest as he looks out of frame in Eva's direction. A matching close-up of Eva registers her growing awareness that she is being watched. But rather than turning to face him and completing an eye-line match, she averts her eyes and modestly turns away, never meeting his gaze, as the composition registers her simultaneous awareness of the libidinous dynamics of the interchange and her refusal to participate. When we return to the original long-shot composition, Charlie catches Lil's eye across the frame, with Eva caught in the middle, her attention still fixed on the new shoes in the display case. Although Eva behaves virtuously in this first scene with Charlie, studiously ignoring his advances, the film's prologue has quite explicitly circumscribed her narrative within this sexual economy. Since viewers know the parameters of Eva's fate from the beginning—she will "sell herself" for a pair of shoes—the film's emphasis shifts toward understanding the conditions under which such young women might barter sexual favors for their attire, an arrangement that surely seems scandalous at first glance, but that begins to be developed here in these opening scenes. Framed against the window, Eva becomes an object on exhibit much like the shoes, but in another visual economy, one in which no glass barrier exists to shield her. Here in this sequence viewers are asked to watch as if through two pairs of eyes, empathizing at first with Eva's longing for the lovely boots, then gradually seeing what she cannot see, the web of winks and implications spun by Charlie and Lil just outside her line of vision. By tracing sight lines within the sequence, the film asks viewers to situate their understanding of Eva's desire within a broader framework of sociological observation.

By underscoring a visual economy of desires, these opening scenes mark a notable departure from the *Collier's* magazine story on which Weber based her screenplay. Whereas Stella Wynne Herron's narrative begins simply with Eva arriving home on a Saturday evening clutching her five-dollar weekly pay, the film devotes substantial energy to the moment between work and home; in particular, the moment when Eva is poised in front of the shopwindow. Before we ever learn of her destitute family and her desperate need to replace her worn boots, viewers are invited to share Eva's interest in the shoes as items of fashion, an interest that is doubly framed: first, by the workday she spends surrounded by consumer goods, and then by her circulation in a heterosexual economy of flirtation and attraction. Whereas consumer desire and sexual desire are underplayed in Herron's story, they play significant, and significantly intertwined, roles in the film. Herron, for instance, has Eva peer into the shopwindow at the boots just once, only when her feet are blistered and soaking wet from a drenching rainstorm late in the story, thus placing sole emphasis on Eva's hardship. Moreover, no extended seduction leads up to Eva's eventual sexual "downfall" in the original *Collier's* story; the flirtatious subplot with Charlie and Lil was an element added entirely by Weber to complicate the circumstances under which Eva trades sex for shoes. Motivation of sorts is furnished by Lil, her jaded friend, who accepts gifts of jewelry and clothing from male admirers in exchange for what we assume to be sexual favors. Although Eva manages to withstand Charlie's advances at first, she becomes increasingly enamored of the trinkets Lil flaunts in front of her co-workers, a key motivating factor that Weber adds to the narrative.

The interdependence between consumer desire and sexual desire in Weber's script was also common to reform discourse of the day, for concerns about young women's participation in the wage labor force were often expressed through anxieties about their sexuality, especially fears that women's paltry earnings might lead to various kinds of "treating" from better-paid male beaus, as historian Kathy Peiss has documented. "Every possible weakness in a girl is detected and traded upon in the retail store," Jane Addams cautioned in her treatise on prostitution and white slavery.[146] In her 1913 study, *The Work-a-Day Girl,* Clara Laughlin told the story of a sixteen-year-old department store clerk, a composite character named Katie who chose a retail job over work in an office or a factory because of its social opportunities: "There's no telling what moment a swell fellow will notice you and, having noticed, fall a victim to your charms," Laughlin writes, paraphrasing Katie and the many others she represents.[147] Soon Katie is courted by a young man she meets over the counter, though she finds herself shocked to learn what he expects of her in return. When told by her friends at work that "ain't no feller goin' t' spend coin on yeh fer nothin" and that all the other girls participate in the treating economy, Katie accompanies her subsequent dates to hotel rooms. Laughlin concludes that this kind of "occasional prostitution" occurs "wherever a girl's desire for ease, luxury, and gay times exceeds her ability to provide these for herself, and her preference for virtue is exceeded by her desire."[148] In this "treating" economy, sexual desire and consumer desire were dangerously conflated. As Constance Balides notes, such case studies gave a "particular visibility" to female workers and consumers, one reformers themselves even associated with "kinetoscope views."[149] Yet, far from demonstrating the commonality of sociological case histories and cinematic representation, *Shoes* reveals cinema's unique modes of spectatorial engagement.

Taking its cue from such literature, the film uses the five-and-dime store as a staging ground for Eva's sexual conquest, as if the very commerce enacted there rehearses a kind of libidinal exchange. After Eva first rejects him, Charlie visits the store several times to flirt with Eva and her knowing co-worker Lil across the counter, posing all the while as a customer. In one such sequence a high-angle shot shows Charlie entering the largely female retail environment and surveying the space. His gaze wanders not toward the merchandise, like those of female shoppers visible in the same image, but toward the women themselves. It is Lil who notices him first, in a medium close-up registering her initial pleasure, followed by her subsequent attempts to draw his attention and catch his eye. When Charlie enters the frame in which Eva and Lil stand behind the counter, Lil meets his gaze, while Eva, ever modest, averts her eyes downward. Not surprisingly, Eva turns down Charlie's invitation to join him at the Blue Goose cabaret, yet he and Lil exchange complicitous glances across the frame, and Eva's co-worker appears to offer him reassurance before he leaves, implicating Eva still further in a bargain of which she remains unaware. Once again, viewers' identification with Eva, fostered here through an appeal to sexual modesty, is set alongside a greater understanding of the social dynamics at work in her environment, an understanding that the film provides through its orchestration of on-screen looking relations. Stepping outside diegetic space in these moments, viewers are invited to share the filmmaker's perspective, a perspective that draws upon a broader understanding of the situation. The choreography of viewers' attention in this sequence thus stands in marked contrast to the composite portrait of "Katie" that sociologist Clara Laughlin drew for her readers in *Our Work-a-Day Girls,* a character brought to life only to serve as an object of readers' scrutiny (and distain). *Shoes* negotiates two alternating modes of identification and address, initiating a unique visual and psychological perspective for viewers.

In addition to framing Eva's desire for fashionable boots within a sexual economy, the film invites viewers to recognize how her desire for the boots is tied to class aspirations, for she sees her tattered footwear as emblems of her family's poverty. Kathy Peiss notes that for many urban working women of this era, fashion and public displays of style became the chief means of expressing dreams of upward mobility, a longing to escape the harsh circumstances in which many of them lived and worked.[150] *Shoes* makes this point especially plain when Eva encounters a group of chic young women in the park where she sits eating lunch one day. As one of them drops a handkerchief to the ground, a point-of-view shot registers Eva's glimpse of the woman's elegantly clad feet. Then a high-angle shot shows Eva quickly tucking her own shabby specimens under the bench where she sits. Representing no character's possible viewpoint, the unusual high-angle composition forcefully evokes Eva's own experience of the scene, the humiliation she feels in front of these well-to-do women. This sequence occurs just after Eva has been asked to admire Lil's new wristwatch at work, a bauble her co-worker most certainly obtained from casual prostitution. The juxtaposition of these two scenes underscores Eva's own investment in fashion, stylishness, and consumer desire. She is not only sick and unhealthy because of her poorly protected feet, but ashamed of her poverty and envious of those who can afford nicer things. That Eva's encounter with the chic young women happens in public, rather than her workplace, accentuates still further the connection in Eva's mind between the coveted footwear and her social status.

Class dynamics are further reinforced in the sequence's structure, for at the outset Eva finds herself sitting on the bench beside two well-dressed older men who object both to the fact that she is eating outdoors (and therefore presumably unable to afford lunch in a restaurant) and to the odor of strong cheese emanating from her sandwich, marking their offense not simply in class terms but presumably in ethnic terms as well. The men get up and leave the bench in disgust, and poor Eva breaks down in tears, overcome by embarrassment. We have seen her kept awake just the previous night, haunted by the specter of poverty, visualized in the form of a huge human hand labeled "Poverty" looming over Eva and her sisters as they slept. Viewers, privy to Eva's innermost fears, now see how those fears manifest themselves in her public interactions.

Still, however much the film asks viewers to empathize with Eva's plight, it remains deeply suspicious of her evident investment in fashionable commodities. This becomes clear early on in the film through a comparison developed between Eva and one of her younger sisters, who we see stealing sugar behind their mother's back in order to sweeten watered-down milk. Suggesting that deprivation breeds both ingenuity and transgression, the comic vignette articulates dual aspects of Eva's desire to adorn her feet. Much like Eva's minimal salary, the family's limited milk supply has been stretched too thinly to provide sufficient nutrition for the girls; and just as Eva needs shoes for her blistered feet, her sister needs calcium for her growing body. But the little one's sweet tooth also finds an echo in Eva's longing for *stylish* boots, rather than merely functional ones. Had Eva's sister been given whole milk to begin with, the film implies, the little girl would not have needed to sweeten it and thereby further diminish its nutritional value. So too with Eva: had she been given money to buy serviceable footwear early on, she would not have invested so much desire in having a more frivolous, fashionable pair of shoes, a yearning that becomes almost erotic—and dangerously entangled in an associated visual and sexual economy.

Reformers worried openly about the fashion tastes and spending habits of underpaid female wage earners for precisely this reason. Noting that salesclerks not only felt pressured to look neat and presentable but found themselves surrounded by merchandise all day long, reformers expressed concern about the women's tendency to spend a disproportionate amount of their wages on clothing. In their 1911 study of New York's "working girls," Sue Ainslie Clark and Edith Wyatt derided the "unreasonable folly," "weak judgment," "absurd excess," and "cheap, hand-to-mouth buying" of one such clerk, troubled that she had purchased too many shirtwaists of poor quality rather than investing her income wisely in fewer articles of better workmanship.[151] They surmised that she likely did not have enough saved at any one time to purchase the higher-quality items; but one might also suppose she had a taste for fashion fueled by the mercantile environment. According to Ruth True, the working girl had "no keener longing than the longing for pretty and becoming clothes," and many would gladly forgo such practicalities as protective outerwear, overshoes, and umbrellas for extravagances such as chinchilla coats, Easter outfits, and elaborate hats.[152] True also documented the struggles that occurred at home when young women who were forced to surrender their wages to their families also harbored modish desires. Barely concealing her disdain, True recounted the story of "Louisa," a young woman very proud of the "flossy" attire she wore out with her friends in the evenings: a brown serge suit with sateen collar she purchased on the installment plan, "a great encircling hat of cheap black straw," and bleached peroxide hair. "But," True noted, "the costume in which she steps out so triumphantly has cost many bitter moments at home."[153] One hears in these studies not simply a concern for the women's finances but a puritanical objection to spending wages on style, rather than substance.

Although few reformers mentioned it overtly, the women's interests in fashion also bespoke an awareness of sexuality, for surely a tacit component of Eva's fixation on the boots in *Shoes* is a wish to make herself attractive. Once Eva's interest in the shoes extends beyond her mere need to questions of fashion and style, the film seems to suggest, she moves one step closer to bartering her sexuality for the coveted pair. After twice surrendering her earnings to her mother without being allowed to purchase new shoes, Eva finally decides to take Charlie up on his offer and meet him at the Blue Goose cabaret, her assumption being that he will provide her with a "token" of his affection following their encounter. Ascribing to theories of contemporary sociologists, the film suggests that women had two avenues of economic currency—labor and sexuality—and that when the first did not yield adequate reward, necessity could lead quickly to the second, more lucrative route. As Kristen Whissel emphasizes in her inspired reading of the film, Eva's boots, worn through from hours of standing behind the shop counter and daily trips back and forth to work, become "emblematic of the thin and fragile barrier that separates the working poor woman's position in legitimate traffic from the proximate traffic in women."[154] Yet even as *Shoes* shares many of the concerns of contemporary reformers, the very means of its cinematic engagement helps to foster an identification with Eva's desires, a structure of empathy wholly absent from these other reform tracts. Eva's eventual participation in the sexual economy she initially resists is presented in a scene that invites our identification with her emotional experience of humiliation and self-loathing, rather than the judgmental views of middle-class reformers so evident in the tracts discussed above.

Rather than focusing on Eva's encounter with Charlie at the cabaret, *Shoes* instead provides a lengthy scene depicting her preparations before the mirror in the moments before she leaves home. Her resigned manner in performing this ritual of self-adornment suggests that she is not anticipating her evening at the Blue Goose with pleasure, but that she now feels as if she must take advantage of her last resort—the one method of attaining nice things that she has known about all along, thanks to her co-worker Lil, but that she has thus far managed to resist. Intercut with Eva's preparations are shots of her father lying on his bed, reading (as usual) one of his many dime novels, and shots of her mother tending (as usual) to her younger sisters in the kitchen as the girls complain of feeling hungry. The familiar, even repetitious, nature of these parallel scenes only reinforces the endless cycle of deprivation in which Eva finds herself. Before replacing her functional, workday shirtwaist with a sheerer, more elaborate one, Eva stands at the mirror pinning up her hair. Her downcast face reflected in the cracked mirror on the wall shows that she cannot bring herself to look at her own image. In a wider framing, we see her turn away from her own reflection, unable to look at it, as both she and the mirror image remain visible, doubling her body in the frame. Unable to make eye contact with the young woman caught in the glass, Eva now sees herself as a marketable commodity, much like the boots she has admired behind glass in the shopwindow or the items arranged in glass display cases at work. Here she places herself for the first time within Charlie's imagined eroticized gaze, a position she has so far refused. Elsewhere in the film, Eva's sight line is used to emphasize her moral judgment, particularly her disgust with her father's self-indulgent laziness. Here, Eva's refusal to meet her own gaze in the mirror suggests that she is now feeling an internalized moral judgment. There is a decided irony here, for she wants the boots not only to look *fashionable* like the young women she has seen earlier in the park, and therefore to mask her poverty, but also to look *desirable* in the heterosexual economy that might one day lift her out of poverty through marriage. Donning the fashionable look in order to enter this economy, she does so on terms that will also ultimately bar her from more "legitimate" forms of marital exchange in the future.

Watching herself as if on screen in this sequence, Eva understands her place in the sexual economy for the first time. She also functions as a stand-in for the film viewer, conceived here not as a reform-oriented middle-class woman struggling to comprehend the plight of poorly paid working women, but as one of those women themselves. This, then, is the film's most radical model of identification: middle-class women, those chiefly targeted by the film's address, are asked to see Eva's image as their own reflection, to ask, Would I be able to look myself in the eye in similar circumstances?

In the end, though, however much the film has invited audience identification with Eva's experience, even including her calculated preparations for the Blue Goose encounter, her ultimate sexual "downfall" casts the narrative within a melodramatic frame, in which individual virtue and vice, rather than larger social and political forces, are held accountable for injustice. Ultimately the film shies away from a forceful plea for women's wage equity, displacing the living-wage issue from the workplace onto the family: it is the father's indolence and the mother's willingness to ignore her daughter's desires that drive Eva to seek recompense outside the traditional labor force in prostitution, the film suggests. Had the father only worked to support his large family, had the mother allowed Eva to spend some of her income on personal items, the film implies, Eva would not have been pushed as far as she was.

In this regard several fantasy scenarios offered at the end of the film are telling, for they do not (or cannot) imagine a resolution whereby both Eva and her father work outside the home, whereby the family prospers, and whereby Eva is able to use her income not only to support her family but also to indulge occasionally in fashionable goods for herself. Instead, we are offered two visions. One presents Eva in a modest small-town setting waiting behind her front gate to welcome both her sweetheart and her father home from work, suggesting that she herself is not in the workforce, but is, rather, almost literally "fenced" in, supported by her father's earnings and preparing for a domestic life at home with her future husband. The second scenario shows Eva in a more upscale setting, seemingly at her society "debut," dressed all in white, trailing tuxedo-clad admirers, almost as if she were being auctioned off to the highest bidder, though the film itself seems to offer no such critique. In both cases Eva is being cared for, rather than exploited, and it is not hard to imagine the appeal of such fantasies, given what has come before. Yet each reinscribes a highly traditional, and rapidly eroding, vision of femininity, one that does not involve labor or political engagement outside the home, nor sexuality outside of marriage—a fantasy given added weight by the horrific vision of working conditions advanced in the preceding scenes. In a reversal of the sobering scenes witnessed by characters in "Life's Mirror," here audiences are treated to pleasant fantasies of life beyond exhausting labor, deprivation, and urban poverty. But viewers are brought back to reality by the film's final moments: Eva returns home to her family's tenement apartment the morning after her night out with Charlie, sporting new boots, then collapses into her mother's lap in tears. The fantasy sequences have literally stood in place of her (unrepresentable) sexual "downfall," allowing viewers to project their desires elsewhere.

This conservative undercurrent in *Shoes,* not fully evident until the film's final moments, was brought to the fore when Weber returned to the shopgirl theme one year later with *The Price of a Good Time* (1917), one of the first offerings of her new company, Lois Weber Productions. While much of the plot remained the same—Linnie, a salesclerk, finds herself seduced by the lure of commodities on display in the store and, in doing so, finds herself sexually compromised with the store owner's playboy son— Weber introduced a critical change in the story structure.[155] In this second iteration of the shopgirl plot, the heroine's predicament is contrasted to that of a fellow salesclerk who, as one reviewer put it, "marries a worthy young chap in her own walk of life and her future happiness is assured."[156] What appears a fairly innocuous substitution actually alters the story's emphasis enormously. By promoting marriage within one's "own walk of life," *The Price of a Good Time* undercuts the argument for women's wage equity mounted, however tenuously, in *Shoes,* claiming instead that women ought to depend on their husbands' income. Moreover, negative associations between consumer desire and female sexuality, redolent in *Shoes,* are magnified further in this second film's suggestion that "good" girls are satisfied with their class station, however humble, and seek only marital stability. Indeed, the implied moral judgment against Linnie in *The Price of a Good Time* is largely absent from *Shoes,* a film that goes out of its way to contextualize Eva's sexual "disgrace" and to blame her indolent father for the family's poverty.

The Price of a Good Time, then, upholds the moralistic tenor of much contemporary reform discourse as it addresses itself both to the disapproving gaze of middle-class women concerned to police the sexual exploits of wayward shopgirls and to those very same saleswomen ever in danger of losing their virtue under the spell of commodity culture. *Shoes,* as we have seen, attempts something more daring. While its ultimate message also upholds the conservative, even alarmist, views of female wage earners fostered by many reformers, its use of cinematic devices, particularly spectatorial identification and address, points to the more radical role that cinema might play in discussions of contemporary social issues. Through an appeal to sociological realism, *Shoes* invites civic-minded middle-class women to reorient their gaze within retail space, away from the merchandise, and toward the young women serving them behind the counter. Aspiring, on the one hand, to the mode of sociological studies, the film holds up working women as objects of scrutiny for others who might be in positions to influence social policy, offering viewers a position alongside the authorial gaze of director Lois Weber and reformer Jane Addams. But woven throughout this address are moments, on the other hand, when viewers are also encouraged to share the heroine's singular viewpoint, moments that counteract this dominant discourse with the promise of understanding what it means to work hard, to feel ashamed of one's circumstances and fearful about the future, and to long for one potent symbol of escape—a new pair of shoes.

BIRTH CONTROL, CENSORSHIP, AND *WHERE ARE MY CHILDREN?*

If *Shoes* demonstrates the complicated cinematic address Weber marshaled in her social-problem films, *Where Are My Children?* furnishes a telling case study of the more public battles that surrounded her efforts to present contentious social issues on screen. In this instance Weber took on the subject of contraception, then making headline news around the country thanks to Margaret Sanger's pioneering campaign to legalize family planning, or "voluntary motherhood," as she called it. Disseminating contraceptive information of any kind remained a felony during these years, and *Where Are My Children?* was a controversial attempt to engage cinema and its patrons in national debates about birth control. The film presented a difficult case for censors, not simply because it took on such a provocative topic, but because of the way the film framed its case for controlling family size in a classist and racist appeal to eugenics and, especially, the way it confused contraception and abortion.

Weber's script, adapted from the stage play *The Unborn*, by Lucy Paton and Franklin Hall, intertwines legal battles around contraception with a more intimate marital struggle over reproduction, by focusing on the character of District Attorney Richard Walton (Tyrone Power).[157] Richard comes to favor family planning under the guise of eugenics during the trial of a doctor accused of circulating contraceptive information to impoverished working-class women overburdened with large families and poor health. Later he prosecutes another doctor for performing abortions after his housekeeper's daughter dies following a botched procedure. During the second trial Richard discovers that his wife and her society friends have been procuring abortions from the same physician. Richard's climactic cry, "Where are my children?" accuses Edith Walton (Helen Riaume) and her set of murder. The film thus makes an argument in favor of birth control for working-class and immigrant populations, while lambasting Edith and her privileged circle of friends for avoiding motherhood, vilifying them further through their association with abortion, rather than contraception.[158]

Weber begins the film's treatment of eugenics and reproductive control with a prologue in which her own editorial views are most pronounced, furnishing a view "behind the great portals of eternity" where the souls of little children wait to be born. Children are stratified from conception, the prologue explains, sanctioned with either God's approval or "the sign of the serpent." This might seem like an odd place for a film on birth control to begin. Family planning pioneers like Margaret Sanger, for instance, rarely discussed the topic in such spiritual terms. But the hierarchy Weber proposes here, whereby some children are sanctioned by God and others not, attempts to add theological weight to the quasi-scientific theories of eugenics that are developed in subsequent scenes as a rationale for population control.

After this prologue, District Attorney Walton, "a great believer in eugenics," is introduced as he stands at the doorway of a courtroom, watching a dispute before the magistrate. Surveying the proceedings, he comments to an associate, "These poor souls are ill-born. If the mystery of birth were understood, crime would be wiped out." A police officer also looks on from the other side of the doorway, his body and Richard's framing the view of the courtroom, hinting that it will be male medical and legal experts who dominate discussions of reproductive politics in the film, a discourse in which women's voices will be noticeably absent. At several later points, *Where Are My Children?* again calls attention to the male spheres of influence in which decisions about family life, human sexuality, and reproduction are made. Following Richard home, the narrative begins a pattern of cross-cutting between different spheres of activity, asking us to consider the relationship between public spaces like the courtroom and private spaces like the Waltons' home, between male spheres and female spheres, and between open, legal forums and more clandestine, illegal activity. The first view of the Waltons' domestic life contrasts sharply with what we have just seen in the courtroom, as the dark, cramped view of the trial gives way to a sunny outdoor locale where we see Richard's wife, Edith, lying on a chaise lounge feeding chocolates to her dogs while books lie abandoned at her side. Edith here evokes at once idleness and privilege—her relative inertia a striking contrast to the dogs' vibrant energy. But intertitles hint that tension underlies the Waltons' cheerful façade, noting that it is "her fault" that they remain childless, a "great disappointment" to her husband. Richard, we learn, is concealing his disappointment from Edith, while she harbors an even darker secret. By furnishing viewers with privileged information in intertitles, and by designing cross-cutting sequences that invite us to compare complementary spheres of activity, the film creates an active viewing position in which we are encouraged to pass moral judgment on the characters.

A visit from Richard's sister and her new baby begins a pattern of doubling and rhyming that is another key feature of the film's narrative structure. Like the cross-cutting, these rhymes invite viewers to make comparisons—and judgments—between characters. Here two marriages, and in particular two wives (Edith and her sister-in-law), are compared. A mirrored composition shows Edith cradling her dog, while her sister-in-law cradles her infant, emphasizing a distinction between the women, one who "neglects" her childbearing obligations (according to the film's logic) while the other embraces them. Edith's dog becomes a perverse surrogate child, a comparison only reinforced when the group moves inside and the Waltons' housekeeper (Cora Drew) takes the animal from Edith's arms just as a nursemaid leaves with the infant. Thus, Richard's sister's visit provides an occasion for the film to champion the positive benefits of reproduction among the white, educated, wealthy elite for, a title tells us, she has "contracted an eugenic marriage." Even as the eugenics movement advocated fertility *control* for certain segments of the population, it strongly encouraged *reproduction* for the "better classes." Faced with the so-called double threat posed by wealthy, U.S.-born white women limiting the size of their families, while working-class and immigrant populations were reproducing at a faster rate, many in the eugenics movement advocated family planning for immigrants, people of color, and the working class, while encouraging the supposedly "threatened" white elite to propagate. In 1905 President Theodore Roosevelt helped popularize the incendiary term *race suicide* to describe this demographic discrepancy.[159]

Richard's private desire for children is paired with his prominent role as district attorney when he finds himself at the trial of Dr. Homer (C. Norman Hammond), who has been charged with disseminating contraceptive information, a practice that remained a felony. *Moving Picture World* found the doctor's trial "plainly indicative of the Margaret Sanger case" currently making headlines across the country.[160] Sanger, the nation's most visible and vocal advocate for reproductive freedom, had been indicted the previous year for distributing birth control information through her pamphlet "Family Limitation," and she had fled the country to avoid prosecution. Sanger returned to the United States late in 1915, then embarked on a national speaking tour during most of 1916, eventually settling in New York City, where she opened the nation's first contraceptive clinic in the Brownsville section of Brooklyn. Police raided the clinic and arrested Sanger after only nine days of operation, and the activist served a thirty-day prison sentence for illegally distributing information on contraception.[161] Indeed, Dr. Homer's objection that he is being tried for circulating "indecent litera-ture" refers to the common practice of filing obscenities charges against family-planning advocates. Sanger herself had been subject to a similar indictment. By foregrounding the criminal nature of birth control in this early trial sequence, *Where Are My Children?* also draws attention to its own status as a text engaging such a controversial, and potentially criminal, subject matter.

Pages from Dr. Homer's treatise on birth control are inserted as interti-tles during the trial scenes, framing his argument for legal contraception within the clear context of eugenics. "When only those children who are wanted are born," he writes, "the race will conquer the evils that weigh it down." Family planning, if used properly, could eliminate crime altogether, he implies, making it clear that the primary targets of fertility control ought to be "the ignorant and the undisciplined." Richard Walton's views on eugenics, which in the previous scene had been used to support an argu-ment that privileged couples like he and his wife ought to raise children, now support the corollary position that other segments of the population ought to control the size of their families. When Dr. Homer writes, "Let us stop the slaughter of the unborn and save the lives of unwilling mothers," his argument mirrors that of many in the family-planning movement at the time who argued that unsafe abortions could be prevented through the use of safe and effective contraception. However, Homer's use of the term *slaughter of the unborn* frames abortion in particularly negative terms, a theme developed later through Edith Walton's story.

To defend himself, Homer offers three stories from his own experience, case histories of patients in desperate need of reproductive control: an impoverished family whose many children are exposed to disease and death; an unmarried mother who is driven to suicide and infanticide after she is rejected by her lover; and a couple whose violent alcoholism endangers their offspring. Each of Dr. Homer's flashbacks highlights the children's suffering, not the women's desire for reproductive choice. In surviving prints of the film, two key images are missing from Homer's story of the unwed mother, rendering it all but unintelligible. Two additional shots described in the script make the connotation plain: in the first, a woman on the bridge approaches a man, is shunned by him, and is then hustled off by the police officer; in the next shot we see her drowned body floating alongside a baby's in the water.[162] All that remains of this shocking vignette in surviving prints is Homer's horrified response and his quick impulse to summon the officer. Although the script is not explicit, we can infer that the woman had conceived a child with a lover out of wedlock and, when rejected by him, felt compelled to kill herself and her child. Why these two images are missing from *Where Are My Children?* is not clear. Censorship records indicate no discussion of them, suggesting that they may have been excised prior to the film's review by the National Board of Censorship. Whether the images were removed for their depiction of suicide or infanticide or illegitimacy, or for some other reason, is not clear. What is clear is that by including the example of an unmarried mother, Homer's testimony raises the issue of female sexuality not only outside marriage but also beyond the context of reproduction. By implication Homer also raises the issue of a cultural "double standard" that holds female sexual "transgression" to a higher order than men's. In its original form, this brief flashback would also have set the backdrop for later scenes involving the housekeeper's daughter Lillian, who also finds herself pregnant and unmarried, adding considerable urgency to her situation. The scene also has a sad, and equally shocking, echo in Weber's 1921 film *What Do Men Want?* in which a single woman, pregnant with her lover's child, commits suicide by jumping off a bridge after the man refuses to support her.

Concluding his testimony, Homer declares, "These conditions prove to me the necessity of world-wide enlightenment on the subject of birth control." The doctor's flashbacks form the nexus of the film's argument in favor of reproductive control, but they do so not by giving women a voice in the courtroom or in the film's narrative, but by using Dr. Homer's testimony, the testimony of a medical expert, to stand in for the women's voices.[163] Significantly, in recounting these sad circumstances, Dr. Homer does not mount a prudish plea for female chastity or sexual virtue; rather his argument seems to acknowledge the importance of human sexuality. But as the final insert from his birth control treatise reminds us, Homer's aims, however progressive, fall in line with contemporary arguments about eugenics that favored limited reproduction within certain segments of the population: "Because men and women are ignorant and undisciplined, does it follow that unwanted children should be born to suffer blindness, disease or insanity?"

Just as Dr. Homer concludes his case for family planning, we are introduced to Edith's friend Mrs. Carlo (Marie Walcamp), who is visited by a "little soul" waiting to be born: an iris-in shows us an image of the heavenly gates opening and closing, then a little winged cherub is superimposed over her head, whispering to her. Lounging on her porch, Mrs. Carlo echoes Edith's posture in the opening scene: here is another wealthy, childless woman idle during the daytime, another vision of privileged whiteness mirroring Edith's own. Bright sunlight shines through Mrs. Carlo's light hair and clothing, standing out against the dark, dank scenes of inner-city poverty presented in the flashbacks that accompany Dr. Homer's testimony. Mrs. Carlo's pouty unhappiness seems especially unwarranted when set against such destitute conditions. Her misery, the comparison insists, cannot be equated with the poverty, disease, abuse, and death suffered by less fortunate women and children.

By introducing Mrs. Carlo's story during Dr. Homer's trial and then intercutting the two storylines, the film once again uses contrast and comparison to put a number of key themes in play. An image of male jurors filing into the courtroom is echoed by the flock of female friends who flood into Mrs. Carlo's house to discuss her predicament. Edith and her friend whisper together as Mrs. Carlo announces her pregnancy, then Edith gestures behind Mrs. Carlo's back when another friend arrives. Women in Mrs. Carlo's set share a common experience from which she has thus far been excluded. Lighting reinforces the theme of secrecy by placing Mrs. Carlo in the spotlight while relegating her friends almost to silhouette. Smoking and drinking, the women are oblivious to the maid who serves them, seemingly unaware of their privileged status, which the film misses no opportunity to emphasize. The life that this status affords them—their social calendars of parties and get-togethers, their personal luxuries and indulgences—has become more important to them than raising children, the compositions insist.

Intercutting sets the women's whispered and secretive communications against the open discourse in the all-male courtroom. Behind the visible network of male power and decision making, the film shows us, is a clandestine network of women. While male doctors, judges, attorneys, and jurors make decisions about human reproduction—decisions from which women are noticeably excluded—affluent women like Edith and her circle take recourse in the shadowy underground world of illegal abortion.

The women's coded language of confidences, euphemisms, and innuendo are echoed later when Edith takes Mrs. Carlo to Dr. Malfit's office for an abortion. When Edith suggests that her friend pay a visit to the doctor, she does not mention abortion, but the inference is clear. In Weber's original script Edith simply said to her friend, "Why don't you see what Dr. Malfit can do for you?"[164] But the title was rewritten in postproduction so that Edith makes a more pointed comment: "If you are determined to evade motherhood, and are willing to take the risk, I would suggest that you see Dr. Malfit." Though spoken by Edith, the revised language makes a clearer moral judgment against the women. No record survives of who made these changes, but it is likely they were made by Universal during the studio's protracted battle with the National Board of Censorship, rather than by Weber herself. In fact, she would complain later during the film's run about changes that had been made to the picture.

A second, even more important distinction is established by cross-cutting between Dr. Homer's trial and the women's gathering at Mrs. Carlo's house—a distinction between medical arguments *in favor of* contraceptive use among poor and disadvantaged women and a simultaneous *condemnation* of wealthy, native-born white women in Edith's circle who, according to the film's logic, reject their childbearing obligations in favor of parties and personal indulgences. Quite unlike birth control advocate Margaret Sanger, who argued that *all* women ought to be able to control their fertility, *Where Are My Children?* makes the case that poverty-stricken women should have the option of limiting the size of their families, while women of wealth and "good breeding," such as Edith and Mrs. Carlo, are selfish if they choose to remain childless. Polarizing contraception and abortion along class lines as it does, the film puts itself at odds with practices at the time, as contemporary reviewers pointed out: as long as birth control remained illegal, affluent women with ties to the medical establishment had access to under-the-table family planning advice, while poor and disadvantaged women, without such connections, were often forced to resort to unsafe, backroom abortions.

Dr. Homer's conviction—by a jury of men, a title reminds us—comes just as Edith and Mrs. Carlo resolve to visit Dr. Malfit (Juan de la Cruz). The juxtaposition reminds us that while forward-thinking physicians like Dr. Homer were convicted for disseminating birth control to needy women, less scrupulous doctors like Malfit profited by furnishing abortions to privileged clients who "ought" to be having children. The scene in Dr. Malfit's office is remarkable for a film of 1916. In fact, it would become the specific target of censorship, even though no mention of abortion is ever made. Edith confidently enters the office and says to Malfit, "Doctor, my friend desires to consult with you privately concerning a serious ailment." She then smiles and picks up a magazine as Mrs. Carlo disappears into an inner room with the doctor. Edith's composure in this scene, her ability to speak about her friend's "serious ailment" in practiced euphemisms, stands out against the emotional distress of a woman visible in the background and, indeed, Mrs. Carlo's own obvious discomfort. Edith's attitude is so cavalier, in fact, that she will soon stifle a yawn. Following Mrs. Carlo's abortion, a white-winged child ascends pillars behind the pearly gates, and a title informs us, "One of the 'unwanted' ones returns, and a social butterfly is again ready for house parties," passing clear judgment on Mrs. Carlo's decision.

Mrs. Carlo's abortion is intercut with a second scene showing Richard's return to his now-empty home, where he watches the children next door and chats with their father across the garden wall. Happy, well-fed youngsters romping on the lawn, just out of Richard's reach, powerfully evoke the loss he perceives, a trope repeated at several other moments in the film when he watches them through the window. "We plan to have half a dozen of these little angels in time," Richard tells his neighbor, a striking turn of phrase given the "unwanted" angel we have just seen ascending to heaven. Intercutting between the backyard scene and Malfit's office, the narrative emphasizes how excluded Richard is from decisions that affect his family, how tragically unaware he is of what his wife is doing at that very moment, and how "unnatural" her actions are.

Here we also have another scene in which men discuss children and family life in the absence of women. Yet in this case it is not doctors, lawyers, and jurors making decisions about contraception in an all-male courtroom, but two husbands talking about their shared love of child rearing. If, earlier, cross-cutting emphasizes women's exclusion from important spheres of decision making, here it condemns Edith's set still further, showing men doting over youngsters while women "evade motherhood." It is also important to recognize that Richard's anguish over his own childlessness in this scene replaces any depiction of the anguish Mrs. Carlo might be suffering over the decision to terminate her pregnancy, a narrative displacement that further underscores the film's eugenics rhetoric: Edith and her friends, the film insists, are selfishly denying their would-be children a life as secure and idyllic as that enjoyed by the "little angels" who live next door to the Waltons.

Following Mrs. Carlo's abortion, the film introduces a lengthy subplot involving the Waltons' housekeeper's daughter Lillian (Rena Rogers), a naïve young woman lured into a liaison with Edith's brother, an unscrupulous lothario (A. D. Blake). Lillian's narrative adds another dimension to the stories of unplanned pregnancy portrayed in the film and complicates still further its overlay of abortion and contraception. If *Where Are My Children?* seems to advocate birth control for the impoverished, unhealthy, and abused women described by Dr. Homer, while simultaneously denouncing women in Edith's circle for their reliance on abortion, Lillian's case is less clear.

In its limited advocacy of birth control, the film does not go so far as to promote reproductive choice for consenting, unmarried adults, a case Margaret Sanger was indeed making during the 1910s, but it does still introduce the topic of sexuality in Lillian's storyline, albeit with a rather clichéd tale of a male predator and his gullible victim. Lillian returns home from school to visit her mother while Edith's brother is also staying with the family. He eyes the young woman as soon as she enters the Waltons' living room. Close-ups isolate his lascivious stare and register Lillian's obvious discomfort as she looks away, refusing to meet his gaze. The class dimensions of this interaction, the brother's sense of privilege and entitlement, are made all the more explicit by the scene's staging in his sister's living room, where a single composition registers intricate power relations between employers and staff, men and women. Here we glimpse an ugly underbelly of class privilege, interesting in a film in which class privilege is otherwise invoked to encourage women to reproduce. Class privilege is evoked further in the following scene when the brother propositions a young maid in the household (Mary MacLaren). It is a prelude of what is to come with Lillian, of course, but the seasoned young domestic in this first scene knows how to respond to such advances and slaps the cad soundly across the face; she is not as easily seduced by his charms as Lillian will be.

Edith's brother's predatory gaze is contrasted with the benevolent attention that Richard Walton showers on Lillian. Watching as she frolics on the lawn with one of Edith's dogs, midway between the Waltons' home and the children he adores next door, Richard clearly sees her as a surrogate daughter. Richard and his brother-in-law, distinguished through their differing interests in Lillian, also exhibit contrary uses of class privilege, one paternal, the other exploitive. This comparison paints the brother's single-minded lust as a perverse inversion of Richard's love for the neighbor's children and his sister's baby, a contrast that deepens toward the end of the sequence when Richard lovingly cradles the infant while his brother-in-law carelessly fathers a child without concern for its welfare or that of its mother. Richard and his brother-in-law's contrasting use and abuse of class privilege are tied, in turn, to the film's condemnation of Edith, for it is implied that she has "squandered" her class privilege by not raising children.

Lillian's story is also important, then, not only for the way it complicates the film's treatment of sexuality and birth control, but also for the way it further vilifies Edith. Edith's repeated abortions are associated with her brother's self-indulgent lechery. Brother and sister are presented as two sides of the same coin, both "selfishly" interested in sexuality beyond its reproductive function. The brother's hedonistic approach to indulging his desires, his careless manipulation of inexperienced young women, is associated with Edith's own extravagances: smoking, drinking, socializing, doting on her dogs all become metaphors for sexual indulgence.

On the one hand, then, the film appears to set Lillian's unplanned pregnancy and subsequent abortion against those of Edith and her wealthy friends, distinguishing between Lillian's sexual naïveté and Edith's confident navigation of the clandestine abortion process, even hinting, perhaps, that young unmarried women like Lillian ought to have access to reliable contraception. Yet, on the other hand, Lillian and Edith are also *connected* through the film's condemnation of female sexuality indulged outside the parameters of reproduction. Abortion, it suggests, is the painful consequence of unbridled feminine desire. Two forces threaten the social order, according to the film's eugenics-based logic: the "lower" elements of society (immigrants, the poor, people of color) and the "baser" elements of human sexuality. Both must be restrained if the culture is to flourish. So while the film reserves its harshest criticism for Edith and her circle, in many ways it also reinforces their own bourgeois hierarchy that valorizes white racial "purity" and feminine sexual virtue.

Lillian's pregnancy also draws attention to her mother, the Waltons' housekeeper. If the film sets Lillian's predicament against Mrs. Carlo's, it also poses a more tacit question about the housekeeper's past, since she is seen raising Lillian as a single mother. Is Lillian's mother simply widowed, or are there aspects to her story that might have a bearing on the film's treatment of sexuality, reproduction, and motherhood? Is it possible that the housekeeper might once have found herself in a situation very similar to the one her daughter faces? Might the young maid who slaps Edith's brother for his improper advances mirror earlier incidents in Lillian's mother's career? But being more like her daughter, perhaps she did not respond so sharply to the advances.

An intertitle describing Lillian's predicament as "the wages of sin" was added to the finished script after the film was completed. It casts harsh judgment on Lillian in a narrative that otherwise strives to present the complexities of her situation: the class dynamics of her mother's employer's household, as well as her own ignorance about sexuality and birth control. Still, Lillian's emotional distress is heartrending, all the more so when set against her lover's indifference—an indifference that parallels Edith's coolly calculating approach to terminating pregnancy. When he approaches his sister for help, the two share a whispered confidence about his friend "in trouble." There is the possibility that this is not the first time Edith has been called upon to help out her brother in this manner.

The excitement Lillian feels meeting her lover after dark, her eagerness for his embrace, is later contrasted with her isolation at the abortion clinic. Lillian, so thrilled to have been courted by Edith's brother, so delighted to have been singled out by him, now stands utterly alone—a fact reinforced by compositions that isolate her in the frame as she leaves Dr. Malfit's office. Doors are closed to her now: a nurse shuts the door and disappears inside the clinic just as Edith's brother helps her into a cab and sends her on her way alone. Lillian's abortion and death provide the film's emotional climax, her demise standing in for the loss of other potential children in the film. If death is Lillian's punishment for her sexual transgression, the ultimate "wages" for her "sin," then it also stands as *Edith's* punishment as well. For it is Edith, not Dr. Malfit, or her brother, who is held directly accountable for Lillian's death. As the Walton household learns of Lillian's fate, compositions isolate Edith from the others, highlighting her horrified reaction to the young woman's death, Edith's role in which remains as yet unknown to anyone other than her brother.

While prosecuting Dr. Malfit for Lillian's death, Richard discovers evidence of abortions the doctor has performed for Edith and her friends, as incidents in his home life and his career again coalesce. "Before sitting in judgment on others," Malfit lashes out at him, "you should see to your own household." Richard's blindness to events in his own household, his own marriage, his own bedroom come to a climax in these final scenes. In a narrative that offers a series of rhymes and doubles—two pregnancies, two abortions, two doctors, two trials—Malfit's case echoes Dr. Homer's earlier trial for disseminating "indecent" literature on family planning. But this second court case contrasts sharply with the first. If the film looks sympathetically upon Homer's plight, using his testimony to advance an argument for reproductive control among the poor, Malfit and his wealthy female patients are accorded no such understanding. Once again, cross-cutting interweaves the public sphere of Malfit's prosecution with scenes of the women gathered privately in Edith's living room monitoring the trial with great interest, fearful their secrets will be exposed, as they soon are. Wielding Malfit's record book that contains evidence of their "transgressions," Richard returns home to confront the women. "I have just learned why so many of you have no children," he cries. "I should bring you to trial for manslaughter, but I shall content myself with asking you to leave my house!" He then challenges Edith with the climactic cry, "Where are my children?"

Following Lillian's death Edith had finally tried to conceive a child, but, as a title explains, "having perverted Nature so often, she found herself physically unable to wear the diadem of motherhood." Weber's original scripted version had explained only that "the portals remained closed to her forever," but this new title invites a much harsher judgment.[165] In the final scene of the film Edith and Richard, now elderly, sit beside a fire imagining the children they might have had now grown: superimposed images of a young woman and two young men dissolve slowly onto the screen, showing the children sitting on the arms of their parents' chairs. Another example of Weber's keen ability to use cinematic techniques to render characters' interior psychological states visible on screen, this scene is meant to evoke a strong emotional response from viewers. A film that begins with a stirring call for legalized contraception ends, then, with a potent image of loss.

Despite its troubling confusion of abortion, contraception, and eugenics—or perhaps even because of this—*Where Are My Children?* stands as a landmark of Weber's Progressive Era filmmaking, a model of cinema vying to take on the challenge of presenting complex social issues through the lens of narrative cinema. A film like *Where Are My Children?* ultimately aimed to do much more than simply capitalize on a topical, even sensational, issue like contraception; it asserted cinema's claim to participate in national debates on an equal footing with newspapers, magazines, and other forms of political commentary. And it did so at a key historical juncture: just one year earlier the U.S. Supreme Court had denied motion pictures protection under the First Amendment, paving the way for much stricter regulation.[166]

At a time when disseminating contraceptive advice remained a felony and when motion pictures were no longer protected by guarantees of free speech, *Where Are My Children?* encountered significant problems with censorship and regulation. Like the white slave films released a few years earlier, contraceptive pictures complicated the film industry's desire for "quality" features on subjects of topical and social import by introducing sexuality into the equation, for reproductive politics engaged questions not only of female sexuality but also of sexuality outside marriage and motherhood, issues that dominated and divided American popular discourse throughout these years. On what grounds might a popular medium like the cinema be permitted to depict a topic that was itself still illegal? Could the industry's desire for "quality" features on weighty subjects encompass questions of sexuality and reproduction? And did motion pictures have a public role comparable to print media in the wake of the Supreme Court's landmark decision?

The National Board of Review took great care in its deliberations over *Where Are My Children?* no doubt mindful of the film's delicate subject matter. The board's executive secretary, William D. McGuire, pointed out that since contraception had been discussed "in magazines and newspapers, the question arises as to whether the National Board are to attempt to deny its discussion upon the motion picture screen."[167] At first, the board's Review Committee voted to pass the picture without requesting any changes. But, to be sure, the board set up a special screening of the film for notable guests who might help advise them on the decision, including famed vice crusader George Kneeland and Dr. William F. Snow of the American Social Hygiene Association.[168] Following this special screening, the board reversed its initial decision and voted unanimously to reject *Where Are My Children?*—not because of its presentation of contraception and abortion per se, but because of what the board considered *incorrect* or, at best, *confusing* information on what it termed "delicate and dangerous topics" like "the actual control of life." With the help of its expert panel, the board determined that *Where Are My Children?* contained medical misinformation in that it presented surgical abortion as "a very simple matter" and implied that Edith Walton would be unable to conceive a child after having had an abortion. The board was also concerned that the film confused contraception and abortion, and that it contained mixed messages about the use of both, seeming to advocate family planning, as the board noted, "in order to protect young girls from the consequences of their misdeeds," while appearing to oppose any form of birth control in the plot involving the Waltons.[169] Summing up the board's view, Chairman Cranston Brenton wrote that *Where Are My Children?* "so confuses the question of birth control and abortion that even a second viewing of the picture failed to make the distinction clear." Brenton stressed that the board's decision not to pass the film had nothing to do with its subject matter. In fact, he maintained that motion pictures were an appropriate forum in which to consider matters of contraception, but portrayals on screen, he said, "must have the unanimous approval of medical men rather than an emotional endorsement, however sincere."[170]

Unwilling to accept the Board of Review's condemnation, Universal fought the board's ruling, insisting that the film carried a viable message to its audiences. Having successfully shepherded the first white slave film, *Traffic in Souls,* through the board's dominion three years earlier, Universal—not part of the powerful Motion Picture Trust of major film production companies that had helped to form the board in 1909—seems to have maintained a more adversarial relation to the organization than other companies, even during these waning years of the board's authority. The studio's general manager, Joe Brandt, met with board executives to discuss the film, but no acceptable compromise was reached.[171] Throughout its dealings with the board, Universal operated as if the agency had censured *Where Are My Children?* solely on the basis of its controversial subject matter, not because of concerns about its potential to mislead viewers. A disclaimer added to the opening titles, asking whether a "subject of serious interest" ought to be "denied careful dramatization on the motion picture screen," only played up such a perception. If the board appealed to concepts akin to responsible journalism in its refusal to pass the picture, Universal employed similar rhetoric in its rebuttal, appealing to concepts of a free press. Reviewer Kitty Kelly agreed, arguing that the film "compares to a straight, clear-cut, well written newspaper story, containing facts and characterization and significance," setting it against the white slave picture *The Little Girl Next Door* and Elinor Glyn's soft-core fiction, both popular at the time.[172]

Looking to circumvent the board's restrictions, and eager for an alternative forum, Universal held two private screenings of *Where Are My Children?* for invited guests, including one at the one-thousand-seat Globe Theater on Broadway during the run of *The Dumb Girl of Portici*, evidently hoping that the cultural cachet associated with the Pavlova film would lend legitimacy to Weber's newest effort despite its more polemical message.[173] Still unapproved by the board, *Where Are My Children?* then began a regular engagement at the Globe following *Portici*'s run, with four daily screenings accompanied by an "augmented" symphony orchestra.[174] Large advertisements in New York's daily newspapers stressed, simultaneously, the film's endorsement by "press, public and clergy" and its spectacular appeal, with one such notice promising an entertainment that was both "dignified" *and* "sensational." Pledging "a powerful portrayal of the premeditated destruction of the un-born" and declaring the picture "society's greatest weapon against race suicide" in terms much stronger than those used within the film itself, the ads emphasized conservative elements of the film's message, while also guaranteeing titillating details on banned topics like contraception.[175] Press coverage only added to the sensation when one paper reported that "nervous feminine spectators" had fainted during a sequence in which the housekeeper's young daughter dies after an unsafe abortion.[176] By early the following week, patrons were being turned away from sold-out screenings, the theater was doing record business, and additional daily showings were being planned.[177] Still eager to gather sufficient "public opinion" on the picture that might refute the board's protective stance, Universal circulated postcards at these initial Globe screenings inviting patrons to comment on the film. Of the more than one thousand cards collected, only four apparently voiced negative views, allowing Universal to argue that the board's decision was "not in line with public opinion."[178] Universal clearly hoped that these New York screenings could secure enough endorsements to guarantee national bookings, with or without the Board of Review's approval.[179]

Industry trade papers chronicled the exhibition battle with great interest, for rarely, if ever, had a major production company flouted the board's

Figure 26. Promotions for *Where Are My Children?* (1916) stressed both its "daring" subject matter and its "dignified" presentation. Courtesy of the Mark Johnson Collection.

condemnation with such untested subject matter. It was still illegal, after all, to disseminate contraceptive information in *any* medium, let alone one designed for such a mass audience. For this reason *Moving Picture World* predicted that *Where Are My Children?* would likely "become one of the most discussed films of the year," not simply because of its topicality but also because of Universal's determination to release the film "whatever the attitude of the National Board of Review."[180] Most writers in the trades felt the subject had been handled with tact and defended the cinema's ability to handle controversial topics on par with other media. Noting that contraception was an issue being addressed by "countless numbers of very prominent persons," *Wid's* maintained that the film would generate a significant amount of discussion around the subject and, for that reason alone, was worthy of presentation.[181] *The New York Dramatic Mirror* congratulated the filmmakers on producing a film that dealt "boldly yet . . . inoffensively" with such a contentious subject.[182] *Variety* praised the film, suggesting that "there isn't much that could be cut even by the most bigoted."[183] *Moving Picture World*'s Lynde Denig was the most enthusiastic, praising the filmmakers' "sincere, courageous and intelligent effort." Not simply a good picture, *Where Are My Children?* provided a model of how photoplays should advance "if they are to contribute to a better understanding of human nature and the complexities of modern society."[184]

While obviously invested in arguments endorsing the cinema's ability to tackle weighty social problems—arguments they could make via *Where Are My Children?*—trade commentators were more reluctant to endorse the film's political agenda. Many recognized the film's conflicted message, complaining, much as the National Board of Review had, that its presentation of the subject was clouded by its confusion of contraception and abortion. "It starts off seemingly as an argument in favor of birth control," *Variety* protested, "and suddenly switches to an argument against abortions."[185] With no differentiation "between birth control, race suicide, and abortion," the *New York Dramatic Mirror* complained, the film ended up with a "confusing" message. "We cannot believe this to be the purpose of the authors."[186] Even Lynde Denig, who provided the most favorable of the trades' reviews, argued that the film "departs from the path of strict consistency" by apparently favoring family planning instruction in its initial scenes, then focusing on a condemnation of Mrs. Walton and abortion in the second. More significantly, Denig maintained, the film contradicted arguments advanced by birth control advocates Margaret Sanger and Emma Goldman, who were careful to stress how class differences affected women's access to contraceptive methods. Hack abortionists of the sort portrayed in the film were not patronized by wealthy women like those in Edith Walton's circle, Denig insisted, since most had ready access to reliable methods of preventing pregnancy. It was impoverished women, lacking access to the medical establishment, who were forced resort to unsafe abortions.[187]

Those within the film industry were not the only ones to condemn the film's apparently contradictory logic. When *Where Are My Children?* played in Portland, Oregon, that autumn, members of the Birth Control League mounted a similar charge, protesting that the film failed to distinguish between "birth control properly speaking and abortion" and generated "misunderstanding and confusion" about their objectives. They pointed out that Sanger, who had brought the term *birth control* into general usage, never intended to include abortion under that rubric, and that one of her chief reasons for advocating family planning was to reduce the number of abortions.[188]

For her part, Weber took great issue with these objections, first blaming censors for forcing her to dilute her original intentions, but then arguing that to make a successful dramatic film about reproductive politics, one had to follow the dictates of effective storytelling much more than rigorous propaganda. "The propagandist who recognizes the moving picture as a powerful means of putting out a creed," she claimed, "never seems to have any conception of the fact that an idea has to come to terms with the dramatic if it is to be successful screen drama."[189] Weber, in other words, defended her film on the grounds that it must serve as entertainment first and propaganda second.

Criticism of the film's political agenda or its "confusing" message appears to have had little effect on its popularity and did nothing to curb Universal's enthusiasm for wide distribution. Shortly after the film's successful run at New York's Globe, Universal put the film into national release, announcing the sale of states' rights in full-page trade ads. The film's New York success was touted in the campaign, which featured a photo of crowds lined up along Broadway outside the Globe during the film's run. If the film could draw such business on "the hardest show street" and "the greatest theatre neighborhood in the world," exhibitors around the country could not go wrong.[190] Following these announcements, *Moving Picture Weekly* claimed the studio had been "literally besieged and bombarded with telegrams, telephone and special delivery communications" from states' rights buyers.[191] Indeed, the film did well around the country, setting box office records in many communities, including Albany, New York, where 24,000 patrons reportedly saw the picture in its first week, with nearly as many returning during the second week of the run. *Where Are My Children?* enjoyed record business at Chicago's La Salle Theater, the best the owners had seen since the venue opened. And "several enthusiastic audiences" saw the film in San Francisco in August. According to National Board of Review records, the film played without incident in cities and towns in many states across the country, including those in the East Coast states of Maine, Vermont, Massachusetts, and Connecticut; the southern states of West Virginia, Kentucky, Arkansas, and Louisiana; and the western states of Wyoming, Idaho, and Utah.[192]

Complaining that *Where Are My Children?* "visualizes in revolting detail the subject of 'Birth Control,'" the Pennsylvania State Board of Censors requested considerable eliminations in the film, including "all views" of the interior and exterior of Dr. Malfit's offices and "all that occurs" within, every mention of the term *birth control* in the intertitles, and a significant reduction in the "seduction" scene involving Lillian and Edith's brother. Even after these changes were made and the film was submitted for a second time, Pennsylvania censors refused to pass it. A Pennsylvania film exchange ultimately sued the board over the case, arguing that it had condemned *Where Are My Children?* "for reasons not pertaining to the morality or propriety of said motion picture play" and that such a decision lay beyond the mandate of the board, which was charged only with regulating material that might be "sacrilegious, obscene, indecent or immoral." The appeal failed and *Where Are My Children?* was banned in Pennsylvania.[193] Weber claimed that "the entire first part of the play" was excised by the Pennsylvania Board of Censorship, including Dr. Homer's flashbacks and "all the incidents going to prove that under certain conditions birth control was justifiable."[194]

Still, Pennsylvania's decision remained atypical. The film was approved by the influential Ohio Board of Censors.[195] Even Boston's censorship commission, notorious for its strict enforcement, did not prevent *Where Are My Children?* from being shown in that city, where it proved to be very popular. Some 2,000 patrons were turned away on opening night and the film continued to generate "enormous business" during a run of several months. In fact, Boston mayor James Michael Curley became an unlikely advocate for Weber's film and even lobbied Pennsylvania senators in an effort to get the picture past the state's censors.[196]

If the punishment enacted upon Lillian for her "sexual transgression" in *Where Are My Children?* seems to condemn female sexuality and to offer no clear argument in favor of reproductive control for unmarried but sexually active women, Weber's second film on birth control, *The Hand That Rocks the Cradle*, suffered less from such melodramatic turns. Whereas the message in *Where Are My Children?* is complicated by the film's confusion of abortion and contraception and its promotion of eugenics, *The Hand That Rocks the Cradle* made a clearer, more forceful argument in favor of family planning.

Weber wrote, directed, and starred in *The Hand That Rocks the Cradle* in early 1917 just after Margaret Sanger's case made front-page news around the country. Weber frankly based her script, originally entitled "Is a Woman a Person?" on Sanger's own story.[197] Suggesting something of her own investment in the topic, Weber herself took on the leading role at a time when she had sharply curtailed her acting work. In what would ultimately be her last appearance on screen, Weber plays Louise Broome, a doctor's wife indicted for distributing information on family planning. When her husband (Phillips Smalley) strikes a deal to prevent Louise's prosecution by agreeing to persuade her to abandon her crusade, she refuses the arrangement, saying, "I am sorry, dear, but we each have our own convictions and must live up to them," and reminding him that he agreed to "limit" their own family out of concern for her health.

When the Broomes discuss family planning with their friends the Grahams, Louise remembers the plight of their former nursemaid, Sarah, whose story is narrated in a flashback. Trapped in poverty, Sarah (Evelyn Selbie) and her husband, John (Harry De More), could not provide for their many children, and their relationship disintegrated until Sarah received Louise's help in preventing pregnancy. The Grahams, however, remain unconvinced by Louise's story. Mr. Graham (Wedgwood Nowell) is embarrassed by the open discussion of such "indecent" matters, and his wife (Priscilla Dean) pleads for "self control" rather than birth control. When Louise later receives word from Sarah, eager to spread contraceptive information to her friends, she decides to defy the arrangement her husband has struck with the police, telling him she "cannot permit" him to be responsible for her good behavior and chastising her husband and the medical profession for keeping knowledge of family planning away from women. "If the law makers had to bear the children," she tells him, "they would change the laws quickly enough."[198]

Meanwhile, the Grahams' marriage collapses under the wife's pleas for abstinence. At the film's climax Louise addresses a group of women, including Sarah and her friends, arguing that "man" ought to control "his own powers of reproduction" in much the same manner that "he" has always "endeavored to direct the forces of nature." Arrested, tried, and imprisoned for disseminating contraceptive information, Louise rejects her husband's pleas that she "give up her public work for the sake of our children," and goes on a hunger strike instead. Pardoned at last, Louise lives to see her husband agree that physicians ought to provide patients with instructions on contraceptive use. At the film's close, newspaper headlines announce that birth control may soon be legal in the state of Illinois. "What do *you* think?" the film's final title asks, inviting audiences to talk amongst themselves, as the two middle-class couples can be seen doing in the last sequence.

The Hand That Rocks the Cradle strikes a very different tone from *Where Are My Children?* Struggles over reproductive control in each of the marriages portrayed in the second film drive the narrative forward, rather than anxieties about female sexuality, which propel events in *Where Are My Children?* Arguing strongly for sexuality in marriage, *The Hand That Rocks the Cradle* makes Mrs. Graham's desire for "self control" seem wholly unreasonable. Weber's second birth control film also does not traffic so heavily in arguments about eugenics, offering instead a case for "intelligent child bearing" for all classes. A publicity herald shows Louise and her nurse,

Figure 27. In her last role on screen, Weber *(center)* plays birth control advocate Louise Broome in *The Hand That Rocks the Cradle* (1917). Author's collection.

Sarah, together, labeling them "Rich and Poor, Sisters in Sorrow."[199] Even so, pregnancy prevention serves a different purpose in each of the stories shown: it protects the fragile mental and physical health of bourgeois women like Louise Broome and her friends, whereas it is promoted for working-class women like Sarah so that society might put an end to what the film calls "murderous operations, insanity, poverty and criminal tendencies in the human race." Eugenics is thus not too far from the surface here, either. Significantly, an educated, white middle-class woman, Louise Broome, serves as the viewer's guide through this landscape, providing a female perspective (as opposed to that of her husband), an educated outlook (as opposed to that of her untutored nursemaid, Sarah), and a healthy approach to sexuality (as opposed to that of her prudish friend, Mrs. Graham).

The Hand That Rocks the Cradle did not fare as well with censors as *Where Are My Children?* had. It was initially passed by the National Board of Review with little fanfare, in stark contrast to the protracted negotiations surrounding *Where Are My Children?*[200] If at first this decision seems counterintuitive—this second picture, after all, included a much more militant call for contraceptive use across different classes—*The Hand That Rocks the Cradle* framed its presentation of reproductive politics within an educational context that assumed the perspective of a middle-class reformer. Such a framework may have appealed to the board's broader conception of cinema's elevated role in cultural debates. However, the board's progressive view of cinema's social mandate was increasingly at odds with those in state and municipal agencies charged with regulating motion picture exhibition. New York's license commissioner, who had not interfered with screenings of *Where Are My Children?* the previous year, took a strong stance against both *The Hand That Rocks the Cradle* and Margaret Sanger's own *Birth Control* when the two films premiered there within a week of each other. Defying the board's decision to pass the films, New York's license commissioner successfully prevented their exhibition in that city.[201] Following their legal troubles in New York, neither film was able to generate much box office revenue across the nation, and neither came close to attaining the record-breaking attendance set by *Where Are My Children?*

When *The Hand That Rocks the Cradle* opened in Los Angeles, Weber spoke at the premiere, complaining bitterly about the treatment the film had received in New York. "The propaganda plays that I have produced have been so unjustly criticized and censored by the rigid boards of censorship in the East that I am discontinuing the production of this type of play," she said. This despite the fact that the film had been toned down during the production for fear of censorship: "It's too tame," Weber complained. "Hardly a jolt in it. I wanted to make it talk right out, only fear of the censors made my managers hold me down and divest it of 'ginger.'"[202] Weber took every opportunity to denounce censorship during these years, often evoking comparisons to regulatory practices in other art forms, tacitly elevating creative work in cinema to the same level as those arts. She decried not only cuts and changes demanded by state and local censorship agencies, but also cuts and changes made in-house, which she felt denigrated her own authorial control:

> For a publisher to cut, distort and change the meaning of the work of an
> established author is inconceivable, yet manufacturers of photoplays
> still believe that, having paid the writer of a scenario, their
> responsibility to the originator of the story ends. Putting aside all

artistic pride, there are sound commercial reasons for objecting to seeing one's name attached to a picture carelessly sub-titled and bereft of plausibility because of the elimination of essential scenes. This must not be taken as a personal grievance, [but] rather as a protest against a condition from which nearly all authors and directors are suffering.[203]

Certainly the tenor of Hollywood was shifting in the late 1910s, away from the kind of Progressive, activist filmmaking Weber had championed in favor of films geared more toward entertainment. Reviewers had praised *Where Are My Children?* for its serious treatment of contraception, with one claiming that the film stood as a model of how photoplays should advance "if they are to contribute to a better understanding of human nature and the complexities of modern society."[204] But less than a year later, the tide had shifted. Reviewers now complained that *The Hand That Rocks the Cradle* was "too preachy" and chastised Weber for having "taken up her club" in defense of family planning.[205] Some even felt compelled to comment on the very suitability of using motion pictures as a public forum. *Moving Picture World* was most strident on this issue, declaring that "persons with serious ethical questions to propound have as much right to utilize the screen as they have to hire a hall and set forth their opinions in more or less eloquent speech; but the family photoplay theater . . . is not the proper place for them." Cinemas should be reserved for "amusement and recreation," the paper concluded, not "propaganda."[206] Weber's model of an activist cinema that challenged moviegoers to ponder complex social problems and spurred them to action outside the theater was, evidently, falling out of favor.

In February 1917, just as she was completing work on *The Hand That Rocks the Cradle*, word began to circulate that Weber was leaving "the U," rumors that Carl Laemmle denied in a telegram sent to *Moving Picture World*. Trades reported early that year that Weber had re-signed a lucrative, long-term contract with the studio, after spending a week with Laemmle and his wife, but internal documents reveal that there was considerable rancor developing between the studio head and his top director.[207] By early March Weber had already taken out a full-page ad in *Moving Picture World* announcing the formation of Lois Weber Productions.[208] Weber officially left Universal that spring, and after a two-month vacation set up shop at her own studio and formed an independent production company. In early comments about what she hoped to achieve at her new studio, she distanced herself from the contentious issues that had made her Universal titles so famous, vowing to abandon those "heavy dinners" in favor of films on marriage and domesticity—"little afternoon teas," as she called them.[209] But, as we shall see, Weber did not really abandon her view of cinema's social mandate in the late teens; rather, she shifted her attention to more intimate matters like sexuality and marriage, exploring the changing relations between the sexes and the blurring boundaries between public and private spheres in the context of the postwar boom in consumer capitalism.

By the time Weber left Universal, the company was in decline. Unlike its competitors Fox, Paramount, and Loew's, Universal had not begun acquiring theaters and was thus losing out on the guaranteed runs and enormous profits that in-house theater chains were generating for other studios. Laemmle also continued to resist fully committing to feature films, preferring to offer a regular "Universal Program" of mixed shorts and features well beyond the point at which his competitors had stopped releasing shorts. He also maintained his reluctance to invest in movie stars, a conservative strategy that ensured the studio a profit in Hollywood's early days but became markedly outdated as star-driven features dominated the box office. Production costs were rising everywhere as the U.S. entry into the First World War drove up prices and Universal became increasingly known for its low wages and heavy production schedule. The year 1917 was a particularly difficult one for the studio, for Weber was not the only notable personality to depart—stars such as Francis Ford, Wallace Reid, Mary Fuller, and Ethel Grandin all left as well. By 1919 all of Universal's other female directors had also gone, making 1920 the first year in the studio's history when it did not release a single title directed by a woman.[210] For a time, however, Universal had been home to the "greatest (woman) director in the world," a filmmaker who leveraged an image of bourgeois feminine propriety to insist not only that cinema was *the* medium of the Progressive Era, capable of editorializing on all of the principal concerns of the day, but that women could be the central visionaries of this period, both as filmmakers behind the scenes in Hollywood and as agents of change in the world at large.

3   Women's Labor, Creative Control, and "Independence" in a Changing Industry

Later in life Weber recalled the time she spent at Lois Weber Productions as the "most productive years" of her career, a period when she thrived "under ideal conditions" at her own studio.[1] After signing one of the most lucrative distribution deals in the business, she leased a large residential estate and in July 1917 began equipping it as a filmmaking studio. Lois Weber Productions released fourteen features over the following four years before folding in 1921. In forming her own studio, Weber took advantage of opportunities in postwar Hollywood, especially for women working on both sides of the camera. Yet the company ultimately fell victim to a wave of studio conglomeration and an era of industry "remasculinization" that, as Karen Ward Mahar describes it, began to shut out female directors. Indeed, the rise and fall of Lois Weber Productions bring aspects of postwar Hollywood into particular relief, especially as they signal narrowing possibilities for working outside vertically integrated studios. Weber's experience as an independent filmmaker also highlights the challenges increasingly faced by women who worked in any position other than star: Weber's talents as a screenwriter and director were now frequently eclipsed by her growing reputation as a "star maker" focused on the careers of her leading women; and the marketing and reception of her films reveal how paradoxical her value as a woman director had become. As female audiences dominated at the box office, Weber's "feminine viewpoint" was prized. Yet she catered to female moviegoers in ways that began to unsettle her critics.

When starting her own production company, Weber had pledged to abandon the "heavy dinners" she made at Universal in favor of "little afternoon teas."[2] While the subject matter of her films certainly shifted toward more nuanced studies of marriage and domesticity, Weber in no way abandoned

Figure 28. With the formation of Lois Weber Productions in 1917 Weber realized her long-held dream "to have a company and studio of my own." Frame enlargement.

social critique, as her examinations of class, sexuality, and gender in films such as *Too Wise Wives, What Do Men Want?* and *The Blot* attest. In these late independent releases Weber reconceived marital, familial, and domestic issues *as social problems,* mapping intimate landscapes of marriage and sexuality in relation to larger social forces such as class mobility, capitalism, and consumption. These films demonstrate that Weber considered marriage and sexuality issues as critical to national discourse in the years following the First World War, as poverty, crime, and social welfare had been during the Progressive Era. Exploiting her position as a female filmmaker, Weber chose to engage with popular discussions of these topics, but on terms markedly different from those of other Hollywood films at the time.

LOIS WEBER PRODUCTIONS

After searching Los Angeles for a suitable production studio, Weber chose a residential estate at the corner of Santa Monica Boulevard and Vermont

Avenue in East Hollywood, set apart from the inner hub of the industry. Using the main house as her administrative offices, she erected a large canvas-covered outdoor stage at the back of the property, converted a gardening shed into her film lab, and built dressing rooms for her players. Formal gardens, winding gravel pathways, and a tennis court remained, all surrounded by tall hedges for privacy.[3] Weber's facilities equaled "any in California for completeness and efficiency," according to one early observer.[4] Still, there was a tendency among early reports to feminize the studio and underscore its origins as a domestic space. Visiting the "cottage studio" for *Motion Picture Magazine* in 1921, Aline Carter surveyed Weber's "cozy study," her eyes moving from "the dancing flames in the fireplace to the great bowls of gorgeous dahlias, the wide couch, heaped with pillows, drawn invitingly near the fire, and the stunning carved teakwood desk," declaring "I felt the definite touch of a woman's hands." "You would never guess this is a studio," another fan magazine "tour" announced. "Nothing suggests business." Noting Weber's penchant for calling the studio "My Old Homestead," *Photoplay*'s Elizabeth Peltret found the atmosphere "reminiscent of some Southern manor house," observing how different it was from the "oh, so sudden" look of modern movie studios. Weber herself, apologizing for sounding "sentimental and feminine," proclaimed "we will make better pictures all the way around from having an inspiring and delightful environment in which to work."[5]

If fan magazines stressed the "homey" and "feminine" aspects of Weber's new studio, Weber described it as the realization of a long-cherished dream "to have a company and studio of my own."[6] "News of Lois Weber Productions," her first publicity bulletin, explained that Weber had considered affiliating herself with another studio after her Universal contract expired, but "instead she chose to head her own individual company, and to have a studio of her own in which she might work entirely unhampered."[7] Indeed, many early publicity items drew attention to the creative control Weber could exercise at her own studio. She now enjoyed "complete individual freedom," one account declared, and was finally able to pursue "some of the pet ideas she has nourished these many months," according to another.[8] Weber herself later echoed this view, saying the films she directed at her own company "were made as I wanted to make them, not 'under orders,'" emphasizing her emancipation from hierarchical studio regimentation.[9] The novelty of such autonomy for any filmmaker, let alone a woman, was repeatedly stressed in press accounts of the start-up. "Entering the field when the whole industry was in its infancy Miss Weber has climbed steadily upwards until now hers is a place held by no other woman and by very few men in the entire picture field," one report announced.[10]

Assuming greater independence, Weber also explicitly rejected the streamlined production methods becoming the norm in larger studios. "System and Efficiency have found their way into the manufacture of motion pictures," one filmmaker had complained the previous year.[11] Weber, by contrast, pledged a more artisanal approach. She attempted to shoot films in narrative sequence whenever possible, privileging a performer's creative process over a more economically efficient (and increasingly preferred) method of shooting out of sequence. Explaining that an actress was often called upon to portray a range of emotions across a character's story arc, Weber argued that "if the picture is taken in proper sequence, she will have experienced those things before she is called upon to display their effect and the characterization can be built accordingly." Directing performers in such a manner, she declared, would go a long way toward "knitting a picture into a more plausible and connected whole."[12] How consistently Weber was able to shoot in sequence is difficult to assess, but it is important to emphasize how significantly her ambitions contravened ongoing efforts to use detailed continuity scripts to enable more economical methods of shooting out of sequence.[13] In another attempt to avoid efficiencies prescribed in major studios, Weber pledged to shoot both exterior and interior scenes on location whenever possible.[14] In doing so, she privileged aesthetic integrity over economy, again contravening practices by this point standard at the major studios, for as Janet Staiger notes, "there was a steady exodus from location shooting into the studio and back lot after the mid-teens."[15] If we cannot verify how frequently Weber shot in sequence, photographs, news reports, and extant film prints do make clear that she did indeed shoot a great deal of her scenes on location, interiors and exteriors alike, both during the day and at night. In fact, she appears to have relied on location shooting at her own company much more than at any other point in her career. To accomplish this ambitious goal, Weber leased one of the largest and best portable generators available at the time.[16] Commending her decision to film interior scenes on location in private homes rather than in fabricated studio sets, *Moving Picture World* gave Weber and her cinematographers considerable credit, noting that such undertakings required "an exceptionally keen sense of light values and technical knowledge of the proper placing of artificial lights." These techniques had enabled her "to secure life-like detail" that leant her productions "an atmosphere of reality."[17]

Weber clearly valued her collaborators and brought many of them with her to the new studio. She initially employed many of the personnel she

Figure 29. Weber *(center)* directing interior locations for *Too Wise Wives* (1921). Courtesy of the British Film Institute.

had worked with at Universal, continuing to operate much the same as she had in the past. Arthur Forde remained as her assistant director, and Frank Ormston served as technical director on at least one production at the new studio. Ormston had worked with Weber on all of her big projects, including her first feature, *The Merchant of Venice,* as well as *Hypocrites* and *The Dumb Girl of Portici* later on.[18] Cinematographer Allen Siegler, with whom Weber had worked at Universal, shot two of the first films produced at Lois Weber Productions, and Dal Clawson, her longtime cinematographer, would shoot almost half of the films made at Weber's company. Together since the early days at Rex, Weber and Clawson had continued their association through her tenure at Bosworth, then Universal. Striking out on her own, then, Weber sought continuity among her technical staff. Although her surroundings were new and she would seek players beyond the Universal stable, important collaborators like Forde, Ormston, Siegler, and, above all, Clawson, remained.

Despite continuities, however, Weber's "independence" was also associated with a shift in her working relationship with her most significant collaborator, Phillips Smalley. Items promoting Lois Weber Productions announced clearly for the first time that Weber was the dominant creative voice behind her films, marking her husband's role as strictly secondary. In doing so, Weber moved decisively away from the couple's joint signature, "The Smalleys," finalizing a process she had begun at Universal. A note at the end of one of her studio's early press releases affirmed that Smalley would be "associated with his wife, as he has been in the past," a statement at once ambiguous in the role it assigned him, and definitive in its marginalization.[19] Smalley would serve as studio manager, the bulletin announced, a position that effectively eliminated his creative input. Smalley was no longer even a performer central to Weber's work; he appeared in only one of the fourteen features she wrote and directed at her company, 1921's *Too Wise Wives*. Trade press commentators were especially blunt about the marked change in Smalley's status: "Why the 'and Phillips Smalley' on the producer's line of the announcement?" one observer quipped when the company released its first production, *The Price of a Good Time*. "It is said to be almost entirely Miss Weber's creation. That her husband's assistance was of a minor character.... Mrs. Smalley is *the* genius of the two."[20] When the couple toured Europe later that year, *Screenland* quipped, "It's getting in Pictureland so that nobody can remember the name of a mere husband."[21] Indeed, Weber's name was so well known to filmgoers at this point that *Wid's Daily* told exhibitors, "If you can't get money today by announcing a Lois Weber production, there is something wrong with your method of exploitation," for "she has had more distinctive successes advertised with her name ... than any other director in the business."[22]

It is worth remembering that Lois Weber Productions put Weber in the vanguard of independent production among directors. Her company was created just as Charlie Chaplin left Mutual for First National, a significant move that not only guaranteed him greater profits but also gave him more creative control and his own production facilities on North La Brea Avenue. That same month Thomas Ince severed his association with Triangle Studios and announced plans to build a large studio of his own, eventually purchasing the land for his Culver City studio the following year. It would be another two years until Chaplin joined D.W. Griffith, Mary Pickford, and Douglas Fairbanks to form United Artists; and eight years before Cecil B. DeMille established DeMille Pictures.[23] These years posed an interesting challenge for directors. There was, on the one hand, growing recognition of their creative vision and evolving awareness, especially in the trades, of the different identities and "signatures" associated with individual filmmakers. Witness the lists of "Important Directors" published by *Wid's Daily* in 1916 and 1917 (lists on which Weber was always included, of course).[24] On the other hand, studios were steadily moving toward a model of centralized production, epitomized by a new producer-unit system in which directors lost a measure of control, providing incentives for well-known filmmakers to strike out on their own. In fact, many of the directors who worked independently during this period, directors whose work became the most celebrated in the industry, largely rejected "efficiency" models instituted by the major studios and instead made films that were, in Richard Koszarski's words, "the dogged creations of an antiquated workshop system" that somehow managed to endure in spite of opposing industry trends.[25] Accordingly, profiles of Weber continued to stress her engagement with every phase of moviemaking. She was "the whole show in her company," one writer declared.[26] "She understands and can herself work out each smallest detail of construction, from grinding the camera-crank to developing film, placing properties, writing continuity, acting and directing. Hers is not mere technical knowledge; she has lived thru [sic] every department of Motion Picture work," according to another commentator.[27] Such devotion and breadth of knowledge, however valued, was becoming associated with an outmoded approach to filmmaking. Contrasting her own working methods with those evolving at the majors, Weber celebrated how her "staff moved with me in the harmony and clear understanding of singleness of purpose." Enjoying "full authority," Weber found herself "free of that vacillating shattering of objectives from which many organizations now suffer where half a dozen executive heads must come to an agreement about their story, director and cast, on which subjects no two of them have the same ideas."[28]

By emphasizing Weber's signature, her creative freedom, her attention to filmmaking craft, and her studio's quasi-domestic, unbusinesslike setting, early publicity set Lois Weber Productions apart from the hierarchical "efficiencies" steadily enforced at major studios and cast Weber as the company's sole artistic force, a significant assertion at a time when centralized management structures were being adopted throughout the industry.[29] Yet a closer look at the varied distribution agreements Weber signed over the five-year lifespan of her studio provides a more complex picture, one that exposes the swiftly shifting parameters of independent film distribution and exhibition in the late 1910s and early 1920s, and defies easy conjecture about creative autonomy and artisanal filmmaking. Weber's independence also illuminates the challenges faced by women working in the industry in any position other than star. Intertext surrounding the three actresses Weber directed during this period—Mildred Harris, Anita Stewart, and Claire Windsor—demonstrates how restrictive ideas about women's work in Hollywood were becoming, as profiles of their working relationships focused less and less on Weber's authority as director, once so coveted by the industry, and gravitated instead toward her glamorous female stars.

Ideas about the exact nature Weber's "independence" were complicated from the outset, since the first films made at Lois Weber Productions were distributed by Universal, a studio with which she had long been affiliated. Just as one trade paper reported that Weber had begun constructing production facilities at her new studio, Carl Laemmle sent a telegram to another denying rumors his top director would be leaving Universal. Adding to the confusion, a third report announced Weber would "produce her photoplays independent of Universal supervision although under Laemmle auspices"— a wholly ambiguous configuration.[30] According to the terms of her contract, Weber would receive an annual salary amounting to $5,000 per week, making her the highest-paid director in Hollywood—"man, woman or child," as one commentator put it.[31] This handsome arrangement allowed Weber to purchase a new home in Beverly Hills the following year, formerly owned by her close friend Frances Marion.[32] In exchange, Universal would release Weber's independently produced titles on a states' rights basis under its prestigious and semiautonomous Jewel arm, rather than as part of the Universal program, an arrangement ensuring her films access to the first-run market.[33] This was critical, for, unlike many other studios at the time, Universal had not begun acquiring theater chains and, as a result, was often shut out of many urban, first-run theaters. Beginning in November 1917, Weber released seven Universal Jewel features, all of them starring Mildred Harris: *The Price of a Good Time* (1917), *The Doctor and the Woman* (1918), *For Husbands Only* (1918), *Borrowed Clothes* (1918), *When a Girl Loves* (1919), *Home* (1919), and *Forbidden* (1919). If Weber's own comments sought to establish her autonomy from Universal, the studio worked hard to maintain her well-established association with its name. These titles were often promoted alongside other Jewel releases in banner ads trumpeting the quality associated with the brand, and in an effort to further associate her with the studio, Weber's 1916 film *Scandal* was rereleased in July 1918, one of the first Universal pictures to receive such treatment.[34]

Mildred Harris was the only star Weber held under contract during this period, tailoring each production to the actress's persona and casting other players as they suited the material. For the first time in her career Weber was not working with either a stock company or a roster of studio actors; instead she now created projects exclusively for a single performer. "Mildred Harris is really my 'company,'" Weber explained. "We carry no stock, but engaged a new lead to play opposite her each time and selected all the others to dovetail around her personality and the play's demands."[35] Weber's strategy aligned with other developments in the industry, according to *Motion Picture Classic*, which noted that the trend toward eliminating stock companies was "assuming alarming proportions." Apparently, many studios found it a prudent method of economizing after so many players relocated permanently in Los Angeles.[36]

Not yet sixteen years old when she signed with Weber, Harris had been a juvenile star known as "dainty Mildred Harris" and "little" Mildred Harris, "the pet" of the Broncho Film Company. Just after she joined Lois Weber Productions, *Photoplay's* feature "Five Years Ago This Month" reminded readers that "Little Mildred Harris" had then been attending convent school and acting in Bison films after hours.[37] Emphasis on Harris's youth persisted throughout her association with Weber, enhancing the director's authority while downplaying Harris's own talent and maturity. According to one critic, Weber should be assigned "much credit for having discovered and developed" the actress's abilities.[38] For her part Harris professed herself "delighted" to work "under the guidance" of the renowned director, a formulation that only enhanced their hierarchical working relationship.[39] "She's the dearest little thing, and whenever she's not posing for the camera, she's busy improving something around the studio," Weber told *Motion Picture's* Fritzi Remont. A childlike Harris could be seen in an accompanying photograph dusting one of Weber's cameras on tip-toe.[40] As late as 1920, Theodore Dreiser would describe her as "very small, very babydollish," a type consistent with many of the other popular female leads of the period—Mary Pickford and the Gish sisters chief among them.[41]

The ingénue roles Weber wrote for Harris only amplified her reputation as an "angel-faced innocent."[42] In *The Price of a Good Time* the actress played "a sullen little department store clerk, unhappy at home and rebellious at work," as one reviewer put it, whose parents falsely accuse her of sexual misconduct.[43] In *The Doctor and the Woman* Harris played a young nurse embroiled in a violent sexual triangle. In *Borrowed Clothes* she was a humble flower shop clerk who falls prey to a conniving playboy. In *Home* she played a boarding school girl hiding her humble origins from her tonier chums. In *Forbidden*, dubbed "the story of a modern Pandora," Harris played a country girl adrift in New York's cabarets and opium dens.[44] Yet, even as Weber's scripts built on Harris's ingénue persona, they also began to craft mature roles for the former child star, giving her more to do and more to work with. Reviewers took note. The *Los Angeles Times* praised Harris's "exceptional work" in her first collaboration with Weber, on *The Price of a Good Time*. Harris was "at her best" in *For Husbands Only* a few months later. And her performance in *Borrowed Clothes* represented "the best opportunities she has yet had to demonstrate

"THE PRICE OF A GOOD TIME"
A LOIS WEBER PRODUCTION.

Figure 30. In *The Price of a Good Time* (1917) Mildred Harris plays a shopgirl seduced by the store owner's playboy son. Author's collection.

her abilities at emotional acting," *Moving Picture World* declared, setting it against the mere "passing personal charm" Harris had exhibited in earlier offerings. The *Los Angeles Times* concurred, calling it "one of the best parts ever assigned her."[45] And Julian Johnson included Harris on *Photoplay*'s 1918 list of notable newcomers, though she was, of course, far from a "newcomer."[46] Just a few years later, when Harris began receiving less-than-enthusiastic reviews in other productions, *Variety* paid oblique tribute to Weber, noting that "it was direction that made [Harris] stand out in a couple of the big features that she did in the more recent past."[47]

Harris's ingénue aura was certainly done no harm when her marriage to megastar Charlie Chaplin was announced in the fall of 1918, with one wry observer dubbing Harris "the champion little child-wife of the screen."[48] The couple had married secretly that October after having denied rumors of an engagement. According to Chaplin biographer Joyce Milton, their wedding had been kept under wraps because it coincided with the release of *Shoulder Arms* and Chaplin was concerned that his underage bride might attract negative publicity. Word only got out when Harris suffered a nervous breakdown in early November and was briefly hospitalized, forcing Chaplin to suspend production on his next picture. Claiming overwork, Harris bowed out of her contract with Weber and temporarily stopped acting, her precarious mental health only contributing to the image of her fragility and youth. It was reported that Chaplin visited Weber hoping to buy out the remainder of his wife's contract. Throughout their courtship and after their marriage Harris repeatedly asserted that Chaplin did not want her to work.[49] In these news reports, two assertive, quasi-parental figures seemed to vie for control of the frail young woman. "Mildred Harris Chaplin depends for comment upon other people," quipped *Photoplay*. "Once it was Lois Weber, her director; now it is Charles the Great, her husband."[50]

Universal wasted no time in capitalizing on Harris's notoriety. Pronouncing her "the most talked about girl in America," the studio rereleased *For Husbands Only* alongside *Borrowed Clothes* and planned an early release for *When a Girl Loves*.[51] Jewel ads encouraged exhibitors to "put on a Mrs. Charlie Chaplin week," featuring all five of the star's collaborations with Weber. "Let's go see the girl who married Charlie Chaplin!" read proposed promotional copy. "She's here for a week in five Lois Weber Jewels."[52] The strategy appears to have been a success. That first week of December eighteen of New York City's twenty-five large Broadway movie theaters booked *Borrowed Clothes*, with Universal reporting "enormous demand" across the country for all of Harris's pictures. When the film opened at the Superba in Los Angeles the following month, it broke weekly attendance records and was held over for an unprecedented second week. *Moving Picture World* speculated that part of the film's appeal lay in the fact that Harris's character appeared in a wedding gown, furnishing viewers with "a realistic vision of how she must have appeared on that epochal occasion." After giving Harris's performance a less-than-favorable review, Chicago's Mae Tinée confessed, "It doesn't matter much what I say about the picture, for you'll want to see it anyhow, just to give Mrs. Charles Chaplin the 'once over.' Am I right?"[53] Some enterprising exhibitors even showed Harris's pictures alongside her husband's comedies. Under the banner "Mr. and Mrs. Chaplin," New York's Broadway Theater ran *Borrowed Clothes* alongside *Shoulder Arms* in November 1918. One reporter present for a Saturday matinee recounted that the packed house "practically 'ate the picture up.'" Screenings were so popular that both pictures were held over for an additional week. Later that spring the theater again paired *When a Girl Loves* with Chaplin's *A Dog's Life*.[54]

Even as Universal took full advantage of the hype surrounding Harris's marriage, the studio also appears to have delayed releasing several Weber

CARL LAEMMLE, *Offers*

Mrs. Charlie Chaplin

(MILDRED HARRIS)
IN LOIS WEBER'S PRODUCTION

"HOME"

UNIVERSAL-JEWEL

Figure 31. Mildred Harris's marriage to Charlie Chaplin
was played up in publicity for *Home* (1918). Author's
collection.

titles featuring the actress. *For Husbands Only,* the pair's third collaboration, was completed in the spring of 1918 and shown to reviewers that April
but held for release, causing one trade reviewer to complain about "the
injustice of allowing such a good picture to lie on the shelf at a time like
this." Finally released in August and September, *For Husbands Only* was
then subsequently rereleased in December with ads now touting the presence of "Mrs. Charlie Chaplin."[55] Weber's two subsequent films with
Harris, completed in June 1918—*Home* and *Forbidden*—were not released
until August and September of the following year, some fourteen months

later, and only after Harris was back in the public eye with tragic news about the untimely death of her infant son. By this point Harris had returned to acting, having secured a new contract with Louis B. Mayer, who launched an extensive publicity campaign, much of it based on Harris's past successes with Weber.[56] Once released, both *Home* and *Forbidden* were well received, so it is not clear why Universal held them back for over a year. In the end, commentators advised exhibitors to rely less on short-lived fascination with Chaplin's bride, promoting instead the long-standing appeal of Weber's pictures and the star power she had cultivated in Harris. It was not only "curiosity on the part of the public to see the actress whom Charlie Chaplin chose for his bride" that accounted for the success of these films, according to the *Los Angeles Times*, but also the fact that they were Lois Weber productions. *Moving Picture World* advised exhibitors to "appeal with the star and the direction. . . . Both mean something to your patrons." Promoting Harris, the paper advised, "can be done even without recourse to the 'Mrs. Charles Chaplin.'"[57]

If the language surrounding both Weber's Universal contract and her work with Harris stressed her authority as filmmaker and studio head against Harris's youth and immaturity, this discourse began to shift subtly when Harris suspended her acting career and Weber suddenly found herself without a leading lady. With Harris out of commission Weber promptly signed on to direct four pictures for Anita Stewart Productions, a company the enterprising actress had formed with Louis B. Mayer the previous year. Once again, it was reported that Weber's salary would be the highest paid to any director in the industry—"with the possible exception of D. W. Griffith"—although figures published in the trades suggest she would actually earn less than she had been paid under her Universal contract.[58] A report at the time noted that Weber was leaving "the U," a misleading turn of phrase since she had already made seven pictures at her own studio, but also a telling one, for Weber's contract with Mayer marked a shift away from established patterns of studio releases to the newer landscape of independent distribution. At least one trade commentator expressed the hope that by finally severing her long association with Universal, Weber might be liberated from lowbrow material and "the flathead picturegoers that Universal caters to." Fully on her own, *Variety* predicted, Weber would be able to "do something really fine."[59] Mayer apparently offered Weber considerable support for her productions, reportedly telling her "spare nothing, neither expense, time, nor effort. Results only are what I'm after."[60]

Anita Stewart's collaboration with Mayer epitomized the reach exerted by actress-driven production companies in the late 1910s, part of a veritable "her-own-company epidemic" documented by Karen Ward Mahar.[61] Mary Pickford initiated the trend in mid-1916 when she negotiated a profit-sharing agreement, along with significant creative control on all of her productions, through the formation of the Pickford Film Corporation. She became, in effect, an independent producer with a say in decisions made during all phases of preproduction, production, and postproduction. Other popular female stars soon followed suit, including Stewart, Norma Talmadge, and Clara Kimball Young in what Benjamin Hampton would shortly dub "the Pickford revolution."[62] Mahar argues that "the challenge posed by these entrepreneurial stars was almost certainly part of the reason larger studios moved toward vertical integration in the 1920s," because both assertive stars and independent production were inimical to the industry's drive toward great efficiency and centralized control. But for a time these star-driven companies represented the possibility that women might exercise considerable creative autonomy over their careers.[63] Anita Stewart titles were released through First National, a new and influential player in the exhibition market catering to independent producers. Formed in April 1917, the First National Exhibitors' Circuit brought together exhibitors located in key cities nationwide. Combining their purchasing power, exhibitors aimed to finance and distribute outstanding pictures made by independents. By the time Mayer signed with First National in mid-1918, the circuit controlled hundreds of theaters across the country and had already inked distribution deals with Chaplin and Pickford, top stars leading the move toward independent production. For Mayer, First National represented the best financial option for ensuring "the making of feature films at the highest quality."[64]

A very different personality from the childlike Mildred Harris, Anita Stewart was associated with early (and controversial) attempts to exert authority over her image, her career, and her workload. Vitagraph's most popular and profitable star in the mid-1910s, Stewart had been sued by the studio when she and Mayer formed an independent company before her contract expired. She later claimed overwork at Vitagraph had compromised her health, saying she had been "unappreciated and unkindly treated" at the studio to the point of nervous exhaustion, making it impossible for her to fulfill the terms of her agreement.[65] At the forefront of the "her-own-company epidemic," Stewart was described by Grace Kingsley as "the first independent woman producer of pictures in the world." However erroneous, Kingsley's turn of phrase demonstrates just how profoundly actress-driven production companies were shaking up Hollywood's accustomed power structures. Indeed, Kingsley framed her portrait of Stewart around the apparent disjunction between the actress's appearance ("exactly like one of her own picture characters") and the "tremendous will power" Kingsley sensed underneath ("goodness, she wasn't one of those characters, not at all!").[66] Accordingly, Stewart had grand ambitions for her endeavor, hoping to produce screen adaptations of socially conscious literary works like Theodore Dreiser's *Sister Carrie* and *Susan Lenox: Her Fall and Rise* by muckraking journalist David Graham Phillips.[67] Stewart's association with hard-won independence, assertive creative control, and highbrow ambitions dovetailed with Weber's own reputation, heralding the possibility of a new era for women in the industry. Indeed, when Weber signed on to direct Stewart's pictures, publicity stressed the fusion of two formidable talents—the value of their collaboration would "be extraordinary in exact proportion to the extraordinary talents of Miss Weber as the director [and] of Miss Stewart as the star," *Moving Picture World* concluded.[68]

Weber ultimately wrote and directed only two films for Stewart, *A Midnight Romance* (1919), adapted from a story by frequent collaborator Marion Orth, and *Mary Regan* (1919), which she adapted from a novel by LeRoy Scott, a social activist with a background in settlement work. Cinematographer Dal Clawson shot both productions, continuing his lengthy association with the director. Both films elaborated issues long connected with Weber's work, particularly the effects of class and social status on young women's sexual relationships, themes she had also explored in her seven films with Mildred Harris. In *A Midnight Romance* Stewart plays a shipwrecked European princess disguised as a maid working at a swanky seaside hotel. A wealthy scion falls madly in love with her after he spots her swimming on the beach at midnight, but she does not reveal her true identity to him until the end. The titular character in *Mary Regan* is the daughter of a wealthy heiress and a handsome crook whom her mother had tried unsuccessfully to reform. Ashamed of her lineage, Mary refuses to marry New York City's upstanding district attorney, fleeing instead to the mountains and hoping to escape members of her father's gang who are trying to embroil her in their criminal exploits. There she falls prey to their schemes; unwittingly repeating her mother's fate by marrying another criminal, Mary is forced to seek help from the district attorney she had originally spurned, consenting to marry him in the end after all.[69]

By all appearances, then, Weber continued to work at Anita Stewart Productions much as she had at her own company, selecting her own material, adapting the screenplays herself, and working with trusted colleagues like Orth and Clawson. And she continued to frame heterosexual romance in relation to broader issues of class and gender. Yet the way these titles were discussed in both publicity and promotional materials records a subtle

Figure 32. Disguised as a maid in a luxury hotel, Marie (Anita Stewart) hides in plain sight while keeping a close watch on the plot to swindle her lover, in *A Midnight Romance* (1919). Frame enlargement.

shift in Weber's authority. Unlike Mildred Harris—and later Claire Windsor—Stewart was not a star whom Weber had "made" or "discovered." In 1916 Stewart had already been included on *Motion Picture* magazine's list of the "Twenty Greatest of Filmdom," fourth behind Thomas Edison, Billie Burke, and Mary Pickford.[70] After Stewart liberated herself from Vitagraph and ventured out at her own company, *Photoplay* noted that though "briefly past twenty, she is, in pictures, a veteran of veterans."[71] Stewart was famous in her own right, then, well before she worked with Weber. A star with sufficient clout to form her own company, she was on a much more even footing with the director than Weber's other female leads. As a result, Weber's name was not featured as conspicuously in promotions for either film as it had been in previous releases; Universal publicity, for instance, had never failed to feature Weber's name (and thus her authorship) prominently. In contrast, *A Midnight Romance* and *Mary Regan* were sometimes referred to as "Stewart-Weber Productions," assigning star and director equal authorship. Both films were also often presented as the second and third pictures in Stewart's contract with Mayer, as publicity stressed the continuity between films that Weber directed and Stewart's first independent release, *Virtuous Wives* (1919), directed by George Loane Tucker.[72] For his part Mayer also asserted an authorial imprint on the productions, telling an interviewer, "I have stinted on nothing—money, time nor energy," and taking credit for pairing his star with great directors and great properties.[73] In fact, several reviews of *A Midnight Romance* and *Mary Regan* failed to mention Weber by name—unthinkable for any picture she had released since her early Rex days. *Photoplay* even erroneously credited Marshall Neilan as the director of *Mary Regan*.[74]

An ad for *A Midnight Romance*, neatly encapsulates the competing claims of authorship that structured Weber's work with Stewart and Mayer. Described as "the great triumvirate," they appear in oval portraits, identified as "The Star," "The Producer," and "The Director." With Mayer's image set between those of Stewart and Weber, positioned slightly higher on the page, and his eyes looking directly at the reader, the primacy of his authorship is unmistakable. In brief profiles that follow, Weber, described chiefly as "a maker of stars," is listed last, her contributions seemingly less significant than either Stewart's or Mayer's.[75] Picking up these cues, reviews of Weber's work with Stewart tended to stress how her direction had, as one reviewer put it, "given the picture many little individual touches that enhance the value of the star." *Variety*'s reviewer praised Weber's direction of Stewart in *A Midnight Romance*, for instance, noting that the actress attained "a subtlety beyond anything she has heretofore done" and concluding, "Miss Weber has handled Miss Stewart admirably."[76] Even as it was celebrated, then, Weber's work as a female director was seen chiefly to enhance her stars.

Despite having signed a four-picture deal with Mayer, Weber left after directing only two films for Anita Stewart Productions. It is unclear whether she was dissatisfied with their working relationship or whether medical issues took precedence. In any event, she terminated her contract with Mayer and traveled east to New York in April 1919 for surgery to reset an arm she had broken badly the previous fall; five bone fragments were eventually removed from her elbow.[77] Writing to a friend, Smalley described the pain his wife had endured throughout the previous months, saying "no one knows the agony [she] has been through during these last two pictures as she is so much the stoic—but it was nothing short of heroism to stick the way she did."[78] Weber stayed in the New York area all that summer, recuperating and traveling through the Catskill Mountains with her husband. While east Weber rented her Santa Monica Boulevard studio to Marshall Neilan, and it is likely that he filmed *In Old Kentucky* there with Stewart, the fourth release from Anita Stewart Productions. Ironically,

Figure 33. Competing claims of authorship colored Weber's association with Louis B. Mayer and Anita Stewart in this advertisement for Anita Stewart Productions.

that same summer Mayer also began wooing Weber's original star Mildred Harris, now pregnant with her first child, using Weber as bait. Mayer signed Harris in June 1919, but just a month later her baby died and the distraught actress gave up working again for an extended period. Stewart, in contrast, went on to make a total of fifteen pictures with Mayer until their contract expired in 1922, working with a roster of top-flight directors including not only Neilan, but John Stahl and Fred Niblo.[79]

In the end, however, the tremendous creative control exerted by popular female stars like Stewart was a short-lived phenomenon. As Mahar has shown, the vogue for actress-driven production companies stood in opposition to ever more vertically integrated studios that favored neither overly powerful stars nor films produced and distributed outside their centralized control. Moreover, however groundbreaking, this new brand of female influence was rooted in the lure of youthful feminine glamour exuded by stars like Stewart, Pickford, and Talmadge—a model of femininity quite at odds with Weber's own persona as matronly, socially conscious filmmaking visionary, increasingly out-of-step in 1920s Hollywood. Weber's subsequent contract with Paramount and her work there with Claire Windsor highlight the final phase of this transition. Highly successful, vertically integrated studios were now spaces where women's work was largely relegated to the care and feeding of feminine celebrity and glamour.

Weber began searching for a new distributor while she was in New York during the summer of 1919 recovering from surgery on her arm. She eventually signed with Famous Players–Lasky to release four films through Paramount-Artcraft.[80] Mayer, never one to miss an opportunity to boast, congratulated himself on having worked with a director later selected to make "specials" for Famous Players.[81] The terms of Weber's Paramount contract were again extremely lucrative and, in a nod to the industry's evolving business model, Weber entered into a profit-sharing agreement that was said to guarantee her an income in excess of $500,000 a year. Such a handsome deal allowed Weber to purchase the studio facilities she had been leasing on Santa Monica Boulevard.[82] With this, her third contract in two years, Weber aligned herself with a central player in the new distribution market: alongside its own productions, Paramount also distributed films made independently by some of the top names in the business, including D.W. Griffith, Maurice Tourneur, Thomas Ince, William Desmond Taylor, Mack Sennett, and George Loane Tucker. For all intents and purposes, it must have seemed an excellent move. Paramount, rapidly expanding its theater holdings across the country, represented the new, vertically integrated Hollywood.[83]

Publicity for Weber's Paramount releases once again focused attention on her authorial imprint, prominently featuring her name or the name of her production company in all promotional material—quite a change from the strategies used to market the films she had directed for Anita Stewart Productions.[84] Yet, at the same time, Weber's films were also framed within the studio's broader branding and marketing efforts. Paramount had initiated an unprecedented nationwide advertising campaign in 1917, promoting its releases through ads in daily newspapers and mass-circulation middlebrow magazines such as *Ladies' Home Journal, Collier's,* and the

Saturday Evening Post. Stressing "the good plays and the good audience" Paramount programs attracted, the studio associated itself with solidly middle-class, white moviegoers, as Kathryn Fuller has demonstrated.[85] An omnibus Paramount ad published in *Ladies' Home Journal* and *Photoplay,* for instance, included two of Weber's films among its current releases, promising "entertainment for the whole family, *undivided.*" A well-dressed family is pictured presenting their tickets at the box office, the happy mother looking on confident in the entertainment she has chosen for her family. The tagline "Letting yourself in for a good time" emphasized the woman's direction of her family's leisure time.[86]

The move to Paramount also afforded Weber an opportunity to work with a new female lead, since both Harris and Stewart remained tied to their contracts with Mayer. When asked whom she would direct for her first Paramount production, Weber replied, "I don't know, but I'm certain of one thing—he or she won't be a star," signaling her deep investment not only in nurturing young talent but also in fashioning them into future stars.[87] Weber's subsequent "discovery" of Claire Windsor in the Paramount cafeteria has become legend in both women's biographies. Determined to find her new leading lady, Weber reportedly looked all over the studio. "I'll not stop at this last minute to spend several days or weeks hunting for another [actress]," she was said to proclaim. "I'm going to comb this lot and find one ready to work."[88] Weber promptly spotted Windsor, then still known as Ola Cronk, in line for lunch at the studio's cafeteria. Windsor had arrived in Hollywood after winning a beauty contest but had only managed to secure bit parts and extra work. Weber signed a contract with Cronk, vowing "to endeavor to cause her to become known as a star in motion picture work."[89] As part of this effort, Weber selected the name Claire Windsor, professing that it emphasized the actress's "English type of beauty," and circulated reports suggesting that Windsor had originally hoped for a career in opera.[90]

Under the terms of their contract Weber retained exclusive rights to Windsor's services for one year, with an option to renew for a second year. Weber, at the height of her power after having signed the lucrative contract with Famous Players–Lasky, was here promoting not only her ability to recognize and develop acting talent but also her capacity to *create* stardom for someone like Windsor with virtually no experience. So well established was this facet of Weber's reputation that Windsor was deemed "worthy of joining the distinguished ranks of Lois Weber discoveries."[91] Indeed, Windsor's performances in five films written for her by Weber—*To Please One Woman* (1920), *What's Worth While?* (1921), *Too Wise Wives* (1921),

The Blot (1921), and *What Do Men Want?* (1921)—did make her a star. By 1922 she was named a Western Association of Picture Advertisers (WAMPAS) Baby Star, alongside Colleen Moore, Bessie Love, Mary Philbin, Lois Wilson, and several others. But in the end, Windsor did not stay with Weber long, signing with Goldwyn in July 1922, just a year and a half after her initial contract with Weber, then signing on with MGM three years later, where she became one of the studio's top stars.[92]

If the discourse surrounding Weber's working relationship with Mildred Harris had stressed the director's ability to nurture young talent, facilitating Harris's growth into more complex, mature roles, and if the discourse surrounding her work with Anita Stewart had stressed the collaboration of two notable, ambitious women in modern Hollywood, the characterization of Weber's association with Claire Windsor now stressed only the fabrication of female celebrity. Discussions of beauty and stardom had largely replaced those of talent and hard work; and Windsor became known primarily as a fashion icon, rather than an actress. Such subtle shifts in accounts of Weber's working relationships with her actresses encapsulate a broader, ongoing reconception of women's work in Hollywood. As I will show in greater detail, narratives of instant discovery undercut both women's efforts, reducing Windsor's expertise to possessing "natural" beauty and Weber's artistry to a kind of marketing acumen. The paradox of such profiles, of course, is that they turned on a language of the "natural" that obscured both women's labor, while in the process also seeming to acknowledge the very construction of that image, foregrounding, for instance, the fact that Weber renamed (and essentially repackaged) Ola Cronk as Claire Windsor. Important, as well, is the fact that so much of Windsor's publicity in this period revolved around fabricated "scandals" apparently designed to keep her name circulating in the press. In a little over a year Windsor engineered her own "disappearance," had a rumored engagement to Charlie Chaplin, was mentioned as a possible suspect in the murder of Screen Directors' Guild president William Desmond Taylor, and saw her son become the target of a supposed kidnapping scheme—stories that, needless to say, ensured her name remained in newspaper headlines throughout 1921.[93] All of this is clear evidence that discussions of women's contributions to moviemaking were focused less on creative endeavors such as acting, writing, and directing than on topics like stardom, glamour, and celebrity. Judged by such profiles, Windsor's creative work apparently revolved solely around the cultivation and circulation of her star text, tasks in which Weber was positioned only as her helpmate.

Despite her success in developing Windsor's stardom, Weber's experience at Paramount was rocky—further indication that the terms under which women worked in Hollywood were being redefined. More than a year elapsed between August 1919, when she returned to California to resume shooting, and December 1920, when Paramount released its first title from Lois Weber Productions, *To Please One Woman*. Shortly thereafter Weber was called to the company's New York headquarters to screen three other unreleased pictures, *What's Worth While?*, *Too Wise Wives*, and *What Do Men Want?* After the screening, Paramount agreed to release only the first two titles, leaving Weber to find another distributor for *What Do Men Want?* even though all three films had already been publicized alongside Paramount's upcoming releases and had been given titles consistent with others on Paramount's program. Anthony Slide concludes that *What Do Men Want?* was simply too politically radical and too dour for Paramount executives.[94] I agree: however coy its title, a film featuring a pregnant single mother who commits suicide simply did not fit on the same roster as other early-1921 Paramount releases such as Cecil B. DeMille's *Forbidden Fruit* and William DeMille's *What Every Woman Knows*. As Weber's relationship with Paramount apparently faltered, a report surfaced in March of 1921 saying she had released all actors under contract. In an effort to deny the story, Weber took out a trade ad proclaiming, "Lois Weber announces that she will continue to Produce Independently in Her Own Studio," and reminding readers that *To Please One Woman*, *What's Worth While*, *Too Wise Wives*, and *What Do Men Want?* would all be distributed by Paramount and had all been "produced in my own studio."[95] In reality, Weber no longer had a distribution contract and Paramount would decline to release the final picture.

So if Weber's Paramount contract had initially appeared both prestigious and lucrative when she signed with the company in mid-1919, a mere eighteen months later it was clear that despite the studio's efforts to shoehorn her productions into the Paramount style using sensational titles and branded advertising, the social issues she explored were not consistent with the studio's image; despite the studio's desire to feature Weber's name prominently in its advertising copy, the real trend in the industry downplayed her creative work as writer and director in favor of celebrating her role as a "star maker"; and despite the appearance of supporting independent production, Paramount was exerting authority in a manner that ensured vertical integration and secured its status as one of the most powerful players in postwar Hollywood. Later that year Lois Weber Productions was named along with several other independent companies in a Federal Trade Commission complaint filed against Paramount alleging "unfair competition" and a studio policy of "conspiracy and combination" to keep independent producers out of the business by controlling exhibition outlets. This was final proof, if any was needed, that the agreement Weber had originally signed with the studio was no longer viable.[96]

Released from her Paramount contract and lacking a distributor for her completed film *What Do Men Want?* Weber signed with newly formed independent distributor F. B. Warren Corporation, a significant step down from Paramount and a sign that the market for independent production was rapidly shrinking as the majors moved decisively toward full vertical integration. Warren, general manager of Associated Producers since its inception, had considerable experience with independent distribution. Modeled on United Artists, Associated had been created by a group of top-flight directors in 1919, including Mack Sennett, Marshall Neilan, Allan Dwan, George Loane Tucker, and Maurice Tourneur. Sacked by Associated in March of 1921, Warren formed his own company a month later, setting up exchanges in more than twenty cities nationwide with the hope of attracting top independent directors. Warren's trade ads celebrated independent production and distribution at a time when it was becoming all the more difficult to compete against the majors.[97] Weber was among the first filmmakers Warren signed, along with Nell Shipman and Reginald Barker. In fact, Weber's first Warren release, *The Blot*, was exhibited in Los Angeles on a double bill with Shipman's *The Girl from God's Country* (1921). Later Wid Gunning joined Warren in the endeavor, eventually taking over the company and renaming it Wid Gunning, Inc. Through his publication *Wid's Daily*, later *Film Daily*, Gunning had been a long-standing champion of Weber, frequently reminding exhibitors to mention her name in their promotions. Gunning eventually also signed George Loane Tucker, late of *The Miracle Man* (1919), and boasted of having "two of the greatest directors in the industry."[98]

Publicity items dwelt on the new creative freedom Weber enjoyed outside the purview of studio control. In the *Los Angeles Times* Edwin Schallert reported that Weber would begin production on a project "long cherished by herself, but which she could not fulfill practically until independent," redefining the notion of Weber's "independence" yet again. This new project would not "deal with the marriage problem" common in Weber's recent Paramount releases, but would instead focus on a subject of interest to clubwomen and churchgoers, groups with which Weber had long felt an affinity and to which she now intended to cater. "It is her desire now that she is independent to make pictures with an especial appeal to these interests," Schallert declared.[99] The unnamed project Schallert described would become *The Blot*, the first film released under her contract with Warren, once again featuring her top stars, Claire Windsor and Louis Calhern. After releasing *The Blot*, Warren distributed *What Do Men Want?* the film Paramount had turned down. Weber was featured prominently in advertising for these two pictures, her name and image circulating widely in promotional campaigns clearly geared toward celebrating the directing talent Warren and Gunning represented. "I am proud of the two productions *The Blot* and *What Do Men Want?*" Weber proclaimed in one ad. "They were made as I wanted to make them, not 'UNDER ORDERS.'"[100] Warren even issued collectible cards featuring Weber's portrait—the first time Weber had been promoted this way since her early days at Universal.

In the end, however, Warren and Gunning could not sustain their business model and the company soon collapsed. Warren went on to found American Releasing in 1922, focusing his energies on the exploitation market, by then one of the few avenues for independent production.[101] Nearly a year after the release of *What Do Men Want?* Weber filed suit against Gunning and Warren, claiming the company had collected upward of $200,000 from exhibitors that remained unaccounted for and that it had "sidetracked" her productions in favor of other titles—further evidence that the market for independent production and distribution had all but vanished.[102] What had seemed the promising horizon of independent distribution in 1918 and 1919 with the rise of giants like First National had by 1921 and 1922 become a nearly unnavigable terrain populated by upstarts like F.B. Warren falsely confident they could compete against juggernauts like Paramount and Metro-Goldwyn.

If nothing else, Weber's varied distribution agreements demonstrate how rapidly the market for independent production emerged—and then disappeared—during Hollywood's postwar boom. Weber's first alliance with Universal exploited an older distribution model whereby studios released "prestige" pictures on a quasi-independent states' rights basis. Her second deal with Stewart and Mayer exploited the new phenomenon of actress-driven production companies, piggybacking on the growing autonomy of popular female stars. Weber's contract with powerhouse Paramount-Artcraft initially represented the height of possibilities for independent production, soon all but gone in the era of studio conglomeration. Her last contract, with F.B. Warren, demonstrates what few options existed by the early 1920s for independents in general and female directors in particular. The march toward vertical integration, with Paramount leading the charge, left little room for filmmakers such as Weber, particularly as she continued to take a hard look at marriage, sexuality, and domesticity.

A concurrent narrative of industry "remasculinization" also began to redefine the terms under which women worked in the movie business.

Weber's early reputation as a visionary filmmaker, a matronly embodiment of Hollywood's best intentions, began to shift during this period, giving way to the perception that she was chiefly a "star maker" whose work consisted of discovering beautiful young women and fashioning them into celebrities. In discussions of Weber's working relationships with her leading actresses—Mildred Harris, Anita Stewart, and Claire Windsor—three distinct paradigms of women's work emerge, paradigms that chart Hollywood's growing investment in female stardom and glamour. Harris's publicity infantilized the actress and cast Weber as chief author and creative visionary, celebrating the artistic command exercised by female directors. This view shifted during Weber's association with Stewart and Mayer since there was legitimate confusion about whose energies were driving the "Weber-Stewart" productions, an indication of how fundamentally female stars came to eclipse female directors during the "her-own-company epidemic." And finally, Weber's work with Claire Windsor was understood to consist of merely "discovering" the actress and packaging her "natural" beauty, with publicity campaigns openly acknowledging, even reveling in, the explicit *manufacture* of the personage "Claire Windsor" by Weber the "star maker." By the early 1920s, then, the female star had finally come to replace the female director as the iconic emblem of women's place in Hollywood. This trajectory marks a profound reconfiguration of women's filmmaking work, one that helps explain not only the demise of Lois Weber Productions but also the fates of Alice Guy Blaché's Solax company and Nell Shipman's production company during this same period. A disappearing market for independent production and a fundamental reconfiguration of women's work in Hollywood together made it virtually impossible for Lois Weber Productions to continue past 1922.

LOIS WEBER, STAR MAKER

Portraits that cast Weber as a "star maker" reached their zenith during her time at Lois Weber Productions, but they had been seeded earlier in her career and endured long afterward until the idea came to dominate her obituaries. We have already seen how the star-maker label emblematized broader efforts to reconfigure women's work in Hollywood. During a period of "remasculinization," as described by Karen Ward Mahar, when the technical, business, and creative sides of moviemaking were becoming exclusively associated with men, women were more narrowly associated with beauty, glamour, and stardom. Even esteemed filmmakers like Weber could not escape this broad brush. As becomes clear below, circumscribing

Weber's filmmaking talents in this manner also obscured the enormous range of alliances she fostered with women throughout the industry and beyond: aspiring actresses, screenwriters, and directors whom she mentored; professional peers with whom she collaborated; and clubwomen, journalists, and activists whom she befriended outside Hollywood. Through these varied alliances not only did Weber cultivate ties with other women in an era of industry "remasculinization," but she forcefully asserted a place for women at all levels of movie culture, resisting a narrowing emphasis on female stardom and glamour quickly pervading Hollywood.

Weber's reputation as a star maker initially developed at Universal, where she was said to have "discovered" Mary MacLaren in 1916, casting her in a small part in *Where Are My Children?* then assigning her starring roles in five subsequent pictures. "Her talents so quickly developed under the tuition of Lois Weber that her future was assured," Universal publicity trumpeted.[103] When Mildred Harris was signed to Lois Weber Productions the following year, reports played up similarities with the director's earlier "discovery" of MacLaren, significantly downplaying Harris's long list of previous screen credits. Items soon began announcing that Weber was "responsible for Miss Harris's entry as a star," that Weber had made her "a star almost overnight."[104] By the time Weber "discovered" Ola Cronk in 1920, fashioning her into Claire Windsor and featuring her in five films, Weber's reputation was well established. Windsor was cast as the filmmaker's "protégé," her "brightest star," and her "latest discovery."[105]

Eventually Weber's ability to discover and nurture young female performers became the sole marker of her stature—not the salaries she commanded or the contracts she negotiated, not even her considerable creative accomplishments as screenwriter and director. By 1921 *Moving Picture World* declared that Weber had "been a star maker for years." She had but "one hobby," another observer pronounced, "finding new photoplay stars." Weber, fans were told, was "gifted with an acumen or instinct which enables her to fairly 'sense' talent and screen ability." Another profile simply cast her as a "film astronomer," so accurate were her celestial predictions. "Lois Weber Understands Girls" proclaimed the headline of one 1927 profile, which noted, "Her directorial career is a procession of triumphs with girls. You cannot count on your ten fingers the girls she has made and the girls she has helped to stardom." Indeed, Carl Laemmle declared Weber's "greatest success has been in developing young actresses," a skill he related to her gender: "A woman can develop an actress just rising to stardom as no man can. Women understand women and respond to them. . . . Girls love her." When he hired her to interview and screen-test potential actresses for

Universal 1933, long after the active phase of her career had ended, Weber's "star-making" abilities were played up once again.[106] Weber's gift for "discovering" female stars had, by then, become the sole feature of her reputation. So entrenched was this view that by the time she died in 1939, her obituaries remembered her chiefly for her role in helping make other women famous, best illustrated in the headline "Lois Weber, Movie-Star Maker."[107] What are we to make of the fact that one of the most respected director-screenwriters in early Hollywood was ultimately remembered only for making other women famous? What were the consequences of framing Weber's achievements so insistently within the rubric of star making?

To begin with, stories of Weber "discovering" young talents almost by accident and elevating them to the ranks of superstardom overnight cast actresses in wholly passive roles, simply waiting to be noticed. Such narratives erased the labor and training involved in acting for the screen, promoting instead the notion that female performers possessed "natural" gifts. Such stories also insisted, rather forcefully, that stardom was the ultimate—often the *only*—goal for women in Hollywood. In doing so, they reasserted highly conventional ideas about femininity in the face of Weber's powerful stature in the industry.

Accounts of Weber's "discovery" of Mary MacLaren, for instance, emphasized the actress's passive investment in being admired and reduced Weber's role to simply recognizing MacLaren's inherent talent. According to a tale spun in promotional literature, one bright day MacLaren's face "arrested" the filmmaker's attention when she happened to spot the young woman in a long line of hopefuls gathered at the Universal gates. Tired of being approached by aspiring actresses, Weber had adopted the habit of burying her face in a book or a script as she passed this parade each morning. But on one particular day, the story goes, the director happened to look up from her work. She "looked directly into the eyes of a girl whose face attracted and held her attention," *Green Book* recounted. "There were other girls there, a bevy of them; but she saw only the one girl. In her face was 'something' magnetic. 'Are you looking for work?' the woman director asked the girl." *Universal Weekly* proclaimed, "The story reads like a fairy tale, and in itself would make an extremely interested photoplay if Lois Weber should ever be at a loss for a striking plot." Another piece compared MacLaren to Cinderella and cast Weber as a fairy godmother who waved "her magic wand" over the aspiring actress. "From Extra to Stardom," *Motion Picture* announced giddily.[108]

In Claire Windsor's case, described earlier, the moment of discovery was set in Paramount's cafeteria, not outside Universal's gates, but otherwise the ingredients of the tale remain largely interchangeable. Veritably cinematic, these encounters both culminate in a dramatic, silent exchange of glances between filmmaker and would-be star. And while they emphasize the passive beauty of these young actresses, they also dramatize Weber's command of whichever studio lot she happened to be working, even as they circumscribe the director's stature within very strict parameters, limiting her authorial gaze to an appreciation of beauty. In contrast, MacLaren's own later recollection of meeting Weber stressed her ambition and drive as an experienced young actress, not the street waif persona played up in Universal publicity. Weber and Smalley had seen her perform on stage in San Francisco, MacLaren recalled, then had arranged for her to meet them in Los Angeles at Weber's offices on the Universal lot.[109] Likewise, Weber's account of her first meeting with Windsor diverges sharply from the tale spun in publicity: she remembered that the actress had been introduced to her by a friend who thought she might appreciate the accomplished young performer.[110] MacLaren's acting talent is foregrounded in the women's own recollections of these events, against the narratives of instant "discovery" that circulated in publicity discourse.

Profiles of this sort also tended to minimize the actresses' considerable professional training and to accentuate their youth, a phenomenon already noted in relation to Mildred Harris. A 1918 *Photoplay* piece titled "Stage Experience? None!" emphasized her lack of theatrical training, adding, "It seems like yesterday that *Photoplay* was running a picture of Mildred in short frocks and long hair."[111] On the contrary, though only sixteen, Harris already had a sizable acting résumé before she signed with Weber, having been a member of Thomas Ince's stock company for three years, where she played principal roles, then at Fine Arts, where she had been featured in several Griffith pictures, including *Intolerance* the previous year.[112] As *Moving Picture World* summed it up, the acclaim Harris finally achieved starring in Weber's films represented "six years of good solid effort."[113] In what sense, then, did the filmmaker "discover" Harris at all?

Indeed, many performers sought to reclaim the talent and training hidden under fables of instant discovery by actively disputing publicity accounts of their rise to fame. In "How I Happened," an article published just a year after she became famous in Weber's films, Mary MacLaren rejected the ingénue guise that had been crafted for her, emphasizing instead her own agency in the drive for professional success and her considerable experience, insisting that her acting talents be valued over the ability of others merely to recognize her "natural" gifts. Working hard at Universal under Weber's tutelage, MacLaren recalled, "[I] soon realized that I had 'found myself' at last."[114] Claire Windsor also frequently countered rumors about her "discovery" by calling attention to her own ambition and talent: "I worked very hard and don't want anyone to believe that I merely fell into good fortune," she declared in 1921.[115] In perhaps the most pointed reassertion of their autonomy, both MacLaren and Harris later sought to be released from studio contracts they had signed as minors, agreements they claimed were exploitive. MacLaren found herself in the ironic position of suing to retain control over the "Mary MacLaren" ingénue persona Weber had fashioned for her, even as her assertive legal stance verily shattered that guise.[116]

Others, too, remained distinctly skeptical about persistent myths of instant stardom circulating in early Hollywood. In a 1922 article, ironically accompanying a contest for new screen personalities, novelist Mary Roberts Rinehart decried the "frenzy for novelty" and "wasteful demand for the new" driving the industry's star system. Such folly had "placed on our silver sheets today so many pretty, vacuous faces, new and young and therefore appealing at first, but as cloying as a milk diet after a time," she said, insisting "no art thrives on immaturity and newness."[117] With great prescience Rinehart hit upon an enduring contradiction of the star system: its reliance, on the one hand, upon established, bankable personalities and, on the other, upon a desire for novelty and an investment in the idea that anyone can be plucked from the realm of ordinariness and elevated to fame. Skepticism about the industry's appetite for youthful talent also began to fuel the star scandals of the 1920s, particularly in the wake of Theodore Dreiser's influential 1921 report on Hollywood, "Morals and Manners," and Adela Rogers St. Johns's notorious characterization of Hollywood as "the port of missing girls" in 1927.[118]

Something of Weber's own resistance to these myths is figured in comments she made about a talent search orchestrated by the *San Francisco Chronicle* in early 1921. Interviewed about her approach to casting in an article promoting the contest, Weber insisted that she selected female players not for their beauty but for the "type" they embodied; certain scripts demanded certain character types, she maintained. Praising Mary Miles Minter for playing characters close to "the sweet, fresh young girlhood which is actually hers," Weber argued, on the other hand, that an actress like Alla Nazimova should not attempt to "impersonate a child."[119] Here Weber moved away from her reputation as a star maker and embraced a more holistic approach to filmmaking that included her creative work as screenwriter and director, rejecting the idea that beauty was the sole qualification for screen work.

Myths of discovery and overnight stardom not only cast actresses in passive roles in which they merely waited to catch a director's eye, but also diminished Weber's considerable creative role as screenwriter and director—reduced it to the task of merely noticing "natural" talent on display outside studio gates or queuing in cafeteria lines. When we remember that *star maker* was also a label frequently used to describe Dorothy Arzner's associations with women she directed, as Judith Mayne has pointed out, it becomes apparent that women powerful in the early industry were often depicted in the role of handmaiden to beautiful stars in order to downplay their own authority. Such characterizations also helped gloss over more complex aspects of the women's interactions that, in Arzner's case, involved same-sex attraction and flirtation.[120]

By all accounts, Weber was a forceful, demanding director who gave precise direction to her performers, expecting considerable effort in return. Visiting Weber on the set in the fall of 1917, just after she opened her new studio, Elizabeth Peltret found an exacting filmmaker, noting, "There are times when everything has to be changed over and over before Miss Weber is satisfied."[121] Indeed, both Weber and performers under her charge described her commanding presence. Claiming her work at Weber's studio constituted "the greatest pleasure I've ever experienced in pictures," Mildred Harris explained how closely she tried to follow the directions of this "true artist," for "she knows just what will make the best effect."[122] Claire Windsor explained:

> All of us in the Weber studio avoid all semblance of acting. . . . Miss Weber insists above all else on naturalness. She is never cross when she directs, but I always know when a scene is not going well, for then she walks up and down the set instead of sitting in her easy chair. While working in a picture I keep my eyes constantly on her. I try to read her thoughts, to anticipate what she wants me to do. My aim is to be as plastic as possible in her hands, and that is not difficult, because Miss Weber literally takes one's personality away from one.[123]

Weber herself declared, "I must have players who will let me lead them; I go so fast they must put their hands in mine and run with me. Both Claire [Windsor] and Louis [Calhern] do this and we work beautifully together."[124] Watching Weber direct Billie Dove several years later, another observer echoed this view, claiming, "Lois Weber is a peculiar type of director. Instead of sketching for a player a general outline of a scene, and allowing that player to inject his or her own personality, she very definitely delineates every move, down to the turning of the head to the very inch, and the flicker of the eyelash. In short, the player has no opportunity to plan out

Figure 34. Weber *(right)* directs Smalley and Mona Lisa on the set of *Too Wise Wives* (1921). Courtesy of the Academy of Motion Picture Arts and Sciences.

anything for his or herself."[125] Critics consistently praised the performances Weber elicited from her players, celebrating the "intelligent interpretation of their roles" and noting that "natural acting is at its height in a Lois Weber production."[126]

If Weber's reputation as a "star maker" diminished her writing and directing talent, it also occulted many significant ties she fostered with women both inside and outside the industry. These included aspiring screenwriters and other young women eager for a chance at movie work; influential female peers working within the industry; and clubwomen, journalists, and educators who held considerable stakes in cinema's future. Throughout her career Weber served as a professional mentor for many women in the industry, exercising a level of support and guidance that far exceeded her reputation as "star maker." Several of the actresses Weber directed at Universal went on to successful directing careers of their own, as shown earlier. It is reasonable to surmise, then, that Weber, Universal's highest-profile filmmaker at the time, played a substantial role in encouraging and supporting these women's own artistic aspirations. That Universal had the largest concentration of female directors and screenwriters of any studio during this era must in some respects be attributable to Weber's stature and influence. And one must not forget Weber's early influence on renowned *male* filmmakers. Rupert Julian acted in many of Weber's Rex shorts before directing such films as *The Phantom of the Opera* (1925); and Anthony Slide reports that both John Ford and Henry Hathaway worked as prop boys for Weber in their early days at Universal.[127]

Noted screenwriters Jeanie Macpherson and Frances Marion worked with Weber early on as well. When writer Lenore Coffee arrived in Hollywood in 1919, one of the first stops she made was Weber's studio on Santa Monica Boulevard, which she remembered as "a rambling, shingled bungalow with a stage behind it."[128] The two women would later collaborate on *The Angel of Broadway* in 1927, and their paths frequently crossed in Hollywood. Coffee started reading scripts for Louis B. Mayer shortly after Weber left Anita Stewart Productions and was later under contract at DeMille Pictures during Weber's tenure there. Weber evidently took great pride in the support she lent to women in the industry, recounting, for instance, that she "had under [her] care many of the girls who are now famous in the writing field," including Frances Marion.[129] Though only nine years older than Marion, Weber immediately assumed the role of mentor. Indeed, Marion credited Weber with giving the writer her first break in pictures, recalling that at their first meeting Weber announced, "I have a broad wing, would you like to come under its protection?" Remembering this stage of her career, Marion concluded, "I owe my greatest success to women."[130] Weber and Marion developed a long-standing friendship that endured at a time when both could easily be counted among the most powerful figures in Hollywood and stood as a testament to the alliances Weber fostered with other women in the industry.[131]

Alongside such individual mentorship, Weber also began to use her public persona to encourage other women in the field, particularly those interested in screenwriting. She served on the Advisory Council for the Palmer Photoplay Corporation, the largest and most respected correspondence school for aspiring screenwriters, most of whom were women. Palmer literature reached out to female pupils "with a particularly welcoming tone," as Anne Morey notes.[132] Board members included prominent women in the industry, such as Weber and Macpherson; students studied scripts and manuals authored by women, including Weber's script of *For Husbands Only;* and successful female graduates, who purportedly outsold their male rivals, were touted in Palmer promotions. If in early trade profiles Weber sought to draw attention to the art of screenwriting and to plead for scripts of greater depth and quality, by this point she began using her renown as a screenwriter to encourage other women in the field. To drum up publicity for her new production company in 1917, Weber sponsored a screenwriting contest, offering $1,000 for a sequel to her first release, *The Price of a Good Time*. Four years later she offered money for "unusual stories, especially those built around worthwhile themes," inviting aspirants to send their scripts to her studio. The response was tremendous. By the end of 1921 some 14,000 scripts had been sent to Lois Weber Productions. Only eight were worthy of consideration, she concluded, vowing from that point onward only to read scripts sent through professional agencies.[133] Through syndicated newspaper columns published in papers such as the *Washington Post,* the *Denver Post,* and the *San Francisco Chronicle* in mid-1921, Weber honed her reputation as an expert on moviemaking and an advocate for quality films. Writing on topics as diverse as screenwriting and three-dimensional filmmaking, she adopted a direct, conversational tone, mixing memories of her father's stereoscopic slide collection with practical advice such as "Don't write photoplays calling for expensive settings" and "Don't have long time elapses in your story."[134]

Weber also took an active interest in young women flocking to Los Angeles in search of motion picture work in the late 1910s and early 1920s, a flood of "movie-struck girls" causing considerable alarm.[135] "Miss Weber is noted for the interest she takes in the younger members of the acting faces at Universal City," the studio's trade paper proudly proclaimed.[136] When she opened her own studio, Weber established a school for "young actor folks" there; an article on the studio highlighted the time she spent with younger members of her company. An accompanying photograph showed Weber leaning over a boy's shoulder to correct his homework, her other arm encircling him in a nurturing posture.[137] Ella Hall, whom Weber directed at Universal, would later recall, "If it hadn't been for Miss Weber's kindness and patience when things seemed most difficult for me, I really don't think I should be where I am today."[138] If at times publicity cast Weber in a maternal relationship with younger performers—MacLaren, for instance, was described as "The Girl with Two Mothers"—the real emphasis of Weber's work in this area seems to have been professional development.[139]

This becomes most evident in her long-standing involvement with the Girls' Studio Club, "Home of Young Ladies Who Make Moving Pictures in Hollywood." Founded in 1916 by the Los Angeles YWCA, the Studio Club served as a residence for young women aspiring to movie work, providing social and educational opportunities for its members, including visits with industry notables such as Weber and actress Geraldine Farrar. Affiliated with the club from its inception, Weber attended dinners there, gave educational talks to its members, and served on its finance committee alongside Los Angeles clubwomen and wives of industry executives. She maintained her involvement with the Studio Club throughout the 1920s and into the 1930s, demonstrating a lasting commitment to providing inroads for young women in the industry.[140] As Heidi Kenaga demonstrates, the Girls' Studio Club emerged in response to concerns that young women might be exploited in Hollywood's sexual economy—"casting couch" stories had been circulating since the early 1910s. Eager to dispel such stories, the Motion Picture Producers and Directors Association became increasingly involved with club activities, tying its support with efforts to regulate the employment of extras on movie sets. Exhibiting similar concern, Weber herself began advocating for a union to protect "extra girls" as early as 1918, using her stature within the industry and her reputation for respectability.[141]

In all of her engagements with the Studio Club, Weber embodied a model of mature, serious-minded—and *feminine*—motion picture work, a persona distinctly and deliberately at odds with the image of naïve young souls exploited by a profit-driven, male-dominated industry. She also modeled a mode of civic engagement long exemplified by clubwomen, providing, in fact, a crucial link between such older forms of activism and the new industry attractive to so many young women. In August 1918 she hosted a tea at the Studio Club for some two hundred guests, giving a talk on the work she was doing with the Motion Picture War Relief Association and urging "studio girls" to become involved. She discussed plans to hold a dance at the Studio Club in honor of soldiers stationed at the Officers' Training School in Hollywood. Later that month Weber led a contingent of smartly outfitted studio girls parading in a massive street pageant organized by the association with Douglas Fairbanks serving as grand marshal.[142] Indeed Weber was highly visible in Hollywood's war relief efforts, a sign of both her esteem in the industry and her continued embodiment of a Progressive Era feminine civic-mindedness. In May 1918 Weber was elected to the governing board of the newly formed War Relief Association, and later served as its chair. At the group's first meeting she delivered a speech appealing to women in the industry to get involved in the war effort. Forefront in the group's campaigns, Weber was pictured in the center of a staged tableau of Hollywood's war efforts, flanked by Charlie Chaplin and D.W. Griffith on one side and Cecil B. DeMille and Mack Sennett on the other, industry leaders all. At the launch of the Fourth Liberty Loan Campaign that fall, Weber and Griffith together unveiled and christened a tank paid for by the Hollywood community. Weber also volunteered to

Figure 35. Weber *(center)* hosting officers of the Girls' Studio Club at her studio in 1918. Courtesy of Hollywoodphotographs.

serve along with several other MPPDA members on the West Coast arm of the Advisory Board of Motion Picture Directors, charged with evaluating film propaganda for the federal government's Committee on Public Information, which had its own Division of Films. Following the war, she was appointed "Mother for the Los Angeles Disabled Veterans of the World War" and donated the use of her studio for a charity revue sponsored by the Post-War Service League.[143] In other words, Weber used her reputation not only to support young women aspiring to careers in Hollywood, but also to embody the kind of womanly civic-mindedness they might find when they got there.

Alongside the mentorship Weber provided to aspiring actresses, screenwriters, and directors, she also worked throughout her career in collaborative relationships with female *peers*, another facet of her professional life obscured by her reputation as "star maker." Probably the best example of this teamwork remains her collaboration with Anna Pavlova on *The Dumb Girl of Portici*, a project celebrated at the time for bringing together Weber's "native ingenuity and Pavlova's theatric sense." So notable was their association that writer H. H. Van Loan suggested the project might very well be considered "suffraget [sic] propaganda."[144] Writer Marion Orth was a frequent collaborator throughout her time at Lois Weber Productions. Weber adapted several of Orth's stories, featuring the author's work in films with all three of her leading women, including *The Price of a Good Time, Borrowed Clothes, A Midnight Romance, To Please One Woman, Too Wise Wives,* and *The Blot.* Orth began her career as a writer of short magazine fiction, but moved to Los Angeles at Weber's invitation after the director purchased and adapted two of her stories. The two then began a close collaboration on several pictures, after which Orth went on to a two-decade career as a screenwriter, attributing her success to the tutelage she received working so closely with Weber early on.[145]

Although Orth remained her closest collaborator, Weber continued to adapt the work of other female writers and to direct screenplays written by women other than herself. Mary Roberts Rinehart's book *K* became the basis for *The Doctor and the Woman,* one of Weber's first scripts for her independent company. Rinehart, who had refused previous offers for rights to the novel, was happy to learn of Weber's interest in adapting the material: "I just shouted for joy, because I knew that *K* (1915) would receive the most artistic and truthful presentation possible at her hands."[146] Weber's pattern of collaborating with female writers continued later in her career as well. Doris Schroeder, a well-established screenwriter at Universal, wrote the adaptation of Clara Louise Burnham's novel *Jewel: A Chapter in Her Life* (1903) that Weber would direct in 1923. And, as noted above, Lenore Coffee penned *The Angel of Broadway* in 1927. Weber and Coffee's collaboration lent *The Angel of Broadway* "alarming feministic tendencies," one observed quipped, echoing Van Loan's earlier comments.[147]

Weber also maintained strong social ties with prominent women in the industry, fostering a network of associations even in the face of the industry's efforts at "remasculinization." Her long-standing friendship with Frances Marion, documented by Cari Beauchamp, endured at a time when both could easily be counted among the most powerful figures in Hollywood, and testified to the alliances Weber fostered with other highly creative women.[148] She hosted a luncheon for Elinor Glyn, for instance, dined with Jeanie Macpherson at the Ambassador Hotel, and attended a host of other engagements where she socialized with figures such as Alla Nazimova, Dorothy Davenport Reid, Lenore Coffee, Louella Parsons, and journalist Grace Kingsley.[149] Weber also likely attended regular Friday-night soirees at Marion's, where stars mingled with female screenwriters, producers, and directors, alongside the wives of influential male filmmakers and studio executives. Dubbed "hen parties" by the press, Marion's gatherings were, in fact, signature elements of women's culture in early Hollywood, events that fostered social and professional connections among women. A photo of one such party shows well-known stars like the Talmadge sisters and Colleen Moore together with Adela Rogers St. Johns, Davenport Reid, and Marion herself.[150]

Weber's partnerships also extended beyond Hollywood where she fostered extensive associations with women's clubs, the premiere activist organizations for middle-class women of her era, as well as journalists, business owners, and intellectuals, acting as a visible embodiment of female leadership within the industry. Weber addressed the Los Angeles chapter of the Federated Clubwomen of America several times on matters such as improving motion picture quality and ensuring the safety of young women who emigrated to Los Angeles looking for movie work.[151] Promoting her efforts working behind the scenes with young women in Hollywood, Weber invited a group of clubwomen to tour the facilities at Universal City in early 1917. They met with some of the young actresses there, "visited the beautiful green room which has been provided for their comfort," and had lunch with Weber afterward, declaring themselves "pleased with the treatment accorded the girls at the film capital."[152] In these ventures Weber served as an ambassador for the industry, providing a visible index of womanly decorum behind the scenes.

In 1921 she embarked on a national speaking tour, addressing women's clubs around the country on the topic "Woman's Influence in the Photoplay World," a talk heard by clubwomen in Pittsburgh, Kansas City, Philadelphia, St. Louis, Cincinnati, and Newark.[153] Weber's efforts to exemplify feminine propriety within Hollywood were evidently successful, for Mrs. Edward S. Bailey, vice-president of the influential Illinois Federation of Women's Clubs and editor of *The Edict*, the group's official publication, professed her belief that opposition to motion pictures among clubwomen had "arisen from a lack of understanding of just such producers as Lois Weber, her objects and ideals."[154] Alternating with her talks on "woman's influence," Weber also spoke to women's clubs about more controversial topics such as moving picture censorship and Sunday blue laws in Denver, Salt Lake City, Topeka, and Indianapolis. A staunch opponent of censorship, Weber lobbied clubwomen at a time when they were stepping up calls for greater regulation of motion pictures. Following their successful campaigns for women's suffrage and prohibition, women's groups were considered extremely effective advocates for social change. Aligned with Protestant and Catholic clergy, clubwomen took on the task of "cleaning up" motion pictures in the 1920s, a project that only intensified after the star scandals. MPPDA head Will Hays courted women's groups aggressively throughout this period, hoping to prevent an escalation of federal motion picture regulation by co-opting the Better Films movement and enlisting clubwomen to serve in the Hays Office. His efforts were not always successful, as many clubwomen became disillusioned with efforts at industry self-regulation.[155] Weber entered this debate, then, hoping to sway clubwomen with the idea that the influence of women such as herself behind the scenes might be the best solution to the censorship question. As someone associated with both feminine propriety *and* controversial films, Weber was uniquely poised to address these issues. She reportedly conceived the idea for her 1921 film *What Do Men Want?* after meeting with clubwomen and agreeing to make a picture under their auspices in order to "offset as far as possible the spirit of unrest so dominant in the lives of many of the younger men of the present generation."[156]

As the star scandals began to erupt that same year, Weber spearheaded a campaign to secure the cooperation of women's clubs, female newspaper editors, and businesswomen in helping to correct the impression that young women emigrating to Los Angeles in search of motion picture work placed themselves in grave danger. "Certain yellow journalists," Weber complained, ". . . would have the rest of the country believe that Hollywood looks like one of Dore's illustrations in Dante's *Inferno* and that the streets of Los Angeles' suburbs are populated by under-world characters."[157] Long-standing fears about Hollywood's sexual economy escalated sharply when Roscoe "Fatty" Arbuckle was implicated in the death of would-be starlet Virginia Rappe, then again when several well-known actresses were drawn into the mystery surrounding William Desmond Taylor's murder. In seeking to counter these narratives, Weber not only mobilized her own considerable renown but summoned traditional voices of feminine propriety installed in positions of leadership in clubs, businesses, and media outlets across the country. Her ongoing work with the Girls' Studio Club, discussed above, moved outward in the wake of the star scandals, as she sought to recruit other powerful women in the campaign to ensure that the filmmaking business remained a safe and welcoming industry for its legions of female aspirants.

While profiles that focused on Weber's star-making abilities drew attention to her many collaborations with women, de-emphasizing her waning partnership with husband Phillips Smalley, they did so at the expense of portraying her as a motherly helpmate to would-be starlets, thereby concealing the rich texture of her associations with many eminent women both within and beyond the film industry. Stories framing Weber as a "star maker," obscured her considerable creative acumen as writer and director in favor of her ability to discover "natural" talent, while at the same time fueling an impression that acting and fame were the sole ambitions of women in Hollywood. Even as they acknowledged Weber's influential stature in the industry, such stories, reiterated at so many different junctures in her career—repeated so often, in fact, that they became the singular note of her obituaries—ultimately cast Weber's authority in considerably diminished terms. If the arc of Weber's associations with her three leading ladies, analyzed in the first section of this chapter, demonstrates a pronounced shift in conceptions of women's work in Hollywood, her reputation as star maker functioned in a similar manner, emphasizing female glamour and stardom over creativity, talent, and hard work, concealing networks of women's motion picture work in an era of "remasculinization."

"A WOMAN'S PICTURE IN A WOMAN'S WAY TO A WOMAN'S TASTE"

Publicity surrounding both the formation of Lois Weber Productions and Weber's interactions with her leading women indicate how narrowly women's contributions to moviemaking were conceived during this phase of industry "remasculinization" and how often they were constrained by an overwhelming preoccupation with beauty and fame. Yet, even as Weber's creative work was so often reduced to "star making," she occupied an unusual position: as Hollywood's most prominent woman filmmaker, she was valued for her potential to speak to female movie patrons prized by exhibitors. Weber's status as a *female* director thus became much more pronounced during this phase of her career and was frequently called out as a topic of note. If anything, Weber's gender became an even more integral part of her public persona. As Karen Ward Mahar demonstrates, directing was increasingly branded a masculine technical craft unsuited to women, whose roles were ever more bound to the ideal of the glamorous female star.[158] Consider Lillian Gish's comments on the subject in 1921. Expressing her own distaste for directing, Gish stated, "I am not strong enough. I doubt if any woman is. . . . Directing requires a man of vigor and imagination."[159] Weber was the lone female filmmaker Gish mentioned, recalling only that Weber "was always ill after a picture," pathologizing the very notion of a woman director even as she acknowledged it. Weber's paradoxical status was perhaps best expressed by her longtime champion Carl Laemmle, who told an interviewer he would "trust Miss Weber with any sum of money . . . to make any picture she wanted to make." But for Laemmle this made her unique: "Miss Weber has the strength of a man," he said, claiming that she "is the only woman I have ever known who could work until two in the morning and be fresh and ready for another day's work at six."[160] Cecil B.

DeMille concurred, noting, "Lois Weber is an exception. Most other women would crumple under the strain."[161]

With film directing steadily reconfigured as a "masculine" occupation, Weber was often erroneously cast as the "only" female director in Hollywood, further marking that role as an aberration. In a nod to Weber's uniqueness, Fritzi Remont dubbed her the "Lady behind the Lens" in a 1918 *Motion Picture* profile—the singular "lady" serving as a telling reminder of Weber's exceptional status. In *Photoplay* Cal York called her "our lady-director," again drawing attention to Weber's singularity.[162] Weber's position was also visualized in ways that drew attention to the assertively masculine character of film directing. The lone woman among eighteen filmmakers pictured in a 1916 newspaper feature titled "The Men Behind," Weber was helpfully described as "not a man" in the caption beneath her photo.[163] Arresting in its illustration of her difference, the layout encapsulated her contradictory status: too respected and well known to be excluded from a short list of prominent filmmakers, she was nonetheless marked as a curious anomaly capable of being understood only in a negative relation to the norm—"not a man." By 1921 *Wid's Daily*'s annual feature, "Biographies of Important Directors," included only 5 women in its comprehensive tally of nearly 250 filmmakers: pictured alongside Alice Guy Blaché, Mrs. Sidney Drew, Frances Marion, and Ida May Park, Weber was one of the few women filmmakers visible in Hollywood. Photos accompanying each profile—a sea of male faces—only underscored how exceptional these women were.[164]

The perception that Weber remained an isolated example—the exception that proved the rule—illustrates how profoundly conceptions of women's work were changing in Hollywood. Earlier in her career, as we have seen, Weber's stature as a matronly, bourgeois white woman was a key ingredient not only in establishing her own legitimacy as a filmmaker, especially one who took on so many controversial subjects, but also in promoting the industry's bid for greater respectability. If upstanding women like Mrs. Smalley worked in the movie business, then it might not be as tawdry as many feared. But by the time she ran Lois Weber Productions, the situation had changed. The industry's cultural cachet had largely been established, and two other important developments had taken hold. First, directors were now usually recognized as the driving creative force behind any production, but this role was increasingly figured as masculine. Second, female stars had emerged as the main feminine face of the industry, accorded a (short-lived) measure of creative agency under the rubric of stardom and celebrity. Profiles of Weber thus sought to trouble out her unclear status as a "woman director" in relation to both the image of the powerful female star-producer and the image of the director, now associated with a particularly masculine command of artistry, technology, and crew. Weber, as a female filmmaker, straddled these boundaries, presenting a paradox for an industry in the throes of "remasculinization."

One further paradox colored Weber's increasingly marginalized status as Hollywood's "only" woman director: as female audiences came to dominate the box office during these years, a female filmmaker, presumably capable of speaking to these moviegoers on their own terms, became highly prized. "Who knows as well as a woman what will ring true for her sisters in the theater?" Ida May Park proclaimed in her spirited call for female directors.[165] Estimates vary widely and such figures are notoriously difficult to track, but the pattern is clear: according to one 1920 assessment, 60 percent of moviegoers were female; another put the figure closer to 75 percent; and in 1927 Moving Picture World determined that women constituted 83 percent of all patrons.[166] Thus, as a female writer-director making female-centered productions aimed at a female audience, Weber held genuine currency. Her status as "foremost director among women"—the descriptor used in ads for Palmer screenwriting programs—said it best, for Weber was simultaneously located "among women" in the audience *and* in the industry.[167]

Reviewers now frequently took note of "Miss Weber's deft feminine touch," her "feminine angle on the making of motion pictures," and the "delicate suggestion of the feminine viewpoint" appreciable in her work.[168] Although it had not been uncommon for critics to mention Weber's "feminine hand" earlier in her career, such comments became much more pronounced in the early 1920s. Suddenly the idea that Weber's films might impart a distinctly female viewpoint became a topic of discussion, a selling point for her work. "One word spells the success of this woman—Women," declared one profile. "Miss Weber studies women. Her photoplays are cross-sections of a woman's soul. They have a feminine touch lacking in most man-made films."[169] There was often, too, an implication that Weber spoke for a larger community of American women; one writer noted that she "keeps in constant touch with woman's organizations everywhere . . . it is from other women that she gets the ideas that are transplanted to the silent sheet."[170]

Female critics seemed particularly cognizant of Weber's feminine viewpoint, many of them setting it against the dominant tenor of the industry. *What Do Men Want?* was "really what women want to see on the screen," Lillian R. Gale declared, distinguishing a project with *genuine* appeal to women from those merely *marketed* to women.[171] Noting that *To Please*

One Woman was "*peculiarly* a story of a woman's character written and directed by a woman," Alison Smith concluded that the film's depictions of female sexuality could be "received with more tolerance than if a man had made them."[172] *Motion Picture*'s Adele Whitely Fletcher offered an especially poignant view. "Always we have felt that it must, of necessity, be a woman who would bring a feminine psychology to the screen—who would picture for us the actions and reactions of women in the drama of everyday," she wrote. "And, after seeing *Too Wise Wives*, we will look to Lois Weber to do this."[173] Uniting journalists, moviegoers, and filmmakers in an inclusive "we," Fletcher tacitly acknowledged that although female fans and critics together produced much of early movie culture, an industry run largely by men risked falling out of step with its core fan base. Fletcher's sentiments betray a longing on the part of both fans *and* journalists for an authentic feminine voice behind the screen.[174]

So striking, sometimes, was the response of female writers to Weber's work that publicity took advantage of the fact. A remarkable ad for *What Do Men Want?* placed in the *New York Times* contrasted disparaging comments made by that paper's male reviewer—"A MAN said"—with praise lavished upon the film by female reviewers at the city's three other dailies—"But Women Say." The ad quotes Harriet Underhill praising "Miss Weber's usual veracity" in the *New York Tribune*, Gertrude Chase applauding Weber's "remarkable fidelity to detail" in the *New York Telegraph*, and the *Daily News'* Miss McElliot celebrating the film's "little feminine touches," which, she claimed, "the more or less superior sex are inclined to pooh pooh."[175] Women, this ad seemed to suggest, were Weber's intended audience, indeed those most able to appreciate her work.

Indeed, Weber's audience was cast as almost exclusively female during these years. At no other point in her career were her films marketed so exclusively to women or associated so pointedly with a feminine authorial viewpoint. Suggesting possible exploitation angles for *To Please One Woman, Moving Picture World* proposed the slogan "Lois Weber Produces a Woman's Picture in a Woman's Way to a Woman's Taste." Wid Gunning's two-page ad for *What Do Men Want?* assured tradesmen that "women love it," proclaiming that there was "no need to tell any exhibitor what this appeal to women . . . means to the box office. No need to tell any exhibitor what it means to start the women *talking*."[176] As a result, many promotions singled out female patrons, drawing their attention to Weber's feminine perspective behind the camera. "Mrs. Wife!" called a newspaper ad for *For Husbands Only* that featured a long line of smartly dressed women entering a movie theater. "With a woman's heart and a woman's eyes and woman's

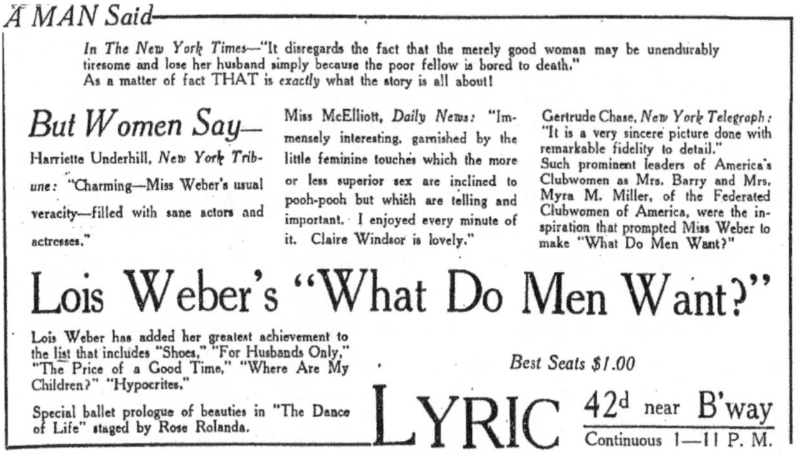

Figure 36. Male and female perspectives on *What Do Men Want?* (1921) are contrasted in the film's advertising campaign.

intuition," the copy promised, Weber "finds the real things that mere man could never discover."[177] The tagline "a woman's answer to women's pleading," used to promote *What Do Men Want?* perfectly encapsulates the way publicity appealed to female moviegoers by drawing attention to Weber's feminine authorship while delineating a marginalized sphere of women's cinema.[178]

Welcome though it was, Weber's "feminine touch" and her potential to appeal to female filmgoers produced some uneasy musings. Might her feminine hand be connected to a feminist brain? Profiling Weber for *Motion Picture* in 1921, Aline Carter hypothesized:

> Just what Miss Weber may think of the Feminist movement, I do not know, for that is one of the few subjects on which we did not touch during the interview. However, I am quite certain that she has never marched in a parade, carried a banner or made speeches in its support, yet she is doing a lion's share toward broadening the horizon of women's endeavors, and her brilliant accomplishments should act as a spur for the ambitious but halting ones who long for the freedom of self-expression found in a vocation of their own, but who shrink from the responsibilities and increased obligations which come when they step out among the world's workers.[179]

Careful to mention that they "did not touch" feminist politics during their interview, Carter confidently asserted that Weber was not a feminist, apparently forgetting that Weber had served as mayor of Universal City after running on an all-female women's suffrage ticket, that she had protested loudly when women were excluded from initial gatherings of professional screenwriters, and that she maintained strong connections to clubwomen throughout the country. Carter walked a fine line, drawing a distinction between outright feminist agitation, presumed to be undesirable, and Weber's embodiment of a forward-looking femininity inspirational to others. Women on the vanguard of social change need not necessarily be radicals, Carter assured her readers. Weber was described in a similarly apologetic (and paradoxical) manner by the *Los Angeles Herald,* which published a poem that same year noting that she "does a man's work; but has never marched in a suffragist parade."[180] Introduced only to be dismissed, the specter of radical feminism evidently haunted profiles of Hollywood's "only" female filmmaker, at once prized and marginalized.

Some of the unease surrounding Weber's status as a feminine—and potentially *feminist*—filmmaker is captured in the mixed notices her films received during these years. Pearl Latteier's careful survey of Weber's reviews documents a marked shift from the near-unanimous acclaim her films garnered during her Universal years to the growing discord that greeted her work in the early 1920s.[181] As her films shifted to subtler portraits of intimate matters, Weber fashioned a style of filmmaking more reliant on subtleties of performance, décor, and mise-en-scène. For some critics this was a welcome development. Praising her ability to render "simple details, simply," reviewer Joseph L. Kelley marveled at how Weber's films "revealed the obvious, the simple little happenings of everyday life." Others praised the "world of detail" captured in her independent productions, the "exceptionally human characterizations and convincing atmosphere" she created, and her ability to generate "human interest arising from trifling domestic happenings" and "the drama of everyday." Even while criticizing Weber's production of *What Do Men Want? Los Angeles Times* critic Edwin Schallert noted her "keen sense of details of domestic life" and her "excellent power for visualizing them on the screen."[182]

But Weber's focus on the quotidian, the domestic, and above all the *feminine* was derided by many critics. Complaining that *What's Worth While?* was "infected with the disease of detail," Schallert disparaged the film's focus on "lackluster sentiment" and the "stupid infatuations of the women." Commending Weber for her attempts to depict the heroine's interior "mental struggle" in the same film, reviewer Norman Clark confessed himself bored by "so little action, so many close-ups, so many soulful glances." Or as another critic put it less charitably, "One does get tired of the woebegone expression [Windsor] assumes all through the picture." As these comments suggest,

Weber was interested in capturing a level of detail that extended beyond mise-en-scène to include subtleties of interior psychology, particularly in her female characters. *What's Worth While? Too Wise Wives,* and *What Do Men Want?,* in particular, feature extended close-ups of Claire Windsor that emphasize her characters' interiority, rather than events around them. "Dull-brained weeping women" at the heart of *What Do Men Want?* ruined that picture, according to the *Times'* Edwin Schallert, a vocal critic of Weber's later work.[183]

The most notorious criticism Weber's work received during these years was that her tone was too preachy, that she indulged a taste for sermonizing. This shift registered much broader changes in American culture through the postwar period, as concerns of the Progressive Era gave way to those of the Jazz Age. Weber's "sermons" on poverty, addiction, wage equity, and capital punishment had been welcomed in the prewar years, when Americans were more amenable to Progressive politics (and Hollywood followed suit). But during the postwar boom Weber's films began to seem unnecessarily dour, especially as she turned her lens inward to studies of heterosexual marriage and feminine psychology. For Lea Jacobs this shift is evidence of a wider "decline of sentiment" in Jazz Age culture. Although Jacobs does not ascribe a gender bias to the anti-sentimentality movement, and finds D.W. Griffith an equal victim, other cultural historians see concurrent trends as evidence of a broader rejection of what might be termed the "maternal" ethos of the Progressive Era, ideas explored in greater depth in the following chapter.[184] Feminine sensibilities once at the heart of Weber's cultural capital, then, were now perceived as outmoded and out of step, as reviewers began to link Weber's heavily promoted feminine viewpoint to her films' shortcomings.

Denigrating *What Do Men Want?* as a "sermon in celluloid," the *New York Times* asked, "Why does Miss Weber devote the really worth while time of herself and her staff to those simplified sermons on the screen?" While this quote has featured prominently in scholarly discussions of Weber's later career, less well known is the reviewer's subsequent complaints about the film's feminist perspective. Weber's sermonizing was less an issue than its feminist tenor. The *New York Times* critic was certainly not alone in his views. Calling the same picture "maudlin," *Photo-Play Journal's* reviewer quipped, "Heaven knows what men want. And Lois Weber certainly does not." Another critic complained that "her pictures some way always make me think of the oldtime books you got from the Sunday school, which were usually about bad little children who did things they shouldn't on the Sabbath day and almost died as the result." This sermonizing, too, was associated with an overly feminine viewpoint. Weber's desire to insert "a strong flavor of moral uplift" into *What Do Men Want?*

had led her to place the story's husband "in a rather uncomplimentary light," Edward Weitzel grumbled. Conceding that "women will pat her on the back" for *What Do Men Want?* Chicago's Mae Tinée, one of the few female critics to join this chorus, could not help but fantasize that Phillips Smalley might stage an intervention with his wife. Smalley "wouldn't be human if . . . a mildly remonstrative 'MY DEAR!' did not escape him" as he valiantly "referees her struggles in the cause of right."[185] With patriarchal authority restored, the fantasy scenario suggested, Smalley would rise from the subjugated position of "Advisory Director" to upbraid his wife for editorializing so vocally on matters of marriage and sexuality in a voice that critics found too strident and ultimately too "uncomplimentary" to their male compatriots. What the industry might have welcomed in a female filmmaker—notably an ability to attract and cultivate cinema's mostly female audience—critics ultimately found troubling, for Weber brought a critical feminist perspective to topics such as marriage, domesticity and sexuality that were otherwise assumed, perhaps, to be "safe" womanly spheres.

Weber's treatments of domesticity and marital sexuality, however strident they were perceived to be, engaged much broader public discussions. If the previous decade had been dominated by debates about sexuality *outside* marriage, evident in handwringing about prostitution, white slavery, modern dating culture, and the venomous "vamp," after the war attention shifted to sexuality *within* marriage, or rather, tensions that modern sexual mores might cause between husbands and wives. Historian Nancy F. Cott argues that "public understandings of marriage were recreated" during these years, shaped by improved opportunities for women outside the home, increased use of family planning, more open discussions of sexuality, and new expectations about personal happiness wrought by consumer culture.[186] Illustrating Cott's argument, Beatrice Hinkle diagnosed "the chaos of modern marriage" for *Harper's Magazine* in 1925, noting the "general uncertainty and instability" surrounding the topic and a "tide of disaffection and disruption" among married couples. Nothing was "agitating the minds of the people of the United States" with greater "insistence and acuteness," she insisted, than "the question of the future of the institution of marriage."[187] Examining the steep rise in divorce rates during this period—by the end of the 1920s one in every six marriages would end in divorce—Elaine Tyler May concludes that pressures on marriage escalated as a result of "great expectations for personal fulfillment" in the modern era. May describes the "ambivalence" of many married men and women who were intrigued by contemporary thinking about sexuality or women's work outside the home but still deeply rooted in older conceptions of heteronormativity based on a male provider and a female homemaker.[188] Out of this uncertainty arose novel ideas about "companionate marriage" based on personal happiness and sexual fulfillment for both partners, an attempt to reconcile old and new. As one observer asked, "Does the husband really want a mere permanent housekeeper, a faithful drudge, an unpaid servant, or does he desire a real companion and a friend?"[189] In the end, despite increased public discussion of new marital ideals, continuities endured. As Christina Simmons points out, "Marriage remained the end point of most long-term heterosexual relationships, the locus of most childbearing, a substantial means of social regulation, and the main work of most women's lives."[190]

Hollywood featured prominently in national conversations about marriage, sexuality, and divorce both on screen and off. A series of scandals swept the industry after the war, fueling long-standing concern about Hollywood's sexual economy: Mary Pickford's "quickie" divorce and marriage to Douglas Fairbanks after a rumored extramarital affair; Charlie Chaplin's divorce from teenaged Mildred Harris; starlet Virginia Rappe's death during a sexual encounter with Fatty Arbuckle; and the murder of Screen Directors' Guild president William Desmond Taylor, the investigation into which uncovered the sex lives and drug habits of his female lovers. On screen too, a rash of popular and notorious "sex comedies" invited moviegoers to find humor in contemporary marital upheavals. The trend began in 1918 with *Old Wives for New*, written by Jeanie Macpherson and directed by Cecil B. DeMille, then continued with two additional comedies produced by the same team—*Don't Change Your Husband* (1919) and *Why Change Your Wife?* (1920)—and a pair of comedies directed by Erich von Stroheim—*Blind Husbands* (1919) and *Foolish Wives* (1921). Billed as a "New Angle on the Ever Present Divorce Problem," *Don't Change Your Husband*, like all of these comedies, waded directly into the fray. Calling them "comedies of remarriage," Charles Musser argues that against a threatening horizon of divorce, these films suggested that husbands—and especially wives—could refashion themselves and their relationships through consumption, self-transformation, and self-realization.[191] Sex comedies were ultimately tied to a broader cult of personality in the 1920s, as Mark Lynn Anderson demonstrates, for they instructed couples to "participate in a process of discovery by appreciating fashionable consumption as a means of communication within matrimony." Such films urged women "to offer themselves as playmates on equal footing in the enjoyment of the expanding consumer marketplace," Anderson notes, while instructing husbands to "let go of preconceived notions about self-sacrificing wives and their duty to provide for home and family, and to honor a woman's right to pleasure."[192]

Weber's films on marriage and sexuality could not help but be swept up in this phenomenon. She signed her distribution contract with Paramount just as the "sex comedy" craze crested, and there is evidence that the studio made an effort to align her pictures with DeMille comedies already on its roster, particularly since they had performed so strongly at the box office. Weber's film "Married Strangers," for instance, was renamed *Too Wise Wives* just prior to its release in an evident bid to capitalize on the sex comedy trend.[193] The new title conjured not only well-known DeMille and von Stroheim pictures but also a rash of other films released that same year, including *Suspicious Wives*, starring Mollie King, and a Marguerite Clark vehicle called *Scrambled Wives*. If Weber's original title telegraphed one of her film's core themes—spousal alienation—the revised title emphasized wry humor instead, consigning *Too Wise Wives* to a place alongside other "comedies of remarriage." Although there is no direct evidence that any of Weber's other Paramount releases were renamed, with titles like *To Please One Woman, What's Worth While?* and *What Do Men Want?* they were, if nothing else, consistent with the cycle.

Changing the title of "Married Strangers" to *Too Wise Wives* is only the most obvious evidence of Paramount's attempts to refashion Weber's marital dramas as sex comedies, for other elements of the studio's marketing campaigns drew visual and thematic parallels between Weber's productions and the DeMille-Macpherson titles on its roster. Advertising graphics for Weber's first Paramount release, *To Please One Woman*, immediately distinguished the film from previous titles released by Weber's company, either as Universal Jewels or Weber-Stewart Productions. Evoking Paramount's earlier campaign for *Old Wives for New* and especially its roughly concurrent campaign for *Why Change Your Wife?* one ad employed bold vertical lines, line drawings, and modern fonts to signal the film's fashionable themes. Ads also played up the films' production values, suggesting Weber's films included the notoriously lavish interiors on display in many DeMille pictures. *To Please One Woman* was described as "a modern American drama that is stupendous in production and in story."[194] Noting the film's similarity to "some of the recent DeMille pictures," a review of *Too Wise Wives* predicted it would appeal to audiences who liked "society dramas with a good display of showy homes and lavish appointments."[195] All of Weber's Paramount releases were also included in the studio's national advertising campaign, her films listed in omnibus ads published in monthlies such as *Ladies' Home Journal* and the *Saturday Evening Post*

Figure 37. Paramount's marketing campaign suggested similarities between *To Please One Woman* (1920) and "sex comedies" released by the studio. Author's collection.

that featured affluent white women directing their families' leisure activities.[196]

Yet, if reviewers noted comparisons between Weber's work and other sex comedies—Wid Gunning, for instance, found that *Too Wise Wives* "closely resembles some of the recent DeMille pictures both in story and production"— they were also quick to distinguish her outlook. Although "Miss Weber shows you love troubles, somewhat on the general order of the domestic tangle dramas of Cecil B. DeMille," one critic noted, she handled "sex themes without going too far." As another reviewer put it, *What's Worth While?* was "not a sordid problem play with the sex element running rampant ... but a play dealing with the problem of just what it is in the average person's life that is most worth striving for." Framing the comparison more negatively, another writer complained that, despite its enticing title, *Too Wise Wives,* lacked the "ginger" that "picture patrons nowadays require ... to keep their interest alive."[197] Even as Paramount sought to pigeonhole Weber's films alongside lavishly appointed sex comedies, reviewers noted the distinct tenor of her offerings and her penchant for taking seriously such topics as marriage, sexuality, and consumption.

In interviews and public comments Weber herself joined the larger public conversation about marriage. Positioning herself as an expert on the topic, she exploited a persona long associated with a modern approach to heterosexual unions based on gender equality and professional camaraderie. In contrast to publicity earlier in her career, when more indirect portraits of her marriage emerged through reporters' visits to her home or her work on set with Smalley, Weber now addressed the topic directly in profiles and promotional materials. In a series of interviews with female journalists, Weber spoke as a long-married woman, someone whose celebrity persona and working life were deeply enmeshed in her own marriage— a union at once conventional and groundbreaking in its combination of professional collaboration and personal intimacy. "There is no doubt that marriage is the most important event in our lives and the least studied or understood," Weber told *Motion Picture*'s Aline Carter. Weber encouraged women to provide spirited companionship for their husbands by cultivating outside interests and activities rather than perfecting domestic tasks. Describing her own marriage, Weber explained how she "found friendship in my husband's love," confessing that "we have developed into the most wonderful friends in the world."[198] Weber's emphasis on "friendship" echoed as much the earlier portraits of her intertwined professional and personal life in which she and Smalley were cast as "chums" and creative collaborators, as it did the wider discourse on companionate marriage. Weber later underscored these sentiments in a conversation with journalist Gladys Hall: "The successful marriage should be nine-tenths friendship and one-tenth attraction. . . . The first question any man and woman should ask of themselves before they take the final marital step is 'Are we friends before we are lovers?'"[199] Framed as an intimate chat between women, Weber's conversation with Hall was staged for the nationally syndicated newspaper column "Diary of a Movie Fan." Throughout the exchange Hall positioned herself as a novice in matters of the heart, consulting Weber the seasoned veteran. In retrospect, it is intriguing to note that Weber's comments on marriage—indeed, the largest segment of her creative work on the topic—

occurred as her marriage to Smalley was disintegrating. In fact, Weber's conversation with Hall was published *after* she had filed for divorce, an irony unremarked at the time. Rather than undercutting Weber's public statements, this knowledge only highlights the need to recognize the profound critique of marriage that lies at the heart of her films.

"DULL-BRAINED WEEPING WOMEN"

If Weber's comments on marriage were framed as intimate chats between female companions, ones movie fans were privileged to "overhear," her films encourage a similar mode of conversational engagement. Weber's focus on feminine psychology and interiority, and on quotidian details of domesticity and married life, which many male reviewers found irksome, might also be considered an attempt to re-create a confidential exchange between women. Yet if Weber now made films openly and explicitly for a female audience, she did so in ways the industry might not have imagined.

Tensions surrounding Weber's appeal to female viewers and her searching treatments of subjects like marriage, sexuality, and class were brought to the fore in three of the last films she made at Lois Weber Productions: *Too Wise Wives*, a film released by Paramount, but renamed and rebranded in an attempt to align it with the era's sex comedies; *What Do Men Want?* the film that likely cost Weber her Paramount contract; and *The Blot*, the last film she made at Lois Weber Productions, one she made completely on her own—"not under orders," as she stressed. Looking at the films themselves puts the disintegration of Weber's distribution contracts in context, demonstrating the degree to which Weber continued to challenge more circumscribed perceptions of women's work in Hollywood and the role of the female director there in particular. Despite Paramount's best efforts to shoehorn Weber's films into the sex-comedy mold, they did not fit, for Weber produced a body of work late in her independent career that addressed active, intelligent female viewers, showcased her strong authorial voice, and provoked fundamental questions about the financial security of marriage, modern sexual mores, childbearing, consumer culture, and capitalism.

The first of these films, *Too Wise Wives*, is structured around a contrast between two married couples: Mr. and Mrs. Graham, comfortably bourgeois newlyweds (Louis Calhern and Claire Windsor), and Mr. and Mrs. Daly, an affluent pair who live in an elegantly appointed home, dress in the latest fashions, and drive the most up-to-date automobiles (Phillips Smalley and Mona Lisa). Neither partnership is a success, we learn in a swift series of parallel scenes. Mrs. Graham, "the martyred kind of wife who lives only for her home and husband," an intertitle informs us, is making her husband miserable with incessant efforts to "domesticate" him. Her counterpart, Mrs. Daly, though "wholly selfish and a poor housekeeper," has "made a very successful wife," in part by letting her husband alone as Mrs. Graham refuses to do. Mrs. Daly's outwardly successful home life is a sham, however, for she secretly yearns for David Graham, her former lover. Burdened by his wife's suffocating attentions, Graham also finds himself reminiscing about Sara Daly, remembering her "broad-mindedness" and her ability "to make a fellow comfortable," clear references to her sexual allure. "One woman loved her husband too much, and burdened his life with her wifeliness. The other loved her husband not at all, and made him blindly happy for her own selfish ends," explained promotional material in Paramount's press kit.[200]

Promotions for *Too Wise* Wives pandered to female viewers whose interests were imagined to be chiefly style and décor. Several items, for instance, mentioned fashions "calculated to cause femininity to gasp with wonder at their beauty and lavishness." Promotions also swooned over interiors shot on location at a Santa Barbara estate, promising a "lavish and opulent setting" with "the most luxurious furnishings and atmosphere." The film "will appeal especially to women," one item concluded, for it satisfied "that distinctly feminine craving" for fashion, style, and design.[201] Accordingly, Paramount's exploitation department recommended that exhibitors make the most of potential tie-ins with neighboring businesses geared toward female shoppers, such as women's wear shops, drugstores, and furniture stores.[202]

Far from the luxury parade imagined in these promotions, however, *Too Wise Wives* offers a pointed critique of modern marriage, beset by conflicting demands of domesticity and sexuality, played out in a sphere infected with reckless consumption and class anxiety, all of which affected women disproportionately. Weber's authorial voice is strongly felt in this critique, as she offers editorial comments in intertitles, sharply contrasts the two marriages in parallel scenes, and solicits active female viewers who bear little resemblance to the awestruck style mavens presumed by Paramount publicists. Weber's presence is evident in the opening moments of the film: "Most stories end: 'And they lived happily ever after—'" a title proclaims. "Our story should begin that way—but—" declares a second. It is clear that Weber intends to break with conventional plotlines that signal narrative closure through the formation of a heterosexual couple. Instead, she proposes to take up where most narratives leave off, finding original subject matter and continuing action in marriage, not courtship. If, early in her screenwriting career, Weber had been a vociferous critic of "happy endings," perceiving them to be too limiting, here Weber explicitly uses marriage, the customary placeholder for a happy ending, as her starting point. Besides drawing attention to a potentially innovative storyline, these opening titles also assert a strong authorial voice, one that assumes a contrary stance in relation to commercial cinema, rejecting what "most" films "should" do, and that addresses viewers directly, inviting their full participation in "our" narrative.

Foregrounded throughout the film, Weber's hand is also evident in the film's structure, which elaborates a series of comparisons between the two wives, their two households, and the threat posed by a potentially adulterous coupling of Sara Daly and David Graham. Parallel editing compares events from the two marriages, most comically perhaps in rhyming breakfast scenes: Mr. and Mrs. Daly enjoy a companionable meal, while the Grahams' morning is ruined as Mrs. Graham frets over fried chicken, a dish her husband neither wants nor consumes. Intercutting underscores the film's critique of Mrs. Graham, juxtaposing her dramatics with Mrs. Daly's nonplussed response to her own husband's lack of appetite: "Don't eat anything you don't want, darling," she says. "You will be just that much hungrier for lunch." After the two men leave for work, cross-cutting continues, setting Mrs. Graham, still moping gloomily about her underappreciated fried chicken, against her counterpart's gleeful enjoyment of the "hours of freedom" that stretch before her. Weber also employs cross-cutting *within* scenes to emphasize alienation in the Graham household. Together in their living room after dinner one evening, the Grahams are isolated in mirrored compositions, each sitting in separate armchairs at opposite ends of the room engrossed in solitary pursuits—Mr. Graham reading a book, his wife sewing. Their sight lines would match, but neither lifts an eye long enough to meet the other's gaze.

Intertitles also frame many events through an editorializing viewpoint, a voice explicitly associated with Weber herself, as decorative borders surrounding many of the title cards remind viewers that *Too Wise Wives* is "A Lois Weber Production." Often placed adjacent to the action as it continues in frame, these titles solicit viewers' participation in evaluating the protagonists. After we have watched Mrs. Graham fussing over her needlessly elaborate fried-chicken breakfast, an intertitle pronounces, "Through a very excess of adoring, unselfish love [she is] unable to reason calmly about how to please him." Later, another title accuses Mrs. Graham of attempting to "nail herself to the cross," asking viewers to see her jealous suspicions as another element of unwarranted self-martyrdom. Weber's well-established reputation as a married middle-class woman, and her well-

Figure 38. Mrs. and Mr. Graham (Claire Windsor and Louis Calhern) are "married strangers" in *Too Wise Wives* (1921). Courtesy of the British Film Institute.

publicized comments on marriage throughout this period, only underscore the authoritative voice she adopts within the text. Alongside quips from an assertive narrator, Weber uses titles to reveal characters' thoughts and wishes, their interior psychological landscapes. Overall, *Too Wise Wives* employs relatively few dialogue titles. Instead, intertitles provide access to unspoken judgments and resentments that fracture the marital terrain, whether it be Mrs. Graham's insecurities, her husband's frustrations and subsequent memories of Sara Daly, or Mrs. Daly's own ambivalence about playing the "role of loving wife." An early scene between the Grahams simultaneously demonstrates the mute tensions eroding many marriages and Mrs. Graham's conscious decision to censor herself. Annoyed by the smoke from her husband's pipe, she waves it away from her face, lifts her head up to meet his gaze, opens her mouth as if to speak, but stops herself before uttering a word. We see her make the decision not to say anything, to silence herself. In lieu of her vocal objection, a title reproduces her complicated thought process, emphasizing as it does her passive-aggressive stance: "She was determined not to nag, but she DID WISH he would discard that dirty, smelly pipe and smoke the nice cigars she had bought him for Christmas." Unspoken elements of both marriages become increasingly problematic—not only David and Sara's pent-up attraction to one another, but also the way Mrs. Graham substitutes tears and door slamming for more direct expressions of her anger and the way Mrs. Daly manipulates both her husband and David Graham, her intended conquest.

Asserting her own viewpoint through parallel editing, trenchant intertitle commentary, and emphasis on the suppressed tensions that fracture relationships, Weber also solicited participation from her female viewers. If promotional schemes sought to channel moviegoers toward fashion, décor, and consumption—supposed realms of womanly interest—the film itself actually provokes fundamental questions about how women are positioned in relation to consumer culture, domesticity, and conventionally masculine realms like politics and business. *Too Wise Wives* engages female viewers directly, there is no question, but it does so less through an appeal to feminine "cravings" for fashion and home furnishings than through a moralizing or disciplinary gaze associated with the filmmaker herself. By challenging conventional viewing habits at the outset, *Too Wise Wives* invites engaged, intelligent viewers, not women prone to "gasp with wonder" at pretty things.

The film also refuses to offer a conventional heroine with whom viewers might identify, presenting instead two equally flawed women. Even while permitted access to their interior thoughts and the unspoken tensions that fracture their marriages and friendships, viewers are invited to scrutinize these women from an external, critical perspective, an outlook they are encouraged to turn inward as well, perhaps recognizing some of their own shortcomings as wives and women. Some of this perspective is captured in reviewer Marjorie C. Driscoll's assessment of Mrs. Graham, whom she found "maddening," not to mention "over-solicitous, over-attentive, and given to weeping when her husband fails to appreciate her efforts as deeply as she thinks he should."[203] This model of an omniscient, judicious female viewer observing both wives with a seasoned eye was even suggested in the film's advertising campaign, which repeatedly featured owls. In one poster, the predators hover over both wives, passing silent judgment from above; in another an owl's body outlines an entire page, with each woman's head appearing in a circle over the bird's eyes, as if reflected in a pair of glasses. The spectator-owl's omniscient viewpoint is reinforced in ad copy promising a film that "peeps behind the scenes in a million homes."[204]

Weber's appeal to female viewers in *Too Wise Wives*, then, is not unlike that in earlier social-problem films such as *Shoes*. There, as we saw, she

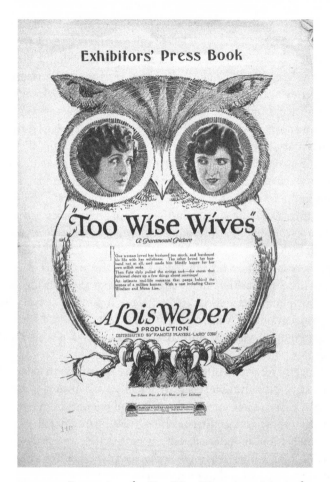

Figure 39. Promotions for *Too Wise Wives* (1921) invited active female viewers. Author's collection.

addressed middle-class women, asking them to split their identification between two perspectives—identifying emotionally with the interior struggles of an impoverished shopgirl like Eva Meyer, while simultaneously adopting a more objective view acknowledging the broader social and economic forces circumscribing Eva's experience. Weber's goal with films like *Shoes* was to push viewers to adopt an activist role in their communities. In *Too Wise Wives* Weber's voluble authorial stance invited women to view both Mrs. Graham and Mrs. Daly with an equally critical eye, to recognize how circumscribed each woman's choices were and how challenged both women were by changing sexual mores, new civic responsibilities, and the incessant demands of a consumer economy. As Maureen Turim points out, insistently referring to the women as Mrs. David Graham and Mrs. John Daly not only reinforces parallels between the two wives and the two marriages, but also lets us see how much their roles are overdetermined by the institution of marriage itself.[205] If Weber's aim with *Shoes* and other Universal social-problem films was to ignite engaged citizens, here she encouraged women to turn their gazes inward and examine their own marriages and their own roles as wives. This may seem a more modest goal, a move away from the "heavy dinners" she concocted at Universal, but it was, in fact, no less radical in its ambitions.

If in DeMille and Macpherson's sex comedies consumer culture became a sphere where women (and men) could recreate themselves, presenting their personalities to best advantage through style, ornamentation, and décor, in *Too Wise Wives*, fashion becomes merely an expression of wealth and status, consumption the hollow terrain of social mobility and class anxiety. Contrasts that develop between the two households highlight this dynamic. The Dalys' union is financially secure, but unloving. Having married solely for wealth, Mrs. Daly has the freedom to spend lavishly on herself and her home, but she has given up her true love in exchange. Although her counterpart Mrs. Graham dotes lovingly on her husband, she is beset with class anxiety and financial insecurity in the new consumer economy, for her husband does not have the resources to appoint them in the luxurious manner enjoyed by her friends. She feels ashamed, for instance, that she must drive her own car while others are ferried about by chauffeurs. The rivalry Mrs. Graham feels toward Mrs. Daly, fueled equally by romantic jealousy and class envy, finds its ultimate expression in consumption. After modestly restraining herself during Mrs. Daly's spending spree, Mrs. Graham later expresses "no hesitation about shopping" for a weekend visit to the Dalys, arriving with a trunkful of fashionable gowns. If Mrs. Graham's spending is covert, Mrs. Daly uses her charm to manipulate her husband into buying her things, sitting suggestively at his feet one evening, then casually dropping into his lap the brochure for a fancy new automobile. "John Daly didn't know it but he was going to buy a certain limousine in the morning," a title observes, emphasizing his wife's machinations in equal measure to her husband's willful blindness. Daly's inability to recognize what is going on in front of his own eyes is reinforced throughout the film in scenes showing him taking on and off his glasses.

Enticements and anxieties produced by consumer culture are set against the changes shaping women's lives following the ratification of the Nineteenth Amendment in 1920, granting them full voting rights. Politics and consumption offered alternate modes of social engagement for women outside the workforce, as Weber makes clear with a scene set in the Woman's Social and Political Club. Mrs. Daly, Mrs. Graham, and their friend Mrs. Wynn all attend a talk there. Asserting her class privilege, Sara Daly confidently navigates this terrain, chatting up the club's guest speaker. Mrs. Wynn remains more hesitant, confessing that while she has obediently followed her family's tradition by voting Republican, she finds herself utterly confused when asked to weigh in on more complex matters such as further constitutional amendments. Mrs. Graham, there simply to spy on her rival, is inattentive and distracted, a passivity in the face of civic matters that viewers are invited to condemn. After the meeting, Mrs. Daly leads her friends on a shopping expedition, a juxtaposition demonstrating how easily class aspirations, mingled with consumer desire, interrupt the women's engagement with politics. A shot of all three taken from inside the window of an automobile dealership pictures the shiny machine reflected on their bodies; Mrs. Daly, placed in the middle, becomes the literal "engine" of their materialism. Linked in this manner, the two scenes illustrate how distractions such as petty jealousy and shopping allow the women to avert their gazes from weightier concerns, how new political freedoms might be erroneously channeled into consumption or sexuality. Changes that swept the nation after the introduction of women's suffrage also provided the backdrop in many sex comedies, both implicitly and explicitly, for as contemporary observers often noted, full voting rights had irretrievably altered relationships between husbands and wives. Acknowledging this radical upheaval, *Old Wives for New* opened with a title announcing, "We wives ... must remember to trim our 'Votes for Women' with a little lace and ribbon—if we would keep our Man a 'Lover,' as well as a 'Husband.'" The sentiment Weber expressed in *Too Wise Wives* could not be more different.

The film's critique of women and consumer culture becomes most apparent late in the film when Sara Daly sets the stage for an illicit meeting with her old flame David Graham. Donning one of her newly-purchased gowns, checking her reflection in a mirror, dimming her bedroom lights, then arranging herself provocatively on a chaise, Mrs. Daly turns herself into a commodity—not a fashionable icon to be admired by female moviegoers, as Paramount's promotions might have it, but a sexual commodity for Graham. Nor is this a triumphant scene of refashioning one's personality, as might be found in *Don't Change Your Husband* or *Why Change Your Wife?* but a scene of pathetic misinterpretation. If Graham has failed to comprehend Mrs. Daly's veiled innuendo leading up to this scene—there are repeated moments of miscommunication—then she has also failed to understand that this kind of self-commodification is no more what Graham wants than his own wife's overbearing self-sacrifice. In fact, if Mrs. Daly is first seen as the wife who sustains her husband's (sexual) interest by remaining interesting herself, here we see the limits of her self-absorption. As Kathleen McHugh points out, *Too Wise Wives* disparages a world in which successful femininity is "now wholly performative and symbolic."[206]

Sexuality remains a prevailing undercurrent throughout the film, a disruptive force in both marriages, and in the end both Mrs. Daly and Mr. Graham must contain their "truant" sexual energies. There is a sense that a certain kind of sexuality can be heightened by the consumer economy: Mrs. Daly's hankering for the latest fashions and products leads her to desire the security of a wealthy husband. And while fashion, décor, and consumption allow her to exhibit her social mobility and exercise her class privilege over her friends, the same forces also fuel her misguided self-commodification. Mrs. Graham is first tempted to fight for her husband's affections in the same arena, going on a shopping spree before her weekend at the Dalys. But she comes to realize that only her moral superiority (and implied sexual restraint) can win him over in the end. Put most bluntly, rampant consumption is associated with unchecked female sexuality leading to unseemly self-display; moderate spending is associated with self-control and sexual restraint.

In the end, then, Sara Daly is called upon to reign in her "hunting instincts," as they are called, setting aside her attraction to David Graham and settling down with her husband, older and admittedly less attractive, but perpetually doting and extremely well-off. Summing up this view, reviewer Marjorie C. Driscoll worried that Mrs. Daly "plays with fire," having "never stopped to consider the relative values of the love of a good husband and the fascination of once more bringing a former admirer to her feet."[207] For his part, Mr. Graham forgoes fantasizing about her former paramour and all of the ways she knew "how to make a fellow comfortable," realizing it was "an illness that might have been dangerous" and choosing instead to take pride in his own wife's strong moral ethos. Like Mrs. Daly, he elects to trim his carnal appetites in the name of marital harmony, coming to value his wife's virtue over his former lover's erotic allure. Mr. Graham also plays a role in suppressing his own wife's sexuality, chastising her when she tries to kiss him in front of the household help.

Conflicting expectations about domesticity, sexuality, consumer culture, politics, and class produce two "failed" wives at opposite ends of the spectrum. Mrs. Daly represents an extreme of conspicuous consumption and self-interested desire; but she is also someone who succeeds in making herself an interesting spouse by leaving her husband alone and cultivating her own avocations. Mrs. Graham represents an extreme of wifely self-sacrifice, demonized as much in the film as Mrs. Daly's narcissism; yet she is less subject to the artificial pressures of fashion and consumption. If Mrs. Daly is a little too savvy about wielding her sexuality to manipulate both her husband and her former lover, Mrs. Graham is "too wise" about trying to domesticate her husband. Writing in 1925, diagnosing the "chaos" of modern marriage, Beatrice Hinkle linked such women to an affluent post-war consumer economy: "Because she has so much idle time on her hands, and no necessity to force her to independent constructive activity, [she] becomes unhappy and neurotic—a waste product without meaning or purpose."[208] In the end, as one reviewer put it, "both women learn the basic errors of their matrimonial ways," each discovering something through the other.[209] Through Mrs. Graham, Mrs. Daly recognizes the worth of honesty, restraint, and sexual modesty, values that seem as rooted in a middle-class ethos as they do in feminine virtue. From Mrs. Daly, Mrs. Graham learns to leave her husband alone, not to domesticate him too much or subjugate her own needs to his. Both come to understand that consumption and self-commodification will get them nowhere.

Although marital harmony is ostensibly achieved in both relationships by the end, questions remain. If *Too Wise Wives* began by rejecting a customary measure of narrative closure—marriage—using it as a beginning point instead, the film concludes with a profound lack of resolution. Each wife is shown to be "too wise" for her own good, and each has seemingly learned a lesson from the other, yet modifications proposed in each household appear unlikely to solve broader structural problems unearthed in the narrative—structural problems that reveal conflicting demands of sexuality and domesticity on married women, as well as conflicting demands wrought by a consumer economy and a fully enfranchised electorate outside the home.

Yet the radical aspects of Weber's views on marital politics are not fully apparent until *Too Wise Wives* is considered alongside *What Do Men Want?* the film that likely cost her the Paramount contract. Evoking the spirit of contemporary sex comedies while abandoning their coy titles, Weber chose to state her question bluntly: *What Do Men Want?* Promotions promised the film would "ask and answer the question that underlies the whole matrimonial structure," calling it "the million dollar question." "What Do Men Want?" another ad asked. "Home? Happiness? Excitement? Babies? Luxuries? Love? Learn why husbands leave home!" The film's poster shows Claire Windsor's character, Hallie Boyd, selecting a dose of "Love" from a range of potions aligned on a shelf labeled "Success," "$,"

Figure 40. The complex chemistry of male desire in *What Do Men Want?* (1921). Author's collection.

"Thrills," and "Happiness."[210] Are these complementary or contradictory ingredients? We do not yet know, and neither, it seems, does Hallie. If *Too Wise Wives* had studied female desire, as did earlier films such as *To Please One Woman* and *What's Worth While?*, here male desire became the central focus of inquiry, configured as an enigma from the start. Still, women remained the target audience, as one theater program made plain: "Through the steps that mark your progress down the vale called life, treading even with you, is the taunting thought, 'What *Do* Men Want?' Your son, your husband, your sweetheart—to hold your man's mind, heart, soul, for yours—it's a woman's answer to man's problem."[211]

Like *Too Wise Wives, What Do Men Want?* is structured around a pair of rhymed couples. We follow Hallie and Frank Boyd (Claire Windsor and J. Frank Glendon) through their youthful courtship, the early days of their marriage, and later years with children. An aspiring inventor, Frank is driven by an incessant desire to get ahead, a desire that pulls him away from Hallie and their home toward greater riches and further sexual conquests. The Boyds' crumbling marriage is contrasted with Frank's brother Arthur's on-again, off-again courtship with Bertha Rider (George Hackathorne and Edith Kessler). As Frank grows restless in his marriage, we realize Arthur's secret longing for his sister-in-law Hallie. But Frank's unceasing disregard for his wife is nothing compared to Arthur's treatment of his girlfriend Bertha. Hoping to fend off Arthur's obvious attraction to Hallie, Bertha initiates a sexual relationship with him, trying to win over his affections and curtail an unspecified "restlessness" that seems to plague all male characters in the film. But Bertha's plan fails miserably. She becomes pregnant, and Arthur abandons her before she has a chance to let him know. "Oh! Why had she—through fear of losing him—put off telling him that marriage was imperative?" a title cries. Later, in utter despair, Bertha commits suicide by jumping into the lake in a public park. Archetypal names given to each character underscore their elemental function in the narrative: Hallie and Frank are "The Girl" and "The Youth"; Arthur and Bertha are "His Brother" and "The Unfortunate." Cross-cutting throughout the film sets the two relationships, the two brothers, and their two female companions against one another.

If contemporary sex comedies frequently found humor in the failure of women to comprehend the sexual companionability essential to modern marriage—or, rather, their failure to express their sexuality through consumption and self-commodification—then *What Do Men Want?* unearths deep-seated currents in modern masculinity, pulled on the one hand by an unceasing drive for capitalist profit and on the other by sexual conquest. Focusing on the Boyd brothers, Weber demonstrates how these two desires are intertwined in corporate America. Weber sets male desire not in relation to the cult of personality, physical culture, or fashion, as DeMille and Macpherson do in their sex comedies, but in relation to the booming postwar economy—where men acquire women, homes, and families like commodities and treat them accordingly. In an early scene of Frank and Hallie's courtship, titles tell us that Hallie "dreamed of years of companionship together," whereas "to him marriage meant—possession." One year into their marriage Hallie begins to notice "a restlessness" in her husband.

Figure 41. The warm intimacy of Hallie and Frank's courtship (Claire Windsor and J. Frank Glendon) is contrasted with the cool distance of their married life in *What Do Men Want?* (1921). Frame enlargements.

"What was the reason for this vague unrest?" a title asks. "He had Hallie—and fair enough prospects! What DID he want anyway?" As the titles make plain, even Frank himself does not know. After his patent finally earns him a fortune, he thinks to himself, "This was what he wanted. Big Business! Money!! Power!!! His days of restlessness were over." But his satisfaction soon wears off, and he finds himself envious of his unmarried pal Yost after the two meet at a nightclub. "It was Freedom he wanted—he had married too young," Frank thinks to himself.

If *Too Wise Wives* found fault chiefly with its female characters, unable to negotiate modern sexual mores, the lures of consumer culture, or the demands of engaged citizenship, male characters fuel the problems in *What Do Men Want?* A masculine ego driven by a desire for fame and fortune, as well as ever-varied sexual encounters, becomes the chief problematic in heterosexual marriage. Weber ties the capitalist drive for innovation and material success to a restless male sexual drive—both of which clash with marriage and domesticity. In this respect Weber's views aligned closely with other contemporary observers. Again, Beatrice Hinkle's analysis of the "chaos" of modern marriage bears witness, for she noted how the affluent postwar economy drove men to work "so hard and intensively" that they neglected their loved ones, even while claiming to be working on their behalf. "Men are caught in a mechanism of their own creating," Hinkle concluded, one "which drives them on regardless of necessity or wish."[212]

Both Hallie, the young wife alienated from her husband's affection, and Bertha, a casualty of Arthur's capricious attention, suffer the consequences of men's wanton "restlessness." If Frank treats Hallie as a decorative commodity in his home, another visual marker of his accumulation of wealth, Arthur treats Bertha as a sexual commodity to be tossed aside when no longer desirable. Bertha's suicide, the film's climactic moment, echoes a brief scene in *Where Are My Children?* when an unwed mother drowns herself and her infant after being spurned by her lover; but in *What Do Men Want?* the *emotional* experience of unwanted pregnancy is explored in far greater detail. No other film from this era treats the experience with such depth, rigor, and compassion. Several adjacent scenes show Bertha watching or eavesdropping on other characters in ways that emphasize both her fragile emotional state and her alienation from the community. In one scene Bertha watches as Hallie walks by with her own newborn. A long shot frames both women together, emphasizing the trajectory of Bertha's gaze, but vertical tree trunks bisect the frame, separating the two characters. In a subsequent scene Bertha overhears men gossiping about her and Arthur. "I never thought he'd have the nerve to break away from the Rider girl," one of them says. Bertha's horrified reaction is shown in closeup in the following shot.

Both men feel trapped in their relationships—Frank by monogamy, domesticity, and fatherhood, Arthur by Bertha's desire to tie him down—

yet the women are imprisoned in comparable ways. Hallie and Bertha's shared experience of pregnancy, albeit under very different circumstances, invites us to draw comparisons between them, just as we are invited to draw parallels between the brothers Arthur and Frank. Bertha lives with her invalid mother and an unmarried older sister, whose work as a seamstress provides meager support for the family—three "generations" of women living together in relative poverty. No father is mentioned, creating the suggestion that Bertha's mother might also have become pregnant outside marriage, like Lillian's mother in *Where Are My Children?* A shot of the three women together stages the bleak horizon of possibilities that lie before Bertha: pregnant and single, she occupies the foreground; her sister sits working in the mid-ground; and their mother lies on a daybed in the background, sick from overwork and endless poverty.

If Bertha's pregnancy is secretive and shameful, a target of furtive dealings between the two families, Hallie's is the object of much public celebration. Yet in the end we come to recognize that Hallie's situation is not so unlike Bertha's, for though she has the security of marriage that Bertha lacks, Hallie experiences another type of entrapment. After early scenes of her courtship with Frank, Hallie is invariably pictured at home, often shot through windows and doorways that emphasize her confinement as she is left to raise her children alone while Frank pours over his inventions, then later cavorts in nightclubs after striking it rich. Like Mrs. Graham in *Too Wise Wives,* Hallie often fails to speak or act in ways that might amend her situation, resorting instead to mute tears. A title reminds us how much her fate resembles that of her counterpart: "Bertha Rider had loved unwisely and lost. [Hallie] had loved wisely but lost just the same." Hallie's unhappiness also reflects contemporary thinking about motherhood. Tinkering with his inventions, Frank finds a measure of fulfillment that Hallie does not achieve in motherhood, a contrast acknowledging that not all women accepted the maternal role "with total delight and absorption," as Elaine Tyler May puts it. Nancy Cott stresses that with more women employed outside the home and family planning options more widely available, options were expanding for women beyond "wifehood and the home."[213] Although marriage might seem the logical solution to Bertha's plight, Hallie's parallel story suggests otherwise. Men like Arthur and Frank will always be driven to further conquests and greater fortunes, the film suggests. Married or unmarried, successful or still striving, both brothers abandon women in the same way.

Reviewer Edwin Schallert's cold disregard for Bertha and Hallie—he described them as two "dull-brained weeping women"—demonstrates how the drama of male desire continued to play out even in discourses surrounding the film.[214] Beginning with the oft-quoted remark, "Why does Miss Weber devote the really worth while time of herself and her staff to those simplified sermons on the screen?" an unnamed *New York Times* reviewer went on to complain that in posing the question, "Why do good men leave good wives for other women?" the film failed to "take into account the human need for intensification of life, which the good home so often fails to provide." A wife may become "unendurably tiresome and lose her husband simply because the poor fellow is bored to death," the reviewer explained, seeming to condone Frank's behavior.[215] Four days later an ad published in the same newspaper quoted that review and retorted, "As a matter of fact THAT is *exactly* what the story is all about!" then went on to contrast the male reviewer's bleak assessment of the film with quotes from three female writers at competing New York dailies, as noted above.[216]

In the end, then, although Frank and Hallie's relationship is putatively salvaged, *What Do Men Want?* raises serious questions about heterosexual marriage, about its abilities to handle the competing demands placed on men and women alike in the postwar boom. Marriage provided women with financial security and the ability to have "legitimate" children, but for their husbands it stifled both capitalist enterprise and sexual conquest—twin engines of their desire. If *Too Wise Wives* had urged married bourgeois women to develop interests outside the home beyond the endless loop of consumption and self-commodification or the nervous energies of homemaking, *What Do Men Want?* shows the challenges of doing either in families still structured around traditional patterns of male breadwinner and female homemaker.

It would not be until *The Blot*, the last film she made independently, that Weber demonstrated that a critique of marital politics and the consumer economy could not be achieved without a focus on class.[217] Both *Too Wise Wives* and *What Do Men Want?* dealt with different aspects of the capitalist economy, with *Too Wise Wives* investigating the negative effects of consumer culture on bourgeois housewives, and *What Do Men Want?* demonstrating perilous links between a "restless" male sexuality and capitalism's constant drive for innovation and profit. Prior to *The Blot's* release, it was announced that the picture would not "deal with the marriage problem" so prevalent in Weber's other recent releases, but would instead present an issue of interest to clubwomen and churchgoers, whom Weber had long considered her core audience.[218] Released from her Paramount contract, Weber evidently sought to capitalize on her outsider status, making a picture she felt she could not have released under the Paramount banner, perhaps even embracing her growing reputation for dour sermonizing. Employing the same performers made famous in her Paramount releases—Claire Windsor and Louis Calhern—Weber openly returned to the terrain of social-problem films, exploring the "blot" of society's disregard for its educators and clergy. As Patricia Mellencamp argues in her discussion of the film, *The Blot* demonstrates the impossibility of disentangling matters of the home from those of the economy.[219]

Weber's critique of the consumer economy highlights its effects on women—not the bourgeois housewives of *Too Wise Wives* and *What Do Men Want?* but the wife and daughter of an underpaid university professor (Philip Hubbard). Professor Griggs's seeming disregard for his family's desperate financial situation is set against the stress it causes his wife (Margaret McWade), the family's homemaker, and his daughter, Amelia (Windsor). Their situation is so precarious that even something as simple as serving tea to their clergyman, Reverend Gates, becomes a burden—a burden that the women bear disproportionately. Mrs. Griggs's position in the home puts her at the forefront of these problems. As a homemaker, she must use her husband's salary to buy goods to feed and clothe her family and maintain their home. Her increasing inability to perform these basic functions propels the film's crises. Many scenes emphasize her optical point of view, inviting audiences to share her humiliation at the family's poverty, her panic when her husband invites Reverend Gates in for tea while her cupboard is bare, and her envy at the luxury enjoyed by the Olsen family next door. Weber underscores these issues by staging so many of Mrs. Griggs's key scenes in her kitchen, her own private domain in the home, a place where she is often alone and where she can relax the brave front she puts up for company. Like those moments when she alone seems to notice the family's tattered furniture and frayed carpets, the scenes in the kitchen emphasize Mrs. Griggs's solitary shame. But given its pivotal place in the consumer economy, the kitchen, traditionally a female domain, also becomes the stress point for the family's poverty. All goods seem to enter the home through the kitchen; and Mrs. Griggs's position at this gateway is crucial. Repeated shopping expeditions emphasize her pivotal role as consumer, poised between home and commercial sphere, a position in which she feels the effects of deprivation more acutely than other members of her family.

While the Griggses live a threadbare existence, barely able to scrape together the makings of an afternoon tea for their clergyman, their neighbors the Olsens live in relative comfort. When first introduced, the Olsens are described as "foreign-born," a qualifier that immediately establishes the threat that up-and-coming blue-collar, immigrant families like the Olsens represented to established white middle-class families like the Griggses. According to the film's logic, it is simply unjust that those who produce consumer goods, such as Olsen the shoemaker, ought to prosper more than educators and clergymen whose labor in shaping minds and souls goes under-rewarded. The Olsens' place in the new consumer economy is signaled when the father drives up in a new Model T Ford to the great delight of his family, marking a notable contrast to Professor Griggs and Reverend Gates, whom we have just seen arriving on foot. As one reviewer put it, *The Blot* contrasts the starkly different economic circumstances enjoyed by "that great army of underpaid brains and overpaid brawn."[220]

Middle-class hardship was a topic that dominated national consciousness in the postwar boom, when skyrocketing prices eclipsed white-collar salaries, as Jennifer Parchesky documents in her own insightful analysis of the film.[221] Professional and managerial "brain workers," as they were called, became a shrinking sector of the workforce, defined against an expanding working-class population and the wealthy bourgeois elite. This conception of a "middle class" of salaried white-collar Americans was quite new, replacing an older, simpler opposition between rich and poor. Professors and clergy were favored examples of such brain workers newly disenfranchised by the consumer economy, for they imbued this class with a genteel moral authority. What is scandalous in *The Blot*, then, is the modern phenomenon of nouveau riche immigrants making a better living producing and selling consumer goods than the educators and clergy charged with sculpting American minds and souls—a system, that is, in which financial reward is completely divorced from either class status or social value.

The contrast between these two ways of life crystalizes in a scene in which the Olsen's toddler casually ruins a pair of satin pumps while tromping in the mud, suggesting that affluence was wasted on blue-collar immigrants like the Olsens who had no basis for appreciating goods they made or purchased. That this sight is framed through Mrs. Griggs's horrified point of view, and echoed in a glance down at her own shabby footwear, only underscores the supposed inequity. This brief but significant interchange is set against a host of other scenes in which footwear, in particular, becomes the index of characters' class status: earlier Amelia tried to conceal her tattered boots from Phil during their first car ride home; later Reverend Gates attempts to shine his worn boots with goose grease with predictably unfortunate results. Such poignant scenes of genteel poverty are contrasted with shots of the Olsen toddler teetering in mud, a grotesque closeup of Mrs. Olsen's wide feet crammed inexpertly into small, delicate shoes, and the elder Olsen girl's blasé reaction to a gift of a new pair of shoes—one in a long line of others, we are led to presume. As Parchesky notes, "Shoes are the perfect commodity to represent deprivation," since they are necessary wardrobe items that can, in their more fashionable incarnations, become objects of consumer desire. This was particularly so in the early 1920s, she notes, when skirt lengths began to rise and footwear became a visible index of one's ability to keep up with the times.[222] In his own, trenchant analysis of *The Blot* Mark Lynn Anderson connects the film to Sinclair Lewis's *Main Street*, the best-selling novel that year, finding an echo of these ideas in Lewis's indictment of consumer culture: "Such a society functions admirably in the large production of cheap automobiles, dollar watches, and safety razors," Lewis wrote. "But it is not satisfied until the entire world also admits that the end and joyful purpose of living is to ride in flivvers, to make advertising-pictures of dollar watches, and in the twilight to sit talking not of love and courage but of the convenience of safety razors."[223] The vacuousness of consumer culture, its closed loop of references, is something that clearly concerned Weber as well.

Family budget woes also exert pressure on Amelia's courtships, for she must consider financial security above all else when selecting a husband. If Weber returned to romance in *The Blot*, rather than the issues surrounding marriage that she had pursued in other recent films, she did so in order to highlight class inequity. Amelia must choose between her longtime beau Reverend Gates—sincere, intelligent, generous, and loving, but deeply impoverished—and a new suitor, society playboy Phil West (Louis Calhern), whose wealth and charm she finds exceedingly attractive. Peter Olsen, a secret admirer next door, offers Amelia the alternative of aligning with newly prosperous immigrant families still learning American ways. By structuring the film around Amelia's courtships, Weber underscores the degree to which her future economic well-being is tied to marriage. Her parents' differing views on the subject illuminate her dilemma—her father wants her to marry an educated man of letters such as himself; her mother values a man who can provide Amelia with the financial security lacking in her own marriage.

Initial contrasts between the shabby Griggs household and their affluent immigrant neighbors are widened to include Phil's wealthy country club set and Reverend Gates's frugal subsistence, as Amelia's courtships begin to dominate the story. If we are encouraged to identify with the emotional struggles of Amelia and her mother, cross-cutting between multiple households also provides viewers with a commanding view, one that underscores structural boundaries of wealth and class. Phil's country club set is shown enjoying a sumptuous feast, while the Griggs and Olsen families each eat around the dinner table at home. Editorializing intertitles remind film viewers how expensive this country club meal is and how labor-intensive its preparation, seeming to echo Phil's own dawning realization about class inequities. Images of the food emphasize not only its decadence—"trout in paper" and "mushrooms under glass"—but also its "unnatural" character, particularly apparent when set against the humble roast chicken so savored by the Griggs. The "unnatural" aspect of these country club scenes is also apparent in the fact that they are fueled by cigarettes and alcohol. Weber's decision to portray Phil's high-society class through the country club setting, rather than his home, for example, denaturalizes the setting, removing it from a family home and showing Phil always in the substitute (false) family he has created, missing the intergenerational wisdom evident in the other two households.

Intercut with this lavish feast is a scene in which Reverend Gates receives his meager wages from church elders, a brief moment encapsulating the social and economic causes of genteel poverty: the church leaders, a butcher and a tailor who, like Olsen the shoemaker, produce consumable goods, are better compensated than those who "fed their souls and clothed their minds," an intertitle reminds us. The congregation's parsimonious treatment of its clergyman is set against Gates's earlier decision to give the last of his own cash to his housekeeper, a woman even more destitute than he is. After the church elders leave, Gates turns to the biblical passage reminding him that it is "more blessed to give than to receive," underscoring the scriptural grounding of his convictions. Nonetheless, set amid images of country club bounty, this scene condemns a society with such misplaced spending priorities that while socialites dine in luxury, their clergyman must occasionally skip meals in order to make ends meet.

In a narrative structured around a series of oppositions—between two neighboring families, between Amelia's two beaus, between impoverished "brain workers" and well-heeled immigrants and society folk—alliances across these class and economic barriers become important for the film's resolution. Phil and Amelia's romance forms the cornerstone of these, of course, but other significant friendships emerge as well. Phil and Reverend Gates discover a common talent for drawing; Mrs. Griggs and Mrs. Olsen find they share a fierce love for their children, sealing their budding friendship with a trip to the movies; Professor Griggs's wealthy students finally come to respect his wisdom in the classroom; and the Olsens recognize the value of a sound education for their son Peter, sending him for tutoring sessions with the professor next door.

Getting to know one another better proves instructive. Characters of all social strata learn valuable lessons and reform their behavior. By the end of the film both Mrs. Griggs and Juanita (Marie Walcamp), Phil's society flame, recognize one of the film's key messages: one's worth has nothing to do with wealth or poverty. Mrs. Griggs lets go of her precious pride, and Mrs. Olsen learns the social damage wrought by her conspicuous consumption. But it is Phil West's transformation that proves most essential and most pivotal; his class, affluent and influential, has both the clout and the resources to affect significant social change. Phil's first step in the right direction is recognizing Amelia's superiority to Juanita, whom he comes to regard as "loud" and "rude." Social stature cannot be measured by prosperity or material goods, but by the quality of one's character, he learns. Phil's social conscience first ignites when he offers Amelia a ride home from the library, as point-of-view shots register his growing awareness of the diminished circumstances in which his professor's family lives. In sharp contrast to the ethereal portrait he sketched of Amelia at the beginning, Phil notices the frayed corners of Amelia's life—the holes in her gloves, her tattered shoes—and begins to come to grips with the real Amelia, a woman whose worn-out clothing and failing constitution do not match his fantasy drawing. Phil soon notices the shabby details of Amelia's domestic environment too, imperfections that only Mrs. Griggs seemed to have noted, and he declares the family's poverty a matter of "everybody's business." Phil's first attempt to help her (bringing an overlarge bouquet of flowers) is immediately set against her very real need for nourishing food. His next attempt to help, by clumsily stowing crumpled bills in the living room, is shown to be nearly as misguided. Here Phil's evolving friendship with Gates becomes central, for the minister plays a fundamental role not only in fostering Phil's intellectual and creative interests but also guiding his charitable instincts, clearly framing them within a Christian ethos. The minister's generosity toward his impoverished housekeeper in an early scene, for instance, is shown through Phil's viewpoint, underscoring the learning experience it serves for him. In the end, Phil is able to convince his father, a wealthy college trustee, to furnish the faculty with salaries more commensurate with their value to society, recognizing and compensating their pivotal role in educating both the sons of wealthy families (society's future leaders) and the sons of immigrant families, like Peter Olsen, who will also play a key role in the country's growing economy. Thus, while the plot hinges on wealthy characters noticing (and remedying) the plight of those less fortunate, it does insist on a social solution—that is, education—alongside individual acts of charity.

Beyond these diegetic alliances, the film also proposes another solution: an informed film public, together with aware artists and filmmakers, can effect social change. Weber appears quite conscious of her own role in sending activist-oriented filmgoers out into the world. Even more so than in *Too Wise Wives* and *What Do Men Want?* cross-cutting in *The Blot* provides viewers with a commanding view of many different scenes happening simultaneously, resulting in a comprehensive knowledge of events unlike any character in the film. We see in close proximity both the secret humiliations of characters such as Mrs. Griggs, Reverend Gates, and Amelia, and an overarching view of inequities between the decadent elite, aspiring blue-collar immigrants, and steadily impoverished "brain workers." In a film structured around what characters see or, more important, fail to see, our omniscience is especially meaningful. We recognize before Phil does the futility of his initial attempts to help Amelia by showering her with expensive gifts; we recognize before Amelia does that her mother maintains a strong ethical core despite the enormous strain she is under; and we recognize the injustice of Reverend Gates's congregation for underpaying their spiritual leader while enjoying their own affluence. The role Weber imagines for her viewers is best illustrated in the scene in which Phil convinces his father that he must use his position as university trustee to fight for better faculty salaries, showing him an article titled "Impoverished College Teaching" published in the *Literary Digest*.[224] Inserts of the actual article are also shown to viewers. This brief, extratextual allusion toward the end of the film encourages moviegoers to educate themselves, to track down a copy of the magazine once they leave the theater, and read more about conditions dramatized in the film.

Although alliances forged in the film prove transformative for many characters, a bleak final image of Reverend Gates walking away from the Griggs home into the nighttime darkness troubles the film's attempts at resolution. Women of "good breeding" like Amelia had the hope of sustaining their social standing, however destitute their own family circumstance, by marrying "up." Producing a new generation of well-bred children, they could help temper an elite class prone to decadence in the postwar boom. But the film suggests that men of her class, such as Reverend Gates, were far less fortunate. Forced to compete (unfairly, in the film's view) with butchers, tailors, and shoemakers for adequate salaries, they were also forced to play a losing game competing with wealthy playboys like Phil West to win the affections of bright young women like Amelia Griggs. Gates, ostracized at the end—from Amelia, from the Griggses' home, from a society that fails to recognize the worth of his ministry—reminds us that many of the problems the film raises cannot be resolved with the tidy conclusion of a Hollywood marriage. Leaving Reverend Gates outside the circle of closure at the end, Weber also leaves room for the viewer to work toward a more comprehensive solution to the problem outside the theater. Interviewed when the film was released, she acknowledged that "the public does not like preachy pictures" and does not wish to be addressed "in primary grade logic." Instead, she said, "I endeavor to have my audience leave the theater with a greater perspective on life. . . . I am to arouse interest to such an extent that the moral does not seem diagrammed."[225]

Looking at the films Weber made on marriage and domesticity in the latter years of her independent production company, Lisa Rudman and Thomas Slater both conclude that Weber's work betrays an "undercurrent of Victorianism," to use Rudman's phrase.[226] Weber's public comments, her films, and the broader persona she evolved in Hollywood leave no doubt that she was keen to participate in debates about marriage, femininity, and sexuality raging in the early 1920s. And certainly she was highly critical of many contemporary trends—an emphasis on romance over friendship, for example, and the reduction of female sexuality to self-commodification— but it would be a mistake to attribute Weber's critique to a Victorian sensibility, as Rudman and Slater have done. On the contrary, an analysis of *Too Wise Wives, What Do Men Want?* and *The Blot* demonstrates how incisively Weber questioned many aspects of modern marriage, heterosexuality, and consumer culture.

In *Too Wise Wives* Weber investigated the twin pulls of consumer spending and political engagement on modern femininity, remaining equally critical of women who frivolously spend on themselves and those who refuse to engage with the world around them, focusing only on their domestic environment. This created a kind of frenzied loop of useless activity, she suggested, while the political realm went critically unattended and unacknowledged. *What Do Men Want?* revisits the modern roles of housewife and mother, this time set against capitalism, rather than its mirror consumer culture. If the previous film had shown how easily female desire could be channeled into self-commodification or feverish homemaking, here she demonstrated how male desire fueled capitalism's drive for profit and innovation with a devastating impact on women and children. In *The Blot* Weber returned to courtship, a subject she had explicitly set aside in her marital dramas, now looking closely at the very real economic choices many women faced before marriage. She continued her scrutiny of the new consumer economy, but now from the perspective of an underpaid professor's family struggling to keep up with their more affluent neighbors. The choice their daughter, Amelia, must make in marriage frames the entire family's circumstances. Far from espousing a Victorian viewpoint, then, these three films look directly at issues central to a more prosperous nation and a successful film industry in the years following World War I. The fact that Weber looked critically at modern sexual mores that emphasized female self-commodification, or at the new consumer economy more generally, should not be equated with a step backward toward Victorianism.

Weber's own public persona had long been associated with a modern marriage, at once "respectable" in its bourgeois propriety and novel in its model of gender equality and creative collaboration. Even as she assumed the central creative role at Lois Weber Productions, Smalley's support as husband and collaborator remained an important element of her persona, with journalists frequently noting his "helpful" presence on the lot. Weber's own observations on the value of "friendship" in marriage were invariably peppered with examples from her relationship with Smalley. Yet, as an analysis of her experiment with independent filmmaking has revealed, conceptions of women's work in Hollywood were shifting rapidly during this period of "remasculinization," as stardom came to eclipse directing as the central image of female labor and as Weber became increasingly pigeonholed as a "star maker" and a "woman's director." Put more simply, the emphasis on self-commodification she questioned on screen was beginning to have a real impact on her own career. Subsequent films such as *The Marriage Clause* (1926), *Sensation Seekers* (1927), and *The Angel of Broadway* (1927) would take an even more critical view of the era's commodification of youthful femininity, drawing modern celebrity culture and Hollywood's star factory even more directly into the mix, as the following chapter reveals. In her public comments about stardom, women's roles on screen, and her own place in the industry, Weber adopted an increasingly oppositional stance toward Hollywood's growing investment in the glamour industry during the Jazz Age.

Lois Weber's experiment with independence coincided with a moment when women's contributions to moviemaking were increasingly circumscribed under the rubric of stardom and glamour. As a result, her own work as writer and director was understood more narrowly than ever, often seen to consist chiefly of helping to make other women stars. This trend occurred despite her sustained investment in mentoring younger women in the movie business and fostering professional alliances with female peers both inside the industry and beyond it. Yet, even as female filmmakers were increasingly marginalized, Hollywood came to recognize the box office clout of its female patrons, and Weber's potential to speak to these women as a woman held tremendous appeal. She did so in a series of films on marriage, gender, and class that, though marketed aggressively to women and tailored to look like contemporary sex comedies, actually critiqued prevailing social norms. Despite claims that she had left her penchant for "heavy dinners" behind, it is clear that Weber remained a trenchant feminist critic of norms surrounding heterosexual marriage, consumer culture, and modern sexuality. She likely lost her Paramount contract as a result, precipitating the collapse of Lois Weber Productions shortly thereafter. In the next phase of her career Weber would find herself even more out of step with Hollywood trends, and more vocal than ever about the industry's treatment of women both on screen and behind the scenes. Consequently, she would find it unusually difficult to secure work.

4 "Exit Flapper, Enter Woman"; or, Weber in Jazz Age Hollywood

Most accounts of Weber's career chronicle nothing but loss and failure following the demise of Lois Weber Productions in 1921. Rehearsed in many iterations, the story goes something like this: "Weber's marriage broke up, she lost her company and she had a nervous break down." Thereafter "she seemed to lose her focus and energy, and her career as a filmmaker essentially ended." Her "life completely fell apart," her "career went to pieces," and she was "never able to regain her career momentum." Some sources will admit that Weber "returned to directing briefly in the late 20s," releasing "one or two minor program features," but, as Anthony Slide put it, "without the strong masculine presence of Phillips Smalley at her side, she could not continue directing."[1] Remarkably consistent across multiple recitations, both scholarly and popular, this wretched narrative suggests, first of all, a synchronicity between personal events and professional downfall so profound as to erase all other effects of the monumental changes that rocked Hays-era Hollywood, changes that had a disproportionate effect on women and independents; and, second, a complete erasure of the work that Weber did, in fact, produce during these years and the leadership roles she continued to assume as a highly visible woman in the industry.

Given this sorry chronicle of events, it is no wonder that Weber's late career has received little scholarly attention.[2] Without downplaying the real consequences wrought by profound changes in Hollywood throughout this period, it is possible to suggest a more nuanced reading of Weber's position in the evolving industry, one that allows for the prospect of *resisting* Hollywood's forward march toward respectability, as it was being recast during the Hays era, and toward glamour, as it was being employed to relegate women to the status of decorative objects. Re-examining the latter phases of Weber's career, it becomes clear that not only was she active in

Hollywood, but she *actively resisted* what was happening to women such as herself who had pioneered creative and leadership roles in the industry—now marginalized as tokens of respectability—and to a newer generation of female performers—employed only as decorative accessories on screen. Looking again at Weber's late career also allows us to see that her accomplishments were neither "lost" nor "forgotten," to use the terms employed by Slide and Richard Koszarski, the two historians most responsible for reviving her reputation.[3] Far from being "lost," Weber's achievements were refigured during the latter phase of her career in a manner consistent with Hollywood's evolving narrative about its own history and women's place there. Weber was effectively written out of history at the same moment she was written in.

A NEW PRODUCTION CLIMATE

To begin, it is important to assert that Weber did, in fact, maintain a relatively active filmmaking career in the 1920s—not only when compared with Smalley but also in relation to many other filmmakers with whom she had risen to prominence in the 1910s, including D. W. Griffith, Rex Ingram, and Marshall Neilan. She did so in a climate of accelerated vertical integration and studio conglomeration, renewed scrutiny of films and filmmakers from the gatekeepers of morality, and an ongoing "remasculinization" of the movie business documented by Karen Ward Mahar. Weber not only continued to defy this "masculinization" but also resisted, as best she could, new strictures of corporate control, working largely outside major studios and continuing her denunciation of censorship within the industry and beyond.

After completing work on *The Blot*, the last film she made at Lois Weber Productions, Weber took an extended vacation with Smalley, sailing for Europe in September 1921 before *What Do Men Want?* had even been released. The couple ultimately traveled for some nine months through Egypt, China, and India.[4] In June 1922, shortly after their return, Weber filed for divorce, citing her husband's "habitual intemperance."[5] After at first attempting to keep the divorce quiet, Weber was dogged by rumors and finally admitted the following year that she and Smalley had "not lived together as man and wife for several years," explaining "our philosophies of life made the marital relationship impossible." Nonetheless, the couple remained friends, attending social events together, dining out, and sometimes sharing rides to work.[6] Smalley did not direct or produce another film after they separated, but continued to act in several pictures every year, appearing as Colleen Moore's philandering father in the early flapper film

Figure 42. Weber and Smalley sail for Europe aboard the *Aquatania,* September 1921, following the collapse of her production company. Author's collection.

Flaming Youth (1923); Weber would cast him in a similar supporting role in her 1927 production *Sensation Seekers,* their last collaboration.

Returning to Hollywood in the spring of 1922, Weber found what Marcia Landy describes as an "industry in transition," evident in the fact that Erich von Stroheim was out of favor, Griffith was ever more marginalized, and Ingram found himself unable to adapt to production changes demanded by newly consolidated studios. A younger generation of directors was emerging, men like Allan Dwan and Sam Wood who accommodated themselves to the evolving studio environment and who would continue to work in the industry for decades as a result.[7] Will Hays, recently installed as head of the Motion Picture Producers and Distributors of America, was also beginning to assert control over studio releases. In an age of conglomeration and vertical integration independent production companies found it increasingly difficult to survive, a reality that hit female filmmakers particularly hard. Lois Weber Productions had collapsed by the time Weber left for Europe in the fall of 1921; both Alice Guy Blaché and Nell Shipman closed their production companies that same year. After initial reports that Weber might resume production at her old studio or travel back to the "far East" to make pictures, in October 1922 Weber returned to her old home at Universal Pictures, signing a contract with the studio to write and direct a remake of one her early features, 1915's *Jewel.*[8]

Although she found herself on familiar ground back at Universal, Weber returned to a very different studio. Without a chain of theaters under its control, as emerging giants MGM and Paramount had built, Universal now occupied a more diminished market position than it had once held. Most urban, first-run theaters owned by the major studios were closed to Universal, so the company now relied on independent theaters located mainly in small towns and rural areas.[9] "Before the age of vertical integration, Universal dominated the motion picture business through sheer size and output," Thomas Schatz argues. "But with the emergent studio era, Laemmle's steadfast program strategy and his aversion to theater acquisition destined Universal to minor status."[10] The studio was also no longer home to the considerable female directing talent that had once thrived there—Weber would now be on her own.[11]

Weber's remake of *Jewel,* retitled *A Chapter in Her Life* (1923), received significant support from the studio. Universal announced its desire to stage a more lavish production than the original, ordering extensive color tests, though ultimately deciding to shoot the picture in black and white.[12] Adapted from Clara Louise Burnham's best-selling 1903 novel, *Jewel: A Chapter in Her Life,* Weber's production was part of a slate of literary adaptations

Universal released that year, headlined by Lon Chaney's appearance in *The Hunchback of Notre Dame*. "Great Pictures made from Great Books with Great Exploitation Tieups," Universal told exhibitors. Promotions made a strong pitch to small-town exhibitors, offering them "quality" pictures at reasonable prices, providing access to first-run pictures many studios reserved for their large urban venues.[13] Ultimately, however, Weber's return to Universal was not a success. Critics praised her direction of *A Chapter in Her Life*, but found the film's subject matter out of step with the times. The story of a young girl whose love and faith transform troubled adults in her life was dubbed "old fashioned" by *Film Daily*, with other critics objecting to the film's "Pollyanna" tone.[14]

Following the poor reception of *A Chapter in Her Life*, Weber left Universal, vowing to take a break from film production. She wrote plays and a novel instead, projects she had long aspired to complete. She traveled to Europe again, socialized with friends including Jeanie Macpherson, and spent time at the Colorado summer home of another friend, novelist Margaretta Tuttle, saying she would remain on vacation until regulators "came to their senses."[15] "I have received many offers, but in each case I'm hampered with too many conditions," she claimed. Clearly troubled by the new industry landscape, Weber objected to the strictures governing Hays-era Hollywood, the control increasingly exerted by consolidated studios, and the ever more strenuous censorship pressures felt both within the industry and without. "The producers select the stories, select the cast, tell you how much you can pay for a picture and how long you can have to make it in," Weber protested. "All this could be borne. But when they tell you that they also will cut your picture, that is too much."[16]

Complaining that Weber had been "wasting her directorial sweetness on the desert air," *Motion Picture* asked, "What's the Matter with Lois?" and concluded, "There must be something wrong with the motion-picture business" if it could not find work for one of the "best six directors in the game." Was she out of work because "producers will not let her hold a megaphone for them or because she will not make the kind of picture that they want?"[17] *Film Mercury* declared, "It would be interesting to know why she has made no films in the past year or so," and continued, "It is almost a crime for such wonderful director material to be lying idle while third-raters flood the screen with junk."[18]

Beyond these speculations little information is available about Weber's activities in the eighteen months following the completion of *A Chapter in Her Life*, but there were later reports that she suffered from severe depression; she may have even experienced a complete mental breakdown. Alice

Williamson, a British journalist who visited Hollywood later in the decade, reported that Weber had withdrawn from the world and "simply disappeared" during this period. Her house, Williamson recounted, "had the air of being completely shut up. Windows were closed, curtains closely drawn. No ring at the door was answered. Newspapers lay uncollected." Williamson surmised that the "dark, stupid microbe of an idea" that women could not direct "nearly ruined" the filmmaker: "She lost faith in herself, and so lost interest in herself."[19] Weber herself never spoke publicly about this period.

Modern sources have tended to connect her mental health crisis with the near-simultaneous collapse of Lois Weber Productions and the dissolution of her marriage, implying that the end of her collaboration with Smalley rendered her deeply depressed and unable to work alone. In the four years Weber ran her production company, she had written and directed fourteen features, managed her own studio, nurtured three leading ladies to mature stardom, and negotiated four different distribution contracts, two of which ended with legal action. Every report of her work habits, beginning with her early days at Rex, suggests that she was both a perfectionist, determined to perform tasks over and over until they were completed to her satisfaction, and an extraordinarily driven worker, supervising every detail of her productions from props and costumes through the final edit and promotional campaign. It is no wonder she was exhausted and depressed after the enterprise failed when the independent distribution market collapsed. Moreover, it is unlikely that her divorce from Smalley had much to do with either her mental health or the downturn in her career. Their split appears to have been amicable, a formalization of years spent living separate lives. Smalley had also assumed a relatively minor role at Lois Weber Productions, having played supporting parts in only two of Weber's fourteen films and having had no other credited role in her productions. It is also worth noting that while Weber wrote and directed five additional features after their divorce, Smalley never again assumed any creative responsibility other than acting, with his roles diminishing from leading man to supporting player to uncredited extra in the end.

Weber appears to have emerged from her depression in early 1925, returning once again to Universal, where she was hired by Carl Laemmle to take charge of all story development for a new $5 million production initiative focused on adapting popular novels for the screen.[20] The success of *The Hunchback of Notre Dame* had encouraged the studio to release more quality features. "Exhibitors want bigger pictures and will pay to get them," announced Al Lichtman, the studio's new sales manager.[21] As part of this effort Universal was also placing renewed emphasis on screenwriting, building up its scenario department with a roster of writers, including at least two women, Olga Pritzlau and Florence Ryerson.[22] Weber evidently took these two under her wing, cajoling Laemmle into paying Ryerson a higher salary after learning the terms of her original agreement.[23] Laemmle and studio general manager Julius Bernheim declared themselves "fortunate in urging [Weber's] return to screen work."[24] Sensing a need to reintroduce Weber in 1925, Universal publicity stressed her long history in the movie business and the years she spent running her own studio. Weber possessed "the experience and executive ability of any man," Bernheim pronounced, coupled, of course, with "the delicate intuition of a woman."[25] Confident in Bernheim's assessment, the Los Angeles Times assured readers that "announcements of important developments in stories are expected soon from Lois Weber."[26]

Even with its new production initiative, Universal continued to struggle in the era of studio conglomeration. Company vice president Robert H. Cochrane complained in 1926 that the studio still suffered from a shortage of first-run houses, even lacking its own venue in the all-important New York market. By the following year, Universal began selling off its modest chain of theaters, its move into theater acquisitions having "come too late," according to Richard Koszarski.[27] Even with the push to produce more "quality" features in the late 1920s, Laemmle continued to promote a varied program, pouring resources into "programmers," inexpensive Westerns and melodramas designed to fill out an evening's entertainment. These two strategies all but ensured Universal's "minor status," according to Schatz.[28]

Putting Weber at the helm of his new production initiative, Laemmle demonstrated his continued faith in her abilities, especially where quality features were concerned. Indeed, she appears to have exerted considerable influence during her time as head of the story department, for it was rumored that she had been called in to recut the studio's megaproduction of The Phantom of the Opera after the film had tested poorly during early screenings.[29] Weber's tenure in the story department was evidently successful, for at the end of the year she signed a lucrative directing contract with the studio, bringing her "back to the Kleigs and the cameras" as one of the highest-paid women in the industry, publicity notices trumpeted.[30] Noting that women had been "noticeably absent" from the director's chair, Film Daily proclaimed that Weber, re-ensconced at Universal, was likely "to give the Griffiths, von Stroheims, Vidors, and others a run for their money."[31] Film Daily's prediction proved not far wrong. The two "specials" Weber subsequently wrote and directed for the studio, The Marriage Clause and Sensation Seekers, were both extremely well received. They established Billie Dove as a star and helped revive the careers of two older leading men, Francis X. Bushman and Warner Oland. Critics noted Weber's reemergence as a director, with one arguing that *The Marriage Clause* "demonstrates that her art has broadened during her absence." *Moving Picture World* heralded Weber's "triumphal return" to the screen. "She is back again now, near the very top," *Motion Picture* proclaimed, with another commentator noting that her "comeback" would "be pleasant to the believers in women's rights."[32] After *Sensation Seekers* received similar accolades, the *New York Times* suggested, "Many other directors would do well to study Miss Weber's style."[33]

In June 1926, amid this career revival, Weber married her second husband, Captain Harry Gantz, a retired army officer who owned a large citrus ranch in Fullerton, southeast of Los Angeles. Director Allan Dwan had introduced the two at the premiere of Cecil B. DeMille's *The Ten Commandments* in December 1923. Weber's close friend Frances Marion and her husband, actor Fred Thomson, served as witnesses at the civil ceremony in Santa Ana.[34] Born in South Dakota, Gantz had been a member of the Army Signal Corps, one of the "early bird" aviation pioneers. He was also a noted polo player. His first marriage to wealthy Santa Barbara socialite Beatrice Wooster Miller had ended in divorce in 1921, after which Gantz rarely saw his son, Peter, born in 1919.[35] In Gantz, Weber found "a companion as well as husband who is avidly interested in her work," according to one observer.[36] The couple frequently entertained Hollywood guests at their Fullerton ranch, dubbed El Dorado. A magnificent 125-acre property set in the hills above the city, the estate included an elaborate Spanish-style home, rose and cactus gardens, a tennis court, and a swimming pool. Weber's writing studio sat atop a tower gatehouse—"a sequestered work room, fixed up in the acme of comfort," glassed in on all four sides, described as her "sanctum," according to visiting reporters.[37] "Nobody can reach me there by telephone or in any other way," Weber explained. "I can thoroughly concentrate on my work— that is, when the lovely view will let me!"[38] "No wonder that girl is doing such excellent work just now," a reporter quipped.[39]

Following the excellent notices Weber garnered for *The Marriage Clause* and *Sensation Seekers, Hollywood Vagabond* wondered openly "why United Artists, Famous Players, Metro-Goldwyn-Mayer, DeMille or one of the other giant companies . . . have failed to avail themselves of the intelligence and experience of Lois Weber."[40] Indeed, shortly after completing *Sensation Seekers* in the fall of 1926, Weber was signed by United Artists' Joseph M. Schenck to write and direct an adaptation of *Topsy and Eva,* a popular vaudeville interpretation of *Uncle Tom's Cabin* featuring

Figure 43. Weber and her second husband, Captain Harry Gantz, at their El Dorado ranch in Fullerton, California, 1926. Author's collection.

legendary performers Vivian and Rosetta Duncan.[41] Schenck had been brought in to United Artists in late 1924 with the authority to reorganize the corporation and improve its fortunes after some poor showings.[42] He had initial successes the following year, securing Gloria Swanson as a partner and signing Samuel Goldwyn to a five-year distribution contract; Schenck also began acquiring a chain of theaters and signing contracts with outside theater franchises in order to improve the company's distribution prospects. United Artists released only eight pictures in 1926, but among them were such highly successful titles as Douglas Fairbanks's *Black Pirate*, Mary Pickford's *Sparrows*, and the Rudolph Valentino vehicle *The Son of the Sheik*. That same year Schenck formed the Art Cinema Corporation, a subsidiary designed to supply productions that would be distributed by

United Artists, setting up headquarters at the Pickford-Fairbanks Studio. *Topsy and Eva* was to be one of three pictures released by Art Cinema the following year. Weber's "come-back as a director was so eminently success-ful," *Photoplay* noted, that she "will join United Artists."[43] Alongside *Topsy and Eva,* UA releases scheduled for 1927 included titles from Pickford, Fairbanks, Charlie Chaplin, Gloria Swanson, Norma Talmadge, Buster Keaton—illustrious company for Weber indeed.[44] So successful were Schenck's efforts to revive the studio that by the end of 1928, United Artists boasted a $1.6 million surplus.

After signing on to direct *Topsy and Eva*, Weber declared, "It has been the dream of my life to make this picture," reflecting an evident fascination with Harriet Beecher Stowe's original novel.[45] In fact, *Topsy and Eva* marked Weber's second attempt to bring Stowe's work to the screen in less than six months. Prior to starting production on *Sensation Seekers* that summer, Weber had briefly been assigned to direct Universal's $2 million "Super-Jewel" adaptation of *Uncle Tom's Cabin*. Carl Laemmle handed Weber the project, Universal's biggest film that year and one of its most expensive productions to date, when Harry Pollard, the studio's top director, took ill early in the production. Press reports suggest that Weber threw herself into this assignment, putting aside *Sensation Seekers,* even interrupting her honeymoon, with the intention of making the picture "completely her own." One report suggested that she might "give the story a slightly differ-ent treatment from the one Pollard was considering," a distinct possibility given that Pollard had only shot a few scenes and had not completed casting; significant roles including Little Eva and Topsy remained to be filled.[46] Grace Kingsley even speculated that Weber might consider casting the Duncan sisters for these parts, given their popular vaudeville act. "They are the offi-cial Topsy and Eva of the world now. And I think she [Weber] thinks so too."[47] But within a month Pollard's health had improved, he was reassigned to direct, and Weber resumed production on *Sensation Seekers.*[48] When given the opportunity to adapt *Topsy and Eva* at United Artists just a few months later, Weber evidently jumped at the chance, taking a leave from Universal to work for Schenck in the hopes of completing her imagined adaptation of Stowe's novel. There are even indications that Weber left for UA before postproduction had been completed on *Sensation Seekers,* for she later claimed she was unhappy with the way the film had been edited.[49]

But in adapting the Duncan sisters' stage act, Weber found herself a far cry from Stowe's original. The Duncans' performance began as a twenty-five-minute vaudeville sketch featuring Vivian Duncan as the saintly, childlike Little Eva and her sister Rosetta in blackface playing a sprightly, mischievous Topsy. Playwright and lyricist Catherine Chisholm Cushing had enlarged the sketch in 1924, turning it into a three-act play featuring an enhanced cast and several song-and-dance numbers with original music and lyrics by the Duncans. One of the most popular musicals of the 1920s, *Topsy and Eva* played long runs in many major cities.[50] Rather than adhering strictly to Stowe's novel, the Duncans' act assumed audience knowledge of the material and focused on the relationship between the two girls, avoiding virtually any discussion of slavery, presenting racial caricature in its stead. While some critics praised the staging—one noted how Cushing's version "preserves the atmosphere" of Stowe's text "without going into any of the harrowing details"—most others objected to the translation, with respected theater critic Burns Mantle calling the production "a freak of the season."[51]

Adapting the Duncan sisters' already-controversial stage act to the screen proved difficult, and it appears there was growing tension between Schenck's conception of the project and Weber's own. If Weber's interest lay primarily in reworking Stowe's novel, Schenck apparently wanted to preserve comedic elements of the stage production, presumably to capitalize on the Duncans' popularity while distinguishing his own release from Universal's high-profile adaptation. Schenck initially hired Clarence Hennecke as "a 'gag' man" to assist Weber.[52] One of the original Keystone Cops, Hennecke received a screen credit for "comedy construction" and likely choreographed much of the physical humor. Weber ultimately left the project, claiming it had veered too far toward physical comedy. "To save my soul I couldn't help its developing into a farce with a great deal of slapstick in it," she said. "That wasn't the original plan, which was to make the story a comedy-drama. . . . I don't feel that I am the one to direct a farce, or a slap-stick comedy."[53] Anthony Slide speculates that the bald racism of the material might also have offended Weber. Del Lord, veteran director of Keystone shorts, was subsequently called in to replace her. Weber was asked to remain on the project to "supervise" dramatic scenes, but it is not clear that she accepted this position.[54] Lord, who had directed only one feature prior to *Topsy and Eva*, was apparently not quite the answer Schenck had imagined, for ten days prior to the film's premiere, none other than D.W. Griffith was called in to "straighten things out," as *Variety* put it.[55] Absent from Hollywood for nearly a decade, Griffith had just been hired by Schenck to work at United Artists. Revising *Topsy and Eva* became his first assignment after relocating to Los Angeles. Griffith's assistant, Raymond Klune, would later claim that the director "shot quite a few additional scenes and recut the greater part of it," but most Griffith scholars agree that this "overstates" the case.[56]

Given the different hands involved in the original stage production and its subsequent adaptation, not to mention Weber's early departure from the project, her contributions to the finished film are impossible to isolate.[57] Indeed, after explaining the material's convoluted path to the screen, *Variety*'s reviewer surmised that "it was just as well that no one was given screen credit for the adaptation as possibly no one would have craved it."[58] Dismissed as "a Sennett comedy *de luxe*," *Topsy and Eva* was considered "a bit crude and grotesque," faulted for its "cheap vulgarity."[59] By contrast, Universal's *Uncle Tom's Cabin*, released a month later, received high praise from critics, including those in the African American press, many of whom viewed it as "the highest achievement of blacks in cinema to date," according to Thomas Cripps, largely thanks to Noble Johnson's notable performance as Tom.[60] It became the sixth most popular film at the box office that year.[61]

Having twice failed in her attempts to adapt *Uncle Tom's Cabin*, Weber declared, "I am going to take my time, and when the chance comes to do that sort of thing I want to do, and know I can do, I'll do it." A report at the time claimed, "Hollywood is watching for her next move with interest."[62] Five months later Weber signed with DeMille Pictures, a relatively new independent studio. A trade piece suggested she had "yielded to an offer" from DeMille after having formally "retired from motion picture direction," but it is more likely that she sought the work herself, as was her pattern.[63] Weber was friendly with DeMille's partner Jeanie Macpherson and had visited the two on the set of *The King of Kings* in 1927. DeMille Pictures furnished Weber with an opportunity to work in a studio setting somewhat outside the control of the large conglomerates, one associated with prestige pictures. Housed in the Culver City studio Thomas Ince had built to resemble George Washington's Mount Vernon estate, DeMille Pictures represented a short-lived experiment in independent production by an influential, if somewhat controversial, figure in 1920s Hollywood. DeMille's "sex comedies," and later biblical epics such as *The Ten Commandments* (1924) and *The King of Kings* (1927), had ensured his reputation as a filmmaker who resisted Hays-era mores. Formed in 1925 after the director left Famous Players–Lasky, DeMille Pictures released forty-one titles in 1926–27, including "twenty-one popular novels, eight successful stage plays, [and] four widely read magazine stories," according to studio publicity, indicating the company's emphasis on presold properties with literary or dramatic heritage. In June 1927, following the success of *The King of Kings*, the company announced a deal with Pathé to produce four "superfeature pictures" for the 1927–28 season at a cost of $10 million.[64]

Visiting DeMille Pictures around this time, journalist Alice Williamson noted that Weber had been "welcomed as if she were a queen."[65] She had

Moguls of the movies — Cecil B. De Mille, Lois Weber, and Jeanie Macpherson, ...ped on the steps of the De Mille Studio. Miss Weber, a prominent producer and director, stopped in to discuss Mr. De Mille's next big production, "The King of Kings", a story of Christ written by Miss Macpherson.

Figure 44. Weber *(center)* visiting Cecil B. DeMille and Jeanie Macpherson at DeMille Pictures, 1927. Courtesy of L. Tom Perry Special Collections, Harold B. Lee Library, Brigham Young University, Provo, Utah.

been assigned to direct *The Angel of Broadway,* a vehicle for DeMille star Leatrice Joy penned by screenwriter Lenore Coffee.[66] After success crafting vehicles for Gloria Swanson and Vilma Banky, Coffee was included among the top screenwriting talents in Hollywood—"frank, interesting, radiating capability," according to one profile.[67] *The Angel of Broadway* was the third script Coffee had written for Joy in short succession. Already an established star for DeMille, Joy had first been noticed for her performance in *Manslaughter* (1922). The role of Babe Scott in *The Angel of Broadway* marked Joy's return to serious drama. "I'm so happy that Miss Weber is to make it," she declared, noting the director's talent for crafting "believable" female characters.[68] The "feminine triumvirate" behind the picture was not lost on a *Film Daily* scribe who dubbed Weber, Coffee, and Joy "L's Belles." Another quipped that the project was manifesting "alarming feministic tendencies" as a result of the women's collaboration.[69]

Figure 45. Weber on the set of *The Angel of Broadway* (1927) with cinematographer Arthur C. Miller. Courtesy of the British Film Institute.

The result received considerable praise: *The Angel of Broadway* was "mighty well staged and brilliantly directed," with one critic citing Weber's "easy, effortless, but shrewd direction" and another noting that she had "done exceptionally well."[70] Special praise was reserved for Weber's direction of Joy, deemed the actress's "best performance since *Manslaughter*" and "the best acting of her career." "Never has Leatrice Joy distinguished her performance by a more sincere faculty for acting," declared the *Los Angeles Times*. "It is to be hoped that Miss Weber will again direct Miss Joy, for the combination of their talents is an admirable one."[71]

Following Weber's success with *The Angel of Broadway* there were reports that she would direct additional pictures for DeMille, but these opportunities did not materialize as DeMille Pictures struggled. According to Robert Birchard, the films DeMille himself directed were successful at the box office, but "the studio's overall program did not perform well enough to sustain the company."[72] *The Angel of Broadway* does not appear to have been an exception. Although made for a relatively modest budget of $172,364, the picture grossed only $157,093.[73] Pathé Exchange absorbed

DeMille Pictures in 1928, and DeMille signed on with MGM, thereby ending his early experiment in independent production. When sound technology swept Hollywood later that year, the production landscape changed dramatically once more. Asked when she might direct again, Weber replied, "When I find a producer who thinks I have intelligence enough to be let alone and go ahead with my own unit."[74] It would be a long wait.

All in all, Weber had a far more active career in the 1920s than she is generally given credit for, proving herself adaptable to an evolving industry by producing well-received pictures for several studios following the breakup of her own production company in 1921. Despite her evident misgivings about an industry now dominated by vertically integrated studios, greater regulation, and the loss of many independent distributors, Weber experimented with the varied filmmaking models possible in this new climate. First she returned to her old studio, Universal, still under the tutelage of aging patriarch (and great Weber supporter) Carl Laemmle, but lately relegated to the status of a minor studio because of Laemmle's resistance to vertical integration. Weber then signed with two quasi-independent studios—United Artists and DeMille Pictures—both operating under the signature of figures powerful in Hollywood a decade earlier. In doing so, Weber managed to stage a comeback of sorts, garnering largely positive critical response while working mostly outside the conglomerates that now dominated the industry.

"EXIT FLAPPER, ENTER WOMAN"

Even as she struggled to find a place in Hollywood's changing production landscape, Weber mounted a vocal critique of the narrowing roles Hollywood offered to women on screen and off. Returning from Europe in 1922, Weber announced her interest in fashioning a new feminine "screen type" to counter the flappers and vamps who clouded Hollywood's imagination, calling them "cute little dolls dressed up in clothes that they do not know how to wear."[75] In contrast, Weber proposed the "womanly woman" who possessed "brains and character," was "neither wild nor prudish," and was, above all, "able to act." She had been inspired, she said, by actresses she had seen in Europe, women whose primary attributes were neither beauty nor glamour, but depth of personality and range of dramatic talent. "The real American girl is not a flapper," Weber contended, proposing instead female characters who were "thoroughly modern, sophisticated and up-to-date," but also "sincere" and "moral."[76] *Sensation Seekers*, she said, offered a counterpoint to other contemporary pictures about "our much discussed 'younger generation,'" which too often resorted to flat stereotypes of party-loving flappers. "The modern girl does not demand jazz parties, cocktails and late hours nearly as much as she demands freedom of thought and action," Weber proclaimed.[77] Summarizing Weber's aims, the headline for one interview pronounced, "Exit Flapper, Enter Woman."

Weber thus took seriously cinema's role in creating and circulating feminine ideals that she considered limiting, even harmful. Forward-thinking filmmakers, she proposed, could reject such hollow templates and fashion female characters capable of shifting expectations about gendered identity. Indeed, by the end of the "Exit Flapper" profile, Weber herself emerged as an embodiment of the modern feminine type she imagined, the "sort of woman she would like to see supplant the flapper and the overdressed Christmas tree on screen."[78] As evidence of Weber's efforts to refashion femininity on screen, consider the trio of films she made in 1926 and 1927—*The Marriage Clause, Sensation Seekers,* and *The Angel of Broadway.* Not only did these films reaffirm her artistic reputation, as we have seen, but they offered leading female roles designed to challenge Hollywood types in stories that contain remarkably reflexive meditations on the performance of femininity in Hollywood's glamour culture. In doing so, they also explored the simultaneous loss of a Progressive, socially engaged ethos with which Weber had been so associated early in her career.

The first of these films, *The Marriage Clause,* offers an object lesson on the fate of talented actresses in the commercialized celebrity culture of Broadway's theater world. Hollywood, though absent, is clearly evoked in the story of stage actress Sylvia Jordan (Billie Dove), forced to forgo marriage in order to pursue her career with near-disastrous results. Renowned theater director Barry Townsend (Francis X. Bushman) initially recognizes Sylvia's potential and helps her develop her talent. The two fall in love and plan to marry, but when producer Max Ravenal (Warner Oland) offers Sylvia a lucrative three-year contract, he inserts a clause forbidding her to marry. Hoping to win Sylvia for himself, the scheming Ravenal simultaneously refuses to renew Barry's directing contract. Sylvia tries to intercede on his behalf, but a jealous Barry sees her alone with Ravenal and assumes the worst. Fleeing to Chicago, he ends up on a path of alcohol-fueled self-destruction. The two are reconciled in the end after Sylvia collapses on opening night, having tried to perform while seriously ill in the hopes Barry would see her. Secretly present in the audience, Barry is able to rush to Sylvia's bedside in time to help her recover.[79] Genuine human relationships, they both discover, are more sustaining than the false intimacies created between star and audience.

Figure 46. Sylvia (Billie Dove) and Barry (Francis X. Bushman) discover the offending clause in her contract, backstage in *The Marriage Clause* (1926). Courtesy of the Billy Rose Theater Collection, New York Public Library for the Performing Arts.

If the plot at first appears to proffer "the old familiar complication of the marriage versus the career," as one critic put it, in fact *The Marriage Clause* rejects this accustomed moral.[80] Rather than showing a woman unable to juggle competing demands of work and family, the film demonstrates that Sylvia's bond with Barry sustains them both, professionally and personally. Ravenal's attempts to sever their union artificially, by firing Barry and preventing the couple's marriage, only produces catastrophe—Sylvia's near-fatal illness and Barry's descent into alcoholism. Rather than warning women *against* combining careers and marriage, Weber's script, in fact, *endorses* such arrangements as mutually beneficial for women *and* men.

Barry and Ravenal, who discover Sylvia together in the film's opening scene, each attempt to control and shape her, but in very different ways. Barry does so as a director interested in nurturing her talent—a relationship that expresses itself in love. Ravenal is interested primarily in Sylvia's beauty and seeks to market her as a star—a relationship that expresses itself principally in lust. Ravenal's lascivious appetite for Sylvia, symbolized as he ostentatiously gnaws and sucks on greasy chicken bones in the opening scene, manifests itself in a desire to possess her sexually, to remove her from supportive personal and professional ties, and to commodify and commercialize her image for profit. Cloaked in the ornate costumes he selects, Sylvia loses the original, "genuine" self that attracted Barry in the first place; Ravenal has constructed an empty star in its place, so hollow that Sylvia herself becomes ill. The triangular configuration between Sylvia and the two men foregrounds the film's withering assessment of stardom and celebrity, a motif clearly referenced in the film's original title, "Star Maker," as well as a later incarnation, "The Show World." Both make plain the film's allegorical portrait of Hollywood's star factory.[81] Universal's marketing campaign played up the film's "alluring atmosphere of back stage life" and "the glitter of luxurious settings" visible therein, but such superficialities are ultimately contested in *The Marriage Clause*, shown to be particularly damaging to female stars vulnerable to exploitation and commodification.[82]

Weber's next project, *Sensation Seekers*, about a high-living socialite who renounces her hedonistic lifestyle for a more ethical path, is less clearly an allegory for Hollywood. The story's heroine, Egypt Hagen (Dove again), is not an actress like the characters in *The Marriage Clause* and *The Angel of Broadway*; yet, as a well-known socialite, Egypt lives her life on a kind of media "stage" where her every move is watched and reported on—written up in newspapers' society columns, then gossiped about by her friends and neighbors. In this context, then, *Sensation Seekers* offers another frank meditation on female celebrity.

Egypt "smokes, drinks and goes bad with six times the diligence of any possible society girl, determined to go to hell as fast as she can get there," according to *Time*'s reviewer.[83] When she meets Reverend Lodge (Raymond Bloomer) at the outset of the film, they seem to have little in common. But after she is arrested in a raid on the "Black and Tan" speakeasy, Lodge appears with her in court at her mother's behest. Deeply embarrassed, Egypt is inspired by his simple act of kindness and becomes eager to learn from his example. When her fiancé, Ray Sturgis (Huntly Gordon), mocks her predicament by showing up in a costume made from newspaper headlines about her arrest, Egypt further distances herself from his set and begins spending more time with Reverend Lodge. The clergyman, sympathetic to her desire to lead a more principled and purposeful life, begins advising her, but parishioners spread malicious gossip, reimagining their intellectual and spiritual conversations as illicit romantic liaisons. Lodge's

Figure 47. Egypt (Billie Dove) taunts her father (Phillips Smalley) in *Sensation Seekers* (1927). Courtesy of the British Film Institute.

reputation is nearly ruined as a result. "Egypt was making the best of her opportunities," an intertitle proclaims. "Gossip was making the worst of them." Seeking to avoid further scandal, Egypt agrees to marry Ray Sturgis after all and leaves with him on his yacht. But Sturgis dies when their boat is caught in a terrible storm; Lodge arrives just in time to save Egypt. With the approval of his bishop, the two are married in the end.

While the film risks being lumped together with the rash of late-1920s indictments of flapper culture, it is worth remembering that the "sensation seekers" evoked in the film's title are just as much Egypt's neighbors and fellow churchgoers (eager for a scandal between their pastor and a handsome young woman) as they are Egypt's own "ultra-jazzy wealthy set."[84] Intercutting equates the younger crowd's social gatherings—at the speakeasy, the Huntington Bay Country Club, and an impromptu ukulele and gin party in the woods—with the ruthless behavior of Egypt's neighbors, gathered on a veranda across from the country club to watch the "sinful" goings on inside, gossiping mercilessly in church, and crowding around to read newspaper coverage of Egypt's arrest. There is little difference, the film asserts, between those who seek sensation through alcohol or sex and those who seek it through scandal and gossip mongering. Egypt's attempts to leave this claustrophobic and limited world demonstrates her desire to transcend the usual narrative about society girls. Hoping to escape both her insular "jazzy" set and the hollow loop of gossip, she is receptive to the alternative that Reverend Lodge represents, just not sure how to achieve it. Weber, explaining the character she intended to create, said, "I think the young women of this country today want to be individuals, and have freedom of thought and action. They have brains and character. That is the kind of girl I am going to show in my story."[85]

Like Egypt and Sylvia Jordan in *The Marriage Clause*, Babe Scott (Leatrice Joy), the jaded nightclub headliner "of doubtful virtue" featured in *The Angel of Broadway*, is a woman challenged by celebrity, theatricality, and performativity.[86] Without principles at the outset of the story, Babe ridicules the Salvation Army in her stage show only to embrace its philosophy in the end. Visiting an army mission to gather material for her routine, she meets truck driver Jerry Wilson (Victor Varconi). The two fall in love, but when Jerry finds out about Babe's parodic nightclub act, he rejects her and seeks out his old friend Gertie, a prostitute. Near death from a suicide attempt, Gertie dispatches a neighbor to find someone who can pray with her; the neighbor stumbles upon Babe, still in her Salvation Army costume. Mistaken for a real evangelist, Babe is brought to Gertie's bedside, where she finds herself moved by the dying woman's plight. As she prays with Gertie in earnest, her own faith is restored. Witnessing this episode, Jerry forgives Babe and asks her to marry him.[87] Electing a life of service and compassion in the end, Babe explicitly rejects the sphere of performance and artifice she had inhabited at the Alla Ba Ba nightclub, a New York speakeasy presided over by Big Bertha (May Robson), a character reviewers compared with real-life contemporary Texas Guinan.[88] Critics such as the *New York Times'* Mordaunt Hall complained that the nightclub scenes were "not in good taste," objecting that "it was hardly necessary to present girls in exaggerated costumes."[89] Yet these scenes clearly demonstrate a pervasive sexual commodification of women that Babe ultimately refuses. Babe's stage persona consists of an elaborate costume and flowing blonde wig. A scene backstage foregrounds the construction of this artifice by duplicating Babe's image in a mirror reflection, showing the performer gazing listlessly at her own likeness. Babe's nightclub routines are staged to show audiences surrounding and encasing identically clad female dancers—a neat visual encapsulation of Babe's commodification. If anything, Hall's prim objection in the *Times* demonstrates how watching these performances on screen, rather than live in a speakeasy, only enhanced the effect. Although

Figure 48. Audiences surround and encase identically clad female dancers at the Alla Ba Ba nightclub in *The Angel of Broadway* (1927). Author's collection.

Hollywood itself is never directly evoked, the Orientalized Alla Ba Ba nightclub is a thinly veiled stand-in for the contemporary film industry, just as the theater world was in *The Marriage Clause* and the gossip industry was in *Sensation Seekers*.

Each film's plot thus offers an explicit commentary on Hollywood glamour culture, presenting a heroine who rejects stardom and artifice in favor of a more genuine engagement with others, choosing intimacy, humanity, and spirituality over a life in the public eye, and choosing altruistic acts over a self-absorbed quest for fame. Weber's veiled indictments of Hollywood star culture were released at a time of heightened scrutiny of Hollywood's sexual economy. In early 1927, *Photoplay* published Ruth Waterbury's two-part exposé, "Breaking into Hollywood," followed shortly thereafter by Adela Rogers St. Johns's series on Hollywood's "port of missing girls."[90] Even so, Weber's critique was not always well received. While she garnered top praise for her direction, reviewers frequently complained about what they perceived to be the films' outmoded or overly sentimental plots. The *Los Angeles Times,* for instance, felt the "regeneration" plot in *The Angel of*

Broadway was "tired," and *Variety*'s reviewer complained that the film was "weepy with religion" and appeared aimed directly "at the tear ducts of the great sentimental American public."[91] This "stuff the hoi polloi likes" might play well in the "hinterland," *Variety* suggested, but for New York audiences it would be "a dud," a sentiment also echoed in *Film Daily*. "Those who know their New York will smile at the antique atmosphere, but it will no doubt go great out in the open spaces."[92] Others complained that "gobs of sentiment" marred *The Marriage Clause* or that *Sensation Seekers* was "a bit too preachy."[93] As Lea Jacobs demonstrates, there was a pronounced decline in American tastes for sentiment during the 1920s, and esteemed directors of the previous decade, such as Weber and Griffith, were now often called on the carpet for playing to the emotions of their audiences.[94] Weber's attempts to refashion her flapper characters into intelligent, thoughtful, and socially engaged citizens smacked to many as "hackneyed" or "antique."[95]

One certainly cannot argue that these films are wholly feminist or progressive by today's standards—each heroine is redomesticated in the end and removed from the workforce and the public eye, her sexuality contained in a marital and familial sphere. Yet Weber's efforts to devise alternative roles for women on screen in the 1920s ought to be recognized. Films like *The Marriage Clause, Sensation Seekers,* and *The Angel of Broadway* explore how women might reject a culture of sensation and commodification in favor of a more genuine, ethical (even Christian) engagement with the world. Even as this trio of films focused on female celebrities and performers, showing how a superficial culture of stardom and glamour separates women from what is truly meaningful in their lives, the films might also be read as figurations of another female artist—the filmmaker—struggling to maintain a progressive filmmaking practice in the face of Hollywood's ascending commercialization. How might a filmmaker who had sworn off the "heavy dinners" she made earlier in her career, and who remained fearful of the control exerted by profit-minded studio heads and moralistic censors, maintain her interest in bringing a sense of social engagement to the screen? Thus Weber's feminine ideal was not wholly "Victorian," as Thomas Slater would have it, but remained invested in the goal of challenging contemporary culture, particularly, in these cases, any suggestion that the commercialization of sexually objectified women might be considered "modern."[96] Instead, Weber proposed an alternate conception of contemporary womanhood, based on an intelligent, socially aware engagement with the world—perhaps best exemplified in the role of a female filmmaker seeking to address the era's mores on screen and working behind the scenes to effect change in Hollywood.

Within her critique of Hollywood glamour culture, Weber also succeeded in refashioning the persona of actress Billie Dove, star of both *The Marriage Clause* and *Sensation Seekers*. Writing in *Picture Play* Myrtle Gebhart observed the new tenor of Dove's roles, praising the "interesting, womanly characters" Weber had fashioned. In the *Los Angeles Times* Katherine Lipke noted that roles Weber had written for Dove helped the actress "break the mold of the sweet young heroines" she had played in the past. Whereas previous directors had "never let her do anything else but look lovely," Weber "saw the vast emotional possibilities in Billie," Alma Whitaker declared. It had taken "a woman to bring out in celluloid the full talent of an actress who heretofore has been more or less purely decorative," another critic noted. Under Weber's direction Dove became "virtually overnight an actress of the first rank."[97] Dove herself remembered that after *The Marriage Clause* was released, she received offers from "every studio in the business."[98] In fact, before filming on *Sensation Seekers* was complete, she had signed a five-year contract with First National to appear in a series of star vehicles. By the end of the decade she would be voted the most popular actress in Hollywood, alongside Clara Bow. Remarking on the "confidence" Weber instilled in her players, Dove claimed she would be happy to work with Weber "any time, all the time."[99] In fact, later in life she remembered Weber as "the best director I ever had. . . . If I'd had anything to say about it, I would have had her direct all my pictures. I had a lot of men directors that I liked too, but she understood women."[100]

Weber's investment in Dove—writing nuanced female characters for her and directing some of her best performances—complicates the filmmaker's narrow reputation as a "star maker" during these years. Yes, Dove did receive greater recognition after working with Weber, but their collaboration was not principally designed to turn Dove into a celebrity. Rather, Weber's interest lay in nurturing Dove's acting talent and creating intelligent roles for women on screen, roles that countered the "cute little dolls" and "overdressed Christmas trees" she saw elsewhere. These roles, moreover, lay at the heart of film plots pointedly critical of Hollywood's star factory. To suggest Weber's primary achievement lay in being a "star maker" was to miss the point of her work entirely. When she discovered a performer's talent, she said, "all my thoughts are to bring it out, make my actors as great as they can be."[101]

On screen and off, then, Weber worked hard to improve conditions for women in Hollywood, writing roles more focused on character complexity than surface beauty, directing actresses in order to achieve their best performances, making films critical of Hollywood's glamour industry, and

Figure 49. Weber directing Billie Dove on the set of *The Marriage Clause,*
1926. Courtesy of the Kobal Collection.

offering herself as a model of an intelligent, socially conscious artist working behind the scenes. Some evidence suggests that attention was paid to
her accomplishments and those of other women prominent in the industry,
especially the growing cadre of female screenwriters who dominated the
field in the late 1920s. Weber, for instance, was included among the "Big
Women of the Screen" profiled in *Screenland,* alongside the likes of screenwriters June Mathis and Jeanie Macpherson—all of whom were said to
possess "talents that are not expressed with long eyelashes," unlike so
many other women showcased in the magazine.[102] Weber also featured
prominently in a lengthy profile of "Women's Work in Motion Pictures"
that dubbed her "one of the most notable contemporary creative figures in
the screen world." Cinema "would be far behind its present state of development, both artistically and commercially, had it not been for the achievements of many women in its ranks," *Motion Picture* reminded its readers.[103] Announcing "Bright Girls Aren't Hiding Their Lights under
Bushels," a newspaper item noted that "many more women than men" had
written the most successful recent films, and it included Weber among their
ranks.[104]

Even as women working in the movie industry received some measure of attention in the late 1920s, particularly those employed as screenwriters, Weber encountered increasing obstacles as a director. She continued to speak out against the sexism rampant in Hollywood, noting the challenges faced by female directors in particular—challenges that, she insisted, were relatively new. Citing her desire to "come forward in behalf of the many talented women," she penned a two-part syndicated newspaper article calling for more female filmmakers. Her thoughts had been sparked in response, she wrote, to one high-ranking industry executive's confident assertion that "women do not make good motion picture directors."[105] So few women had been accorded an opportunity to direct, Weber pointed out, that "we have no average by which to judge" their suitability. "Women entering the field now find it practically closed," she lamented, noting that when she had started in the business two decades earlier, everyone was so busy that "no one had time to notice whether or not a woman was gaining a foothold." Now, she said, "men bosses are a bit self-conscious about engaging women for any line of work that they consider men's work," including directing. They were less inclined to give women directing opportunities routinely accorded male camera operators or assistant directors, and then less likely to tolerate mistakes when those opportunities were given to women.

Setting her recent experiences against the years she spent under "ideal conditions" at her own production company, Weber described how alien it now was to be working with men who did not know her and furthermore "suffered resentment and hurt pride at being placed under a woman's direction."[106] Having become accustomed to the "royal welcome by any man of the older generation of studio workers," she found herself having to "'show them' all over again." It took the first ten days of production to win over a recent crew, she confessed. Few women directing for the first time could withstand this "battle ground," Weber noted. "A male beginning would not be so handicapped." Weber's advice to aspiring female filmmakers in another interview from this period—"Don't try it"—has been taken to indicate that she did not believe most women capable of directing. She was, instead, pointing out how difficult it had become for women to break into directing. So "few get the opportunity," she said, that one must approach the task with "superabundant vitality" and a "hard mind"; otherwise, as woman, "you'll never get away with it."[107]

During this period of sustained critique of the industry both on screen and off, Weber maintained her long-standing ties with women's organizations outside Hollywood. In speeches and appearances before clubwomen, she promoted twin objectives: improving the climate for women working in the movie industry and, thereby, expanding the female types produced and circulated by that same industry. A guest of honor at the annual banquet of the Southern California Woman's Press Club in 1927, Weber allied herself not only with a group of influential women but also with a body that recognized, as she did, the interconnectedness of media and progressive reform. A professional organization for more than two hundred newspaper and magazine journalists, the club included such politically active figures as Clara Shortridge Foltz, publisher of *New American Woman,* and Harriet Barry, editor of *Woman's Bulletin,* a publication of the Woman's Progressive League of California.[108] Seeking to advance women in journalism, the Press Club provided a professional network for female writers, editors, and publishers while furnishing opportunities for members to educate themselves on a range of topics including women's suffrage, international peace efforts, and media technologies such as radio and cinema. The club's educational mandate "often dovetailed with its members' interests in reform," according to historian Nan Towle Yamane.[109] At a 1929 luncheon meeting of the Women's University Club of Los Angeles, Weber participated in a panel of women who spoke about their experiences working in the film industry, including actress Anita Page and others who worked as publicists, theater managers, script readers, and researchers. An affiliate of the American Association of University Women, the Los Angeles chapter had more than five hundred members, all college-educated.[110]

For all the work Weber put into challenging industry orthodoxies and insisting on a place for women in the movie business, there were constant reminders that Hays-era Hollywood was becoming a bastion of male power. Efforts to "masculinize" the industry begun a decade earlier had been almost entirely successful. Weber remained, for instance, one of only two women admitted to the Motion Picture Directors' Association—a membership granted to her in 1916 as an exception to club policy.[111] (Ida May Park was made an honorary member in 1923.) When the Academy of Motion Picture Arts and Sciences was formed in 1927, Weber was its only female director and one of only a few women in positions of leadership in what Pierre Sands stresses was "an exclusive, invitational, honorary organization."[112] Weber had a prominent role as secretary to the Executive Committee for the Directors' Branch from its inception in the spring of 1927, serving alongside Reginald Barker, Sidney Olcott, Rowland V. Lee, and J. Stuart Blackton, who chaired the committee. The committee took on tasks such as drafting a standard contract for freelance directors.[113] Weber also participated in a conference sponsored by the Academy in July 1927 to discuss industry cost-cutting measures; she was the only woman present at the "man-to-man

Figure 50. Weber's early involvement with the Academy of Motion Picture Arts and Sciences marked her continuing influence in Hollywood, as well as her increasingly isolated status as a female director.

discussion," which brought together twenty top directors, as well as leading producers and studio heads.[114] Into the late 1920s, then, Weber continued to exert influence and command respect among her peers, even as she exercised her authority in an increasingly masculine field.

Not only was Weber more active in the 1920s than has previously been thought—writing and directing critically acclaimed films, continuing to develop acting talent, assuming leadership roles in the fledgling Academy, and maintaining high-profile public appearances—but she also used her position to resist many of the changes sweeping the fully consolidated, vertically integrated movie business. Uneasy with Hollywood's glamour culture and the limited opportunities available to women outside stardom, she wrote allegorical scripts critical of this culture, crafted complex roles for female protagonists, and spoke openly about the limits of a movie culture defined largely by hollow flappers at the expense of women with "brains and character." Critical of a production climate she felt was becoming hostile to female directors, she wrote newspaper columns and spoke up repeatedly in interviews, lamenting the changes she saw in the industry, calling on everyone from executives to crew members to again give women opportunities in the director's chair.

"A CHILD SHALL LEAD THEM"—JEWEL AND LITTLE EVA

Weber's interest in promoting alternative visions of modern femininity on and off screen was complicated by two films from this period that betray a fascination with an older, strikingly different, female type. Alongside alt-flappers like Egypt and Babe, Weber's heroines included two young girls: Little Eva, featured in both of her attempted adaptations of *Uncle Tom's Cabin*, and Jewel, the preadolescent heroine of *A Chapter in Her Life*. At first glance Weber's depiction of asexual and sentimentalized girls might appear retrograde, a remnant of Victorian child worship, but it becomes more legible when framed against her broader commentary on Jazz Age femininity. Far from marking a retreat to outmoded Victorian ideals, youthful heroines like Jewel and Little Eva staked a place for a female-centered culture resistant to the effects of consumption and self-commodification. In fact, *A Chapter in Her Life* might even be considered a prelude to the critique of Hollywood's glamour industry that Weber would launch a few years later in *The Marriage Clause, Sensation Seekers,* and *The Angel of Broadway*.

Young heroines like Jewel and Little Eva emerged within sentimental popular fiction of the late nineteenth century, material written by, for, and about women, as Jane Tompkins famously put it.[115] Though nearing the end of its influence by the 1920s, sentimental culture represented a strong resistance to masculinist modernism. One of the most influential texts of the period, Harriet Beecher Stowe's *Uncle Tom's Cabin* (1852) remained popular well into the early decades of the twentieth century, circulating in multiple formats in print, on stage, and on screen, so familiar it could easily be considered "the best-known story of the era," according to Linda Williams.[116] Weber's attachment to two cinematic adaptations of this material—*Topsy and Eva*, with the Duncan sisters, and Universal's 1927 megaproduction—marked a brief resurgence of Stowe's text on screen after a lull of nearly a decade. In fact, Universal's adaption was, according to Barbara Tepa Lupack, "the last of the significant Tom films," for though new versions were invariably discussed over the coming decades, none were made—an indication that Stowe's novel had reached the peak of its cultural influence.[117]

The central place that *Uncle Tom's Cabin* maintained in women's culture of this era was affirmed when one observer noted how significant it was that Weber, a woman, had been granted an opportunity to "paint the stirring sequences on the screen" from Stowe's "Nation-rending novel."[118] Sentimental fiction like *Uncle Tom's Cabin* has often been taken to task for failing to engage real political action and effect real political change, despite its inclination to take on weighty issues like human slavery. Yet, as Shirley Samuels explains in *The Culture of Sentiment*, there is an essential "paradox of sentimentality," a "double logic of power and powerlessness." Set apart from the realm of overt political action, sentimental culture nonetheless presented an "affective alternative" that gave "emotional significance" to social change, she argues.[119] Indeed, tracing the varied iterations of *Uncle Tom's Cabin*, Williams stresses that it "revolutionized the American melodramatic stage" by introducing challenging subjects such as slavery and racism and featuring African American characters in central, not marginal, roles.[120] Viewing *Uncle Tom's Cabin* in this light, it is not difficult to imagine the appeal it must have held for Weber: it was one of the most respected and influential novels in American history, had been central to the abolitionist movement, and was firmly rooted in women's culture. This was Weber's métier. She, too, aspired to create popular, melodramatic, even sentimental narratives by, for, and about women, narratives that tackled the most sensitive cultural debates and were ultimately able to inspire profound social change. One can understand why Weber described adapting Stowe's novel as the "dream of my life."[121]

Less familiar now than *Uncle Tom's Cabin*, *Jewel: A Chapter in Her Life* (1903) was a best-selling novel by Clara Louise Burnham, part of a trilogy that proselytized Christian Science and was endorsed by the movement's founder, Mary Baker Eddy. A popular and prolific author, Burnham promoted the faith in her fiction and explained the positive impact it had had on her own life in her 1912 book, *A View of Christian Science*.[122] Weber was evidently keenly interested in Burnham's work, for her 1923 adaption of *Jewel* marked a return to the author's oeuvre: not only had she made a previous film version for Universal—1915's *Jewel*—but she had also penned the screenplay for Universal's 1914 production of Burnham's novel *The Opened Shutters* (1906).[123] Weber's attraction to Burnham's novels has led some to surmise that she was herself a Christian Scientist, but Anthony Slide found little evidence to support this claim. Weber apparently attended some Christian Science services in Los Angeles, along with other women prominent in the industry, but showed no further commitment to the cause.[124] Rather, Weber's attraction to the work of "matriarchs" like Stowe, Burnham, and Eddy might be seen as an attempt to preserve a form of feminine influence in popular culture.

Eddy's teachings, Burnham's popularization of them, and subsequent screen adaptations were all part of a larger "New Thought" movement in the late nineteenth and early twentieth centuries promulgated by many women, Eddy's followers and rivals alike. Historian Beryl Slatter frames the New Thought movement in relation to struggles between white middle-class men and women for cultural dominance, arguing that New Thought discourse offered "explicitly gendered concepts of mind, matter, selfhood, and desire." Through the New Thought movement, she claims, "women struggled to create a new kind of white woman's self or ego in the midst of a culture that was rapidly changing the ground rules of gender."[125] Interest in Christian Science and other New Thought paradigms spread quickly in the early decades of the twentieth century, receiving considerable attention in the popular press.[126] It reached a zenith in 1908 when, seeking an even wider platform, Eddy founded the *Christian Science Monitor* newspaper, part of what Stephen Gottschalk describes as a "significant reorientation" of the movement "away from the personal and private to the social and universal." In doing so, he says, Eddy aligned Christian Science with "the ideal of social concern then assuming so important a place in Protestantism."[127] Cast in this light, then, Weber's interest in Burnham, Eddy, and the wider field of New Thought becomes clear, for it coincides with her long-standing commitment to woman-centered social justice, dating back not only to the cycle of social-problem films she produced at Universal in the mid-1910s, but ultimately to her background in "Church Army work," an experience she frequently framed as her point of origin as a politically engaged filmmaker.

Promoting a woman-centered culture focused on social change, *Jewel: A Chapter in Her Life* and *Uncle Tom's Cabin* are also notable for their child heroines. With girls like Jewel and Little Eva at the heart of their narratives, Burnham and Stowe employ what Karen Sánchez-Eppler calls "the rhetorical power of childhood," investing their young protagonists with a profound capacity to influence adults in their lives. Many forms of nineteenth-century American popular culture, she explains, drew on the "immanence and innocence" of children, valuing the "emotional work" they could perform in expressing an "idealized capacity for love and joy."[128] Burnham's novel, for instance, begins with the title-page inscription "And the child shall lead them," a quote from the Old Testament Book of Isaiah that neatly encapsulates late-Victorian attitudes toward children—girls in particular. As preadolescent protagonists, both Jewel and Little Eva occupy a space beyond modern forms of capitalism and sexuality, a locus from which they can question many basic assumptions. They each possess a naïve innocence that enables them to see beyond strictures that bind adults around them—human slavery in Little Eva's case, and in Jewel's case a more subtle emotional vacancy caused by fixations on wealth and social status. Although Jewel and Little Eva evoke older, more sentimental modes of girlhood that might seem at odds with Weber's avowed determination to present women of substance on screen, their status apart from adult society provides a space from which to challenge it.

Still, sentimental, child-centered narratives produced by women like Burnham and Stowe faced mounting disapproval in the first decades of the twentieth century. Indeed, Ann Douglas finds a "revolt against the matriarch" at the heart of modernist discourse. Rejecting a culture they felt had been overly "feminized," she contends, "the moderns aimed to ridicule and overturn everything the matriarch had championed," including middle-class piety, racial superiority, and sexual repression. "Opposing every form of 'sentimentality,' they prided themselves on facing facts, the harder the better."[129] Perhaps not surprisingly, *Uncle Tom's Cabin* became an object of particular scorn, singled out by critic H. L. Mencken in his critique of "sentimental romanticism."[130] It had become, by then, "the apotheosis of sentimental narrative," according to Amy Schrager Lang.[131] Lea Jacobs traces a similar shift in critical taste surrounding popular movies in the 1920s, noting a "rejection of sentimentality" by many reviewers and commentators.[132] Although Jacobs does not attribute any particular gender bias to these discussions, she includes several examples demonstrating that reviewers disparaged particular titles by suggesting they were suitable only for women and children, as if these patrons occupied a distinct minority among moviegoers, rather than an overwhelming majority.

"Mother" Eddy herself also came under attack during these years, as the subject of a less-than-flattering 1929 profile subtitled *The Biography of a Virginal Mind*. Eddy's supposedly "frustrated" sexuality, menopausal mood swings, and general "hysteria" all featured prominently in the book, exemplifying the repudiation of femininity Douglas finds building throughout the decade.[133] Flapper culture, that icon of Jazz Age modernity, was itself anti-maternal, Douglas points out. A *New York Times* piece titled "Flapping Not Repented Of" celebrated the flapper's ability to "take a man's view as her mother never could," she notes. A feminist symposium published in the *Nation* in 1926 included pieces such as "Confessions of an Ex-feminist," "The Autobiography of an Ex-feminist," and "The Harm My Education Did Me," complaining about the "bitterness" of maternal rule.[134] Even flapper fashion was relentlessly masculine, Douglas notes: short hair, cloche "helmet" hats to mimic soldiers of the Great War, open consumption of cigarettes and alcohol once solely for men, and a newly popular hipless, flat-chested androgynous silhouette.[135] Decidedly nonflapper, Jewel and Little Eva marked an alternative embodiment of femininity, rooted in an older, woman-centered popular culture now so keenly disparaged.

Weber developed her girl heroines in the mid-1920s, between the apex of Mary Pickford's phenomenal popularity in the late 1910s and Shirley Temple's rising stardom in the early years of the Great Depression. At the time, reviewers were already beginning to question Pickford's continued preference for playing juveniles on screen.[136] In praising Weber's decision to cast eleven-year-old Jane Mercer in the role of Jewel, rather than a "juvenated" adult, *Moving Picture World*'s reviewer made a sly allusion to Pickford's recent screen appearances. By then thirty-two, the actress had played a teenage Tess in *Tess of the Storm Country* the previous year and the nine-year-old title character in *Little Lord Fauntleroy* the year before that. As Gaylyn Studlar puts it, by this point Pickford had effectively become "a child impersonator," an object of nostalgic and pedophilic longing.[137] Jane Mercer's Jewel, by contrast, was "not the usual frolicsome, curly-haired darling of the screen," the reviewer noted, suggesting not only a favorable comparison with Pickford but a more instrumental use of a child performer.[138]

A Chapter in Her Life demonstrates Weber's complex investment in childhood, best understood when read in relation to her critique of feminine norms then emerging in celebrity culture. At the outset of the film Jewel (Mercer) comes to stay with her grandfather Everingham (Claude Gillingwater) while her parents are traveling overseas, setting the story in motion. Estranged from his son and daughter-in-law, the old man has never met his granddaughter and does not know that her parents, a former "drunkard" and "working girl," have reformed themselves through an unnamed "faith." Carrying this faith with her into her grandfather's cold, emotionless household, Jewel manages to transform not only Everingham, but all of the other adults living there as well—his other son's aged widow, Madge (Frances Raymond), and her grown daughter, Eloise (Jacqueline Gadsden); his prim, stern housekeeper, Mrs. Forbes (Eva Thatcher); and her son, Ezekiel (Ralph Yearsley), secretly an alcoholic. In the end Everingham comes to value love and familial bonds over his single-minded pursuit of wealth. Mrs. Forbes, cold to Jewel from the beginning and blind to her son's drinking problem, comes to place her maternal responsibilities above her obsession with social propriety. Madge stops trying to marry her daughter off to the highest bidder, finally approving of Eloise's beloved suitor, Nat Bonnell (Fred Thomson). Eloise also finds fulfillment not only in her love for Nat but in caring for the little girl. And with Jewel's help Ezekiel combats his drinking problem. Though never identified as such, Christian Science is the religion that enables these profound transformations.

The Everingham household is bleak, cold, and emotionless, its gloomy, restrictive spaces filled with heavy wooden furniture and dark-paneled walls. So large are the furnishings and vast are the rooms that human figures appear dwarfed and isolated there. In her design of the film Weber

Figure 51. Madge (Frances Raymond) and Eloise (Jacqueline Gadsden) eavesdrop as Mrs. Forbes (Eva Thatcher) directs Jewel (Jane Mercer) to her room, in *A Chapter in Her Life* (1923). Courtesy of the British Film Institute.

appears to have closely followed illustrations from the 1903 edition of Burnham's novel by well-known illustrators Maude and Genevieve Cowles, lending the settings a period character. Indeed, were it not for Eloise's modern gowns, the story might take place at the turn of the century, rather than the early Jazz Age. The older inhabitants of this forbidding household—Mr. Everingham, Madge, and Mrs. Forbes—are all associated with emotional distance, an overinvestment in social propriety, and an accumulation of wealth at the expense of meaningful, loving relationships. Charged with caring for Jewel after she arrives, Mrs. Forbes refers to her only as "the child," constantly scolding the girl and withholding her affection. Madge is a similarly repressive force within the household, rejecting her daughter Eloise's attraction to her beau, Nat. Deeming him "poverty-stricken" and therefore unsuitable, Madge puts her daughter on display at every opportunity, hoping to secure an alternate engagement to wealthy Dr. Ballard (Robert Frazer)—or, as Eloise puts it, "dressing me up to throw at that man's head." Later Madge even tries to suppress the maternal instincts that overcome her daughter when young Jewel falls ill.

Depression and alcoholism are the effects of this repression, if Eloise and Ezekiel are any indication. Kept from her sweetheart and trotted out, silently, for Dr. Ballard, poor Eloise is miserable. She channels her suppressed emotions inward, filling the house with maudlin piano music and pouring her heart out in letters to Nat. Like Eloise's music, Ezekiel's drinking simultaneously represses and expresses his deepest insecurities and is associated with dangerously suppressed emotions. Covering his breath with a supply of onions he keeps readily at hand, he too is the victim of a repressive force more concerned with class decorum and wealth than individual happiness or spiritual fulfillment. If his mother, Mrs. Forbes, is associated with a disciplinary gaze, she ultimately falls victim to a kind of blindness. The voice of propriety in the home and a self-appointed authority on raising children, she fails to recognize her own son's alcoholism until it is almost too late.

Arriving at the Everingham estate, Jewel proves an energizing antidote, questioning its routines and cheerfully upending all of its accustomed hierarchies. When told she's sitting in her grandfather's chair, thereby breaking house rules, she tilts her head in amazement, smiles, and says, "They are *all* his, aren't they?" as the sun creates a halo effect around her head. In a household stymied by emotional repression, Jewel is a novelty, saying exactly what she feels at any moment and pointing out assumed structures of power. After Mrs. Forbes cruelly informs her that "young ladies cannot expect attention from gentlemen unless they are pretty," Jewel, looking quizzical, replies, "Somebody married *you*, Mrs. Forbes." Jewel's honesty and openness are associated with natural surroundings and many of her scenes are staged outdoors on estate grounds, rather than inside the dim, confining mansion. Sitting near a waterfall with her doll, Anna Belle, Jewel says "Castle Discord is far away now," delineating both a literal and figurative distance from her grandfather's house.

Jewel's sheer physicality also challenges the stifling environment: she climbs into Everingham's lap at every opportunity and aggressively plants kisses on his face. Whereas other characters cluck their tongues or roll their eyes instead of speaking up, play maudlin tunes on the piano instead of voicing their sorrow, or disguise the smell of alcohol with onions, Jewel's straightforward expression of emotion and love are particularly pronounced. This is no more so than in her interactions with Anna Belle, for she speaks candidly with the doll and showers her with an affection missing in her own life. After Mrs. Forbes has refused to let Jewel say goodnight to her grandfather and has turned out the girl's light without so much as a word, Jewel turns to her doll, kisses her warmly, and says, "Darling Anna Belle, did you think I had forgotten you? Did you think you were not going to have anyone kiss you good-night?" As Marcia Landy stresses, Jewel's "imaginative power" to breathe life into her doll, to invent the fairy-tale world of Castle Discord, and to evoke her mother's absent presence are all key to her redemptive force, her ability to transcend her current, desperate situation, and her ability to inspire others to do the same.[139]

It is significant not only that Jewel arrives from outside the household with a fresh perspective but also that her perspective is explicitly a child's. She belongs neither to the older generation of Everingham and Madge nor to Eloise's and Ezekiel's younger generation—those young adults suffering the full consequences of emotional and spiritual repression. As a young girl, Jewel is in a liminal state, on the verge of transformation herself but clearly capable of transforming others as well. Ultimately, Jewel's tendency to utter simple yet powerful truths is associated with her pure, unassuming faith. When Madge expresses concern for Jewel's parents overseas, she replies, "I know God will take care of father and mother." After her grandfather advises her not to spend all of her money, she tells him, "More will come to me when I need it."

Although Christian Science is never explicitly named in the film, its principles are clearly espoused and would likely have been recognized as such by contemporary viewers. Much of the philosophy, however sketchily cast, is conveyed by Jewel herself, her innocent intentions and pure faith lending authenticity to the teachings. The girl's mother is frequently invoked as the conduit for these sentiments. In a letter to Jewel she advises her daughter to make "a stepping-stone of every trial," stressing the importance of "helping others" who are "unhappy in their hearts"—a central tenet of Christian Science. When helping Eloise recover from her depression, Jewel says simply, "This is how my mother learned to be glad," handing her a book, presumably Mary Baker Eddy's *Science and Health with Key to the Scriptures*. Later Eloise describes only "Jewel's wonderful faith," but the transformation it has enabled is profound. She is emboldened to set things right with Everingham and to reunite with her sweetheart against her mother's wishes. Jewel is also able to help Mrs. Forbes and her alcoholic son, saying, "This seems very terrible, but my father had this sickness and it can be healed." Most striking, of course, is Jewel's insistence on self-healing over medical intervention. Believing that "hate" had crept into her heart and made her ill with a fever, she politely but resolutely refuses all treatment from Dr. Ballard, then miraculously recovers. In the final moments of the film we see Jewel sitting on her grandfather's lap surrounded by the fruits of her efforts: Eloise happily canoodling with her beloved Nat, Ezekiel sober at last and still at work in the stables, and Madge sent away from the estate with a modest income. Surveying all of this, Jewel sings the first bars of a Christian Science hymn: "How blest are those whose hearts are pure, from guile their thoughts are free." The next refrain, not transcribed on the intertitle, would be, "To them shall God reveal Himself, they shall Love's glory see."

References to Christian Science in *A Chapter in Her Life*, then, are both obscure *and* plainly evident. Viewers familiar with the faith or with Burnham's novels would recognize the philosophy immediately. Yet, by not naming Christian Science outright, Weber and her co-writer, Doris Schroeder, left open the possibility that other faiths, other programs, other approaches could effect the same dramatic change. The point of the story seems less to proselytize Christian Science per se than to promote a woman-centered value system that embraces a maternal caregiving ethos while rejecting capitalism and class propriety. These are associated with a commodification of women on the marriage market and a weakening of masculinity by alcohol abuse and emotional distance. Valuing wealth and social status above all else has caused Everingham to single-mindedly pursue profit over familial bonds; Madge to auction off her daughter to the highest bidder, suppressing all happiness in the poor young woman; and Mrs. Forbes to snobbishly deny Jewel any human affection while neglecting her own son. These failed parents—failed *mothers* in particular—are redeemed by and through Jewel's love. If Eloise provides a glimpse into a bleak future, a preview of what might happen to Jewel if her genuine emotions, "pure" faith, and imaginative power are stifled at the hands of Madge and Mrs. Forbes, the key to Eloise's "recovery" lies in embracing her own maternal instincts by loving and caring for Jewel. Jewel, then, is the vehicle for this much more than Christian Science.

If *A Chapter in Her Life* remained coy about Christian Science, reviewers did not. *Moving Picture World* noted helpfully that the film portrayed "that modern religion which teaches that faith and right living is a safeguard against physical and spiritual ills" and that "many people have read the book." In Los Angeles the *Times* bluntly decried the film's "unmasked propaganda in favor of Christian Science."[140] As Lea Jacobs notes of many reviews during this period, critics often distinguished between their own (cultured) sensibilities and less cultured views presumed prevalent among the filmgoing public. Admitting "probably there will be a lot of folks who will think 'Jewel' the picture is quite a picture," Chicago's Mae Tinée declared, "Myself? Wasn't crazy about it."[141] Railing against the film's "gospel of cheer, peace, and good will" and claiming it had "no place" on the screen, the *Los Angeles Times'* reviewer announced, "I do not like that kind of thing," once again personalizing a distaste for sentimentality.[142] *Variety's* review is especially revealing in its frankness. Calling the production "too sweet for words," the trade suggested its "saccharine Pollyanna theme ... may appeal to the matinee children and women but is rather tepid for average consumption."[143] Women and children did, of course, constitute the vast majority of moviegoers during the early 1920s, but in *Variety's* telling construction, they were cast outside the mainstream as tangential filmgoers, at best, whose tastes were wholly questionable and antithetical to the modern medium. The rhetorical alignment of women and children—*matinee* children, no less—with *A Chapter in Her Life* demeans the film through association with femininity and sentimentality. Moreover, the specter of Pollyanna, that ever-optimistic youngster from Eleanor H. Porter's bestselling 1913 novel had already become shorthand for the sort of feminized, sentimental culture so despised by "cultivated" movie reviewers. Her specter was evoked not only in *Variety's* review but by the *Los Angeles Times* as well, both critics evidently haunted by the 1920 production starring none other than Pickford herself.

Perhaps anticipating criticism of this sort, Universal's marketing campaign generally downplayed the film's child heroine and its sentimentality, focusing instead on Burnham's novel and its female-centered storyline. Most ads and posters featured Eloise, rather than Jewel, with taglines implying a rather conventional story about sexuality and romance in the life of an adult woman. "Why was she ashamed of this chapter in her life?" one ad asked. "Was it a secret love affair? bitter hate? jealousy?" Another proclaimed, "Now she learned the bitter truth! The pages of her life were blank."[144] Not only do these ads steer potential filmgoers far from the actual plot, but they suggest that a chapter from Eloise's life will be portrayed, rather than from Jewel's, as the novel's original title makes clear. Jewel is not even pictured in many of the surviving ads and posters; if she is, her gaze, like that of other characters, is directed toward Eloise. Burnham's novel was highlighted in virtually all publicity, as design concepts played on the meaning of "a chapter in her life" and championed Universal's 1923 "Big Ten" program of literary adaptations. Yet not once did studio publicity mention Christian Science or even a generic term such as *faith*. Following the studio's lead, many press notices also emphasized themes of "love" and "personal transformation," with the *Chicago Defender* describing the film, rather typically, as "a lesson in happiness."[145]

Appearing in 1923, not long after such films as *Too Wise Wives, What Do Men Want?* and *The Blot, A Chapter in Her Life* was promoted much as those titles had been—with an emphasis on the woman-centered narrative and ties to women's fiction. Weber's name featured prominently as author. Universal elected not to stress the shift this production represented, away from the subject of bourgeois marriage and femininity and back toward broader social themes, preferring to suggest continuity instead. Perhaps most significant, none of the surviving promotional materials note that the film was a remake of Weber's highly successful 1915 Universal production, *Jewel*. When the studio distributed films made by Lois Weber Productions in the late 1910s, Weber's earlier Universal releases had often been touted, *Jewel* usually included among them. In the late teens, Weber's earlier social-problem films had retained their currency; but by 1923, this was apparently no longer true. Although Weber's name continued to feature prominently, her earlier productions were not listed. She had become just another filmmaker under contract at Universal, nothing like the star director she had been at the studio seven years earlier. Her persona had been successfully transformed into that of a "woman's director" making films for a marginal audience.

Universal's marketing department sidestepped the thorniest aspects of *A Chapter in Her Life*—its child heroine, its sentimentality, its connections to Christian Science, and its rebuke of the vain pursuit of wealth and social status—and instead promoted another, bland woman's picture on love and romance. But Weber evidently had something else in mind. When considered alongside the trio of films she made later in the decade—*The Marriage Clause, Sensation Seekers,* and *The Angel of Broadway*—*A Chapter in Her Life* might also be seen as a film that scrutinizes the effects of capitalism and a consumer economy on young women. Like later titles, *A Chapter in Her Life* turns away from materialism toward spirituality, rejecting a consumerist objectification of women in favor of social and political engagement.

At first glance, Weber's interest in youthful heroines like Little Eva and Jewel may seem contrary to her desire to put women of substance on screen, female characters who countered the "decorative" flappers then dominating popular culture. However, a closer look reveals that Jewel and Little Eva are not so far removed from later heroines such as Egypt, Babe, and Sylvia. Each opposes a femininity rooted in sexuality, one associated almost exclusively with self-commodification, in favor of a femininity rooted in social consciousness and progressive change. A femininity, in other words, that rejects surface qualities of glamour and wealth in favor of a "genuine" ethos. Moreover, girls like Jewel and Little Eva counter the anti-maternal spirit of both oversexed flappers *and* older women like

Maude Everingham and Mrs. Forbes, more concerned with social propriety and class privilege than caregiving. Both of these young heroines represent a maternal ethos as it is most broadly conceived, embodying the best qualities of a woman-centered politics rooted in civic caretaking and social justice. Weber's depiction of figures like Jewel and Little Eva, though ultimately less successful than her other projects in the 1920s, suggests her continued investment in woman-centered progressive movements. It shows her continued attempts to find a path around Jazz Age consumer culture, which she perceived to be antithetical to women, families, and spiritual health. Her interest in these characters resonates not only with her condemnation of Hollywood flapper culture, but also with the significant ties she maintained with women's organizations outside the industry and her ongoing critique of the ever more male-dominated business culture of the studios.

RETURN TO SCREEN WORK

After the transition to sound in 1927–28 and the industry's economic collapse in the early years of the Depression, Weber found it unusually difficult to find work. In fact, she did not work at all for nearly five years after she finished *The Angel of Broadway* in 1927, despite the favorable notices it had received. Living in semi-retirement on the El Dorado Ranch she shared with Harry Gantz in Fullerton, Weber regularly hosted figures from the entertainment industry—"many a gay Sunday afternoon party has been held there," one observer remarked.[146] At one such event Weber and Gantz served barbequed meats to guests gathered informally at long outdoor tables placed under the trees. Guests included women with whom Weber had worked, including Lenore Coffee, Leatrice Joy, Priscilla Dean, and Claire Windsor, as well as actor Jean Hersholt and novelist Margaretta Tuttle.[147]

Without film work Weber focused her energies on a growing real estate empire. Since the mid-1920s she had been investing her considerable fortune—estimated at around $2 million—in properties throughout the Los Angeles region. In addition to El Dorado and her Ivar Avenue home in Los Angeles, Weber invested in the new "Castellammare" development overlooking the ocean in Pacific Palisades, and the Miramar Estates Country Club in Santa Monica, and in 1929 she purchased the Park Lane Apartments in Los Angeles. She had become, according to the *Los Angeles Times,* "an extensive holder of realty in Southern California."[148] An avid gardener, Weber was also active in the Los Angeles Plant, Flower, and Fruit Guild; the magnificent succulent gardens Gantz designed at El Dorado were twice fea-

Figure 52. As opportunities to direct became harder to come by, Weber turned her attention to a growing real estate empire, a detour noted in this 1930 cartoon from the *Los Angeles Times* (February 2, 1930).

tured in gardening magazines.[149] She also devoted significant time to high-profile philanthropy, raising money for the Los Angeles Art League; working with the Assistance League, a charitable organization run by prominent Angeleno women; continuing to devote time to the Girls' Studio Club; and serving as one of the official state hostesses for the 1932 summer Olympics, held in Los Angeles.[150]

Weber's real estate transactions were at first associated with her renown—she was named among the "film notables" purchasing properties at Castellammare, for instance.[151] So much so that by the time she bought the Park Lane Apartments, Weber was known almost as much for her property holdings as her filmmaking career, as a 1930 newspaper cartoon makes clear. Two fashionable young women gathered outside the building exclaim excitedly, "Miss Weber is directing it too!"[152] But Weber's real estate ventures did not always prove successful, and she was shortly consumed with financial woes and legal struggles. She and Gantz had purchased property in the Castellammare development, intending to build a "palatial home" there, but the development did not progress as planned, and Weber and Gantz chose not to build on the site.[153] Weber's investment in the Park Lane Apartments was particularly fraught. She had purchased the large six-story, sixty-five-unit apartment hotel on the corner of New Hampshire and Fourth Streets with plans to renovate and redecorate each unit and thus generate substantial rental income. However, she soon filed suit against the realtors, alleging she had been misled about the property's value and its monthly revenue and claiming financial losses in excess of $300,000. Weber ultimately lost the suit in 1930.[154] That same year her Hollywood home was robbed for the fourth time in less than twelve months. Thieves made off with $25,000 worth of valuables, jewelry, and furs while she was staying at the El Dorado Ranch in Fullerton.[155] Liquidating some of their real estate holdings, she and Gantz eventually sold El Dorado to a wealthy orange grower in 1931.[156]

With the help of her friend Frances Marion, Weber's professional fortunes began to reverse in the spring of 1932 when she was signed to help write a screen adaptation of the stage play *Cynara*. Nearly five years after she had wrapped production on *The Angel of Broadway*, Weber finally returned to full-time screen work. *Cynara* had enjoyed a successful Broadway run that season, and Samuel Goldwyn purchased the rights, intending it as a vehicle for his stalwart male lead Ronald Colman.[157] Marion, recovering from what she later described as severe "nervous tension" following a divorce from her fourth husband, was easing back into work and had loaned herself out to Goldwyn to adapt *Cynara* on the condition that Weber also be hired to assist. Marion was at an influential point in her career, having recently won two Academy Awards: Best Adapted Screenplay for *The Big House* (1930) and Best Story for *The Champ* (1932).[158] As Marion's renown grew, she often acknowledged her friend and mentor, telling an interviewer in 1930, "My beloved Lois Weber encouraged me to write for the screen."[159]

Weber did not receive credit on the final script for *Cynara*, and it is difficult to determine the extent of her work on the project, but reports at the time indicate that Marion built her own script on an earlier adaptation penned by Weber.[160] A press release noted that Weber's experience with scripts involving "triangular marriage complications" had prompted Marion to enlist her help. "Samuel Goldwyn was so impressed by Miss Weber's enthusiasm and the first rough treatment," the press release continued, "that he invited her to become a member of his staff."[161] Press notices soon trumpeted Weber's "comeback" and her "return to screen work," describing how she emerged from the "retirement of ranch life at Fullerton." Grace Kingsley speculated, "She may later direct for Goldwyn." Weber herself was more cautious: "Just what I shall do following the completion of this contract, I don't know as yet. But I expect to come back to the film business."[162]

A story of marital infidelity, the script for *Cynara* is structured around a flashback in which a husband tells his wife about an affair he had with a shopgirl, a liaison that nearly ruins their marriage. When his lover commits suicide, the husband refuses to divulge information about her multiple sexual partners, leaving himself open to accusations of her "ruination" as he gallantly preserves her "reputation," under the film's outmoded mores. Ready to leave him at the outset of the story, the man's wife forgives him in the end and decides to remain married. Despite a sexual double standard that modern audiences might find trying, the material includes themes that had historically interested Weber, such as the ruinous effects of male philandering on women—wives and mistresses alike—and the hazards of a double standard for young, unmarried women, themes she had explored as recently as *What Do Men Want?* in 1921, in Universal features like *Shoes* and *Where Are My Children?* and as far back as her Rex shorts. The pre-Code environment of 1932 would have allowed the script to be especially frank about issues such as female sexuality and suicide in ways that would not be possible under the Production Code Administration just two years later. King Vidor directed the project when it began production in August, starring Colman as the husband and Kay Francis as his wife. The picture evidently underwent some revisions after less-than-successful test screenings in the fall, then was finally released in December to generally favorable reviews.[163]

Despite speculation that Weber's work on *Cynara* marked something of a comeback for the fifty-three-year-old filmmaker, offers did not immediately flood in. Industry trade papers contained reports of Weber having been signed to various directing contracts, but none seemed to have borne fruit. She was, for instance, reportedly signed to direct for the Aubrey M. Kennedy Pictures Corporation in mid-1932; the company was said to be planning a roster of pictures with "idealistic themes," according to its general manager, Jules Bernstein, an old ally of Weber from Universal. Jeanie Macpherson had also been signed to write "Power of the Cross."[164] Influential figures a decade earlier, both women found themselves struggling in the early 1930s. In the end, Weber had to wait almost a year until she was hired once again at Universal in the spring of 1933, this time as a talent scout "to interview and test screen aspirants" under Carl Laemmle, Jr.'s plan to "develop as many potential stars during 1933 as possible," according to the studio's press release.[165] "Junior," Laemmle's son, had taken over production at the studio in 1928 and had begun a program of offering "opportunity contracts" to actors, many of whom had significant background on the stage but were new to the movies. Weber tested and recommended both male and female performers, signing at least two players, though press reports often stressed her experience discovering and cultivating female talent. The *Hollywood Reporter*, for instance, claimed that she would "find and develop only feminine players" under her new contract."[166]

This new, rather unusual assignment framed Weber's talents in a particular manner. Universal publicity drew attention to her long association with the studio, noting she had started there twenty years previously in 1912, but stressed "her remarkable reputation for finding new faces for the screen," rather than her long record of successful writing and directing. Press items noted that Weber had been "one of the three women successful as film directors" (the others being Dorothy Arzner and Dorothy Davenport Reid) and that in this capacity her main achievement had been as the "discoverer" of Ella Hall, Mary MacLaren, Claire Windsor, and Billie Dove.[167] So this new assignment amplified Weber's already-considerable reputation as "star maker," while obscuring her other accomplishments as screenwriter and director. Indeed, some press accounts went so far as to *equate* screen testing with directing, at least for women, presenting female directors as little more than talent scouts for pretty, able young starlets.

Shortly after she was hired, Weber interviewed some 250 young women from drama schools, universities, and amateur and professional stock companies, a dozen of whom were deemed promising enough for screen tests. Assessing these aspirants, Weber maintained the importance of proper voice training and "cultural refinement," the former being far more important since the latter could be more easily overcome. "Girls with beautiful faces and forms seem to be able to register emotions—but when they open their mouths, they completely spoil the effect," Weber stated, noting that the project of finding suitable acting talent had been significantly complicated by the introduction of recorded dialogue. "Until 1926, picking potential stars and even making them in one picture was a simple matter. Since the coming of talkies this is impossible. The voice breaks down the illusion."[168] Famed Yale Drama School instructor Constance Welch endorsed

Weber's comments later that year in an article published in the journal *American Speech*.[169]

Weber's assignment screen-testing young women thus built on her long-standing interest in encouraging stage actors to enter motion pictures—a cause she had championed since the early 1910s when she and Smalley left the theater to make movies. And though the appointment capitalized on her reputation as a "star maker," Weber herself pushed against this narrative, stressing instead the need to look beyond surface beauty for acting talent, a trained voice, and "cultural refinement." This latter comment marks Weber as dated, even classist, but it demonstrates her continuing effort to populate the screen with educated and intelligent women, not just decorative bodies, an objective she had begun in earnest over a decade earlier with her "Exit Flapper, Enter Woman" interview.

Weber's work on a script for Universal the following year—an adaptation of Edna Ferber's short story "Glamour: 24 Hours in the Life of a Great Actress"—indicates that Weber's growing critique of gender, fame, and sexuality in Jazz Age Hollywood were literally written out of the picture. Ferber's original story, "Glamour," had been published in *Hearst's International Cosmopolitan Magazine* the previous year, then had appeared in her 1933 short-story collection, *They Brought Their Women*, as the film adaptation was being prepared.[170] Ferber, a best-selling author and Pulitzer Prize winner, had a string of popular novels to her name, among them *Show Boat* (1926) and *Cimarron* (1929), along with several successful stage plays co-written with George S. Kaufman, including *Stage Door* (1926) and *Dinner at Eight* (1932). In what J. E. Smyth dubs "the Ferber franchise," her literary and dramatic works were frequently adapted for the screen, becoming celebrated films as well.[171]

Universal's adaptation of "Glamour"—always referred to as *Edna Ferber's Glamour*—was part of an ambitious program of new features planned for the 1933–34 season; the studio aimed to release thirty-six pictures, considerably more than the previous year's crop of twenty-six. Many were to be adaptations of well-known novels, stage plays, and musicals. Within this program *Glamour* was conceived as one of the studio's grander efforts, alongside an adaptation of Fannie Hurst's *Imitation of Life*, pictures based on the work of celebrated women writers and calculated to appeal to female viewers.[172] It was first announced that Sarah Y. Mason would write the adaptation of "Glamour."[173] Mason had recently completed an adaptation of *Little Women* (1933) for George Cukor at RKO and would go on to pen some of the decade's most prominent women's pictures, including *Imitation of Life* (1934) and *Magnificent Obsession* (1936), both directed by John Stahl at Universal, as well as King Vidor's *Stella Dallas* (1937). Early reports also suggested that Universal had approached Gloria Swanson about playing the lead, another sign of their ambitions for the project, but the role was ultimately played by Constance Cummings, then briefly affianced to "Junior" Laemmle.[174]

It is significant, therefore, that Weber was assigned to adapt such a high-profile project. But telling, as well, is that she remained associated with women's pictures, rather than the social-problem films she had made for the studio nearly two decades earlier, especially during these pre-Code, early-Depression years when some in the industry turned back to social-issue films. Reports at the time indicate that Weber had been originally slated to direct the project as well, and that her contract with Universal now included the possibility of her directing "one or more pictures for that company during the coming year." But that task was ultimately handed to William Wyler, and Weber took over the screenplay adaptation instead.[175] It is not clear what happened, but given that Weber had not directed a picture for six years and had never directed a sound film, it is reasonable to surmise that the studio was more confident entrusting the project to the younger Wyler, who had been directing steadily at Universal since 1926. Wyler's biographer Jan Herman suggests that though the filmmaker had been pitching an adaptation of *Jezebel* to Junior Laemmle, a project he would go on to direct at Warner Brothers five years later, Wyler was instead assigned to direct *Glamour*.[176]

Weber's interest in adapting Ferber's story must have been keen, for the author explored many themes Weber had addressed in her own scripts and public comments over the past decade. A behind-the-scenes portrait of stage actress Linda Fayne, the story is ultimately a deconstruction of the concept of glamour. Ferber's opening line places this theme front and center: "Of all the words in the English (or any other) language, Linda Fayne most hated the word glamorous."[177] Later Ferber adds, "Like most successful actresses, Miss Fayne was not beautiful. That is, she possessed few of the attributes which the adolescent taste of America usually demands of its beauties ... her great following, baffled by this mask which gave the effect of beauty without actually being beautiful, fell back on the trite word, glamorous, and clung to it."[178] By presenting a twenty-four-hour snapshot of the life of a busy actress rehearsing a new production while still performing on stage in another, the story deconstructs the façade of "glamour," revealing instead the labor, sacrifice, self-doubt, and sheer exhaustion that goes into maintaining an actress's career. The frontispiece accompanying the story's original publication featured an actress pulling off a mask, highlighting Ferber's attention to masquerades of beauty and glamour.

During the spring of 1933 Weber wrote three drafts of a continuity script adapted from Ferber's story, which at one point was apparently to have been renamed "Footlights." Weber's drafts contain a considerable amount of dialogue not included in the original story, suggesting her facility with writing dialogue—a new craft for the silent-era screenwriter. The three drafts also contain very detailed camera directions absent from later drafts, suggesting Weber's continued interest in directing and old habits of writing projects that she would later direct, indicating her practice of thinking about projects visually and cinematically as she was writing.[179]

While Ferber's original story had been restricted to a twenty-four-hour period, Weber expanded this original concept to produce a more sustained portrait of the conflicting demands of work and family life on a successful actress. In many ways Weber's script harkened back to the themes she had explored in *The Marriage Clause,* the last picture she had adapted and directed for Universal back in 1926. *Glamour's* heroine, Linda Fayne, is a renowned stage actress whose husband, Chet, a ruined "wheat king," resents her success and is often left to care for their son on his own. "Poor thing," Linda says of their boy, Sonny, "he hardly knows me." After the premiere of yet another successful play, the couple argues and they discuss the possibility of a divorce. Chet leaves the next morning. But Linda soon gets word that he is dying. Although she rushes to his side and vows to give up acting for good, her husband dies in the final scene.

If Weber's adaptation of *Glamour* recalls themes familiar from *The Marriage Clause,* in fact the two projects could not be more different. The earlier picture, as demonstrated above, rejects shallow ideas about how it is impossible for women to combine a successful career with family life, insisting instead upon the *necessity* of combining the two. In contrast, Weber's adaptation of *Glamour,* however ironic its title, suggests just the opposite, reinforcing platitudes about husbands and children "neglected" by working women, even punishing Linda by having her husband die in the end. Weber's screenplay was certainly not her best, yet it does show her interest in themes omitted from subsequent drafts: the stress placed on a marriage when the woman is the major breadwinner; male feelings of inadequacy as a result; the conflicted loyalties of a professional woman, highly focused on her craft, but also committed to her family. If the death of Chet in the end seems to punish Linda for harboring interests and ambitions outside family life, the body of the film does allow viewers to ponder her situation with considerable sympathy.

Weber submitted a third and final draft of the continuity in May 1933 and was subsequently removed from the project for reasons that remain unclear, her work uncredited in the final print. Screenwriter Doris Anderson submitted an entirely new continuity draft in December 1933, with rewrites added by Gladys Unger the following January; shooting began later that month.[180] The film ultimately made from this final screenplay bears little relation to Weber's initial drafts. Rather than focusing on challenges faced by married working women, the plot shifts predictably to a story about the rise of a young would-be stage star, charting her romances along the way. Although Linda becomes estranged from her husband, the man who had originally propelled her career, she reconciles with him in the end, but only after giving up her own career and watching the death of their son—a typical Hollywood ending, perhaps, but a significant departure from both Ferber's original and Weber's initial adaptation. As one reviewer summed it up, the final version of *Glamour* served up a lesson about "a woman mistakingly [*sic*] following the will-of-the-wisp—the glamour of the theater and its personnel—rather than a truer and more rational course to love and happiness." In the end, *Variety* dismissed the production as "unoriginal" and "just a good woman's picture."[181] For his part, Wyler later remembered it only as "kind of a screwy picture" and "a real disappointment."[182]

After she had been dropped from *Glamour*, Weber quickly signed on to co-write and direct a low-budget independent film, *White Heat*, in the summer of 1933, seizing her first opportunity to direct in six years. Despite the *Hollywood Spectator*'s confident assertion that the assignment would ensure Weber's "restitution to the ranks of directors who can be entrusted with important pictures," *White Heat* became her last film, the only one she directed in synch sound.[183] An interracial love story, *White Heat* was the first film shot on the Hawai'ian island of Kaua'i, one of only a handful of Hollywood features filmed on location in the Hawai'ian islands in the 1930s, and one of the few to use its location as the actual setting for the story, rather than as a stand-in for a more generic "tropical" locale.[184] Dismissed in recent histories and undervalued at the time of its release, *White Heat* was an unusually ambitious production, noteworthy for the way it tackled complex themes of interracial relationships, class, and femininity within the formulaic constraints of a "B" production.

Sometimes described as an "exploitation" film, *White Heat* is best understood within the context of B-film production in the early sound era. Produced by Seven Seas Corporation and released by Pinnacle Productions, a low-budget distributor for several other racially charged melodramas in the early sound era, *White Heat* was made at "the height of quickie filmmaking" in the early 1930s. As Brian Taves explains, the voracious need to fill double bills and Saturday matinees created a ready market for quickly and inexpensively made films. Indeed, close to three-quarters of all features produced in the 1930s were low-budget productions, made either by "B" units at major studios or by one of hundreds of low-budget outfits like Seven Seas and Pinnacle on so-called Poverty Row. It was these pictures, not high-profile "A" features, that fueled Depression-era Hollywood, Taves points out. Many actors, directors, and other personnel moved back and forth between low-budget independents and the major studios in these years, as "B films became the domain of numerous individuals with long, prolific careers."[185] Weber's contemporary Marshall Neilan, for instance, also wrote and directed a feature for Pinnacle in 1934, a "voo doo" picture called *Chloe, Love Is Calling You,* and Dorothy Davenport Reid was also directing on Poverty Row, making exploitation films like *The Road to Ruin* and *The Woman Condemned,* both also released in 1934. "B" productions also provided experienced directors and cinematographers with opportunities for creative freedom outside the constraints of studio filmmaking. Director Robert Florey recalled, "As long as I remained on schedule, I could shoot all the angles and set-ups I wanted, and move the camera whenever and wherever I wanted to, in the limited time I had."[186] Like many of her contemporaries, then, Weber evidently seized the opportunity to write and direct a film on such a weighty topic as interracial romance, however limiting the constraints of a B production, especially given the opportunity to work on a sound picture. Seven Seas Picture Corporation had been recently formed by William Fiske III and Count Alfredo Carpegna, the latter described as a "famous Italian sportsman and aviation enthusiast" and a friend to Douglas Fairbanks. Knowing Weber was looking for work, Fairbanks's wife, Mary Pickford, and her close collaborator Frances Marion, recommended their mutual friend be hired as the company's first director. Given Weber's track record they assured Fiske and Carpegna that she would complete the picture on time and on budget.[187]

Weber adapted the script for *White Heat* from a screenplay originally written by James Bodrero, later known for his work on such Disney musicals as *Fantasia* (1940) and *The Three Caballeros* (1944). As a boy, Bodrero had spent summers at his grandparents' sugar plantation in Hawai'i, a likely source for the story material.[188] Originally to have been called "Cane Fire," *White Heat* made extensive use of location shooting on Kaua'i, utilizing spectacular local scenery and existing structures in place of expensive sets. Some thirty actors, crew members, and technicians traveled to the island by steamship for the three-week shoot, bringing with them cameras, lighting equipment, sound trucks, and electrical generators, since the island's own electrical current was unreliable. Isadore Bernstein, former general manager at Universal and a longtime Weber ally, served as general manager for the production. Weber's husband, Harry Gantz, was on hand to sign checks and manage the finances. Also sailing with the cast was the film's wealthy backer, Alfredo Carpegna.

Weber, along with Bodrero and Seven Seas producer William Fiske III, arrived a week ahead of the cast to scout locations and hold casting sessions for local talent. Hundreds of local extras were cast in the film, including many native Hawai'ians, and several Hawai'ian performers were chosen for minor roles in the film, including noted hula dancers and female chanters.[189] Scenes were shot at a local homestead, an old Hawai'ian house in Waimea Valley, and at the Waimea Sugar Company, along with many outdoor locations in Waimea Canyon and Olokele Falls. A local newspaper noted at the time that many of the sites selected for the film were "visited by only ambitious hikers and adventurers." "When the picture is shown on Kaua'i," the report speculated, "most of the people on this island will for the first time view these places, accesses to which are dangerous even to the most courageous."[190] A *New York Times* reviewer later noted that although the low-budget production was "technically inferior to the studio product," it "compensates for this by the reality and beauty of its Hawaiian setting"; *Film Daily*'s reviewer added, "Among independent productions, this rates way up near the top of the ladder." *Billboard* dubbed it "one of the best South Seas pictures to hit the screen in a long time."[191]

Weber shot *White Heat* with noted cinematographer Alvin Wyckoff. Known for his groundbreaking work on *The Cheat* (1915) and many other early DeMille pictures, Wyckoff had been blacklisted by the majors following his efforts to unionize cinematographers in the late 1920s. He subsequently brought his considerable talent to low-budget productions like *White Heat* and several features and serials produced at the Poverty Row outfit Mascot Pictures in the early 1930s.[192] Amid the picturesque Kaua'i locales, Weber and Wyckoff staged ambitious large-scale action, such as rainstorms and a spectacular final blaze in the sugarcane fields. Actress Virginia Cherrill remembered particularly grueling shooting conditions, especially scenes in which her character was assaulted by torrential rains and raging winds that swept up mounds of red dust.[193] Apparently proud of what she was able to accomplish with her modest production budget, Weber said afterward that the film "was not a hit but will not lose any money."[194] Based on her success, producer William Fiske elected to shoot two subsequent Seven Seas productions "against their natural background," in Hawai'i as Weber had done with *White Heat*.[195]

Working within the parameters of a low-budget, sensationalized "South Seas" production, Weber managed to make a film that dealt with interracial

Figure 53. Leilani (Mona Maris) holding William (David Newell) after she rescues him from a fire in the sugarcane field in *White Heat* (1934), Weber's last film. Courtesy of the British Film Institute.

romance in an unconventional manner and to make a woman of color the film's active heroine. Although the claim is difficult to confirm with absolute certainty, one historian believes *White Heat* to be the very first Hollywood film to present a successful interracial relationship that survives the end of the film. At the outset of the story William Hawks (David Newell), foreman of a Hawai'ian sugar plantation, falls in love with Leilani (Mona Maris), a native Hawai'ian, and begins living with her as his wife. Called back to company headquarters in San Francisco, William subsequently falls in love with and marries a white woman, his boss's socialite daughter, Lucille Cheney (Cherrill). When William returns to Hawai'i with Lucille, Leilani is displaced. But bored and unhappy on the island, Lucille reignites a romance with her visiting ex-fiancé (Hardie Albright), who promises to take her back to San Francisco. As the two men begin fighting over her, Lucille sets fire to the cane fields, escaping with her lover. William is hurt as he battles the blaze, trying to save the crop and the plantation. Leilani rescues him and the couple is reunited in the end.[196] Initially produced under the title "Cane Fire," the film was renamed *White Heat* for release, a baldly sensational title whose double entendre simultaneously drew attention to the story's inter-racial dynamics, its tropical locale, and its sexual tension.[197]

Sensational it surely was, for interracial romances were officially forbid-den by the Hays Office during these years. But relationships between white men and brown women were often overlooked, especially if contained in exoticized "South Seas" locales, as Susan Courtney has demonstrated. By infantilizing native women, rendering them passive and servile, such films "reinforce and eroticize white male privilege through their tropical sce-narios of master and servant, voyeur and spectacle," she argues.[198] Among such films there are few other contemporary examples in which a native woman is shown to be a love interest and domestic partner superior to a white woman. Here *White Heat* appears relatively unique in its treatment of race. Indeed, the *New York Times'* reviewer objected that the film suc-cumbs to an "easy but unfair method of vilifying the white girl" in order to play up Leilani's "loyalty and unselfishness," a complaint that underscores the film's unaccustomed racial dynamics. Compare the plot of *White Heat*, for instance, to that of the better-known 1932 South Seas romance *Bird of Paradise*, starring Joel McCrea as an American playboy who falls in love with a Pacific Islander, Luana, played by Dolores del Río. In the final scene, Luana sacrifices herself in order to save her lover, dying in a fiery volcano—a convenient plot twist that disrupts the interracial coupling.[199] Tellingly, actor Peter Hyun, a Kaua'i resident who played the butler Soong in *White Heat*, misremembered the film in his memoir, erasing Leilani from the plot and reimagining the film as a tragic love story about two white tourists in Hawai'i.[200] *Photoplay's* discussion also reimagined the plot as one in which William "affairs [sic] with a native," then later marries his white girlfriend, the writer forgetting the subsequent disruption of that relationship.[201]

At the risk of overstating the case for *White Heat*—by all indications a low-budget effort that garnered mixed reviews—it is worth noting that few other women besides Dorothy Arzner were directing in Hollywood in the 1930s; indeed few of Weber's early male contemporaries, apart from DeMille, were working at all. Securing work co-writing and directing *White Heat*, Weber clearly surmounted limitations of both her gender and her generation. Moreover, by taking on such an ambitious project—her first dialogue picture, the first Hollywood feature shot on Kaua'i, a production with hard-to-reach locations and complex stunts, and one of only a handful of Hollywood features shot on the Hawai'ian islands during this period—Weber showed herself working hard to maintain a position in the industry. She continued moving forward, in other words, determined to keep direct-ing in the sound era and to keep making relevant pictures with strong

female leads, even if that meant shooting on a shoestring for a B production. Yet, even as she continued to work, Weber was becoming increasingly
invisible in the industry. As Anthony Slide notes, few of those reviewing
White Heat "thought it pertinent to mention the name of the director," an
indication of how thoroughly Weber's career had already been erased from
industry history, even as it continued.[202] Within a few short months Weber
would be described as someone "formerly active in the pictures," her career
pronounced over.[203]

Alongside her efforts to continue working in Hollywood in whatever
capacity she could—screen-tester, uncredited screenwriter, B director—
Weber also worked hard throughout this period to initiate a national program of visual instruction for schoolchildren, a goal she had long cherished.
Finding it more difficult to work in the commercial industry, she focused
instead on nontheatrical film culture. Indeed after completing *White Heat,*
she declared that promoting visual instruction in schools had become "my
job now."[204] With backing from Carl Laemmle she devised a complete
school curriculum and began contacting boards of education around the
country, proclaiming that "ideas can be absorbed with more facility from
motion picture screens than from books and lectures."[205] Motion pictures
were suitable for a wide range of subjects, she declared. "Their adaptation
to history, for instance, is easily seen. But what about astronomy, geology,
physiology, botany, economics, geography, art, music, natural history, and
all the other subjects that somehow lose their great essential interest when
hedged about by small printed words on a cold, uninspired page?"[206] Much
earlier in her career she had pronounced cinema an "ideal medium" in
which to promote learning, because of "its direct appeal to the eye and its
absorbing interest."[207] With this new initiative Weber now aimed to "supplant the blackboard with the screen" once and for all, as one commentator
put it.[208] She even attempted to trademark the Aladdin's lamp symbol she
had used at Lois Weber Productions, presumably with the aim of reviving
it for her visual instruction program.[209]

Visual instruction and nontheatrical cinema more broadly were ideas to
which Weber had long been attracted. Making social-problem films at
Universal more than a decade earlier, she had described them as "living
newspapers," explaining that moviegoers "want educational pictures—they
want pictures with sermons, pictures which stimulate the soul as well as
appeal to the heart and the senses."[210] She had always been particularly
interested in the egalitarian possibilities of cinema, believing that commercial features on serious subjects contributed to the "education of millions
of people." With cinema, she said, "the boundary lines of ignorance and

poverty are taken down, and the intellectual reservations of centuries are thrown open to millions of new settlers."[211] She had advocated the circulation of films in nontheatrical settings such as churches and had at least twice been approached by women's organizations seeking a filmmaker to "produce instructive and welfare pictures."[212] The possibilities for the use of cinema in schools, she felt, were endless. In 1916 she predicted that "the day would come when every public school in America would have its own projection room and the classes studying history, botany, physiology, religions of different countries, geography and literature could learn more from the actual film visualizations than from a thousand text books of scientific description."[213] Citing psychological research, Weber explained that material was learned best when the senses were stimulated, emotional interest piqued, and visual attention maximized.[214] "It is one of the greatest surprises of my life that the educational value of the motion picture has not been more generally recognized. I thought that the schools would take immediate advantage of this marvelous method of teaching," she declared.[215] Returning to this concept years later, she stressed that visual instruction was especially important for schoolchildren from disadvantaged backgrounds or immigrant families, particularly those learning English. Cinema, she said, "is the Universal Language," employing a truism commonplace in the film education movement but one that also betrayed her deep commitment to social justice.[216]

Weber was by no means alone in her enthusiasm for visual instruction during these years. As Jennifer Peterson notes, "The dream of an educational role for cinema" had been "an undercurrent in discourses about film since its inception."[217] A movement that began in earnest during the Progressive Era picked up steam in the 1920s and early 1930s, especially after the development of 16mm. Organizations formed to promote the cause, including the Society for Visual Education (1920) and the Visual Instruction Association of America (1922), many of them sponsoring accompanying journals such as *Visual Education* and *The Educational Screen*. Guides such as Don Carlos Ellis and Laura Thornborough's *Motion Pictures in Education: A Practical Handbook for Users of Visual Aids* (1923) and A. P. Hollis's *Motion Pictures for Instruction* (1926) became available. And the National Education Association formed a Department of Visual Instruction in 1923. Scholars also began to conduct academic research on the effectiveness of visual instruction, including an influential 1929 study entitled *Motion Pictures in the Classroom*.[218] As Peterson notes, "Moving pictures, once scorned as a bad influence for children, were becoming a new feature of the classroom in the 1920s."[219]

Promoting visual education in schools, Weber aligned herself with female librarians, classroom teachers, and distributors who were leading the cause of visual education, mounting a significant challenge to Hollywood's domination of commercial circuits of exhibition.[220] The visual education movement, broadly defined, became a noted sphere of women's engagement with movie culture in the late twenties and early thirties, a trend especially clear if we consider visual education alongside the little theater movement, the increasing use of films in museums and other cultural institutions, and the growing interest in home theaters—all of which marked notable engagement by women as both film producers and consumers. As opportunities for women and socially engaged filmmakers declined in Hollywood in the 1920s, Weber cast her sights toward noncommercial and nontheatrical avenues, renewing her early investment in cinema's social mandate.

After the changes that swept Hollywood in the late twenties and early thirties, Weber found herself increasingly marginalized, relegated to screen-testing and script adaptations, and more reliant than ever on support from old collaborators such as Carl Laemmle and Frances Marion. Opportunities to direct proved particularly elusive. Even when assigned to work on women's pictures, she was passed over for directing jobs in favor of newcomers like William Wyler and King Vidor. Her only directing job materialized on Poverty Row, where several others of her generation also found themselves. Even so, Weber managed to infuse the work she found casting, writing, and directing with her campaign against Hollywood's glamour industry, its preference for decorative female stars over intelligent actresses, and its sexual double standards. She also devoted considerable attention to ensuring her historical legacy, for Hollywood was beginning to look backward during these years of transition, chronicling its own history in a manner that quickly excluded pioneers like Weber.

"END OF THE CIRCLE"

During her years at Lois Weber Productions, as we have seen, Weber had been prematurely pronounced the "only" woman directing in Hollywood, her creative labor reduced to that of "star maker." Over the following two decades the process of marginalizing, then ultimately "forgetting" Weber's work, alongside that of many other women active in early Hollywood, only accelerated. Throughout the 1920s Weber's ongoing career continued to be marked an aberration; hers was the exception that proved the rule. Even when she still enjoyed an active career, Weber was cast as the "only woman director in cinemaland." Virtually every news item, profile, or review mentioned this "fact" from 1922 onward. On the one hand, it was partly true: Weber *was* one of very few women directing in Hollywood in the twenties; on the other hand, this repeated characterization marked the female director as oddly anachronistic. In 1927 *Moving Picture World* went one step further, describing Weber as "the only woman *ever* to achieve success as a motion picture director," an astonishing erasure of the historical record. By 1933 Weber was paired with Dorothy Arzner as "the only women *anyone can remember* as having directed." In 1937 Weber became the "lone woman movie-maker of silent days." And by 1939, the *Los Angeles Times* set Weber's success in "the good old days," effectively sealing her career in a lost era.[221] So while Weber's accomplishments were acknowledged, even celebrated, in these early histories, they were almost immediately cast as singular exceptions possible only in a distant, soon-to-be-forgotten past, noted for experiments like having female directors.

If remembered at all, Weber's work was cast in a particular vein, associated not with tackling social issues such as poverty, birth control, and state executions, or critiquing institutions such as capitalism and heterosexual marriage, but with addressing "problems of the home and children in the silent era."[222] *Where Are My Children?* her most popular and controversial film, was eventually misremembered as one of the sensational "white slave" films of the early teens, not a pioneering film on contraception and abortion—a telling conflation of issues related to female sexuality.[223] Not only was Weber's work consigned to the past, then, deemed the lone exception that proved "motion-picture directing is a man's realm," but her films were erroneously associated with women's issues and thus deemed less relevant to film history.[224]

As Weber's career slowed down in the 1930s, the possibilities for women directing in Hollywood became all the more isolated and all the more remote. "The executive field of motion pictures has never been one for women," *Los Angeles Times* critic Edwin Schallert pronounced in a 1932 piece entitled "The Eternal Masculine." Weber, Pickford, and Marion came "closest to arriving at the goal" in the past, he admitted, but none of the women currently active in Hollywood could fit the bill. Others took a more defensive posture. "Why Can't Women Be Good Directors?" Philip K. Scheuer asked. Weber, he remembered, had been one of the few "ladies who could make a camera sit up and talk." When Mary Pickford announced plans to head a production unit in 1935, Weber was predictably cited as the only woman who "ever got away with it on a big scale." Pickford would "Deny Old Filmdom Jinx," a headline proclaimed, as if some mystical phenomenon, not gender bias, had denied women opportunities.[225]

Even articles about an emerging cohort of women directors, including Leontine Sagan, Germaine Dulac, Esther Shub, and Dorothy Arzner, emphasized their uniqueness, often citing Weber as the previous generation's lone precedent. Announcing Arzner's directorial debut in 1927, *Photoplay* bid "Goodbye to Another Tradition," casting Arzner as "the first woman director in ten years." Weber was, predictably, noted as "the exception." Before Arzner, "Lois Weber was the solitary woman executive in Hollywood," though that had been "long ago," another piece noted. Arzner, another claimed, "may go over as the second one of her kind." When Sagan arrived in Hollywood in 1934, reports noted that "Lois Weber had been uniquely active in that way," resorting almost to euphemism to describe the curious phenomenon of female directors. In his 1932 celebration of Dulac, Harry Alan Potamkin noted "how few women have ever created films," listing Weber, Arzner, and Shub as remarkable exceptions to this seemingly hard-and-fast rule.[226]

Weber aggressively fought this erroneous narrative, taking steps to help ensure her place in Hollywood history. Even so, she was repeatedly cast as an anomaly, a lone, prized rarity among women. When her career revived in 1926 and 1927, following the positive notices she received for *The Marriage Clause, Sensation Seekers,* and *The Angel of Broadway,* profiles and interviews appeared in daily newspapers, mass-market monthlies, and fan magazines. All stressed her notable record of accomplishment in the industry, while also suggesting how unusual her accomplishments were becoming for women. One piece noted how long Weber had been associated with the industry, "emerging with motion pictures from the animated lantern slide stage," how hard she had worked, and how thoroughly she understood every facet of filmmaking, having worked "writing scenarios, starring and co-directing at the same time, handling negatives with white kid gloves, and cutting film with shears." Another, entitled "The Gate Women Don't Crash," stressed how few women could now achieve such success. "Though the field has been open, theoretically, to all comers, [Weber] has stood alone of her sex among the wielders of the megaphone."[227] Weber herself penned a two-part syndicated newspaper piece reflecting on her own career in light of diminishing opportunities for women.[228]

When sound technology swept the industry in 1928, Weber was eager to establish her role in the early days of synch sound recording. She took out a full-page ad in the trade journal *Film Mercury* touting her work directing sound films at American Gaumont two decades earlier—"Lois Weber in Talking Pictures" the headline proclaimed.[229] That same year the *Los Angeles Examiner* published a letter to the editor written by her husband, Harry Gantz, promoting Weber's early experience with synch sound. Gantz was responding to an article that Louella Parsons had written on Dorothy Arzner. Claiming that Arzner's work had not yet approached the quality of Weber's, Parsons suggested this "was probably due to the fact that Miss Weber did not have the talkies to contend with." In fact, Gantz pointed out, Weber had directed some of the very first sound films ever made.[230] In a more substantial and conventional act of historiography, Weber began work on a memoir, entitled "The End of the Circle."[231]

Weber was not alone in her efforts to ensure her legacy; many other female pioneers went to great—and considerably varied—lengths to insert themselves into the evolving narrative of Hollywood's history in the late 1920s and early thirties. Linda Arvidson Griffith published *When the Movies Were Young* in 1925; that same year Nell Shipman's account of her experiences filming in northern Idaho was serialized in the *Atlantic Monthly*. Gene Gauntier published her memoir, "Blazing the Trail," in *Woman's Home Companion* three years later. Taking another tack, Mary Pickford purchased a good portion of her Biograph titles in the 1920s in order to control their destiny—and her legacy. In 1928 Colleen Moore constructed a bejeweled dollhouse that soon toured the country—an act, Amelie Hastie argues, designed to narrate a particular history of Hollywood, one in which women controlled their own fortunes.[232] Taken together, these women's efforts mark a struggle against a historical narrative already emerging.

At this same moment, the industry was beginning to mark a series of anniversaries and milestones, the discourse surrounding which crafted a narrative about Hollywood's past in which an older filmmaking generation was distanced from its modern counterpart. Weber, for instance, was among a group of Hollywood "pioneers" who attended Carl Laemmle's sixtieth birthday party in 1927, complete with screenings of "old" films. When Universal City celebrated its twentieth anniversary in 1935, Weber joined a host of other "former Universalites" invited back for a "family reunion," honored alongside Grace Cunard, Francis Ford, Mary Fuller, and Florence Turner. "Remember these names?" the *Los Angeles Times* quipped. This earlier generation was associated with a "prehistoric" period characterized by all manner of "hijinks" including, apparently, the novel idea that women might write and direct.[233] Books such as Terry Ramsaye's *A Million and One Nights: A History of the Motion Picture through 1925* and Benjamin Hampton's *A History of the American Film Industry from Its Beginnings to 1931* say virtually nothing about women's contributions to early Hollywood or to film culture more generally, save for mention of the most prominent female stars.[234]

Cast as a "prehistoric," "forgotten" "pioneer," Weber became ever more invisible in Hollywood's early self-chronicles. One potent example of how this evolving narrative simultaneously wrote Weber *into* Hollywood history while writing her *out* is a 1927 photo essay entitled "Now They Do the Bossing," a profile of former actors who had made the leap into directing.[235] An accompanying illustration showed Weber acting with Rupert Julian in one of the hundreds of Rex shorts she wrote and directed some fifteen years earlier. Julian was by 1927 primarily known for his work as a director, most notably *The Phantom of the Opera* (1925). "And here we have two who forsook acting for directing," read a caption under the photo. "Lois Weber and Rupert Julian appeared opposite each other in many early films—and now both are with de Mille [sic]." "Now They Do the Bossing" accomplishes several feats simultaneously. First, by casting Weber's directing—or "bossing"— as a recent career shift, the profile effectively erases not only the directing she did at Rex, but also the more than forty features she wrote and directed afterward. The article makes it seem as if Weber is just beginning her directing career at DeMille Pictures in the late 1920s. Moreover, Julian is presented as Weber's equal and costar—two former actors now trying their hand at directing—instead of an actor who began his career working under her direction and from whom he likely learned a great deal.[236] While Julian was already known as an actor before he began directing, Weber's fame had always circulated around her writing and directing career, not the roles she played on screen. The film still selected to illustrate the article adds an additional layer of nuance, for it shows Julian's character strangling a passive and immobilized Weber, effectively reversing the power dynamic between (female) director and (male) star to that of male aggressor and female victim. The pair's relationship is complicated still further by rumors that Weber had been called in to recut *The Phantom of the Opera* when the two were both at Universal.[237] Finally, by announcing that Weber and Julian were now "with" DeMille, the caption renders DeMille in a fatherly relation to Weber, infantilizing her relationship with him and deemphasizing their role as industry equals a decade earlier. "Now They Do the Bossing," like so many other profiles at the time, linked Jazz Age Hollywood to its earlier incarnation, drawing attention to the long-standing participation of artists such as Weber, Julian, and DeMille and to the opportunities for advancement that the early industry provided. Yet, in doing so, the profile supplied an astounding rewriting of history in which Weber became, remarkably, another aging actor trying her hand at directing in the late 1920s with help from the master, DeMille, when not so long ago she had been not only Julian's director and mentor, but, alongside Griffith, DeMille's only peer.[238]

Perhaps the best illustration of Weber's escalating invisibility is *The Unshod Maiden*, Universal's 1932 sound parody of *Shoes*, Weber's 1916 feature on urban poverty and women's wage equity.[239] Recut with an added sardonic voice-over, *Shoes* became *The Unshod Maiden,* a comic short written and directed by Albert DeMond, the first of the *Universal Brevities.* *Shoes* was certainly not the only silent feature to receive such treatment; Mack Sennett's landmark comedy *Tillie's Punctured Romance* (1914) was parodied the following year. In fact, many studios repurposed their back catalogues in the early sound era, issuing compilation films in series such as Warner Brothers' *Movie Album,* MGM's *Goofy Movies,* and the *Movie Memories* and *Screen Souvenirs* series released by Paramount. As William M. Drew documents, these comedies tended to mine silent films of the prewar era, rather than more recent features of the 1920s, thereby exaggerating differences between sound cinema and its silent counterpart. "The dramatic situations, old-fashioned mores, and 'antique' costumes were seen as vestiges of an increasingly remote, absurd past," he writes. A past made all the more comical when films shot at slower camera speeds were projected at twenty-four frames per second, rendering human movement mechanistic and unnatural.[240]

Parodies of this sort were apparently a great success. Mentioning nothing of the original and noting that *The Unshod Maiden* had been "photographed in real old fashioned style," *Film Daily* rated the film "a wow," predicting it "will sure get laugh results." The *Los Angeles Times* reported that "more and more cause for amusement is being discovered in reviving old silent films with (more or less) caustic and kidding comments," citing *The Unshod Maiden* as an exemplar of this phenomenon. The film "created a furor" when shown to critics and journalists, according to the *Hollywood Herald,* meaning, apparently, that it was well received.[241] After his success with *The Unshod Maiden,* DeMond went on to create a number of other *Universal Brevities,* most notably *Boo!* (1932), which included footage from the 1929 American release of F. W. Murnau's *Nosferatu* (1922), and the studio's own *Frankenstein* (1931).[242]

If silent-film parodies allowed sound-era Hollywood to distance itself from its seemingly "ancient" past, the strident misogynist tone of *The Unshod Maiden* suggests something more particular about how Weber's brand of filmmaking challenged Hollywood's evolving self-conception. Most pronounced in the comic repurposing of *Shoes* is the shift in its address to viewers. The original film, as we have seen, had been presented from an explicit position of female authorship, with Weber's authority framed in and through that of renowned reformer Jane Addams. Viewers looked "objectively" at the effects of urban poverty on young women like the film's heroine, Eva Meyer, while also being invited to share her subjective experiences of grueling labor, consumer longing, and ultimately, sexual humiliation. Reworked as *The Unshod Maiden,* however, the film assumed an unequivocally masculine address. Not only did a male actor perform the vocal track, but his snide comments seem geared almost entirely to a male audience, with off-color jokes about "bosoms" and male "saxophones." Weber's nuanced consideration of the new consumer economy and its relationship to female sexuality was reduced to a series of crude jokes about sexual assault. And with *The Unshod Maiden* credited only to DeMond, Weber's authorship was erased entirely and completely. This process was apparently so effective that when she was briefly assigned to direct the adaptation of Edna Ferber's *Glamour* at Universal the following year, the *Hollywood Reporter* noted that it would be her "first directorial job for that company," an astounding pronouncement, given not only Weber's relatively recent success with *The Marriage Clause* and *Sensation Seekers,* released by Universal five and six years earlier, but her status as that studio's top director and top moneymaker of either gender just fifteen years prior.[243]

Despite her marginalization, Weber continued to work on projects throughout the latter years of her life, her "erudite mind . . . a-buzz with further plans for screen creations," according to one report.[244] At work until the end, Weber sent a story outline to DeMille just a few months before she died, writing, "If this is as good as I think, it will make a sensational success."[245] She must have felt honored when her 1916 epic *The Dumb Girl of Portici* was donated to the Museum of Modern Art's fledgling film library in 1935, part of a gift from Universal that included other notable studio titles, including *Blind Husbands* (1919), *Foolish Wives* (1922), *The Cat and the Canary* (1927), and *All Quiet on the Western Front* (1930).[246] Although allegedly "forgotten," Weber was included among the studio's most renowned filmmakers: Erich von Stroheim, Paul Leni, and Lewis Milestone. With an eye to her legacy, Weber also continued work on her memoir, "The End of the Circle." It was to have been published shortly before she died,, but, for unknown reasons, never appeared in print and is presumed lost.[247]

Throughout her final years Weber maintained strong friendships with other women prominent in the industry—Lenore Coffee, Ruth Roland, and her close comrade Frances Marion. She also frequently socialized with her sister, Ethel, whose husband, Lou Howland, had died in 1931. Their mother, Tillie, who lived with Ethel in Miami, had died in 1935.[248] Weber separated from her second husband, Harry Gantz, sometime that same year, after which he relocated to India, where he apparently continued his interest in filmmaking and eventually married his third wife, Katherine Goldthwaite.[249] In May 1939 Weber's first husband and original collaborator, Phillips

Smalley, died at the age of seventy-three. Smalley had been playing small parts, often uncredited, in films like F. W. Murnau's *Sunrise* (1927), in which he appeared as a waiter, and in the Marx Brothers' comedy *A Night at the Opera* (1935). Featured in a profile of former stars and directors now resigned to playing bit parts or working as extras, Smalley became yet another marker of his generation's demise. "Stars Become Spear-Bearers" blared the article's sensational headline. Veterans of the "good old days" were glad of any chance to appear on screen at all, the author decreed.[250] When mentioned at all in reviews, which was rare, Smalley was described as someone "remembered for his directorial association with Lois Weber." Still, when it came time for Smalley's obituary, the *Los Angeles Times* described his ex-wife only as an "actress and writer," completely eclipsing her career as director.[251] Weber's great champion Carl Laemmle died four months later, another reminder that her generation of early Hollywood veterans was vanishing. Weber was "one of the saddest" at the funeral, Hedda Hopper reported, an indication of how close the two colleagues had remained and how deeply Weber felt the loss of her peers.[252]

Weber herself took ill early in November 1939, hospitalized with a stomach ailment that had plagued her for years. Frances Marion, her friend Veda Terry, and her sister, Ethel, remained with her in the hospital until she died on November 13, at sixty years of age.[253] Some three hundred Hollywood friends and colleagues attended her funeral later in the week. Short obituaries were published in *Variety*, the *Los Angeles Examiner*, the *New York Times*, and other outlets.[254] Only the *Los Angeles Times* accorded Weber a substantial front-page tribute written by Hedda Hopper, who declared, "I don't know any woman who has had a greater influence upon the motion-picture business." Describing Weber's prodigious output in writing, directing, and producing pictures in the early decades of the industry, Hopper asked readers to "imagine her endurance and ability" when compared with "directors of today who feel put upon if they turn out one picture a year with the aid of a measly 25 writers and the United States mint!"[255] Even so, the central focus of Weber's obituaries, including Hopper's, remained her role as a "star maker" to a younger generation of actresses, her own considerable accomplishments as director and screenwriter almost completely sidelined—evidence that women had, even by then, been consigned a wholly marginal role in Hollywood history.

Weber had a far more active career in the 1920s than has previously been acknowledged, and she continued her efforts to write and direct until the final months of her life. But in looking carefully at these two final decades of Weber's career, it becomes clear that the process of forgetting her accomplishments "with a vengeance," as Richard Koszarski puts it, began while she was still actively writing and directing films in the late 1920s.[256] This "forgetting" took place during a moment when Hollywood was engaged in a rewriting of its own history in a manner that sanitized past revelry as "hi-jinks"; cast the period before big-studio consolidation as one of "play" and "infancy," rather than artistic experimentation and freedom, or social and political engagement; undercut the achievements of women in order to employ femininity in the service of the industry's new drive for respectability; and, as Karen Ward Mahar argues, engineered a "remasculinization" of business practices that excluded the idea of female filmmakers.

Even as Weber aligned herself with men such as Carl Laemmle, his son "Junior," Joseph Schenck, and Cecil B. DeMille—all still relatively powerful in the industry—she resisted corporatized Hollywood, criticizing the greater control exercised by conglomerates and censors alike, while working largely outside the major studios. Her resistance took several other forms as well. She launched a relentless critique on and off screen of a Hollywood glamour culture centered on the use of young women as decorative, eroticized objects. She forged deepening alliances with women's groups outside Hollywood, in an appeal toward older models of feminist-oriented civic leadership. She offered generous support for women working at all levels of the film industry. She continued to assume leadership roles within the industry, epitomized by her early and prominent association with the Academy of Motion Picture Arts and Sciences. And she made a sustained and conscious effort to ensure that her own narrative was written into the history of American filmmaking. She did so, moreover, at a time when Hollywood was actively engaged in crafting its own historical narrative by celebrating various anniversaries and comparative legacies. Such histories cast Weber as one of Hollywood's "pioneers," limiting memories of her participation and insistently casting her work in the *past*, assigning her a career that had already been eclipsed, a marginalized role that Weber continually resisted.

Conclusion

"Forgotten with a Vengeance"

Although this photoplay artist is never seen on the screen, she—
Writes her own photoplays.
Puts them in story form.
Chooses and contracts her own players.
Operates a Bell-Howell camera on many of her scenes, and
Plans her own lighting effects.
Bosses her own property "gallery."
Sometimes "shoots" with a still camera.
Plunges occasionally into chemicals in her developing laboratory.
Writes her own titles, inserts, prologues.
Knows how to operate a printing machine.
Is her own film cutter, "splicer" and editor.
Plans her own publicity and advertising campaigns for her finished pictures.
Is her own business manager and signs all her checks.
Owns her own studio.
Was the first to "work" her players to the strains of an orchestra.
Was the first woman in filmdom to get $2500 a week (and that was years
    ago).
"Discovered" Mary MacLaren, Mildred Harris, Lois Wilson, Claire Windsor,
    Priscilla Dean and a half dozen other "stars."
Believes that "the play's the thing" and not the players.
Does her own cooking and raises her own vegetables.
Knows every branch of the film business from actual experience as player,
    director and business manager.
Supervises the marketing and distribution of her photoplays.
Is financially independent of the movie magnates.
Does a man's work; but has never marched in a suffragist parade.
Has made nearly 100 photoplays.
Was one of the first five actresses to leave the speaking stage for picture
    work.
Who is she?
She is Lois Weber, qualified voter.

Los Angeles Herald, February 21, 1921

Figure 54. The process of "forgetting" Lois Weber began during her lifetime, even as she continued to work in Hollywood. Courtesy of the Martin S. Quigley Collection, Georgetown University.

By 1921, apparently, Lois Weber was simultaneously everywhere and nowhere in Hollywood, omnipotent yet imperceptible. A catalogue of astonishing accomplishment, the poem quoted above fashions Weber as an enigma, unrecognizable even after such an exhaustive accounting. "Who is she?" the verse asks, seemingly confident that few readers will have guessed.

Indeed, if this poem were to be read aloud even today at any gathering of film scholars or filmmakers, few would be able to identify its subject. The litany of Weber's achievements, piled here as they are line by line, makes her invisibility all the more poignant. Portrayed through an accumulation of muscular verbs—she writes, chooses, operates, bosses, shoots, and plunges—Weber appears in command of every phase of moviemaking: single-handedly writing, casting, dressing, and directing her pictures; shooting, developing, and editing her footage; managing her studio; then marketing and distributing the finished products. Fiercely self-sufficient, she is "independent of the movie magnates," drafts "her own" photoplays, contracts "her own" players, plans "her own" lighting and props, writes "her own" titles, cuts "her own" films, and is "her own" business manager in "her own" studio. On one level, this frenzied résumé insists upon Weber's multifaceted technical and artistic expertise in a male-dominated industry, showing that she is not a "director" in name only, but a hands-on practitioner with enviable authority. Even so, by 1921 this model of unilateral mastery had become outdated, a relic of earlier, artisanal modes of production jettisoned by studio conglomerates whose mass-production "efficiencies" demanded a stricter division of labor. So even as the elegy charts Weber's stellar position in Hollywood history, it casts her as already an anachronism, already outmoded, already surpassed—and, crucially, already unknown.

Something of this paradox is conveyed in the way that Weber inhabits both past and present in the poem's fictive space. She simultaneously "is" and "was"—"the first" to have achieved significant milestones in the industry, yet still very much active. Indeed, Weber emerges from a nexus of contradictions—a filmmaker who takes still photographs, an actress who no longer appears on screen, a star maker for whom the play is more important than its players, a female voter who is not a suffragist, and a successful businesswoman who cooks her own meals, tends her own garden, and does not consort with feminists. Most paradoxical of all, Weber is a woman doing "a man's work," a woman famous in filmdom for something other than being "seen on the screen." As if to emphasize this particularly vexing phenomenon, the poem begins apologetically, insisting on her importance *even though* she does not appear on screen. This reminds us of how ubiquitous was the view, even then, that women belonged more properly on the screen than behind the scenes. Working off screen, Weber's contributions to early Hollywood are much less visible—not because she is a director or a screenwriter or a studio owner, but because she is a *woman* assuming these unaccustomed roles. Most striking is the way Weber is figured as an enigma, the way such a dizzying list of accomplishments ends with the riddle "Who is she?" That is, ultimately, the most arresting contradiction in the poem, a portrait of a figure simultaneously everywhere and nowhere, peerless yet anonymous. It is remarkable, too, for the way it foreshadows Weber's marginal place in histories of American filmmaking. The question, then, is not "Who is she?" but how could a figure of such renown remain so unknown?

"History has not been kind" to Lois Weber, Richard Koszarski reminds us; or, as Anthony Slide puts it, she "lost her way." For Koszarski, Weber has been "forgotten with a vengeance."[1] She is not alone, of course. Metaphors of loss pervade the discourse on early female filmmakers: Alice Guy Blaché is "the lost visionary of cinema," as Alison McMahan puts it, her life and work a "lost garden" for those trying to document it. Gene Gauntier is "cinema's forgotten pioneer." Nell Shipman, Canada's "forgotten star." Elvira Notari is "lost in male-dominated culture," so obscured that Giuliana Bruno must play cartographer to map not only Notari's presence but also the traces of her absence.[2]

What is clear in Weber's case, at least, is that this process of "losing" and "forgetting" began during her lifetime, began even as she continued to work in Hollywood. An industry in the throes of "masculinization" and corporate conglomeration accelerated by the transition to sound distanced itself from an "ancient" past, a past that included such incredible "hi-jinks" as letting women direct. Weber and her contemporaries tried valiantly to insert themselves into narratives of Hollywood history being written in the 1920s and thirties, but their efforts had little impact. Terry Ramsaye, Benjamin Hampton, and Lewis Jacobs, Hollywood's first historians, wrote only about female stars in their early tomes, fashioning a template that persists even today.[3] Despite significant research by Slide and Koszarski dating back to the 1970s, Weber's career is still overlooked in most major histories of American silent cinema, marginalized in relation to her contemporaries Mack Sennett, Marshall Neilan, Maurice Tourneur, Rex Ingram, and Thomas Ince, let alone Griffith and DeMille.[4] The most prominent histories of American cinema barely consider her work at all.[5] And with the notable exception of Mark Garrett Cooper's revisionist study, *Universal Women*, virtually all modern histories of Universal Pictures are silent on Weber—the director whom Carl Laemmle considered his "best man" on the lot; co-head of the studio's celebrated Rex brand; mayor of Universal City; the studio's highest-paid and most respected director in the mid-1910s; the first director released from contract to form her own production company; and the figure later appointed to head Universal's story department and develop new talent during a period of transition in the 1920s. Astonishingly, Weber receives *absolutely no mention* in standard histories of Universal's early years, and in one other case is remembered only for the role she reportedly played in re-editing Rupert Julian's *Phantom of the Opera*, at best a footnote to her celebrated career.[6]

Weber's marginalization is figured most graphically in introductory texts that, if they allow for the impact women had in early Hollywood at all, insist on framing those accomplishments in a box literally set apart from the main narrative, a postscript, an addendum with no possibility of ever being incorporated into that narrative, let alone changing it. Weber and her contemporaries are highlighted and sidelined in the same gesture. In one striking example, Weber receives passing mention in an introductory film history text that informs readers about "a brief vogue" for female filmmakers in early Hollywood, a trend the authors dub "the feminine mystique," ensuring its anachronism and enshrining it in enigma.[7] Evidently the story Hollywood began telling about itself in the 1920s—that female filmmakers were an anomaly, that women chiefly served the glamour industry, and that female viewers and female subject matter were marginal to the box office—has been so indelibly imprinted that generations of historians have repeated and reinforced the story for nearly a century.

In marked contrast to her striking obscurity in standard histories of American cinema, early Hollywood, and Universal Pictures, Weber assumes a prominent place in any tally of women filmmakers.[8] Should she be recognized principally for her achievements as a woman, or does she warrant broader recognition as a pioneering filmmaker? The answer, most certainly, is both. Regardless of her gender, Weber was a figure of seminal importance in the evolving U.S. film industry. It should be clear by this point in the book that histories of American silent cinema can no longer be written without considering Weber's legacy. She was one of the era's most respected directors, one of its leading filmmakers alongside Griffith and DeMille. Like them, Weber was invested in cinema's "uplift," but she chose an alternate tack, emphasizing a popular cinema of social engagement over highbrow literary adaptations and historical epics. Unlike her contemporaries, she wrote or adapted her own screenplays and was one of the first to form an independent production company after World War I. Recognized as one of the most eminent filmmakers in the industry, she was accorded top salaries, lucrative contracts, hyperbolic press coverage, and enormous creative freedom. An industry leader, she was instrumental in the professionalization of screenwriting in the 1910s, then in the late 1920s helped lead the professionalization of directing through her work on the first director's committee at the newly formed Academy of Motion Picture Arts and Sciences. A groundbreaking celebrity director, arguably the first of her generation to achieve such fame, Weber spoke tirelessly on behalf of the industry, testifying to its artistic and cultural potential in the early years, then coming to its defense during the star scandals of the early 1920s. An intrepid pioneer in the field of social-problem films, through her work Weber spawned landmark censorship cases that tested early regulatory practices, and she emerged, alongside Griffith, as a steady voice against efforts to censor the movies. A proponent of realism and naturalistic acting, she was also a visual stylist particularly adept at conveying psychological interiority, marshaling details of gesture, expression, and props, and experimenting with lighting, location shooting, and multiple exposures.

Essential as she was to the fledgling movie business and its evolving crafts of directing and screenwriting, Weber's career and legacy cannot be understood without taking her gender into account. Active female protagonists were central to her films from the very beginning. These include the struggling wives, daughters, and mothers she played in her Rex shorts; memorable characters like Portia and Fenella in her adapted works; women grappling with poverty, addiction, and scandal in her Universal features; married women and single working women jointly navigating modern sexual mores in the postwar years; and performers juggling fame, glamour, and commodification in the Jazz Age. With female protagonists at their center, Weber's scripts grappled with issues close to women. Marriage and domesticity, to be certain, but her films also grappled with sexual violence, abusive relationships, contraception, wage equity, prostitution, unplanned pregnancy, and the sexual double standard. What is more, her social-problem films made it clear that *any* issue, from capital punishment to poverty to addiction, not only affected women but necessitated women's engagement in order to effect social change.

Conscious of her prominent role in the industry, Weber helped foster a safe, educational space for young women at the Girls' Studio Club, maintained strong ties with feminist clubwomen, and mentored several generations of aspiring actresses, screenwriters, and directors. So marked were her collaborations with other creative women that Weber's films were sometimes referred to as "suffraget [sic] propaganda," accused of harboring "alarming feministic tendencies." Nurturing the talents of Mary MacLaren, Mildred Harris, Claire Windsor, and Billie Dove, Weber wrote mature parts for them, characters explicitly designed to counter dominant images of women on screen. In interviews and public statements she spoke with mounting frustration about the limited roles offered to women in Hollywood films. Weber also spoke out against discrimination in the industry, insisting on a place at the table when the Photoplay Authors' League formed in 1912, protesting the growing climate of hostility toward women directors in the 1920s, and trying against all odds to ensure her own historical legacy in the last years of her life.

Weber's celebrity persona, uncommon for a director of this era, also fed on ideas about femininity, whether in early accounts of creative collaborations with her husband, used to smooth the bold image of a woman filmmaker, or in later tales of her role as "star maker," used to align the female director with the production of glamour and fame. Later in her career, as she became isolated as the "only" woman director in Hollywood, she was valued for her presumed ability to cater to cinema's overwhelmingly female audience, while simultaneously sidelined solely as a director of "women's pictures." As the poem reminds us, Weber embodied a puzzling paradox throughout her career, a "domestic directress" at once Lois Weber and Mrs. Phillips Smalley, a filmmaker who matched the "strength of a man" with "feminine intuition." If Weber's status as a bourgeois married woman leant the movies some credibility in their early days, by the end of her career Weber's reputation as a lone female filmmaker had become a pretext for marginalization. A peerless figure in American silent cinema, Weber's place in early Hollywood and in subsequent histories of that period can be understood only by taking account of her gender. Femininity explains not only her successful navigation of the fledgling movie business but also her subsequent obscurity. It makes her a figure of fascination for feminist historians, yet invisible to many others.

In the end, then, *Lois Weber in Early Hollywood* considers two questions simultaneously. It seeks to demonstrate once and for all that Weber was a pivotal figure in American movie culture, that histories of silent cinema, early Hollywood, and American filmmaking can no longer ignore her films, her career, and her legacy. At the same time, by examining Weber's public persona, the study evaluates how Weber, her work, and her working relationships were understood during her lifetime and how they have come to be understood, forgotten, or lost in subsequent years. At issue is not only the question of why Weber deserves study and recognition, but also the inverse question—how and why she became "lost" and "forgotten" in the first place. Even now, as industry executives and pundits continue to find themselves amazed that women make popular, profitable, and interesting films—even that women watch movies at all—when female filmmakers still negotiate the awkward terrain of "chick flicks," and when being "seen on the screen" is still considered women's primary role in Hollywood, it is essential to remember that these fictions have a long tail. A vengeful "forgetting" of women such as Lois Weber yields a skewed narrative with profound consequences for subsequent generations of filmmakers and filmgoers.

Notes

ABBREVIATIONS

ACSC   Audrey Chamberlin Scrapbook Collection, Margaret
            Herrick Library, Academy of Motion Picture Arts and
            Sciences, Los Angeles

AMPAS   Margaret Herrick Library, Academy of Motion Picture
            Arts and Sciences, Los Angeles

BRTC   Billy Rose Theater Collection, New York Public Library for
            the Performing Arts.

Chic Trib   *Chicago Tribune*

CWSBC   Claire Windsor Scrapbook Collection, Cinematic Arts
            Library, University of Southern California, Los Angeles

FD   *Film Daily*

LAT   *Los Angeles Times*

LAX   *Los Angeles Examiner*

LAXC   *Los Angeles Examiner* Collection, Special Collections,
            University of Southern California, Los Angeles

MoMA   Museum of Modern Art Film Study Center, New York

Mot   *Motography*

MPMag   *Motion Picture Magazine*

MPN   *Motion Picture News*

MPW   *Moving Picture World*

MPWkly   *Moving Picture Weekly*

NBR   National Board of Review Collection, Rare Books and
            Manuscripts Division, New York Public Library

NYDM   *New York Dramatic Mirror*

NYT   *New York Times*

RLC   Robinson Locke Collection, New York Public Library for the Performing Arts

SF Chron   *San Francisco Chronicle*

UW   *Universal Weekly*

Var   *Variety*

Wash Post *Washington Post*

INTRODUCTION

1. Similar portraits of female directors and screenwriters at the typewriter became something of a cliché by the mid-1920s, as Antonia Lant has shown. See Lant, *The Red Velvet Seat: Women's Writings on the First Fifty Years of Cinema* (London: Verso, 2006), 575.

2. See Hilary A. Hallett, *Go West, Young Women! The Rise of Early Hollywood* (Berkeley: University of California Press, 2013); and Shelley Stamp, "Women and the Silent Screen," in *The Wiley-Blackwell History of American Cinema*, Vol. 1: *Origins to 1928*, ed. Roy Grundmann, Cynthia Lucia, and Art Simon (Malden, MA: Wiley-Blackwell, 2012), 181–206.

CHAPTER 1

1. For more general discussion of this pivotal period, see Eileen Bowser, *The Transformation of Cinema, 1907–1915* (New York: Scribner, 1990); Charlie Keil, *Early American Cinema in Transition: Story, Style, and Filmmaking, 1907–1913* (Madison: University of Wisconsin Press, 2001); Charlie Keil and Shelley Stamp, eds., *American Cinema's Transitional Era: Audiences, Institutions, Practices* (Berkeley: University of California Press, 2004); and Richard Abel, *Americanizing the Movies and "Movie-Mad" Audiences, 1910–1914* (Berkeley: University of California Press, 2006).

2. My understanding of Weber's early life is deeply indebted to Martin Norden, whose diligent research has uncovered many of the elusive details of Weber's early days in Pittsburgh and New York. See Martin F. Norden, *Lois Weber: Interviews* (Jackson: University Press of Mississippi, forthcoming). Other information is drawn from Lois Weber (Mrs. Smalley), "How I Became a Motion Picture Director," *Paramount Magazine*, Jan 1915, 12; Robert Florey, "The Screen's First Woman Director," *Motion Picture Director* 2, no. 6 (Jan 1926): 60–61; Elizabeth Peltret, "On the Lot with Lois Weber," *Photoplay*, Oct 1917, 89–91; Aline Carter, "The Muse of the Reel," *MPMag*, Mar 1921, 62–63, 105; Fritzi Remont, "The Lady behind the Lens: Lois Weber, Photo-Genius, in Front of, or Back of, the Camera," *MPMag*, May 1918, 59–61, 126; Mayme Ober Peak, "Only Woman Movie Director Owes Her Career to a Broken Piano

Key," *Boston Sunday Globe,* 12 Sept 1926, C11; and Charles S. Dunning, "The Gate Women Don't Crash," *Liberty* 4, no. 2 (14 May 1927), 29–35. (Weber's *Paramount Magazine* article was later republished in *Static Flashes,* 24 Apr 1915, 8.) Also useful for filling in details of Weber's early life were records from the U.S. Census in 1880 and 1900, as well as city directories for Pittsburgh and Allegheny in 1880–81, 1881–82, and 1900. Thanks to Mark Lynn Anderson for helping with the Pittsburgh connection.

3. Peak, "Only Woman Movie Director," C11; Remont, "The Lady behind the Lens," 60.

4. Peltret, "On the Lot with Lois Weber," 90.

5. Peak, "Only Woman Movie Director," C11.

6. Ibid.

7. Dunning, "The Gate Women Don't Crash," 29.

8. Ibid.

9. Florey, "The Screen's First Woman Director," 60; "Lois Weber Producer and Star," *Detroit Tribune,* 10 June 1917, n.p., env. 2518, RLC; Bertha H. Smith, "A Perpetual Leading Lady," *Sunset* 32, no. 3 (Mar 1914): 635.

10. "High Standard of Pictures Is Urged," *Exhibitors' Times,* 9 Aug 1913, 20; Smith, "A Perpetual Leading Lady," 636.

11. Mabel Condon, "Sans Great Paint and Wig," *Mot,* 24 Jan 1914, 58. The actual date of their marriage was April 29, 1904. Martin Norden's research on the production dates for *Why Girls Leave Home* turned up the three-to-four-month span between the couple's first meeting and marriage. See Norden, *Lois Weber: Interviews.*

12. "Phillips Smalley," *MPMag,* May 1915, 108.

13. Carter, "Muse of the Reel," 105.

14. H.H. Van Loan, "Lois the Wizard," *MPMag,* July 1916, 42.

15. Carter, "Muse of the Reel," 105.

16. L.H. Johnson, "A Lady General of the Picture Army," *Photoplay,* June 1915, 42.

17. Weber, "How I Became a Motion Picture Director," 12.

18. Dunning, "The Gate Women Don't Crash," 31.

19. On Gaumont Chronophone productions, see Alison McMahan, *Alice Guy Blaché: Lost Visionary of the Cinema* (New York: Continuum, 2002), ch. 2; Rick Altman, *Silent Film Sound* (New York: Columbia University Press, 2004), 159–65; and Laurent Mannoni and Alison McMahan, "Chronophone Gaumont," in *The Encyclopedia of Early Cinema,* ed. Richard Abel (New York: Routledge, 2005), 118.

20. Alice Guy Blaché, *The Memoirs of Alice Guy Blaché,* ed. Anthony Slide, trans. Roberta and Simone Blaché (Lanham, MD: Scarecrow Press, 1996), 79.

21. Weber, "How I Became a Motion Picture Director," 12.

22. Lois Weber, "Many Women Well Fitted by Film Training to Direct Movies," *San Diego Evening Tribune,* 24 Apr 1928, 3.

23. Smith, "A Perpetual Leading Lady," 636.

24. H.F. Hoffman, "The Rex Director," *MPW,* 24 Feb 1912, 674.

25. Keil, *Early American Cinema*, 25–26; "The First Birthday of Rex," *MPW*, 24 Feb 1912, 672. Rex's London office was established in July 1911, and by early the next year the outfit was supplying prints to offices in Berlin, Paris, Moscow, Brussels, Copenhagen, Turin, and Barcelona. *Moving Picture World* claimed that Rex's European business was "phenomenal" and that the company was "better represented on the other side than any other American picture firm."

26. George Blaisdell, "Phillips Smalley Talks," *MPW*, 24 Jan 1914, 399; "Rex Company Success," *NYDM*, 23 Aug 1911, 20; *MPW*, 27 Jan 1912, 269; Hoffman, "The Rex Director," 674; "The First Birthday of Rex," 671; and Charles Musser, *Before the Nickelodeon: Edwin S. Porter and the Edison Manufacturing Company* (Berkeley: University of California Press, 1991), 459–65.

27. Unident. clipping, 1915, n.p., env. 2518, RLC; Johnson, "A Lady General," 42; "Miss Weber Has Record of One Script a Week for Three Years," *UW*, 14 Feb 1914, 17; "Lois Weber's Remarkable Record," *MPW*, 21 Feb 1914, 975; Smith, "A Perpetual Leading Lady," 636.

28. "Rex Company Success," 20.

29. "The Rex First Release," *MPW*, 4 Mar 1911, 464.

30. H.C. Judson, "The Civilizing Value of the Photoplay," *MPW*, 27 May 1911, 1182.

31. "The First Birthday of Rex," 671.

32. See "Silhouetted Moving Pictures," *MPW*, 11 Mar 1911, 518; "Toning and Tinting as an Adjunct to the Picture," *MPW*, 18 Mar 1911, 574.

33. *Mot*, July 1911, 40–41.

34. Blaisdell, "Phillips Smalley Talks," 399.

35. "Too Near the Camera," *MPW*, 25 Mar 1911, 633–34; H.F. Hoffman, "Cutting Off the Feet," *MPW*, 6 Apr 1912, 53. On the controversy surrounding focal length in the early teens, see Bowser, *The Transformation of Cinema*, 97–102. Bowser points out that Porter maintained an even more conservative stance toward full-body long shots when he left Rex to direct for Famous Players.

36. Keil, *Early American Cinema*, 173.

37. Musser, *Before the Nickelodeon*, 459–65.

38. "Rex First Release," 463.

39. Musser, *Before the Nickelodeon*, 463. Smalley acted alongside Leonard in many of her Rex pictures. See "Players' Personalities—Phillips Smalley," *Photoplay*, Oct 1912, 86.

40. Florey, "The Screen's First Woman Director," 60.

41. Musser, *Before the Nickelodeon*, 468–70.

42. Unident. clipping, 1915, n.p., env. 2518, RLC.

43. Blaisdell, "Phillips Smalley Talks," 399.

44. "E.S. Porter Resigns from Universal," *MPW*, 2 Nov 1912, 44; Musser, *Before the Nickelodeon*, 463–65.

45. "Taylor and Leonard," *MPW* 27 July 1912, 329.

46. "E.S. Porter Resigns," 44; Musser, *Before the Nickelodeon*, 463–65; George Blaisdell, "Edwin S. Porter," *MPW*, 7 Dec 1912, 961–62.

47. "Ready to Resume," *MPW*, 12 Oct 1912, 129; "Players' Personalities," *Photoplay*, Oct 1912, 86; "Lois Weber on Scripts," *MPW*, 19 Oct 1912, 241.

48. *MPW*, 22 Apr 1911, 916; *MPW*, 29 Apr 1911, 940.

49. Bowser, *The Transformation of Cinema*, 117.

50. Unident. clipping, 1915, n.p., env. 2518, RLC.

51. See David Robinson, *From Peep Show to Palace: The Birth of American Film* (New York: Columbia University Press, 1996), 113–19. Also see Richard V. Spencer, "Los Angeles as a Producing Center," *MPW*, 8 Apr 1911, 768. When Rex moved its headquarters westward to Los Angeles, its old, New York studio was occupied by IMP, the company originally founded by Carl Laemmle. See "Smalley Is Back at Hollywood," *UW*, 31 Jan 1914, 9.

52. "All Aboard for Universal City, No. 3," *UW*, 31 Jan 1914, 4–5.

53. "Smalleys at Fishing Village—Entertained by Townspeople," *UW*, 1 Nov 1913, 5; "Smalleys and Company Live at Fishing Village to Make Great Film Drama," *MPMag*, December 1913, n.p., RLC; *MPW*, 6 Dec 1913, 1161; "Miss Weber and Company Off for Monterey," *UW*, 7 Feb 1914, 16; "Jottings from Universal City," *UW*, 16 May 1914, 8; "Smalley, in Octopus' Grasp, near Drowning," *UW*, 23 May 1914, 8.

54. I.G. Edmonds, *Big U: Universal in the Silent Days* (South Brunswick, NJ: A.S. Barnes, 1977), 39.

55. "Smalleys Back with Universal," *MPW*, 3 Apr 1915, 76.

56. "Lois Weber's Remarkable Record," *MPW*, 21 Feb 1914, 975.

57. Edmonds, *Big U*, 40. See also Ella Hall," *MPW*, 9 May 1914, 797; "Ella Hall a Bluebird," *MPW*, 17 June 1916, 2018; and "Popular Picture Personalities," *MPW*, 14 Apr 1917, 279.

58. "Rupert Julian," *MPW*, 21 Mar 1914, 1515; "Elsie Wilson and Rupert Julian with Rex," *MPW*, 4 July 1914, 79; "Julian to Direct Exclusively," *MPW*, 8 July 1916, 269; "Julian Combines Acting and Directing," *MPW*, 16 July 1917, 1769.

59. "The Rex Has 'Come Back,'" *MPW*, 22 Feb 1913, 739; "Lois Weber and Phillips Smalley Are Again with the Rex," *NYDM*, 26 Mar 1913, 32.

60. Blaisdell, "At the Sign of the Flaming Arcs," *MPW*, 5 Apr 1913, 59; *UW*, 6 Dec 1913, 14; *MPW*, 31 May 1913, 921; *MPW*, 26 July 1913, 429.

61. Mark Garrett Cooper, *Universal Women: Filmmaking and Institutional Change in Early Hollywood* (Urbana: University of Illinois Press, 2010), 22.

62. Keil, *Early American Cinema*, 126.

63. *MPW*, 30 Dec 1911, 1074.

64. "Lois Weber Most Gifted of Scenario Writers," *Montgomery Journal*, 27 Dec 1913, n.p., env. 2518, RLC. The wording of this article is lifted directly from a piece in *Universal Weekly*, suggesting that the studio also endorsed this view of the couple's productions. See "Dreaded Leprosy and Power of Fear Theme of New Smalley Play," *UW*, 20 Dec 1913, 25.

65. "Shadows of Life," *MPW*, 4 Oct 1913, 51; Blaisdell, "At the Sign of the Flaming Arcs," 59.

66. *MPW*, 13 June 1914, 1541.

67. Janet Staiger, "Mass-Produced Photoplays: Economic and Signifying Practices in the First Years of Hollywood," *Wide Angle* 4, no. 3 (1981): 12–27; Staiger, "'Tame Authors' and the Corporate Laboratory: Stories, Writers and Scenarios in Hollywood," *Quarterly Review of Film Studies* 8, no. 4 (1983), 33–45. See also Larry Ceplair, "The Movie Industry and the Scenario Writer," in *A Great Lady: A Life of the Screenwriter Sonya Levien* (Lanham, MD: Scarecrow Press, 1996).

68. Keil, *Early American Cinema*, 36–38; David Bordwell, Janet Staiger, and Kristin Thompson, *Classical Hollywood Cinema: Film Style and Mode of Production to 1960* (New York: Columbia University Press, 1985), 146; Lizzie Francke, "'No Finer Calling for a Woman': The Silent Era," in *Script Girls: Women Screenwriters in Hollywood* (London: British Film Institute, 1994), 6.

69. Gene Gauntier, "Blazing the Trail," *Woman's Home Companion* 55, no. 10 (Oct 1928), 7. Gauntier's memoirs were serialized in *Woman's Home Companion* beginning in September 1928 and running through June 1929. Many of the installments are gathered at http://www.cinemaweb.com /silentfilm/bookshelf/4_blaze1.htm (accessed 10 June 2013).

70. Francke, "'No Finer Calling for a Woman,'" 6. Anthony Slide has disputed this figure. See Slide, "Early Women Filmmakers: The Real Numbers," *Film History: An International Journal* 24, no. 1 (2012): 114–21.

71. Blaisdell, "Phillips Smalley Talks," 399.

72. Keil, *Early American Cinema*, 38.

73. Weber quoted in Carter, "Muse of the Reel," 126.

74. "Lois Weber on Scripts," 241.

75. Gertrude M. Price, "Should All Plays End Happily? Woman Movie Director Says 'No'; 'Yes' is Dictum of Managers," *New Orleans Statesman*, 26 Sept 1913, n.p., env. 2518, RLC.

76. "Lois Weber on Scripts," 241.

77. "Lois Weber's Remarkable Record," *MPW*, 21 Feb 1914, 975.

78. Torey Liepa, "Figures of Silent Speech: Silent Film Dialogue and the American Vernacular, 1909–16," Ph.D. dissertation, New York University, 2008, 140.

79. "Lois Weber—Mrs. Phillips Smalley," *UW*, 4 Oct 1913, 9.

80. Price, "Should All Plays End Happily?" n.p.

81. Liepa, "Figures of Silent Speech," 194–95; Epes Wintrop Sargent, "The Dinner," *MPW*, 7 Sept 1912, 972; Sargent, "The Literary Side of Pictures," *MPW*, 4 July 1914, 202.

82. *Mot*, 4 Apr 1914, 250; *MPW*, 28 Mar 1914, 1674; Sargent, "The Literary Side," 199–202.

83. *MPW*, 28 June 1913, 1361. Some historians have attributed the film, mistakenly, to Smalley. See Kevin Brownlow, *The Parade's Gone By ...* (Berkeley: University of California Press, 1968), 23.

84. "All Aboard for Universal City, No. 3," 5.

85. Condon, "Sans Grease Paint," 58; "Phillips Smalley Talks 'Pictures,'" *MPN*, 17 Jan 1914, 22.

86. Peak, "Only Woman Movie Director," C11.

87. "All Aboard for Universal City, No. 3," 5.

88. Smith, "A Perpetual Leading Lady," 635.

89. "'Movie' Actress Runs for Mayor of Infant Town," *LAX*, 12 May 1913, n.p., env. 2518, RLC; "Miss Weber Heads Slate of Movie Actresses That Oppose Men at Election," unident. clipping, n.d., n.p., env. 2518, RLC; "In Woman's Realm," *NY Telegraph*, 10 June 1913, n.p., env. 2518, RLC; *Photoplay*, Sept 1913, 73.

90. *Mot*, 12 July 1913, 16.

91. "'Movie' Actress Runs for Mayor," n.p.

92. "In Woman's Realm," n.p.

93. *Photoplay*, Sept 1913, 73.

94. William Foster Elliot, "Exit Flapper, Enter Woman: Lois Weber Describes Next Screen Type," *LAT*, 6 Aug 1922, 26.

95. "Lois Weber—Mrs. Phillips Smalley," 8–9.

96. This profile appeared six weeks before the release of *Traffic in Souls*, Universal's soon-to-be-controversial feature-length white slave film. Weber's refined persona contrasted sharply with the film's reputation.

97. *Photoplay*, Sept 1913, 73; "Lois Weber—Mrs. Phillips Smalley," 8.

98. Price, "Should All Plays End Happily?" n.p.

99. Richard Abel, "Fan Discourse in the Heartland: The Early 1910s," *Film History* 18, no. 2 (2006): 140–53. See also Gertrude M. Price, "Charming Little Woman Runs 'Movie' Business by Herself, and Makes Big Success," *Des Moines News*, 9 Feb 1913, 2; "Lucky Thirteen Word Proves to Be a New Money Making Position," *Des Moines News*, 15 May 1913, 8; and Richard Abel, letter to author, 13 Dec 2000. Thanks to Abel for sending these clippings my way.

100. Hallett, *Go West, Young Women!*, 70. See also Richard Abel, *Menus for Movieland: Newspapers and the Emergence of American Film Culture* (Oakland: University of California Press, 2015), ch. 4.

101. "Lois Weber of Movies," *Nashville Democrat*, 13 Apr 1913, n.p., env. 2518, RLC.

102. Smith, "A Perpetual Leading Lady," 634–36.

103. Van Loan, "Lois the Wizard," 44.

104. None of these Rex titles survive. Plot summaries were taken from the following reviews and commentaries: *A Heroine of '76, NYDM*, 22 Feb 1911, 32, and *MPW*, 25 Feb 1911, 373; *The Dragon's Breath, MPW* 26 Apr 1913, 381; *Woman's Burden, MPW*, 28 Feb 1914, 1089; *The Final Pardon, MPW*, 9 Mar 1912, 868; *The Spider and Her Web, UW*, 21 Mar 1914, 13, and *MPW*, 28 Mar 1914, 1682; *On Suspicion, UW*, 11 Apr 1914, 11, 24, and *MPW*, 25 Apr 1914, 518.

105. *UW*, 17 Aug 1912, 15, 23.

106. *MPW*, 15 Feb 1913, 681.

107. *MPW*, 22 June 1912, 1164.

108. *MPW*, 8 Mar 1913, 998.

109. *MPW*, 26 July 1913, 429; *UW*, 5 July 1913, 12, 25.

110. *MPW*, 27 Sept 1913, 1393; *UW*, 27 Sept 1913, 21.

111. *MPW*, 22 Feb 1913, 812.

112. *UW*, 23 May 1914, 7; *UW*, 13 June 1914, 20–21; *MPW*, 20 June 1914, 1690.

113. *UW*, 26 July 1913, 21–23; *MPW*, 9 Aug 1913, 638.

114. *UW*, 10 Aug 1912, 3, 9–10; *MPW*, 17 Aug 1912, 674.

115. *MPW*, 7 June 1913, 1033.

116. *MPW*, 26 July 1913, 430.

117. *MPW*, 29 Nov 1913, 1050; *MPW*, 6 Dec 1913, 1152; *UW*, 29 Nov 1913, 22, 24; "Smalleys at Fishing Village," 5; "Smalleys and Company Live at Fishing Village," n.p.

118. *MPW*, 14 Oct 1911, 131.

119. "Smalley Feature a Masterpiece," *UW*, 13 Sept 1913, 8; "Two Kinds of Love Strongly Contrasted in 'Smalley' Drama," *UW*, 4 Oct 1913, 16; "Shadows of Life," *MPW*, 4 Oct 1913, 51.

120. *MPW*, 20 Jan 1912, 244.

121. *MPW*, 22 Nov 1913, 869; *UW*, 1 Nov 1913, 22, 25.

122. *MPW*, 23 May 1914, 1118.

123. *MPW*, 9 Mar 1912, 868.

124. *MPW*, 10 Feb 1912, 492.

125. Ibid.

126. "Clawson Works Out New Photographical Effects," *MPN*, 19 June 1915, 75; "All Aboard for Universal City, No. 3," 5. Clawson appears in a self-reflexive short that the couple directed in 1914 called *The Career of Waterloo Peterson*. Rupert Julian plays an innocent who desires to work as camera operator and happens to show up on the day that Dal Clawson, the Smalley's camera operator, is sick. His comic adventures ensue, with many views of the Universal lot along the way. See *MPW*, 11 Apr 1914, 226; *UW*, 2 May 1914, 25; and *MPW*, 9 May 1914, 821.

127. Keil, *Early American Cinema*, 69–72. Also see Bordwell, Staiger, and Thompson, *Classical Hollywood Cinema*, 179. Thompson argues that such episodes were rarer than Keil finds.

128. Tom Gunning, "Weaving a Narrative: Style and Economic Background in Griffith's Biograph Films," *Quarterly Review of Film Studies* 6, no. 1 (1981): 11–25.

129. *MPW*, 16 Mar 1912, 1004–6.

130. Tom Gunning, *D.W. Griffith and the Origins of American Film: The Early Years at Biograph* (Urbana: University of Illinois Press, 1994), 188–232.

131. Keil, *Early American Cinema*, 173, 235 (quote from 196).

132. Statistics compiled from *MPW* release charts in December 1914 by Eileen Bowser. See *The Transformation of Cinema*, 213.

133. *MPW*, 19 Apr 1913, 282; *MPW* 26 Apr 1913, 381.

134. Blaisdell, "At the Sign of the Flaming Arcs," 59.

135. *MPW*, 26 July 1913, 430; "Smalley Feature a Masterpiece," 8; "Two Kinds of Love Strongly Contrasted in 'Smalley' Drama," 16; "Shadows of Life," *MPW*, 25 Oct 1913, 382.

136. *MPW*, 7 June 1013, 1033.

137. George Blaisdell, "A Jew's Christmas," *MPW*, 6 Dec 1913, 1132; *MPW*, 20 Dec 1913, 1414; *UW*, 6 Dec 1913, 18–19; *UW*, 13 Dec 1913, 13, 16.

138. "'Smalleys' to Film Merchant of Venice for Universal-Rex," *UW*, 6 Dec 1913, 25; Robert Hamilton Ball, *Shakespeare on Silent Film: A Strange Eventful History* (New York: Theatre Arts Books, 1968), 206.

139. Ball, *Shakespeare on Silent Film*, 50–51, 122–25, 146–47.

140. William Uricchio and Roberta E. Pearson, *Reframing Culture: The Case of the Vitagraph Quality Films* (Princeton: Princeton University Press, 1993), 65–74.

141. Ball, *Shakespeare on Silent Film*, 135.

142. "Merchant of Venice Completed," *UW*, 3 Jan 1914, 9; "'Merchant of Venice' Is Supreme Adaptation of Shakespeare," *UW*, 14 Feb 1914, 5.

143. Handford C. Judson, "The Merchant of Venice," *MPW*, 14 Feb 1914, 813.

144. William Shakespeare, *Shakespeare's Comedy of The Merchant of Venice*, with illustrations by Sir James D. Linton (London: Hodder & Stoughton, 1909).

145. Uricchio and Pearson, *Reframing Culture*, 88, 91.

146. *UW*, 7 Feb 1914, 35; *MPW*, 14 Feb 1914, 764–65; *MPW*, 21 Feb 1914, 908–9.

147. "Phillips Smalley Visits New York," *UW*, 10 Jan 1914, 8; Blaisdell, "Phillips Smalley Talks," 399.

148. Judson, "The Merchant of Venice," 813; *Var*, 7 Jan 1914, 32.

149. "Strange Objections to 'The Merchant of Venice,'" *MPW*, 7 Mar 1914, 1245; Ball, *Shakespeare on Silent Film*, 208.

150. Laemmle quoted in Edmonds, *Big U*, 33–34.

151. Ibid., 29, 54.

152. Anthony Slide, *Lois Weber: The Director Who Lost Her Way in History* (Westport, CT: Greenwood Press, 1996), 53.

153. *The Opened Shutters* was relatively well received when it was released in November 1914, several months after Weber and Smalley had left Universal. See *MPW*, 14 Nov 1914, 941; "A Powerful Universal," *Mot*, 14 Nov 1914, 660; *Var*, 21 Nov 1914, 27.

154. Remont, "The Lady behind the Lens," 60.

155. "The Smalleys Join Bosworth," *MPW*, 13 June 1914, 1550; "Progress of Bosworth-Morosco," *MPW*, 10 Apr 1915, 217; "To Sue for Accounting," *LAT*, 10 May 1915, II, 2; Henry Christeen Warnack, "Burbank Makes Rare Offering," *LAT*, 27 July 1914, III, 4.

156. "Hobart Bosworth Directing," *MPW*, 10 Aug 1912, 554; "Progress of Bosworth-Morosco," 217; "Bosworth's Rapid Rise," *NYDM*, 31 Mar 1915, 32; "Bosworth, Incorporated," *MPW*, 13 Aug 1913, 848; Rufus Steele, "In the Sun Spot," *Sunset* 34 (April 1915): 696; Cari Beauchamp, *Without Lying Down:*

Frances Marion and the Powerful Women of Early Hollywood (Berkeley: University of California Press, 1998), 36, 38.

157. *MPW*, 13 June 1914, 1590.

158. "Feature Producers Affiliate," *MPW*, 30 May 1914, 1268–69, quoted in Rob King, "1914—Movies and Cultural Hierarchy," in *American Cinema of the 1910s: Themes and Variations*, ed. Charlie Keil and Ben Singer (New Brunswick, NJ: Rutgers University Press, 2009), 118.

159. "Hobart Van Zandt Bosworth," *The Motion Picture Blue Book*, ed. B.M. Woods (Los Angeles: Cinema Publishing Co., n.d.), n.p.; "Bosworth, Incorporated," *MPW*, 13 Aug 1913, 848; "Paramount Pictures Corporation," *MPW*, 11 July 1914, 264; "Feature Producers Affiliate," 1268–69; Richard Koszarski, *An Evening's Entertainment: The Age of the Silent Feature Picture, 1915–1928* (New York: Scribner, 1990), 69; Anthony Slide, *The American Film Industry: A Historical Dictionary* (New York: Limelight Editions, 1990), 46–47.

160. "Paramount Pictures Corporation," 264; "Morosco and Cort Enter Picture Field," *MPW*, 21 Nov 1914, 1093.

161. King, "1914," 118.

162. "Paramount to Try National Advertising," *MPW*, 5 Sept 1914, 1376.

163. *MPW*, 5 Sept 1914, 1318–19.

164. *MPW*, 7 Nov 1914, 737; *MPW*, 5 Dec 1914, 1330.

165. King, "1914," 117.

166. "Problems of Feature Production," *MPW*, 3 Oct 1914, 37.

167. Stephen W. Bush, "Over Their Heads," *MPW*, 2 Jan 1915, 44.

168. Warnack, "Burbank Makes Rare Offering," 4.

169. "Smalleys Are Most Unusually Gifted Pair in Pictures," *New York Telegraph*, 6 Dec 1914, n.p., env. 2117, RLC; "Lawyer Turns Director, *LAX*, 21 May 1916, n.p., env. 2117, RLC.

170. "Elsie Janis," *MPW*, 16 Jan 1915, 388.

171. "Smalleys Are Most Unusually Gifted Pair," n.p.

172. *MPW*, 28 Nov 1914, 1182.

173. "Doings at Los Angeles," *MPW*, 4 July 1914, 50; Grace Kingsley, "Film Flams," *LAT*, 23 Sept 1914, III, 4; "Film-Flams," *LAT*, 6 Dec 1914, III, 3; "Studio Built in Two Days," *Mot*, 9 Jan 1915, 54; "Progress of Bosworth-Morosco," 217; "Bosworth's Rapid Rise," 32; "Morosco-Bosworth: A Peep at the Studio Where Big Feature Subjects Are Produced," *MPW*, 10 July 1915, 242.

174. Grace Kingsley, "Film Flams," *LAT*, 3 Mar 1915, III, 4; "Making Extensive Improvements," *Mot*, 13 Mar 1915, 390.

175. "Progress of Bosworth-Morosco," 217.

176. "Elsie Janis with Bosworth," *MPW*, 14 Nov 1914, 940; "Elsie Janis Here to 'Film,'" *LAT*, 7 Nov 1914, II, 6.

177. "Morosco and Cort Enter Picture Field," 1093. See also "Oliver Morosco Enters Motion Picture Field," *LAT*, 6 Nov 1914, III, 4.

178. Quoted in Beauchamp, *Without Lying Down*, 36.

179. Ibid., 36, 38–39.

180. Three of the film's five reels survive at the Library of Congress in somewhat incomplete form. Remaining details of the plot have been reconstructed from the script, available in the Paramount Script Collection, AMPAS, and from plot summaries published in the trades. See *MPW*, 12 Dec 1914, 1590; and *Mot*, 26 Dec 1914, 915.

181. "Doings at Los Angeles," *MPW*, 20 Feb 1915, 1124; unident. clipping, 6 Mar 1915, n.p., env. 2518, RLC.

182. Only three of the film's five reels survive. Additional information about the plot is drawn from a script synopsis in the Paramount Script Collection, AMPAS; *Sunshine Molly* publicity herald, c. 1915, author's collection; and reviews published at the time. See *MPW*, 13 Mar 1915, 1625; *MPW*, 20 Mar 1915, 1770; and "Sunshine Molly," *Var*, 12 Mar 1915, 23, 24.

183. *MPW*, 20 Mar 1915, 1770.

184. *Sunshine Molly* publicity herald, c. 1915.

185. "Sunshine Molly," 23, 24.

186. Julian M. Solomon, Jr., "'Hypocrites,'" *MPN*, 10 Oct 1914, 45.

187. "'Hypocrites,'" *Var*, 7 Nov 1914, 23; unident. magazine clipping, 30 Jan 1915, n.p., env. 2518, RLC; unident. clipping, unident. Washington newspaper, 2 Mar 1915, n.p., env. 2518, RLC; unident. clipping, unident. Baltimore newspaper, 23 Feb 1915, n.p., env. 2518, RLC; *LAT*, 24 Mar 1915, II, 7; *NYT*, 21 Aug 1916, 9.

188. "Speaking of the Nude in Advertising," *New York Mail*, 23 Jan 1915, n.p., env. 2518, RLC.

189. "'Hypocrites' Put on at Long Acre Theatre," *MPN*, 23 Jan 1915, 32; "'The Hypocrites' Screened," *Mot*, 6 Feb 1915, 204; "'Hypocrites' Enjoys Successful Broadway Run," *MPN*, 6 Feb 1915, 28; "Remarkable Record of 'Hypocrites,'" *MPW*, 13 Feb 1913, 998.

190. Hanford C. Judson, "'Hypocrites,'" *MPW*, 6 Feb 1915, 832.

191. Advertisement, *MPW*, 5 June 1915, 1561.

192. Unident. clipping, *Pittsburgh Dispatch*, 8 June 1915, n.p., env. 2518, RLC; "'Hypocrites' Returns Here; Now Shown in the Victoria," *Philadelphia North American*, 11 May 1915, n.p., env. 2518, RLC; "'Hypocrites' Open at Globe," *Philadelphia Telegraph*, 13 Apr 1915, n.p., env. 2518, RLC; "Hypocrites," *Atlanta Constitution*, n.d., n.p., env. 2518, RLC.

193. Unident. clipping, *Pittsburgh Dispatch*, 8 June 1915, n.p., env. 2518, RLC.

194. "Nude Figure Barred from Movie Screen," *NYT*, 22 Jan 1917, 9; Kitty Kelly, "If You Can't See It Here—Go to Oak Park," *Chic Trib*, 20 July 1916, I, 5; "Mayor Bans Three Pictures," *MPW*, 1 May 1915, 761; "Nashville Censorship Passes 'Hypocrites,'" *MPW*, 3 Apr 1915, 74; "No State Censorship," *MPW*, 22 May 1915, 1293; "Some Facts of Censoring," *MPW*, 29 May 1915, 1461.

195. "No Naked 'Truth,'" *NYDM*, 14 Apr 1915, 24.

196. *NYDM*, 6 Oct 1915, 32.

197. "'Hypocrites' Sensation All over Country," *MPW*, 1 May 1915, 732; "Taking Denver out of Jitney Class," *MPW*, 1 May 1915, 709; "Michigan Short

Items," *MPW*, 12 June 1915, 1802; "Other San Francisco Notes," *MPW*, 3 Apr 1915, 95; "Variety Offered in Picture Land," *SF Chron*, 20 Mar 1915, 18; "In the Southwest," *MPW*, 8 May 1915, 941; "'Hypocrites' Returns Here."

198. "'Hypocrites' Breaks Records in Crescent City," *MPN*, 10 Apr 1915, 46; "Gulf States Notes," *MPW*, 24 Apr 1915, 599; "Ogden's Alhambra Opens," *MPW*, 10 Apr 1915, 263; "Blaising a Trail through Los Angeles," *MPW*, 22 May 1915, 1242; "Doings in Los Angeles," *MPW*, 10 April 1915, 221; "Doings in Los Angeles," *MPW*, 17 Apr 1915, 378; "New Line of Paper for Hypocrites," *MPW*, 29 May 1915, 1449; "Hypocrites," Paramount Script Collection, AMPAS.

199. Quoted in Beauchamp, *Without Lying Down*, 39; "Portola," *SF Chron*, 14 Mar 1915, 17; unident. clipping, *Ohio State Journal*, 2 Sept 1915, n.p., env. 2518, RLC; unident. clipping, *New York Telegraph*, 24 May 1915, n.p., env. 2518, RLC; "Woman Is Writer of 'Hypocrites,'" *San Francisco Call and Post*, 9 Mar 1915, n.p., env. 2518, RLC.

200. Paul D. Young, "Yours Sincerely, Lois Weber: *Hypocrites* and the Passionate Recognition of Authorship," *Cinema Journal* 55, no. 1 (2015). Young points out that Browning's poem, *The Ring and the Book*, is actually misquoted in the film. The original reads, "What does the world, told *the* truth. . . ."

201. Moya Luckett, *Cinema and Community: Progressivism, Exhibition, and Film Culture in Chicago, 1907–1917* (Detroit: Wayne State University Press, 2013), 83.

202. M.C. Larkin, "Price of Success in Movies Is Sacrifice, Says Thrill Creator," *Milwaukee Journal*, 2 Jan 1916, n.p., env. 2518, RLC.

203. Unident. clipping, 6 Mar 1915, n.p., env. 2518, RLC.

204. "Doings in Los Angeles," *MPW*, 5 Dec 1914, 1363; "Making Extensive Improvements," *Mot*, 13 Mar 1915, 390; Beauchamp, *Without Lying Down*, 41; Slide, *Lois Weber*, 55; "To Sue for Accounting," 2.

205. Quote from Larkin, "Price of Success," n.p. See "Smalleys Back with Universal," *MPW*, 3 Apr 1915, 76; and Gordon Trent, "The 'Smalleys' Now with 'Big U,'" *New York Telegraph*, 1 Apr 1915, n.p., env. 2518, RLC. Announcing their deal, Laemmle called Weber "one of the brightest minds I have ever come in contact with." See *UW*, 3 Apr 1915, 38.

CHAPTER 2

1. Ernestine Black, "Lois Weber Smalley," *Overland Monthly* 68 (Sept 1916): 199.

2. Hugh C. Weir, "Behind the Scenes with Lois Weber," *MPWkly* 31 July 1915, 28; Mlle. Chic, "The Greatest Woman Director in the World," *MPWkly*, 20 May 1916, 24–25; "Ruth Ann Baldwin Directing a Picture," *MPWkly*, 13 Jan 1917, 23.

3. See, for example, "Great Directors and Their Productions," *NYDM*, 15 July 1916, 26, 35. Weber was "ranked second among American photoplay directors," after Griffith, according to another piece. Unident. clipping, *Ohio State Journal*, 2 Sept 1915, n.p., env. 2518, RLC.

4. "Directors' Association Honors Lois Weber," unident. clipping, 21 Nov 1916, MoMA; *Photoplay*, Mar 1917, 87; *MPN*, 24 Mar 1917, n.p., reprinted in *Taylorology: A Continuing Exploration of the Life and Death of William Desmond Taylor*, ed. Bruce Long, no. 95 (Nov 2000), http://silent-movies.com /Taylorology/Taylor95.txt (accessed 15 Feb 2013).

5. Edmonds, *Big U*, 46, 54, 57.

6. "'Jewel,'" *MPWkly*, 28 Aug 1915, 44.

7. "Universal Growing," *MPW*, 21 Nov 1914, 1050; "The Strangest City in the World: A Town Given Over to the Moving Picture," *Scientific American* 112 (17 Apr 1915), 365; Clyde L. Clarke, *Inside a Movie Studio* (Los Angeles: n.p., c. 1920), 1–8; Rufus Steele, "Behind the Screen: How the 'Movie' is Made in the Valley of the New Arabian Nights," *Ladies' Home Journal*, Oct 1915, 16, 80–81; Steele, "In the Sun Spot"; Richard Koszarski, *Universal Pictures: 65 Years* (New York: Museum of Modern Art, 1977), 7; Thomas Schatz, *The Genius of the System: Hollywood Filmmaking in the Studio* Era (New York: Pantheon, 1988), 17–18.

8. "The Spectator," *Outlook* 110 (4 Aug 1915): 822.

9. Koszarski, *Universal Pictures*, 7; Koszarski, *An Evening's Entertainment*, 86; Schatz, *The Genius of the System,* 16, 21.

10. Koszarski, *Universal Pictures*, 7.

11. Cooper, *Universal Women*, 17.

12. Edmonds, *Big U*, 80–81; Koszarski, *Universal Pictures*, 7; Schatz, *The Genius of the System*, 22.

13. Margaret I. MacDonald, "'Wanted—A Home,'" *MPW*, 30 Sept 1916, 2102.

14. "Ida May Park, Director," *MPW*, 14 July 1917, 222, quoted in Mark Garrett Cooper, "Studio History Revisited: The Case of the Universal Women," *Quarterly Review of Film and Video* 25, no. 1 (2007), 28.

15. Cooper, *Universal Women*, 24. See also Anthony Slide, "Universal Women," in *The Silent Feminists: America's First Women Directors* (Lanham, MD: Scarecrow Press, 1996), 41–60.

16. Frances Denton, "Lights, Camera! Quiet! Ready! Shoot!" *Photoplay*, Feb 1918, 50.

17. Black, "Lois Weber Smalley," 200.

18. Koszarski, *Universal Pictures*, 7; Koszarski, *An Evening's Entertainment*, 87.

19. Clifford quoted in Slide, "Universal Women," 42.

20. Cooper, *Universal Women*, 49–89.

21. Denton, "Lights, Camera!" 8.

22. Mlle. Chic, "The Greatest Woman Director," 24–25.

23. Weber "How I Became a Motion Picture Director," 12.

24. Johnson, "A Lady General," 42.

25. Alice Guy Blaché, "Woman's Place in Photoplay Production," *MPW*, 11 July 1914, 195.

26. Denton, "Lights, Camera!" 49.

27. "Lois Weber Talks Shop," *MPW*, 27 May 1916, 1493.

28. Johnson, "A Lady General," 42.

29. Unident. clipping, 1915, n.p., env. 2518, RLC.

30. Unident. clipping, *Chicago Herald*, c. 1915, n.p., env. 2518, RLC.

31. Unident. clipping, 1915, n.p., env. 2518, RLC.

32. "Lois Weber's Graphic Screen Conception for 'Scandal,'" *UW*, 8 May 1915, 14; Peak, "Only Woman Movie Director," C11.

33. Dunning, "The Gate Women Don't Crash," 31.

34. Peltret, "On the Lot with Lois Weber," 90.

35. Mlle. Chic, "The Greatest Woman Director," 25.

36. Van Loan, "Lois the Wizard," 42–43 (quote on 42).

37. "Pavlowa [*sic*] Enthusiastic Worker in Universal Feature Studio," *Mot*, 31 July 1915, 193.

38. *MPW*, 8 Apr 1916, 278.

39. Mlle. Chic, "The Greatest Woman Director," 24.

40. Weber, "How I Became a Motion Picture Director," 12.

41. Dal Clawson was profiled as a "cameraman of international reputation" in *MPN*, 17 July 1915, 129. Clawson's anecdotes informed a contemporary discussion of cinematography published the following month. See Leo Owen, "Camera Stunts: How the Motion-Picture Photographer Turns Things Topsy-Turvy," *Saturday Evening Post*, 14 Aug 1915, 14–15, 30, 32.

42. *Var*, 31 Mar 1916, 25.

43. *Var*, 6 Apr 1917, 22.

44. *MPW*, 22 Apr 1916, 640.

45. Weir, "Behind the Scenes," 28.

46. Kitty Kelly, "Another Step in Photoplay Progress," *Chic Trib*, 31 Jan 1915, n.p., env. 2518, RLC. *The Dumb Girl of Portici* was included in a feature titled "Great Directors and Their Productions," which also showcased *The Birth of a Nation, Civilization, The Battle Cry of Peace, The Eternal City,* and Dixon's *The Fall of a Nation*. See *NYDM*, 15 July 1916, 26, 35.

47. For an account of DeMille's production of *Carmen* with Farrar, see Sumiko Higashi, *Cecil B. DeMille and American Culture: The Silent Era* (Berkeley: University of California Press, 1994), 20–25.

48. "Prominent People Visit Universal City Cal.," *UW*, 29 May 1915, 14.

49. H.H. Van Loan, "Pavlowa's [*sic*] 'The Dumb Girl of Portici,'" *Mot*, 16 Oct 1915, 802; "Notes Written on the Screen," *NYT*, 2 Apr 1916, 11.

50. Another report suggests that Pavlova was paid $40,000, still a considerable sum. See Samuel M. Greene, "The Hay-Day for Universal City," *MPWkly*, 29 Apr 1916, 33.

51. Van Loan, "Pavlowa's 'The Dumb Girl of Portici,'" 801.

52. Ibid., 802. Exactly the same week that Weber and Smalley began shooting *The Dumb Girl of Portici* in Chicago, dancer Maud Allan appeared on screen in *The Rugmaker's Daughter*. See Elizabeth Weigand, "*The Rugmaker's Daughter*, Maud Allan's 1915 Silent Film," *Dance History* 9, no. 2 (1986): 237–51. After shooting the film but prior to its release, Pavlova appeared in an

operatic production of *The Dumb Girl of Portici*, jointly mounted by the Boston Opera Company and her own Ballet Russe, which toured the country during the fall of 1915. See Eric De Lamarter, "Musical Joys in Prospect: Resurgent Opera and Such," *Chic Trib*, 26 Sept 1915, G1; and "Notes Written on the Screen."

53. "Pavlowa [*sic*] Film Screened," *Mot*, 6 Nov 1915, 946.

54. "'Dumb Girl of Portici' Is Given Premiere in Chicago," *MPN*, 12 Feb 1916, 822.

55. *Var*, 7 Apr 1916, 21.

56. "Pavlowa [*sic*] Dimmed in Film," *NYT*, 4 Apr 1916, 11.

57. *Var*, 7 Apr 1916, 21. See also "Too Much Wild-Eyed Rioting Makes This Miss Fire," *Wid's*, 13 Apr 1916, 500; *NYDM*, 15 Apr 1916, 28; and *MPW*, 22 Apr 1916, 640–41.

58. Van Loan, "Lois the Wizard," 44.

59. *NYDM*, 11 Nov 1914, n.p., env. 2518, RLC.

60. Black, "Lois Weber Smalley," 198; unident. clipping, *Columbus Dispatch*, 12 Mar 1916, n.p., env. 2518, RLC; Smith, "A Perpetual Leading Lady," 636; Remont, "The Lady behind the Lens," 126.

61. *MPW*, 21 Nov 1914, 1028.

62. Carter, "The Muse of the Reel," 105.

63. Remont, "The Lady behind the Lens," 60.

64. Richard deCordova, *Picture Personalities: The Emergence of the Star System in America* (Urbana: University of Illinois Press, 1990), 98–107.

65. Kathryn Fuller, *At the Picture Show: Small-Town Audiences and the Creation of Movie Fan Culture* (Washington, DC: Smithsonian Institution Press, 1996), 115–32.

66. Gaylyn Studlar, "The Perils of Pleasure? Fan Magazine Discourse as Women's Commodified Culture in the 1920s," *Wide Angle* 13, no. 1 (1991): 28.

67. Amelie Hastie, "Circuits of Memory and History: *The Memoirs of Alice Guy-Blaché*," in *The Feminist Reader in Early Cinema*, ed. Jennifer Bean and Diane Negra (Durham, NC: Duke University Press, 2002), 29–59.

68. Carter, "The Muse of the Reel," 105; Remont, "The Lady behind the Lens," 126.

69. "Lois Weber, Film Genius, Has Spectacular Rise to Fame," n.d., n.p., env. 2518, RLC.

70. Van Loan, "Lois the Wizard," 42.

71. "Lois Weber, Film Genius," n.p.

72. Smith, "A Perpetual Leading Lady," 636.

73. Mark Lynn Anderson, "Shooting Star: Understanding Wallace Reid and His Public," in *Headline Hollywood: A Century of Film Scandal*, ed. Adrienne L. McLean and David A. Cook (New York: Rutgers University Press, 2001), 86.

74. Johnson, "A Lady General," 42.

75. "The Smalleys," *Photoplay*, Jan 1916, 152.

76. Richard Willis, "Lois Weber and Phillips Smalley—A Practical and Gifted Pair with High Ideals," *Movie Pictorial*, May 1915, n.p., reprinted in

Taylorology, no. 59 (Nov 1997), http://silent-movies.com/Taylorology /Taylor59.txt (accessed 14 Mar 2013).

77. Higashi, *Cecil B. DeMille and American Culture,* 7–8.

78. For analyses of the fan discourse surrounding the Pickford-Fairbanks marriage, see deCordova, *Picture Personalities,* 121–24; and Christina Lane, "Pickford and Fairbanks: Winning and Losing at the Game of Marriage," in "Hollywood Star Couples: Classical-Era Romance and Marriage" (Ph.D. dissertation, University of Texas at Austin, 1999).

79. Unident. clipping, n.p., n.d., env. 2518, RLC; Black, "Lois Weber Smalley," 198; Van Loan, "Lois the Wizard," 42.

80. Peltret, "On the Lot with Lois Weber," 90.

81. Samuel M. Greene, "The Hay-Day of Universal," *LAT,* 9 Apr 1916, II, 14.

82. Unident. clipping, *Columbus Dispatch,* 12 Mar 1916, n.p., env. 2518, RLC.

83. *LAT,* 9 Apr 1916, II, 14.

84. Van Loan, "Lois the Wizard," 43.

85. Ibid., 44.

86. *Photoplay,* July 1917, 81.

87. Black, "Lois Weber Smalley," 198.

88. Remont, "The Lady behind the Lens," 60. For information on other Progressive Era social-problem films, see Kay Sloan, *The Loud Silents: Origins of the Social Problem Film* (Urbana: University of Illinois Press, 1988); Kevin Brownlow, *Behind the Mask of Innocence: Sex, Violence, Prejudice, Crime; Films of Social Conscience in the Silent Era* (New York: Knopf, 1990).

89. "The Smalleys Have a Message to the World," *UW,* 10 Apr 1915, 17. Weber compares cinema to a "voiceless language" in *MPW,* 9 Aug 1913, 640.

90. Weber, "How I Became a Motion Picture Director," 12.

91. Luckett, *Cinema and Community,* 2, 7, 9.

92. Arthur Denison, "A Dream in Realization," *MPW,* 21 July 1917, 418; "Lois Weber Talks of Film Future," *NYDM,* 23 June 1917, 30.

93. Marjorie Howard, "'Even As You and I,' A Drama of Souls at Bay," *MPWkly,* 14 Apr 1917, 18.

94. See, for example, Constance D. Leupp, "The Motion Picture as Social Worker," *Survey,* 27 Aug 1910: 739–41; "Motion Pictures to Be Social Workers," *Survey,* 6 May 1911: 206–7; Jane Stannard Johnson, "Woman's Duty to Motion Pictures," *Ladies' World,* Jan 1915, 18; and Helen Duey, "The Movement for Better Films," *Woman's Home Companion,* Mar 1915, 3, 64.

95. For an interesting discussion of DeMille's use of intertext during these years, see Higashi, *Cecil B. DeMille and American Culture,* 10–20.

96. "Daily Talks by Mary Pickford: Personalities I Have Met; Lois Weber," unident. clipping, McClure Newspaper Syndicate, 1916, n.p., env. 2518, RLC.

97. *NYDM,* 9 June 1915, 37.

98. Only two reels of the film's five survive. Plot summaries can be found in "'Saving the Family Name'—Bluebird," *MPWkly,* 2 Sept 1916, 16–17, 31; and *MPW,* 16 Sept 1916, 1891–92. The film's plot is fictionalized in Claire Marand, "Saving the Family Name," *Photoplay,* Nov 1916, 91–98, 168.

99. Margaret I. MacDonald, "'Wanted—A Home,'" *MPW*, 30 Sept 1916, 2102. The film does not survive; my plot synopsis is drawn from the following sources: *MPW*, 7 Oct 1916, 134–35; and "'Wanted—A Home,' Bluebird Photoplay," *MPWkly*, 30 Sept 1916, 16–17.

100. The film does not survive. For a plot summary, see *NYDM*, 14 Apr 1917, 26.

101. Van Loan, "Lois the Wizard," 43.

102. See Howard Wayne Morgan, *Drugs in America: A Social History* (Syracuse: Syracuse University Press 1982), 88–117; and Diana L. Ahmad, *The Opium Debate and Chinese Exclusion Laws in the Nineteenth-Century American West* (Reno: University of Nevada Press, 2007), 51–76.

103. "Local Chinatown Makes Film Play," *San Francisco Post and Call*, 10 Mar 1916, n.p., env. 2518, RLC; *MPN*, 13 Nov 1915, 172; "Steele's 'Hop' Stories Screened," *NYDM*, 5 Feb 1916, 25.

104. *MPN*, 13 Nov 1915, 172; "Steele's 'Hop' Stories Screened," 25; "Phillips Smalley and Lois Weber in 'Hop, the Devil's Brew,'" *MPWkly*, 12 Feb 1916, 5.

105. *MPW*, 26 Feb 1916, 1308.

106. The film's plot is summarized in the following sources: *Var*, 4 Feb 1916, 29; "Phillips Smalley and Lois Weber in 'Hop, The Devil's Brew,'" 5; and *NYDM*, 11 Mar 1916, 31.

107. *NYDM*, 11 Mar 1916, 31.

108. *Var*, 4 Feb 1916, 29; Kitty Kelly, "Flickerings from Filmland," *Chic Trib*, 25 Mar 1916, 14. For information on other Progressive Era films on drug addiction, see Brownlow, *Behind the Mask of Innocence*, 96–106.

109. "'Room for Long and Short Pictures'—Lois Weber," *MPN*, 22 May 1916, 3222.

110. Mlle. Chic, "The Greatest Woman Director," 24.

111. "Capital Punishment Film Play's Theme," *NYT*, 11 Dec 1916, sec. 7, p. 3.

112. Stuart Banner, *The Death Penalty: An American History* (Cambridge, MA: Harvard University Press, 2002), 208–23; Richard B. Dressner and Glenn C. Altschuler, "Sentiment and Statistics in the Progressive Era: The Debate on Capital Punishment in New York," *New York History* 56, no. 2 (1975): 191–209 (Osborne quoted on 196). Progressive efforts to limit the death penalty were short-lived. Banner reports that of the fifteen states that had abolished execution, only eight remained by 1920 and no additional states would eradicate capital punishment until 1950.

113. Only one reel of *The People vs. John Doe* is known to survive. My plot summary is drawn from the following sources: "Tense Gripping Human Drama Hammers Home Big Thought," *Wid's*, 21 Dec 1916, 1183; *NYDM*, 23 Dec 1916, 26–27; *MPW*, 30 Dec 1916, 1973; and *Mot*, 30 Dec 1916, 1456. For information on other Progressive Era capital punishment films, see Brownlow, *Behind the Mask of Innocence*, 255–61.

114. Stielow's ordeal was one of several highly publicized death penalty cases at the time, including those of Leo Frank and Charles Becker, both of whom proclaimed their innocence and, like Stielow, attracted a sizable

community of supporters agitating for clemency. Becker was a New York police lieutenant accused of murdering a gambler. Frank, convicted of murdering a young factory worker under his employ in Georgia, was widely viewed to have been a victim of anti-Semitism. Two months after his sentence was commuted in June 1915, Frank was abducted from prison and lynched. See Dressner and Altschuler, "Sentiment and Statistics," 197–98; and Gerald S. Henig, "'He did not have a fair trial': California Progressives React to the Leo Frank Case," *California History* 58, no. 2 (1979): 166–78.

115. "The Celebrated Stielow Case," *MPWkly,* 18 Nov 1916, 8–9, 21; Frank Marshall White, "Where There Are Women, There's a Way," *Good Housekeeping,* Aug 1918, 54–56, 130, 133.

116. William D. McGuire to members of the General Committee, 17 Nov 1916; Joe Brandt to McGuire, 20 Nov 1916, both in box 106, NBR.

117. "'The People vs. John Doe,'" *MPWkly,* 25 Nov 1916, 26.

118. "Governor Saves Life of Stielow," *NYT,* 4 Dec 1916, 6; Slide, *Lois Weber,* 86; Edmonds, *Big U,* 88.

119. "What New York Newspapers Said about 'The People vs. John Doe,'" *MPWkly,* 23 Dec 1916, 7; *MPN,* 30 Dec 1916, 4214.

120. *MPW,* 30 Dec 1916, 1973; *NYDM,* 23 Dec 1916, 26.

121. "Still Fight for Stielow," *NYT,* 13 Oct 1916, 7; advertisement, *NYT,* 25 Nov 1916, 6; "Capital Punishment Filmplay's Theme," *NYT,* 11 Dec 1916, 7; *Var,* 15 Dec 1916, 35; *MPW,* 30 Dec 1916, 1973.

122. "Woman Takes Fling at Man-Made [illegible]," *Philadelphia Ledger,* 7 Apr 1917, n.p., env. 2518, RLC.

123. "Tense Gripping Drama Hammers Home Big Thought," 1183.

124. "Notes Written on the Screen," *NYT,* 17 Dec 1916, sec. 10, p. 8.

125. Grace Kingsley, "Frivols," *LAT,* 4 Apr 1917, II, 3.

126. "Notes Written on the Screen," sec. 10, p. 8.

127. "The Celebrated Stielow Case," 9.

128. Several other films took up the cause of capital punishment during these years and also tended to focus on the plight of innocent men. In *And the Law Says* (American, 1916) a judge sentences an innocent man to death on the basis of circumstantial evidence, then finds out that the prisoner is his own "illegitimate" son. See *MPW,* 11 Nov 1916, 806. *Conscience* (Universal, 1915), another film centered on wrongful conviction and execution, featured scenes apparently shot on location at Sing Sing prison. See *MPW,* 12 June 1915, 1784; *MPW,* 19 June 1915, 2004; and *MPN,* 26 June 1915, 73. And *Thou Shalt Not Kill* (Circle Film, 1915) professed to be based on the notorious Leo Frank case. See *Var,* 30 July 1915, 19; *MPN,* 31 July 1915, 97; and *MPW,* 4 Dec 1915, 1920.

129. *Providence Journal,* 26 Sept 1916, n.p., env. 2518, RLC. *The Eye of God* does not survive; my plot summary is derived from the following sources: *Wid's,* 25 May 1916, 600; *Var,* 26 May 1916, 21; *MPW,* 3 June 1916, 1708–9; *MPN,* 3 June 1916, 3427; and *MPWkly,* 3 June 1916, 16–17.

130. *Var,* 26 May 1916, 21.

131. Black, "Lois Weber Smalley," 198.

132. Louise De Koven Bowen, *The Department Store Girl* (Chicago: Juvenile Protection Association of Chicago, 1911), 1.

133. Jane Addams, *A New Conscience and an Ancient Evil* (New York: MacMillan, 1912).

134. Stella Wynne Herron, "Shoes," *Collier's*, 1 Jan 1916, 8–9, 25.

135. "Lois Weber Talks Shop," 1493.

136. Smith, "A Perpetual Leading Lady," 636.

137. "Lois Weber Talks Shop," 1493.

138. "*Shoes*," *MPWkly*, 24 June 1916, 34.

139. *MPW*, 24 June 1916, 2257–58; "A Pair of Shoes," *LAX*, 17 July 1916, n.p., env. 2518, RLC; *Var*, 16 June 1916, 24; Parsons quoted in "*Shoes*," 12.

140. Only two reels of *Idle Wives'* seven reels survive. My discussion of the film is therefore based largely on contemporary reviews and a detailed plot summary. See "Idle Wives," *MPWkly*, 18 Nov 1916, 25–26; *Var*, 22 Sept 1916, 36; *Wid's*, 28 Sept 1916, 996; *MPW*, 7 Oct 1916, 65; *MPN*, 7 Oct 1916, 2231; and *Photoplay*, Dec 1916, 84.

141. William D. Routt, "Lois Weber, or the Exigency of Writing," *Screening the Past* 12 (2001), http://tlweb.latrobe.edu.au/humanities/screeningthepast/firstrelease/fr0301/wr1fr12a.htm (accessed 15 Sept 2014).

142. Sue Ainslie Clark and Edith Wyatt, *Making Both Ends Meet: The Income and Outlay of New York Working Girls* (New York: MacMillan, 1911), 5–6, 37; Bowen, *The Department Store Girl*, 8.

143. *Is This Living?* (New York: Consumers' League of New York City, 1919).

144. Quoted in Bowen, *The Department Store Girl*, 13.

145. Ibid., 4–5.

146. Kathy Peiss, *Cheap Amusements: Working Women and Leisure in Turn-of-the-Century New York* (Philadelphia: Temple University Press, 1986); Addams, *A New Conscience and an Ancient Evil*, 64.

147. Clara E. Laughlin, *The Work-a-Day Girl: A Study of Some Present-Day Conditions* (New York: Fleming H. Revell Co., 1913), 47.

148. Ibid., 51.

149. Constance Balides, "Making Ends Meet: 'Welfare Films' and the Politics of Consumption during the Progressive Era," in Bean and Negra, *A Feminist Reader in Early Cinema*, 167, 186.

150. Peiss, *Cheap Amusements*, 56–76.

151. Clark and Wyatt, *Making Both Ends Meet*, 7–8.

152. Ruth S. True, *The Neglected Girl* (New York: Russell Sage Foundation, 1914), 59–60.

153. Ibid., 54–55.

154. Kristen Whissel, *Picturing American Modernity: Traffic, Technology, and the Silent Cinema* (Durham, NC: Duke University Press, 2008), 188.

155. Since *The Price of a Good Time* does not survive, my analysis is based entirely on plot elements outlined in reviews. See *NYDM*, 17 Nov 1917, 18; *Wid's*, 22 Nov 1917, 743; *Var*, 23 Nov 1917, 43; *MPW*, 24 Nov 1917, 1184–85;

MPN, 24 Nov 1917, 3363–63; and "'The Price of a Good Time' a Winner," *MPN*, 21 Jan 1918, 279.

156. *MPW*, 24 Nov 1917, 1184.

157. *MPW*, 8 Jan 1916, 230.

158. A more detailed analysis of the film can be found on my audio commentary for the DVD release of *Where Are My Children?* on *Treasures III: Social Issues in American Film, 1900–1934* (National Film Preservation Foundation, 2007).

159. Theodore Roosevelt, "On American Motherhood," speech before the National Congress of Mothers, Washington, D.C., 13 Mar 1905, http://www.nationalcenter.org/TRooseveltMotherhood.html (accessed 9 Aug 2007).

160. *MPW*, 29 Apr 1916, 817.

161. The best analysis of the early-twentieth-century birth control movement remains Linda Gordon's *Woman's Body, Woman's Right: Birth Control in America*, rev. ed. (New York: Penguin, 1990), 93–242. For information on Sanger, in particular, see Ellen Chesler, *Woman of Valor: Margaret Sanger and the Birth Control Movement in America* (New York: Simon and Schuster, 1992); and Margaret Sanger, *Margaret Sanger: An Autobiography* (New York: W.W. Norton, 1938).

162. Original continuity script for *Where Are My Children?* Kevin Brownlow collection.

163. Ironically, Margaret Sanger would employ a similar technique in her own film, *Birth Control*, the following year.

164. Original continuity script for *Where Are My Children?*

165. Ibid.

166. See Garth S. Jowett, "'A Capacity for Evil': The 1915 Supreme Court *Mutual* Decision," *Historical Journal of Film, Radio, and Television* 9, no. 1 (1989): 59–78.

167. William D. McGuire to the General Committee, 18 Mar 1916, box 107, NBR.

168. McGuire to invited guests, 18 Mar 1916, box 107, NBR. For a more detailed discussion of the board's treatment of *Where Are My Children?* see Shelley Stamp, "Taking Precautions, or Regulating Early Birth Control Films," in Bean and Negra, *A Feminist Reader in Early Cinema*, 270–97. The board's treatment of other sensitive issues during these years is well documented in Francis G. Couvares, "The Good Censor: Race, Sex, and Censorship in the Early Cinema," *Yale Journal of Criticism* 7, no. 2 (1994): 233–51; and Lee Grieveson, *Policing Cinema: Movies and Censorship in Early-Twentieth-Century America* (Berkeley: University of California Press, 2004).

169. McGuire to Executive Committee, 11 Apr 1916, box 107, NBR.

170. Unident. correspondence, n.d., box 107, NBR.

171. McGuire to Universal, 10 Apr 1916; Hal Reid to McGuire, 17 Apr 1916, both in box 107, NBR.

172. Kitty Kelly, "A Clean Photoplay Despite the Ads," *Chic Trib*, 31 July 1916, 11.

173. "Smalley's Picture Endorsed," *MPW*, 15 Apr 1916, 413; "'Rejected' Film Seen at the Globe," *New York Morning Telegraph*, 17 Apr 1916, n.p., box 107, NBR.

174. *New York Tribune*, 13 Apr 1916, 14; "Women Faint at Photoplay of Birth Control," *New York Herald*, 13 Apr 1916, 9; "Birth Control in Films," *New York Tribune*, 14 Apr 1916, 11; *New York Tribune*, 15 Apr 1916, 7; *New York Tribune*, 16 Apr 1916, 2.

175. *New York Tribune*, 13 Apr 1916, 14; 15 Apr 1916, 7; 18 Apr 1916, 16.

176. "Women Faint at Photoplay of Birth Control," 9.

177. "U. Film's Big Business," *Var*, 21 Apr 1916, 25.

178. Reid to McGuire, 17 Apr 1916; Joe Brandt to Cranston Brenton, 17 Apr 1916, both in box 107, NBR.

179. "Birth Control Discussion with Conditions Plainly Pictured," *Wid's*, 20 Apr 1916, 524.

180. "Smalley's Picture Endorsed," 413.

181. "Birth Control Discussion," 524.

182. *NYDM*, 22 Apr 1916, 42.

183. *Var*, 14 Apr 1916, 26.

184. *MPW*, 29 Apr 1916, 817.

185. *Var*, 14 Apr 1916, 26.

186. *NYDM*, 22 Apr 1916, 42.

187. *MPW*, 29 Apr 1916, 817–18.

188. "Control League Differs," *Portland Oregon News*, 18 Nov 1916, n.p., box 107, NBR.

189. Black, "Lois Weber Smalley," 200.

190. *MPW*, 3 June 1916, 1615.

191. *MPWkly*, 3 June 1916, 47.

192. *Albany Journal*, 7 June 1916, n.p., env. 2518, RLC; "Pictures in Chicago," *Var*, 22 Sept 1916, 32; Mildred Joclyn, "Sordid Tale of Unborn Featured at La Salle," *Chicago Post*, n.d., n.p., env. 2518, RLC; "*Where Are My Children?* Is Market Street Theater Offering," *San Francisco Post*, 21 Aug 1916, n.p., env. 2518, RLC; "Statement Regarding the Exhibition of *Where Are My Children?*" box 107, NBR.

193. Record Group 22, Pennsylvania State Board of Censors (Motion Pictures), Pennsylvania State Archives. Some of the records are undated and others date from 1921, when the film was resubmitted for consideration by the board. See also "Pennsylvania Turns Down 'Where Are My Children?,'" *MPN*, 7 Oct 1916, 2206, 2208.

194. Black, "Lois Weber Smalley," 200.

195. *MPW*, 3 June 1916, 1615.

196. "'Children' Film in Boston," *Var*, 7 July 1916, 22; "Boston's Mayor Accused," *Var*, 22 Sept 1916, 32.

197. No known print of *The Hand That Rocks the Cradle* survives; my analysis is based on the film's printed screenplay, published in "Continuity and Subtitles: 'Is A Woman a Person?,'" *Film History* 1, no. 4 (1987): 343–66.

Although there is no way to compare this script to finished versions of the film, plot summaries printed at the time appear to confirm that the film was shot and released much as it was written. See *MPW*, 2 June 1917, 1501; and *The Hand That Rocks the Cradle* publicity herald, c. 1917, Martin F. Norden Collection.

198. *The Hand That Rocks the Cradle* publicity herald.

199. Ibid.

200. Undated report by Secretary W. M. Covill; undated affidavit prepared for William D. McGuire, both in box 104, NBR.

201. "Film That Was Banned Is Shown," unident. newspaper clipping, 12 May 1917, n.p., env. 2518, RLC; *New York Tribune*, 13 May 1917, IV, 4. For a more detailed analysis of censorship battles surrounding *The Hand That Rocks the Cradle* and *Birth Control*, see Stamp, "Taking Precautions," 284–92. For a discussion of Sanger's film, see Martin F. Norden, "Revisionist History, Restricted Cinema: The Strange Case of Margaret Sanger and *Birth Control*," *Cultural Sutures: Medicine and Media*, ed. Lester D. Friedman (Durham, NC: Duke University Press, 2004), 263–79.

202. "Lois Weber, Film Genius," n.p.; Florence Lawrence, "'The Hand That Rocks the Cradle' Says Laws React against Race Benefits," *LAX*, 24 June 1917, n.p., env. 2518, RLC.

203. "Lois Weber Talks Shop," 1493.

204. *MPW*, 29 Apr 1916, 817.

205. *Wid's*, 31 May 1917, 349; *MPW*, 2 June 1917, 1458; *Wid's*, 31 May 1917, 349; *NYDM*, 26 May 1917, 28.

206. *MPW*, 2 June 1917, 1458.

207. *MPW*, 6 Jan 1917, 84; "Carl Laemmle Denies Lois Weber Rumors," *MPW*, 3 Mar 1917, 1366; Robert Cochrane to Siegfried Hartman, 15 Mar 1917 (thanks to Mark Garrett Cooper for sharing this letter).

208. *MPW*, 10 Mar 1917, 1615.

209. Remont, "The Lady behind the Lens," 60.

210. Edmonds, *Big U*, 80, 90; Koszarski, *An Evening's Entertainment*, 87; Schatz, *The Genius of the System*, 21; Cooper, "Studio History Revisited," 18.

CHAPTER 3

1. Lois Weber, "Hostility of Men Drawback to Women Making Success in Picture Directing, Claim," *San Diego Tribune*, 25 Apr 1928, 13.

2. Remont, "The Lady behind the Lens," 60.

3. *Var*, 15 June 1917, 28; "News of Lois Weber Productions," *Lois Weber Bulletin*, no. 1 (June 1917), env. 2518, RLC.

4. "Lois Weber, Film Genius," n.p.

5. Carter, "The Muse of the Reel," 62; Remont, "The Lady behind the Lens," 59; Peltret, "On the Lot with Lois Weber," 89; Denison, "A Dream in Realization: Interview with Lois Weber," 417. Denison was the new studio's publicist.

6. Denison, "A Dream in Realization," 417.

7. "News of Lois Weber Productions," n.p.

8. "Lois Weber Talks of Film Future," *Dramatic Mirror*, 23 June 1917, 30; "Good Luck to Ye, Lois," *Reeland* 1, no. 6 (29 Jan 1917), n.p., http://www.silentfilmstillarchive.com/brooklyn_madison_monroe_jan_29_1917.htm (accessed 24 Apr 2014).

9. *Wid's Yearbook, 1921–22*, n.p., quoted in Slide, *Lois Weber*, 125.

10. "Lois Weber, Film Genius," n.p.

11. Quoted in Bordwell, Staiger, and Thompson, *Classical Hollywood Cinema*, 135.

12. Denison, "A Dream in Realization," 418.

13. Bordwell, Staiger, and Thompson, *Classical Hollywood Cinema*, 134–39.

14. Denison, "A Dream in Realization," 418.

15. Bordwell, Staiger, and Thompson, *Classical Hollywood Cinema*, 125.

16. H.G. O'Brien, "Portable Power Plants for Motion Picture Studios," *Transactions of the Society of Motion Picture Engineers*, no. 11 (1920): 128.

17. "Lois Weber Sails for Europe; Plans Production of Big Films," *MPW*, 8 Oct 1921, 676.

18. "News of Lois Weber Productions," n.p.

19. "Lois Weber Starts Production," *MPW*, 30 June 1917, 2106.

20. *Dramatic Mirror*, 8 Dec 1917, 9.

21. *Screenland*, Jan 1922, 14.

22. Review of *Borrowed Clothes*, *Wid's Daily*, 19 Dec 1918, n.p.

23. "Ince to Build Los Angeles Studio," *MPW*, 7 July 1917, 73.

24. Weber was also included among a 1916 list of "prominent directors." See *NYDM*, 15 July 1916, 26, 35. For an analysis of how filmmakers like DeMille and von Stroheim became "touchstones for the creation of a director-centered cinema" during these years, see Gaylyn Studlar, "Erich von Stroheim and Cecil B. DeMille: Early Hollywood and the Discourse of Directorial 'Genius,'" in Grundmann, Lucia, and Simon, *The Wiley-Blackwell History of American Film*, Vol. 1, *Origins to 1928*, 293–312.

25. Koszarski, *An Evening's Entertainment*, 110. Staiger makes a similar point. See Bordwell, Staiger, and Thompson, *Classical Hollywood Cinema*, 139–40.

26. "Lois Weber Is Whole Show in Her Company," n.d., vol. 2, CWSBC.

27. Remont, "The Lady behind the Lens," 61.

28. Weber, "Hostility of Men Drawback to Women," 13.

29. Koszarski, *An Evening's Entertainment*, 108–10.

30. "'Lois Weber Productions' Latest Organization," *MPN*, 24 Mar 1917, 182; "Carl Laemmle Denies Lois Weber Rumors," 1366; Grace Kingsley, "Lois Weber Arranging for Studio Site," *LAT*, 18 May 1917, II, 3.

31. Cal York, "Plays and Players," *Photoplay*, Apr 1917, 124.

32. "Lois Weber Breaks Arm," *MPW*, 12 Oct 1918, 207.

33. For more on *Jewel*, see Slide, *American Film Industry: A Historical Dictionary*, 179; Cooper, *Universal Women*, 13.

34. See, for example, *MPW*, 10 Nov 1917, 782; and "Universal Branch Managers Meet in Chicago," *MPW*, 27 July 1918, 529.

35. *Motion Picture Classic*, May 1918, n.p., env. 621, RLC.

36. Ibid.

37. "Mildred Harris," *MPW*, 7 Nov 1914, 768; "Mildred Harris with Griffith-Mutual," *MPW*, 20 Feb 1915, 1127; "Five Years Ago This Month," *Photoplay*, Oct 1917, 79.

38. "Mildred Harris with Lois Weber," *MPW*, 27 Oct 1917, 511.

39. "Among the Women," *Var*, 3 May 1918, 44.

40. Remont, "The Lady behind the Lens," 61.

41. Dreiser quoted in Kenneth Schuyler Lynn, *Charlie Chaplin and His Times* (New York: Simon and Schuster, 1997), 212.

42. "For Husbands Only—Jewel," *Photoplay*, Oct 1918, 76–77.

43. "'Price of a Good Time' Shown at Superba; Genuine Drama in Lois Weber's Girls Film under Her Own Management," *LAX*, 25 Nov 1917, n.p., env. 621, RLC.

44. "Lois Weber at Work on Drama," *MPW*, 18 May 1918, 1007.

45. "Lois Weber's 'Price of a Good Time,'" *LAT*, 25 Nov 1917, III, 4; *MPN*, 6 April 1918, 2031; Robert C. McElravy, "Borrowed Clothes," *MPW*, 7 Dec 1918, 1115; "'Borrowed Clothes,'" *LAT*, 30 Dec 1918, II, 4.

46. Julian Johnson, "The Shadow Stage: An Analytical Review of the Year's Acting," *Photoplay*, Nov 1918, 81.

47. Review of *The First Woman, Var*, 28 Apr 1922, n.p., reprinted in *Variety Film Reviews* (New York: Garland, 1983).

48. Truman B. Handy, "Gossip of the Pacific Coast," *Motion Picture Classic*, July 1920, 50.

49. "Chaplin Engaged," *LAT*, 19 Aug 1918, II, 1; "Mildred Harris Wife of Chas. Chaplin since Oct. 23," *MPW*, 23 Nov 1918, 810; "Chaplin's Bride in Hospital," *LAT*, 13 Nov 1918, II, 1; Grace Kingsley, "Au Revoir, Charlie," *LAT*, 31 Jan 1919, II, 3; Joyce Milton, *Tramp: The Life of Charlie Chaplin* (New York: Harper Collins, 1996), 147–49.

50. Johnson, "The Shadow Stage," 112.

51. *MPW*, 14 Dec 1918, 1141–43; "Lois Weber Supplies Western to Program," *MPN*, 22 Feb 1919, 1183.

52. *MPN*, 1 Mar 1919, 1244; *MPN*, 22 Mar 1919, 1729.

53. "Exhibitors Quick to Seek Film of Chaplin's Bride," *MPW*, 7 Dec 1918, 1104; *MPN*, 8 Feb 1919, 780; "Drama," *LAT*, 5 Jan 1919, III, 1; *LAT*, 2 Jan 1919, II, 8; "Chaplin and His Bride Appear on Same Screen," *MPW*, 30 Nov 1918, 970; "Bride of Comedy King on Display in 'Borrowed Clothes,'" *Chic Trib*, 21 Nov 1918, 14.

54. "'When a Girl Loves'—Jewel," *MPN*, 29 Mar 1919, 2010; "Borrowed Clothes," *Dramatic Mirror*, 30 Nov 1918, 810; *NYT*, 19 Nov 1918, 11; "Charlie

Chaplin and Mildred Harris Stay on at the Broadway," *NYT,* 25 Nov 1918, 11; *Wid's Daily,* 19 Dec 1918, n.p.; "The Screen," *NYT,* 10 Mar 1919, 9.

55. "For Husbands Only," *MPN,* 6 Apr 1918, 2031; *MPW,* 14 Dec 1918, 1141–43.

56. "Director for Mrs. Chaplin," *LAT,* 4 Sept 1919, III, 4; "West Permanently Gets Mayer," *MPN,* 8 Nov 1919, 3468; "Great Campaign on Mrs. Chaplin," *MPN,* 15 Nov 1919, 3606.

57. Just Four Belated Midweek Notices," *LAT,* 2 Jan 1919, II, 8; Robert C. McElravy, "Forbidden," *MPW,* 6 Sept 1919, 1528; McElravy, "Home," *MPW,* 23 Aug 1919, 1179.

58. "Weber Directs Anita Stewart," *MPN,* 23 Nov 1918, 3048; "Lois Weber to Direct Anita Stewart," *MPW,* 7 Dec 1918, 1056; Grace Kingsley, "Lois Weber Leaves U; Anita Stewart Engages the Noted Woman Director," *LAT,* 13 Nov 1918, II, 3.

59. "Borrowed Clothes," *Var,* 22 Nov 1918, 44.

60. Quoted in Mark A. Vieira, *Irving Thalberg: Boy Wonder to Producer Prince* (Berkeley: University of California Press, 2010), 18.

61. Karen Ward Mahar, *Women Filmmakers in Early Hollywood* (Baltimore: Johns Hopkins University Press, 2006), 154–60.

62. Benjamin Hampton, *A History of the Movies* (1931; repr., New York: Arno Press, 1970), 146.

63. Mahar, *Women Filmmakers,* 154–55.

64. Tino Balio, "Artists in Business, 1919," in *United Artists: The Company That Changed the Film Industry, 1951–78* (Madison: University of Wisconsin Press, 2009), 11; "Stewart Pictures Go to First National," *MPW,* 10 Aug 1918, 819.

65. Gladys Hall, "Ex-tra! The Story of Anita Stewart's Hoodoo Year, as Told for the First Time," *MPMag,* Aug 1918, 98. See also "Anita Stewart Ill; Is in Sanitarium Suffering from Nervous Breakdown," *NYDM,* 16 June 1917, n.p., env. 2170, RLC; "Anita Stewart Must Prolong Rest Indefinitely," *NYDM,* 30 June 1917, n.p., env. 2170, RLC; "Vitagraph Settles Anita Stewart Case," *MPW,* 3 Aug 1918, 667; DeWitt Bodeen, *From Hollywood: The Careers of 15 Great American Stars* (New York: A. S. Barnes, 1976), 117–27.

66. Grace Kingsley, "Anita Stewart, Producer," *LAT,* 5 Jan 1919, III, 1.

67. Ibid. See also "Better Pictures for 1917 Is Ambition of Anita Stewart; By Anita Stewart, Vitagraph Star," *NYDM,* 27 Jan 1917, n.p., env. 2170, RLC.

68. "Lois Weber to Direct Anita Stewart," 1056.

69. "Mary Regan," *Var,* 9 May 1919, 53; Edward Weitzel, "Mary Regan," *MPW,* 17 May 1919, 1071; "Excellent Character Studies in Distinctive Production; Sages in Middle," *Wid's Daily,* 11 May 1919, 7; "Mary Regan— First National," *MPN,* 17 May 1919, 3274.

70. Robert Grau, "The Twenty Greatest of Filmdom," *MPMag,* May 1916, 110.

71. *Photoplay,* Jan 1919, n.p., env. 2170, RLC.

72. "Weber Directs Anita Stewart," 3048.

73. "West Permanently Gets Mayer," 3468.

74. "Mary Regan," *Photoplay*, July 1919, 78.

75. *MPMag*, Mar 1919, 93.

76. "A Midnight Romance," *Var*, 14 Mar 1919, 46.

77. "Broken Arm Causing Trouble," *MPW*, 8 Feb 1919, 754; "Lois Weber's Arm," *MPW*, 12 April 1919, 218.

78. Phillips Smalley to Pat Powers, 21 March 1919, Harry and Roy Aitken Papers, Wisconsin Center for Film and Television Research, Wisconsin Historical Society, Madison. My thanks to Eric Hoyt for discovering this.

79. "Mrs. Chaplin Free Agent," *Var*, 27 July 1919, n.p., env. 621, RLC; Grace Kingsley, "Lois Weber's Plans," *LAT*, 14 Aug 1919, III, 4; "Lois Weber Returns to Coast to Resume Work," *MPW*, 6 Sept 1919, 1458; Bodeen, *From Hollywood*, 117–27.

80. "Lois Weber Here," *Var*, 30 May 1919, 82; "Lois Weber Signs with Famous Players–Lasky," *MPW*, 2 Aug 1919, 644; "Lois Weber Returns to Coast," 1458.

81. "West Permanently Gets Mayer," 3468.

82. Slide, *Lois Weber*, 109; "Lois Weber Buys Studio She Has Leased for Past Three Years," *MPW*, 2 Oct 1920, 635.

83. *NYT*, 27 July 1919, 44; Hampton, *A History of the Movies*, 207; Koszarski, *An Evening's Entertainment*, 69–72.

84. See, for example, the press kit for *Too Wise Wives*, private collection.

85. Fuller, *At the Picture Show*, 108–10.

86. *Ladies' Home Journal*, January 1921, 34; *Photoplay*, Feb 1921, 4.

87. Grace Kingsley, "Lois Weber's Plans," *LAT*, 14 Aug 1919, III, 4.

88. "Why Be an Extra? Claire Windsor, She Waited—and Worried—And Won!" unident. clipping, n.d., vol. 1, CWSBC.

89. Signed contract between Lois Weber and Ola Cronk, 12 Jan 1921, vol. 2, CWSBC. Windsor had already appeared in *To Please One Woman* before the contract was signed.

90. Maude Cheatham, "The Heroine," *Motion Picture Classic*, Apr 1922, n.p., oversize scrapbook, CWSBC; Stuart Oderman, *Roscoe "Fatty" Arbuckle: A Biography of the Silent Film Comedian, 1887–1993* (Jefferson, NC: McFarland, 2005), 173.

91. Helen Rockwell, "The Girl You Never Know," unident. clipping, n.d., vol. 1, CWSBC. See also "Olga [sic] Cronk in the Movies Is Protégé of Lois Weber," unident. clipping, n.d., vol. 1, CWSBC; "A Very Real Message Conveyed in 'The Blot,'" unident. clipping, n.d., vol. 2, CWSBC; and "'The Blot' Great American Drama of Today," unident. clipping, n.d., vol. 2, CWSBC.

92. "Goldwyn Signs Claire Windsor," *MPW*, 15 July 1922, 216; "Signs New Contract," *MPW*, 11 July 1925, 196; Denise Lowe, *An Encyclopedic Dictionary of Women in Early American Films, 1895–1930* (New York: Haworth Press, 2005), 589.

93. "Hunt Actress by Plane; Chaplin Offers $1,000 Reward," *Los Angeles Record*, c. July 1921, n.p., vol. 1, CWSBC; "May Be Next Mrs. Charlie Chaplin," *Toledo Blade*, 26 Oct 1921, n.p., env. 2626, RLC; "Clues Point to Director and

Actress," *Toledo Blade*, 4 Feb 1922, n.p., env. 2626, RLC; "Claire Windsor's Son Foils Kidnapping Plot," *LAX*, c. Oct 1921, n.p., oversize scrapbook, CWSBC.

94. Grace Kingsley, "Lois Weber to Flit," *LAT*, 14 Jan 1921, III, 4; "Lois Weber Coming East," *Wid's Daily*, 15 Jan 1921, 2; "Lois Weber Here," *Wid's Daily*, 4 Feb 1921, 1; "Lois Weber Returns to Los Angeles," *Hollywood Informer*, 18 Mar 1921, 15; Slide, *Lois Weber*, 112.

95. "Lois Weber Denies Report," *Dramatic Mirror and Times*, 5 Mar 1921, 421; *Wid's Daily*, 7 Mar 1921, 3.

96. "Attacks Big Firm as Film Monopoly; Federal Trade Board Declares Famous Players–Lasky Corporation Violates Trust Laws," *NYT*, 1 Sept 1921, n.p., http://www.cinemaweb.com/silentfilm/bookshelf/9_ftc_1.htm (accessed 26 Nov 2001).

97. "F.B. Warren Out," *Wid's Daily*, 30 Mar 1921, 1; "Warren's Company Formed," *Wid's Daily*, 18 Apr 1921, 1; "Ten to Start," *Wid's Daily*, 20 Apr 1921, 1; "Screen People and Plays," *NYT*, 1 May 1 1921, 79; "Unit Price Rating," *Wid's Daily*, 10 June 1921, 1, 3; advertisement, *Wid's Daily*, 28 June 1921, 9; advertisement, *Wid's Daily*, 29 June 1921, 11; "Film Industry Flourishing," *LAT*, 18 July 1921, I, 6; "Large Film Firm Will Come Here," *LAT*, 13 Aug 1921, II, 1.

98. "Name of F.B. Warren Corporation Has Been Changed to Wid Gunning, Inc.," *MPW*, 3 Dec 1921, 549; advertisement, *FD*, 9 Mar 1922, 4. Wid Gunning was the great-uncle of film scholar Tom Gunning.

99. Edwin Schallert, "Seeks Ideal Themes; Lois Weber Now Fulfilling Cherished Project," unident. clipping, n.d., vol. 2, CWSBC.

100. *Wid's Yearbook*, *1921–22*, n.p., quoted in Slide, *Lois Weber*, 125.

101. "Buys Gunning Films," *FD*, 7 Apr 1922, 1; "New Distributor," *FD*, 13 Jan 1922, 1.

102. "Gunning Sued by Lois Weber," *LAT*, 5 Nov 1922, I, 4.

103. "Saving the Family Name—Bluebird," *MPWkly*, 2 September 1916, 16–17.

104. "Mildred Harris with Lois Weber," *MPW*, 27 Oct 1917, 511; *MPN*, 30 Aug 1919, 1873; "Mildred Harris in 'Home,'" *Toledo Blade*, 7 Dec 1919, n.p., env. 621, RLC.

105. "Olga Cronk in the Movies"; "A Very Real Message Conveyed in 'The Blot'"; "'The Blot' Great American Drama of Today."

106. "Lois Weber Sails for Europe; Plans Production of Big Films," *MPW*, 8 Oct 1921, 676; unident. clipping, n.d., vol. 2, CWSBC; "Rialto," unident. clipping, n.d., vol. 2, CWSBC; "Claire Windsor Started Career as Film Extra," unident. clipping, n.d., vol. 2, CWSBC; Josephine MacDowell, "Lois Weber Understands Girls," *Cinema Art*, Jan 1927, 18; Dunning, "The Gate Women Don't Crash," 31; *Daily News* (New York?), 3 Feb 1933, n.p., BRTC.

107. *NYT*, 14 Nov 1939, n.p., BRTC; "Lois Weber Movie Star-Maker," unident. clipping, n.d., BRTC; "Lois Weber, First Woman Director, Dies," *LAX*, 14 Nov 1939, n.p., LAXC.

108. "Discovering Mary McLaren [*sic*]: How One Girl Got Her First Big Chance," *Green Book*, Mar 1917, 404–5, env. 1280, RLC; "The Strange Case of Mary MacLaren," *MPWkly*, 24 June 1916, 9; *Theatre Magazine*, Apr 1919, n.p., env. 1280, RLC; "From Extra to Stardom," *MPMag*, Sept 1917, 39. See also Ruth Kingsley, "How Mary Made Her Eyes Behave," *MPMag*, Feb 1918, 38–39, 107.

109. Quoted in Richard Koszarski, "A Few Thoughts on Mary MacLaren's Shoes," *Griffithiana* 40–42 (1991): 82.

110. Carter, "The Muse of the Reel," 126.

111. "Stage Experience? None!" *Photoplay*, Oct 1918, 43.

112. "Mildred Harris," *MPW*, 7 Nov 1914, 768; "Mildred Harris with Griffith Mutual," *MPW*, 20 Feb 1915, 1127; "Mildred Harris with Lois Weber," *MPW* 27 Oct 1917, 511.

113. "Mildred Harris with Lois Weber," 511.

114. Mary MacLaren, "How I Happened," *MPW*, 21 July 1917, 427.

115. Rockwell, "The Girl You Never Know," n.p.

116. "Mrs. Chaplin Free Agent," *Var*, 27 July 1919, n.p., env. 621, RLC; "Actress Says Her Youth Was Sold for $50 a Week," 9 Mar 1917, n.p., env. 1280, RLC; *Photoplay*, May 1917, n.p., env. 1280, RLC; *Photoplay*, Aug 1917, n.p., env. 1280, RLC; "MacLaren Returns to the Universal," *MPW*, 16 Feb 1918, 972. MacLaren eventually returned to Universal under undisclosed terms.

117. Mary Roberts Reinhart, "Faces and Brains," *Photoplay*, Feb 1922, 47–48, 107, reprinted in *They Also Wrote for the Fan Magazines: Film Articles by Literary Giants from e.e. cummings to Eleanor Roosevelt, 1920–1939*, ed. Anthony Slide (Jefferson, NC: McFarland, 1992), 123–28.

118. Theodore Dreiser, "Hollywood: Its Morals and Manners," *Shadowland*, Nov 1921, n.p., reprinted in *Taylorology*, no. 41 (May 1996), http://silent-movies.com/Taylorology/Taylor41.txt. St. Johns's articles appeared in *Photoplay* from February to July 1927.

119. "'Chronicle' Screen Contest Nearing Close," *SF Chron*, 7 Jan 1921, 11.

120. Judith Mayne, *Directed by Dorothy Arzner* (Bloomington: Indiana University Press, 1994), 45–49.

121. Peltret, "On the Lot with Lois Weber," 90.

122. Marguerite Sheridan, "The Girl from Wyoming," *MPMag*, Nov 1918, 123.

123. Windsor quoted in Rockwell, "The Girl You Never Know," n.p.

124. Carter, "The Muse of the Reel," 126.

125. Whitney Williams, "Under the Lights," *LAT*, 31 Oct 1926, I2.

126. *NYT*, 14 Nov 1921, 18; *Dramatic Mirror*, 8 Dec 1917, 9.

127. Slide, *Lois Weber*, 152.

128. Lenore Coffee, *Storyline: Recollections of a Hollywood Screenwriter* (London: Cassell, 1973) 16. Coffee misremembers the studio being on Melrose Avenue.

129. Remont, "The Lady behind the Lens," 60.

130. Frances Marion, *Off with Their Heads! A Serio-comic Tale of Hollywood* (New York: MacMillan, 1972), 11–13; Elizabeth Benneche Petersen, "Frances Marion Goes Over: An Appreciation," *MPMag*, Dec 1918, 54.

131. Cari Beauchamp details the pair's friendship in *Without Lying Down*.

132. Anne Morey, *Hollywood Outsiders: The Adaptation of the Film Industry, 1913–34* (Minneapolis: University of Minnesota Press, 2003), 106. See also Morey, "'Have You the Power?' The Palmer Photoplay Corporation and the Film Viewer/Author in the 1920s," *Film History* 9, no. 3 (1997): 300–319.

133. "The Experience Exchange," *Editor*, 25 Mar 1918, 204; *Chic Trib*, 15 May 1921, F3; "What's the Matter with My Story?" *Screenland*, Dec 1921, 54.

134. With help from Martin Norden, I have found the following items: Lois Weber, "Three-Dimensional Films," *Wash Post*, 15 May 1921, 63; Weber, "Want to Write Movies? Here's a Lesson by One Who Knows the Game," *Denver Post*, 5 June 1921, n.p. (versions of which were also published in the *Washington Post* and the *San Francisco Chronicle*); and Weber, "What's Worth While?" *Wash Post*, 19 June 1921, 49.

135. I analyze this phenomenon in more detail in my article "'It's a Long Way to Filmland': Starlets, Screen Hopefuls and Extras in Early Hollywood," in Keil and Stamp, *American Cinema's Transitional Era: Audiences, Institutions, Practices*, 332–52. Also see Hallett, *Go West, Young Women!*

136. "Lois Weber Club Women's Hostess," *MPWkly*, 7 Jan 1917, n.p., RLC.

137. Remont, "The Lady behind the Lens," 61.

138. *Moving Picture Stories*, 1915, n.p., quoted in Edmonds, *Big U*, 40.

139. "The Girl with Two Mothers," *MPWkly*, 27 Jan 1917, 19.

140. "Studio Club Reception," *LAT*, 10 Dec 1916, III, 3; "In the Capital of Movie-Land," *Literary Digest* 55 (10 Nov 1917): 86; "Studio Club Notes," *Hollywood*, 7 Sept 1918, 20; "Studio Club Winter Plans," *Hollywood*, 26 Oct 1918, 6; "Notes from the Studio Club," *Hollywood*, 31 Aug 1918, 31; "After Hours in Hollywood," *Photoplay*, June 1919, 32–33; Tip Poff, "That Certain Party," *LAT*, 9 May 1935, A1.

141. Heidi Kenaga, "'Making the Studio Girl': The Hollywood Studio Club and Industry Regulation of Female Labor," *Film History* 18, no. 2 (2006): 131, 137; "Some Christmas Wants," *Wid's Daily*, 24 Dec 1918, n.p.

142. "Studio Club Gives Tea," *MPW*, 17 Aug 1918, 969; "Los Angeles War Service Members Parade," *MPW*, 24 Aug 1918, 1091.

143. *New York Telegraph*, 9 June 1918, n.p., reprinted in *Taylorology*, no. 20 (Aug 1994), http://silent-movies.com/Taylorology/Taylor20.txt (accessed 18 Dec 2012); Raymond B. West, "When the Boys Come Marching Home," *MPMag*, Oct 1918, 94–95, 110; Kenneth McGaffey, "Have the Movies Fulfilled Their War Obligation?" *MPMag*, Dec 1918, 30–31; Slide, *Lois Weber*, 152; "Working Together," *Wid's Daily*, 10 Aug 1918, n.p.; "Studio Revue Next Large Film Show," *LAT*, 4 June 1922, III, 33; "Complete Plans for Studio Review," *FD*, 17 June 1922, 4. The organization Weber joined was alternately called the War Relief Association and the War Service Association. For more on the film industry's war efforts,

see Leslie Midkiff DeBauche, *Reel Patriotism: The Movies and World War I* (Madison: University of Wisconsin Press, 1997), 104–36.

144. Julian Johnson, "*The Dumb Girl of Portici*," *Photoplay,* Apr 1916, 102; Van Loan, "Lois, the Wizard," 44.

145. "New Blood," *Scenario Bulletin-Digest* 4, no. 4 (June 1923): 14. For a description of three "working girl romances" that Orth wrote for other directors in the 1920s, see Donna R. Casella, "Feminism and the Female Author: The Not So Silent Career of the Woman Scenarist in Hollywood, 1896–1930," *Quarterly Review of Film and Video* 23 (2006): 225.

146. "Lois Weber to Film 'K,'" *MPW,* 21 July 1917, 478.

147. Rosalind Shaffer, "News of Films and Players," *Chic Trib,* 17 July 1927, F3.

148. Beauchamp, *Without Lying Down,* 38–39.

149. See Alma Whitaker, "Sugar and Spice," *LAT,* 6 Mar 1927, C13; Mildred Spain, "Movie News from Hollywood," *Chic Trib,* 25 Mar 1923, D13; Spain, "Mary Receives Kind Offer of Introduction to Doug," *Chic Trib,* 18 Nov 1923, E1; Isabel Stuyvesant, "Society of Cinemaland," *LAT,* 4 July 1926, C11; Myra Nye, "Society of Cinemaland," *LAT,* 2 Jan 1927, C16; Grace Kingsley, "And Joy," *LAT,* 16 Mar 1930, I4; Myra Nye, "Society of Cinemaland," *LAT,* 21 Dec 1930, B20.

150. Beauchamp, *Without Lying Down,* 231.

151. *Photoplay,* Sept 1913, 73; "Lois Weber Club Women's Hostess," n.p.

152. "Lois Weber Club Women's Hostess," n.p.; *MPW,* 6 Jan 1917, 88.

153. "Nationally Known Club Woman Endorses Lois Weber's Photoplays," *Hollywood Informer,* 18 Mar 1921, 19.

154. Quoted in ibid. Evidence also suggests that leaders of the Better Films Movement sought out Weber as a potential ally. See "Ten Million Women Unite for Fight on Censorship," *Var,* 2 May 1919, 65.

155. See Alison M. Parker, *Purifying America: Women's Cultural Reform and Pro-censorship Activism, 1873–1933* (Urbana-Champaign: University of Illinois Press, 1997), 213–16; Leigh Ann Wheeler, *Against Obscenity: Reform and the Politics of Womanhood, 1873–1935* (Baltimore: Johns Hopkins University Press, 2007), 79–83.

156. "'What Do Men Want?'" unident. clipping, n.d., vol. 2, CWSBC.

157. "Stars Defend Hollywood," unident. clipping, n.d., vol. 2, CWSBC.

158. Mahar, *Women Filmmakers,* 179–203.

159. Ada Patterson, "The Gish Girls Talk about Each Other," *Photoplay,* June 1921, 29.

160. Quoted in Dunning, "The Gate Women Don't Crash," 31.

161. Ibid., 33.

162. Remont, "The Lady behind the Lens," 59–61, 126; Cal York, "Plays and Players," *Photoplay,* Oct 1919, 86.

163. "The Men Behind," *Chic Trib,* 23 July 1916, D3.

164. "Biographies of Important Directors," *Wid's Daily,* 24 Apr 1921, 97–112.

165. "Women Best Suited to Direct Pictures, Says One of Them," *Camera!* 10 Jan 1920, 8.

166. Gaylyn Studlar, "The Perils of Pleasure? Fan Magazine Discourse as Women's Commodified Culture in the 1920s," in *Silent Film,* ed. Richard Abel (New Brunswick, NJ: Rutgers University Press, 1996), 263; Koszarski, *An Evening's Entertainment,* 30.

167. See, for example, *McClure's,* Mar 1921, 42.

168. "Ample Variety in Grauman Program," *LAT,* 31 May 1921, III, 4; "To Please One Woman," *Photoplay,* Mar 1921, 62; Schallert, "Seeks Ideal Themes."

169. "Lois Weber Is Whole Show in Her Company," unident. clipping, n.d., vol. 2, CWSBC.

170. "'What Do Men Want?,'" vol. 2, CWSBC.

171. Lillian R. Gale, "'What Do Men Want?'" *MPN,* 26 Nov 1921, 2811.

172. Alison Smith, "Worth While Pictures of the Month," *Theater Magazine* 33 (Mar 1921), 186 (emphasis added).

173. Adele Whitely Fletcher, "Across the Silversheet: The New Screen Plays in Review," *MPMag,* June 1921, 68.

174. On the striking role that female journals played in defining American movie culture in the 1910s, see Abel, *Menus for Movieland,* ch. 4.

175. *NYT,* 18 Nov 1921, 24.

176. *MPN,* 26 Nov 1921, 2784–85.

177. *Fort Wayne News and Sentinel,* 8 Jan 1919, 4.

178. Unident. advertisement, n.d., vol. 2, CWSBC.

179. Carter, "Muse of the Reel," 62.

180. *Los Angeles Herald,* 21 Feb 1921, n.p., quoted in Anthony Slide, *Early American Cinema,* rev. ed. (Metuchen, NJ: Scarecrow Press, 1994), 161–62.

181. Pearl Latteier, "Griffith, Weber, and the Decline of Progressive Filmmaking," unpublished paper, University of Wisconsin–Madison, 2005.

182. Joseph L. Kelley, "The Doctor and the Woman," *MPN,* 4 May 1918, 2719; "Borrowed Clothes," *Var,* 22 Nov 1918, 44; review of *Borrowed Clothes,* *Wid's Daily,* 19 Dec 1918, n.p.; Schallert, "Seeks Ideal Themes," n.p.; Fletcher, "Across the Silversheet," 69; Edwin Schallert, "Lois Weber Film," *LAT,* 12 Dec 1921, II, 7.

183. Edwin Schallert, "Lois Weber Film at Grauman House," *LAT,* 15 Feb 1921, III, 4; Norman Clark, "'What's Worth While?' at The Wizard and The Parkway," unident. clipping, n.d., vol. 1, CWSBC; "'What's Worth While?' Is Splendidly Received at the Imperial," n.d., vol. 2, CWSBC; Schallert, "Lois Weber Film," II, 7.

184. Lea Jacobs, *The Decline of Sentiment: American Film in the 1920s* (Berkeley: University of California Press, 2008).

185. "The Screen," *NYT,* 14 Nov 1921, I, 18; "What Do Men Want?" *Photo-Play Journal,* Feb 1921, 42; "Bride of Comedy King on Display," 14; Weitzel, "'What Do Men Want?'" 459; Mae Tinée, "Again Miss Weber Wrestles with a Problem," *Chic Trib,* 5 Dec 1921, 20.

186. Nancy F. Cott, *Public Vows: A History of Marriage and the Nation* (Cambridge, MA: Harvard University Press, 2000), 156–57.

187. Beatrice Hinkle, "The Chaos of Modern Marriage," *Harper's Magazine* 152 (Dec 1925): 3.

188. Elaine Tyler May, *Great Expectations: Marriage and Divorce in Post-Victorian America* (Chicago: University of Chicago Press, 1980), 158.

189. Sherman Eddy, *Sex and Youth* (Garden City, NY: Doubleday, 1929), 149, quoted in Christina Simmons, *Making Marriage Modern: Women's Sexuality from the Progressive Era to World War II* (New York: Oxford University Press, 2009), 133.

190. Simmons, *Making Marriage Modern*, 137. See also Rebecca L. Davis, "'Not Marriage at All, but Simple Harlotry': The Companionate Marriage Controversy," *Journal of American History* (March 2008): 1137–63.

191. Charles Musser, "Divorce, DeMille, and the Comedy of Remarriage," in *Classical Hollywood Comedy*, ed. Kristine Brunovska Karnick and Henry Jenkins (New York: Routledge, 1995), 282–313. See also Sumiko Higashi, "The New Woman and Consumer Culture: Cecil B. DeMille's Sex Comedies," in *The Silent Cinema Reader*, ed. Lee Grieveson and Peter Krämer (New York: Routledge, 2004), 305–17.

192. Mark Lynn Anderson, "1921: Movies and Personality," in *American Cinema of the 1920s: Themes and Variations*, ed. Lucy Fischer (New Brunswick, NJ: Rutgers University Press, 2009), 55.

193. Carter, "Muse of the Reel," 63.

194. Quoted in Latteier, "Griffith, Weber, and the Decline of Progressive Filmmaking," n.p.

195. *Wid's Daily*, 22 May 1921, 7.

196. *Ladies Home Journal*, Jan 1921, 34.

197. "Story Is Slight, But Interest Is Well Sustained," *Wid's Daily*, 22 May 1921, 7; unident. review of *What's Worth While?* n.d., vol. 1, CWSBC; "'What's Worth While?' Is Splendidly Received at the Imperial"; unident. item, n.d., vol. 2, CWSBC.

198. Carter, "The Muse of the Reel," 105.

199. Gladys Hall, "Diary of a Movie Fan: Lois Weber," *Toledo Blade*, 1 May 1923, n.p., env. 2518, RLC. For more information on Hall's career, see Anthony Slide, *Inside the Hollywood Fan Magazine: A History of Star Makers, Fabricators, and Gossip Mongers* (Jackson: University Press of Mississippi, 2010), 37–38.

200. Press kit for *Too Wise Wives*, private collection.

201. "Rialto," vol. 2, CWSBC; unident. clipping, n.d., vol. 1, CWSBC; *Wash Post*, 24 July 1921, 43; "This Week's Attractions," *Wash Post*, 24 July 1921, 42; "Women 'Love' Clothes," *Wash Post*, 24 July 1921, 42.

202. Quoted in unident. clipping, n.d., vol. 1, CWSBC.

203. Marjorie C. Driscoll, "Motion Picture Entertainment for Week Offers Photoplays of Unusual Merit and Wide Variety of Theme," *SF Chron*, 16 May 1921, 6.

204. *Wash Post*, 24 July 1921, 43.

205. Maureen Turim, "Women's Films: Comedy, Drama, Romance," in *Chick Flicks: Contemporary Women at the Movies,* ed. Suzanne Ferriss and Mallory Young (New York: Routledge, 2008), 35.

206. Kathleen McHugh, *American Domesticity: From How-To Manual to Hollywood Melodrama* (New York: Oxford University Press, 1999), 112.

207. Driscoll, "Motion Picture Entertainment for Week," 6.

208. Hinkle, "The Chaos of Modern Marriage," 4.

209. "Stars of Screen Appear at Local Picture Houses," *Wash Post,* 25 July 1921, 10.

210. "Coming to the Theater," *Wash Post,* 12 Jan 1922, 15; *MPW,* 12 Nov 1921, 121; *MPN,* 12 Nov 1921, 2511; unident. advertisement, n.d., vol. 2, CWSBC; *What Do Men Want?* poster, author's collection.

211. Unident. program, n.d., vol. 1, CWSBC. Weber drew her title quite self-consciously from George Bernard Shaw's 1919 play, *Heartbreak House,* an indictment of class politics and sexual mores in post–World War I Britain. Hesione Hushabye, mistress of Heartbreak House, poses the question "What do men want?" adding, "They have their food, their firesides, their clothes mended and our love at the end of the day. Are they not satisfied?" Weber's allusion to Shaw's play is marked in the film when Hallie's husband, Frank, reads the quotation in a book. *Heartbreak House* was first published in 1919 and had its U.S. premiere at the Garrick Theater in New York in 1920.

212. Hinkle, "The Chaos of Modern Marriage," 4.

213. May, *Great Expectations,* 88; Cott, *Public Vows,* 157.

214. Schallert, "Lois Weber Film," II, 7.

215. *NYT,* 14 Nov 1921, 22.

216. *NYT,* 18 Nov 1921, 24.

217. A more detailed analysis of the film can be found in my audio commentary for the DVD release of *The Blot,* Milestone Video, 2004.

218. Schallert, "Seeks Ideal Themes," n.p.

219. Patricia Mellencamp, *A Fine Romance: Five Ages of Film Feminism* (Philadelphia: Temple University Press, 1995), 223.

220. "Much Better Than Its Name," unident. clipping, n.d., vol. 1, CWSBC.

221. Jennifer Parchesky, "Lois Weber's *The Blot:* Rewriting Melodrama, Reproducing the Middle Class," *Cinema Journal* 39, no. 1 (1999): 23–53.

222. Ibid., 38.

223. Sinclair Lewis, *Main Street* (New York: P. F. Collier and Son, 1920), 267, quoted in Anderson, "1921: Movies and Personality," 59.

224. "Impoverished College Teaching," *Literary Digest,* 20 Apr 1921, 27.

225. Unident. clipping, n.d., vol. 2, CWSBC.

226. Lisa Rudman, "Marriage—The Ideal and the Reel; or, The Cinematic Marriage Manual," *Film History* 1, no. 4 (1987), 327. See also Thomas Slater, "Transcending Boundaries: Lois Weber and the Discourse over Women's Roles in the Teens and Twenties," *Quarterly Review of Film and Video* 18, no. 3 (2001): 259.

CHAPTER 4

1. Barbara Koenig Quart, *Women Directors: The Emergence of a New Cinema* (New York: Praeger, 1988), 20; Carey Ostergard and Kim Worley, "Lois Weber," http://womenshistory.about.com/gi/dynamic/offsite.htm?site=http://www.tecomm.com/MMTC%2DWeber.html (accessed 15 Feb 2010); ibid.; "Lois Weber," *The St. James Women Filmmakers Encyclopedia: Women on the Other Side of the Camera*, ed. Amy L. Unterburder (Farmington Hills, MI: Visible Ink Press, 1999), 446; Hal Erickson, "Lois Weber," *All Movie Guide* http://www.allmovie.com/artist/lois-weber-116181 (accessed 5 May 2010); Ally Acker, *Reel Women: Pioneers of the Cinema, 1896 to the Present* (New York: Continuum, 1991), 15; *St. James Women Filmmakers Encyclopedia*; Slide, *Lois Weber*, 131.

2. Anthony Slide is one of the few scholars to examine Weber's output and career after 1921 in any detail. See the chapter "A Decade of Uncertainty," in his *Lois Weber*, 127–44.

3. Weber had been "forgotten with a vengeance," Richard Koszarski declared in a "The Years Have Not Been Kind to Lois Weber," *Village Voice*, 10 Nov 1975, 40, reprinted in in *Women and the Cinema: A Critical Anthology*, ed. Karyn Kay and Gerald Peary (New York: E. P. Dutton, 1977), 147. Slide's 1996 book dubs Weber "the director who lost her way in history."

4. "Lois Weber has Sailed for Long Tour of the World," *MPW*, 1 Oct 1921, 535; Grace Kingsley, "Flashes: Lois Weber Home," *LAT*, 16 May 1922, II, 11.

5. "Lois Weber Happier in Free State," *LAT*, 13 Jan 1923, II, 2; *Var*, 19 Jan 1923, quoted in Slide, *Lois Weber*, 128.

6. "Lois Weber Happier in Free State," II, 2; *MPMag*, April 1923, 70; "Re: Lois Weber and Phillips Smalley," unident. clipping, n.d., n.p., MoMA.

7. Marcia Landy, "1923: Movies and the Changing Body," in Fischer, *American Cinema of the 1920s*, 97.

8. "Lois Weber Starts Soon," *FD*, 3 July 1922, 1; "Lois Weber Plans Trip," *FD*, 2 Sept 1922, 2; "To Again Make 'Jewel,'" *FD*, 11 Oct 1922, 1; "Lois Weber with Universal," *LAT*, 14 Nov 1922, III, 3.

9. Clive Hirschhorn, *The Universal Story* (New York: Crown, 1983), 14–15; Koszarski, *An Evening's Entertainment*, 86–89; Schatz, *The Genius of the System*, 21–22.

10. Schatz, *The Genius of the System*, 28.

11. See Slide, "Universal Women," 41–60; Cooper, *Universal Women*, 128–72.

12. "To Again Make 'Jewel,'" 1; "Lois Weber with Universal," 3. One reel of tests for the two-color process survives at the UCLA Film and Television Archive.

13. "Twelve Universal Features to Be Displayed," *MPN*, 27 Oct 1923, 2024; *MPN*, 27 Oct 1923, 2025; *MPN*, 13 Oct 1923, 1708–9.

14. "'A Chapter in Her Life,'" *FD*, 9 Sept 1923, 10; "A Chapter in Her Life," *Var*, 27 Sept 1923, 24; "And a Little Child Shall Lead Them . . . ," *LAT Pre-View Weekly Film Magazine*, 12 Sept 1923, WF 10.

15. Remont, "The Lady behind the Lens," 126; Grace Kingsley, "Flashes: She Rebels; Lois Weber Says Too Many Film Restrictions," *LAT,* 7 July 1923, I7; *Motion Picture Classic,* Oct 1923, n.p., author's collection; Isabel Stuyvesant, "Society of Cinemaland," *LAT,* 7 Mar 1926, 38. I have found no evidence that plays written by Weber were ever staged or that she ever published a novel; no manuscript of such writing survive.

16. Kingsley, "Flashes: She Rebels," I7.

17. "What's the Matter with Lois?" *MPMag,* Sept 1923, 90.

18. *Film Mercury* (October 2, 1925), n.p., quoted in Slide, *Lois Weber,* 132–33.

19. Alice Williamson, *Alice in Movieland* (New York: D. Appleton and Co., 1928), 239, 240. See also "Lois Weber Is Again at Work," *LAT,* 4 Apr 1926, C16; Dunning, "The Gate Women Don't Crash," 31; Winifred Aydelotte, "The Little Red Schoolhouse Becomes a Theatre," *MPMag,* Mar 1934, 35. All except Williamson use the term *nervous breakdown.*

20. "Lois Weber Engaged," *MPW,* 31 Jan 1925, 487; "Universal Program Running High," *LAT,* 23 Jan 1925, A9; unident. clipping, 7 Jan 1925, n.p., MoMA; "Universal Will Spend Millions for Productions," *LAT,* 6 May 1925, A9.

21. Quoted in Koszarski, *An Evening's Entertainment,* 89.

22. "Scenarists Are Winning Recognition," *LAT,* 26 July 1925, B3.

23. Lee Shippey, "The Lee Side o'L.A.," *LAT,* 24 Mar 1934, A4. Ryerson is best known for her later adaptation of *The Wizard of Oz.*

24. Unident. clipping, 9 Jan 1925, n.p., MoMA.

25. Unident. clipping, 7 Jan 1925, n.p., MoMA.

26. "Universal Program Running High," A9.

27. Koszarski, *An Evening's Entertainment,* 89.

28. Schatz, *The Genius of the System,* 28.

29. Robert S. Birchard, *Early Universal City* (Charleston, SC: Arcadia, 2009), 111.

30. "Busy U City," *LAT,* 3 Dec 1925, A11; "The Screen's First Woman Director," Florey, 60; "A Fine Theater Story," *Motion Picture Classic,* Aug 1926, 87.

31. "Lois Weber's Latest," *FD,* 6 July 1926, 7.

32. "The Marriage Clause," unident. clipping, ACSC, vol. 8, p. 118; "'The Marriage Clause'—Universal," *MPW,* 3 July 1926, 39; Dwinelle Benthall, "Poverty Row," *MPMag,* Dec 1926, 113; Don Ryan, "The Screen Observer Has His Say," *Motion Picture Classic,* Aug 1926, 60.

33. "The Minister's Romance," *NYT,* 16 Mar 1927, 2. For other positive reviews, see "Sensation Seekers," *Var,* 16 Mar 1927, 17; and "'Sensation Seekers,'" *MPW,* 29 Jan 1927, 370.

34. "Lois Weber, Film Producer, Wed to Wealthy Rancher," *Chic Trib,* 2 July 1926, 31; "Film Work Shortens Honeymoon," *LAT,* 2 July 1926, A2; "Lois Weber Bride of Ex-Army Flyer," 2 July 1926, n.p., MoMA; "Lois Weber to Become Bride Again," 15 June 1926, n.p., MoMA.

35. Peter Gantz, interview with author, 25 Oct 2007; "Harry Gantz, 1888–1949," *The Early Birds of Aviation,* http://earlyaviators.com/egantz.htm (accessed 12 May 2010); "Harry Gantz" http://www.findagrave.com/cgi-bin/fg.cgi?page=gr&GRid=49186502 (accessed 19 Sept 2014). Harry Gantz and his first wife, Beatrice Wooster Miller, built and designed the home together; it is likely that her family gave them the property, since they were large landowners in the area.

36. "Island Film Ready for Cutting," n.d., n.p., MoMA.

37. Grace Kingsley, "So Lois Weber Entertains!" *LAT,* 20 Mar 1927, I, 6; Alma Whitaker, "Sugar and Spice," *LAT,* 6 Mar 1927, C13; Frances Duncan, "He Has Made His Garden Blossom like the Desert," *LAT,* 31 July 1927, K2; "Captain Harry Gantz Has Developed an 'El Dorado' out of a Badly Treated Ranch," *LAT,* 3 Jan 3 1928, D27.

38. Quoted in Kingsley, "So Lois Weber Entertains!" I6.

39. Whitaker, "Sugar and Spice," C13.

40. "Lois Weber: An Asset," *Hollywood Vagabond,* 5 May 1927, 7. Also quoted in Slide, *Lois Weber,* 139.

41. Grace Kingsley, "Duncan Sisters Get Director," *LAT,* 6 Nov 1926, A6.

42. Tino Balio, *United Artists: The Company Built by the Stars* (Madison: University of Wisconsin Press, 1976), 51–72.

43. "Studio News and Gossip," *Photoplay,* Jan 1927, 98.

44. "U.A. to have Minimum of 18 during 1927," *FD,* 31 Jan 1927, 1–2.

45. Kingsley, "Duncan Sisters Get Director," A6.

46. Grace Kingsley, "Lois Weber for 'Uncle Tom,'" *LAT,* 24 June 1926, A8; "Cupid Beaten by Picture Demand," *LAT,* 2 July 1926, A2; Grace Kingsley, "Lois Weber's Own Uncle Tom," *LAT,* 2 July 1926, A8; "Film Work Shortens Honeymoon," A2. By comparison, the budget for *Topsy and Eva* was reported to be $300,000, less than a third of the money Universal spent on its adaptation. See "Topsy and Eva," *Var,* 22 June 1927, 30. For a detailed account of the production, see David Pierce, "'Carl Laemmle's Outstanding Achievement': Harry Pollard and the Struggle to Film *Uncle Tom's Cabin,*" *Film History* 10, no. 4 (1998): 459–76.

47. Grace Kingsley, "Oh, These Marriages!" *LAT,* 18 July 1926, I5.

48. "Pollard to Resume," *FD,* 14 July 1926, 6; "Universal Starts Feature Productions," *LAT,* 26 July 1926, A9; "'Uncle Tom' and the Jinx," *NYT,* 24 July 1927, 5; "'Sensation Seekers' Started," *FD,* 5 Aug 1926, 15.

49. Dunning, "The Gate Women Don't Crash," 35.

50. John Sullivan, "Topsy and Eva Play Vaudeville," in *Uncle Tom's Cabin and American Culture,* ed. Stephen Railton, online exhibit and interpretation available at http://utc.iath.virginia.edu/interpret/exhibits/sullivan/sullivan.html (accessed 26 Jan 2010); David Mayer, *Stagestruck: Filmmaker D.W. Griffith and the American Theater* (Iowa City: University of Iowa Press, 2009), 241–42.

51. Both reviews quoted in Slide, *Eccentrics of Comedy* (Lanham, MD: Scarecrow Press, 1998), 50.

52. "Assign Lois Weber to Direct Duncan Girls," *MPW*, 4 Dec 1926, 351.

53. Grace Kingsley, "Lois Weber Not to Direct," *LAT*, 12 Feb 1927, A6; Kingsley, "Del Lord with Duncans," *LAT*, 16 Feb 1927, A8.

54. Slide, *Lois Weber*, 12; Kingsley, "Del Lord with Duncans," A8; "'Topsy and Eva' Switched," *FD*, 20 Feb 1927, 6; Kingsley, "Lois Weber Not to Direct," A6. Weber evidently continued to socialize with the Duncans after Lord took over directing the film, for she and Gantz attended a lavish party at the sisters' Hollywood Hills home the following month. See Grace Kingsley, "Topsy and Eva," *LAT*, 27 Mar 1927, H5.

55. "Topsy and Eva," *Var*, 22 June 1927, 30; Grace Kingsley, "D.W. Griffith at Work," *LAT*, 9 June 1927, A8.

56. Richard Schickel, *D.W. Griffith: An American Life* (New York: Simon and Schuster, 1984), 529–32. Klune is quoted in Scott Simmon, *The Films of D.W. Griffith* (Cambridge: Cambridge University Press, 1993), 127. For other assessments of Griffith's involvement in the project, see Simmon, *Films of D.W. Griffith*, 127–28; J.B. Kaufman, "Topsy and Eva," in *The Griffith Project*, Vol. 10, *Films Produced in 1919–46*, ed. Paolo Cherchi Usai (London: BFI, 2006), 204–6; and Mayer, *Stagestruck*, 242.

57. The AFI Catalog credits Weber with writing the screen adaptation for *Topsy and Eva*, but she does not receive a screen credit on extant prints of the film.

58. "Topsy and Eva," *Var*, 22 June 1927, 30.

59. "Topsy and Eva," n.d., ACSC, vol. 23, p. 29; "Topsy and Eva," *Var*, 22 June 1927, 30; "Topsy and Eva," n.d., ACSC, vol. 23, p. 28.

60. Thomas Cripps, *Slow Fade to Black: The Negro in American Film, 1900–1942* (New York: Oxford University Press, 1977), 150; see also 159.

61. Koszarski, *An Evening's Entertainment*, 33.

62. Dunning, "The Gate Women Don't Crash," 31.

63. "Lois Weber Signed by DeMille to Direct 'Angel of Broadway,'" *MPW*, 9 July 1927, 98.

64. "Picture List Announced by DeMille," *LAT*, 2 May 1926, C34; "Superfilms for De Mille [sic]," *LAT*, 3 June 1927, A10; "Heavy Schedule at the Pathe-DeMille Studio," *FD*, 19 Aug 1927, 2.

65. Williamson, *Alice in Movieland*, 243.

66. "Lois Weber Signed by DeMille," 98. See also Coffee, *Storyline: Recollections of a Hollywood Screenwriter*, 138–39.

67. "Emerges from Ranks," *LAT*, 3 Oct 1926, C19–C20.

68. "Star Concerned over New Drama," *LAT*, 13 June 1927, A8.

69. *FD*, 18 Sept 1927, 10; Rosalind Shaffer, "News of Films and Players," *Chic Trib*, 17 July 1927, F3.

70. Mae Tinée, "This Broadway Film Is Unusual, Vivid, Gripping," *Chic Trib*, 11 Oct 1927, 35; unident. review of *The Angel of Broadway*, n.d., ACSC, vol. 23, p. 49; "Angel of Broadway," *Var*, 2 Nov 1927, n.p., reprinted in *Variety Film Reviews*.

71. Unident. review of *The Angel of Broadway*, 49; Tinée, "This Broadway Film," 35; Whitney Williams, "Tears and Laughter Blended in 'The Angel of Broadway,'" *LAT*, 2 Oct 1927, 17.

72. Robert Birchard, "Biography," in *Cecil B. DeMille*, http://www.cecilbdemille.com/bio.html (accessed 12 Mar 2013).

73. M.C. Levee, "The Commercial Requirements," in *Introduction to the Photoplay: A Course in the Appreciation of Motion Pictures* (Los Angeles: University of Southern California; Academy of Motion Picture Arts and Sciences, 1929), quoted in Anthony Slide, "Those Elusive Budget Figures," in *Silent Topics: Essays on Undocumented Areas of Silent Film* (Lanham, MD: Scarecrow Press, 2005), 28.

74. Grace Kingsley, "Night—with Day Trimmings," *LAT*, 1 Apr 1928, 18.

75. Elliot, "Exit Flapper, Enter Woman," III, 25. Weber's comments occurred at a pivotal juncture, just as the cycle of flapper films began and just as European stars such as Pola Negri were beginning to make a splash in Hollywood. See Sara Ross, "1922: Movies and the Perilous Future," in Fischer, *American Cinema of the 1920s*, 70–94; and Diane Negra, "Immigrant Stardom in Imperial America: Pola Negri and the Problem of Typology," *Camera Obscura* 48 (2001): 159–95.

76. Grace Kingsley, "Busy U City," *LAT*, 3 Dec 1925, A11.

77. "New Angle to Old Story," *Wash Post*, 6 Feb 1927, F1.

78. Elliot, "Exit Flapper, Enter Woman," III, 25.

79. The Library of Congress holds a very incomplete and evidently reordered 16mm print of *The Marriage Clause*. My analysis thus also relies on information available in reviews, including *National Board of Review Magazine* 1, no. 3 (July 1926): 7–8; "'Marriage Clause' Theater Life Romance," *LAT*, 15 Aug 1926, I4; Mordaunt Hall, "The Rocky Road of Love," *NYT*, 28 Sept 1926, 30; "New Pictures," *Time*, 11 Oct 1926, n.p., http://www.time.com/time/magazine/article/0,9171,729554,00.html (accessed 25 Jan 2010.

80. "'Marriage Clause' Theater Life Romance," I4. The story's "marriage clause" element was added by Weber and played no part in the original short story. There, Barry and Sylvia are married throughout, and the action focuses on Barry's struggle when Sylvia's fame eclipses his own, an element largely absent from Weber's adaptation. See Dana Burnet, "Technic," *Saturday Evening Post*, 16 May 1925, 14–15, 80, 85, 87.

81. Early items on the production mention these alternate titles. See Grace Kingsley, "Flashes," *LAT*, 22 Feb 1926, A7; "Lois Weber's Next Production," *MPW*, 5 June 1926, 459.

82. *FD*, 18 July 1926, 1.

83. "New Pictures," *Time*, 28 Mar 1927, n.p., http://www.time.com/time/magazine/article/0,9171,730268,00.html (accessed 10 Feb 2010).

84. "'Sensation Seekers,'" *MPW*, 29 Jan 1927, 370.

85. Grace Kingsley, "Will Rogers in Picture," *LAT*, 21 July 1926, A10.

86. "The Angel of Broadway," *Billboard*, 12 Nov 1927, 57.

87. No print of *The Angel of Broadway* is known to survive. My analysis is based on material available in original reviews, as well as production stills in my

collection and those reproduced in promotional materials. James Robert Parish also provides a very detailed plot summary in *Prostitution in Hollywood Films: Plots, Critiques, Casts and Credits for 389 Theatrical and Made-for-Television Releases* (Jefferson, NC: McFarland, 1992), 17. I also consulted the following reviews: Whitney Williams, "Tears and Laughter Blended in 'The Angel of Broadway,'" *LAT*, 2 Oct 1927, 17; "Regeneration Theme of Film," *LAT*, 24 Oct 1927, A7; Mordaunt Hall, "The Screen," *NYT*, 1 Nov 1927, 21; "Angel of Broadway," *Var*, 2 Nov 1927, n.p.; "The Angel of Broadway," *Photoplay*, Nov 1927, 55; "The Angel of Broadway," *FD*, 30 Oct 1927, 12; Tinée, "This Broadway Film," 35; and unident. review, ACSC, vol. 23, p. 49.

88. Texas Guinan's club became a favored haunt for Hollywood stars visiting New York. Well-known guests included Gloria Swanson, Clara Bow, Pola Negri, Rudolph Valentino, John Gilbert, and even, apparently, Leatrice Joy herself. See Louise Berliner, *Texas Guinan, Queen of the Night Clubs* (Austin: University of Texas Press, 1993), 74.

89. Hall, "The Screen," 21.

90. Ruth Waterbury's series "The Truth about Breaking into the Movies" was published in three installments of *Photoplay* in December 1926, January 1927, and February 1927. Adela Rogers St. Johns's series "The Port of Missing Girls" was published in six monthly installments of *Photoplay* beginning in March 1927, the month after Waterbury's series ended.

91. "Regeneration Theme of Film," A7; "Angel of Broadway," *Var*, n.p.

92. "Angel of Broadway," *Var*, n.p.; "The Angel of Broadway," *FD*, 30 Oct 1927, 12. See also "The Marriage Clause," *Var*, 29 Sept 1926, 14.

93. Herbert Moulton, "'The Marriage Clause,'" n.d., ACSC, vol. 8, p. 116; "Sensation Seekers," unident. clipping, n.d., ACSC, vol. 5, p. 139.

94. Jacobs, *The Decline of Sentiment*, 84–85.

95. "The Sensation Seekers," *MPMag*, Jan 1927, 119; "The Angel of Broadway," *FD*, 12.

96. Slater, "Transcending Boundaries," 257–71.

97. Myrtle Gebhart, "A Pot of Gold for Billie Dove," *Picture Play*, April 1927, 71, quoted in William M. Drew, *At the Center of the Frame: Leading Ladies of the Twenties and Thirties* (New York: Vestal Press, 1999), 11; Katherine Lipke, "Marriage First with Her," *LAT*, 15 Aug 1926, C19; Alma Whitaker, "Billie Dove Is Grateful for Big Chance at Success," *LAT*, 20 Feb 1927, C17; Moulton, "'The Marriage Clause.'"

98. Drew, *At the Center of the Frame*, 11, 33–34.

99. Quoted in Lipke, "Marriage First with Her," C19.

100. Quoted in Drew, *At the Center of the Frame*, 32.

101. Peak, "Only Woman Movie Director," C11.

102. "Big Women of the Screen," *Screenland*, Jan 1922, 14.

103. Frederick Van Vranken, "Women's Work in Motion Pictures," *MPMag*, Aug 1923, 89.

104. "Bright Girls Aren't Hiding Their Lights under Bushels," *LAT*, 2 Jan 1927, C33.

105. Weber, "Many Women Well Fitted by Film Training to Direct," 3.

106. Lois Weber, "Hostility of Men Drawback to Women Making Success in Picture Directing, Claim," *San Diego Evening Tribune*, 25 Apr 1928, 13.

107. Dunning, "The Gate Women Don't Crash," 33. Anthony Slide interprets Weber's comments differently. See Slide, *Lois Weber*, 153.

108. Myra Nye, "What Women Are Doing," *LAT*, 16 Mar 1927, A7; Nan Towle Yamane, "Southern California Women's Press Club (1893–1939)," in *Women's Press Organizations, 1881–1999*, ed. Elizabeth V. Burt (Westport, CT: Greenwood Press, 2000), 199–206. Other film industry guests present at the banquet included Lule Warrenton, Hobart Bosworth, and Sidney Olcott, one of the featured speakers. The following year Louella Parsons founded the Hollywood Women's Press Club, an organization for the many women who wrote regularly on cinema for newspapers, fan magazines, and other monthlies. See Samantha Barbas, *The First Lady of Hollywood: A Biography of Louella Parsons* (Berkeley: University of California Press, 2006), 124–25.

109. Yamane, "South California Women's Press Club," 202.

110. Myra Nye, "Of Interest to Women," *LAT*, 6 Mar 1929, A7; "The Women's University Club," in *Who's Who among the Women of California*, ed. Louis S. Lyons and Josephine Wilson (Los Angeles: Security Publishing Co., 1922), 37.

111. Mahar, *Women Filmmakers*, 181.

112. Pierre Norman Sands, *A Historical Study of the Academy of Motion Picture Arts and Sciences, 1927–1947* (New York: Arno Press, 1973), 30. Three women were among the thirty-six original founders of the Academy in 1927: Mary Pickford, Jeanie Macpherson, and Bess Meredyth.

113. *Academy Bulletin* 2 (2 June 1927): 1, AMPAS; "Film Academy Keeps Officers," *LAT*, 21 Oct 1927, A5; "Free Lance Contract for Directors," *Academy Bulletin* 5 (25 Nov 1927): 2, AMPAS; "Academy Drawing Up Form for Gen'l Use," *FD*, 26 Oct 1927, 7. See also Sands, *A Historical Study*, 82–83. Weber resigned from the Executive Committee of the Directors' Branch in March 1928, along with Sidney Olcott; William K. Howard and Donald Crisp filled their vacancies. See *Academy Bulletin* 8 (1 Mar 1928), 2, AMPAS.

114. "Film Heads in Conference," *LAT*, 15 July 1927, A1, A8; "Producers Holding Series of Meetings to Reduce Overhead," *FD*, 17 July 1927, 1; "Producers and Directors Confer on Economy Measures in Film Industry," *LAX*, 15 July 1927, I, 20, in General Clippings, 1927, AMPAS.

115. Jane Tompkins, "Sentimental Power: *Uncle Tom's Cabin* and the Politics of Literary History," in *Sensational Designs: The Cultural Work of American Fiction, 1790–1860* (New York: Oxford University Press, 1985), 126, cited in Linda Williams, *Playing the Race Card: Melodramas of Black and White from Uncle Tom to O.J.* (Princeton: Princeton University Press, 2001), 47.

116. Ibid., 89. For a broader discussion of the multiple adaptations of the material, see Barbara Tepa Lupack, "Uncle Tom and American Popular Culture: Adapting Stowe's Novel to Film," in *Nineteenth-Century Women at the*

Movies: Adapting Classic Women's Fiction to Film, ed. Barbara Tepa Lupack (Bowling Green, OH: Bowling Green State University Press, 1999), 207–56; Michele Wallace, "*Uncle Tom's Cabin:* Before and after the Jim Crow Era," *Drama Review* 44, no. 1 (2000): 140–42.

117. Lupack, "Uncle Tom and American Popular Culture," 236.

118. Peak, "Only Woman Movie Director," C11.

119. Shirley Samuels, ed., *The Culture of Sentiment: Race, Gender, and Sentimentality in Nineteenth-Century America* (New York: Oxford University Press, 1992), 3–4.

120. Williams, *Playing the Race Card,* 78.

121. Kingsley, "Duncan Sisters Director," A6.

122. Grant Martin Overton, "Clara Louise Burnham," in *The Women Who Make Our Novels* (New York: Moffat, Yard & Co., 1918), 267–83 (quote on 277); Dorothy McLeod MacInerney, "Clara Louise Root Burnham," *American National Biography Online,* Feb 2000, http://www.anb.org/articles/16/16–00227 .html (accessed 22 Apr 2013). The other two Christian Science books in Burnham's trilogy were *The Right Princess* (1902) and *The Leaven of Love* (1908).

123. Weber's screenwriting partner for the 1923 remake of *Jewel,* Doris Schroeder, had also written a previous screen adaptation of *The Opened Shutters* in 1921.

124. Slide, *Lois Weber,* 39; Slide, "Christianity Hollywood Style: Reverend Neal Dodd," in *Silent Topics,* 31. As popular interest in Christian Science peaked during the 1920s and early thirties, many in Hollywood either explored the movement or openly promoted its tenets. Leatrice Joy, whom Weber directed in *The Angel of Broadway,* was probably the industry's most prominent Christian Scientist during this period; Mary Pickford's best-selling 1934 book, *Why Not Try God?* (ghost-written by Adela Rogers St. Johns), later helped propagate many of Mary Baker Eddy's teachings.

125. Beryl Slatter, *Each Mind a Kingdom: American Women, Sexual Purity, and the New Thought Movement* (Berkeley: University of California Press, 2001), 13, 17.

126. Ibid., 3–8.

127. Stephen Gottschalk, *The Emergence of Christian Science in American Religious Life* (Berkeley: University of California Press, 1973), 259.

128. Karen Sánchez-Eppler, *Dependent States: The Child's Part in Nineteenth-Century American Culture* (Chicago: University of Chicago Press, 2005), xv, xiv, xviii.

129. Ann Douglas, *Terrible Honesty: Mongrel Manhattan in the 1920s* (New York: Farrar, Straus and Giroux, 1995), 6–9.

130. Quoted in Jacobs, *The Decline of Sentiment,* 16.

131. Amy Schrager Lang, "Class and the Strategies of Sympathy," in Samuels, *The Culture of Sentiment: Race, Gender, and Sentimentality in Nineteenth-Century America,* 133.

132. Jacobs, *The Decline of Sentiment,* ix.

133. Douglas, *Terrible Honesty*, 44.

134. Ibid., 247.

135. Ibid., 248.

136. For a more detailed analysis of Pickford, Temple, and other "juvenated" stars, see Gaylyn Studlar, *Precocious Charms: Stars Performing Girlhood in Classical Hollywood Cinema* (Berkeley: University of California Press, 2012).

137. Gaylyn Studlar, "Oh, 'Doll Divine': Mary Pickford, Masquerade and the Pedophilic Gaze," *Camera Obscura* 48 (2001): 199.

138. "A Chapter in Her Life," *MPW*, 15 Sept 1923, 263.

139. Landy, "1923: Movies and the Changing Body," 99.

140. "A Chapter in Her Life," 263; "And a Little Child Shall Lead Them . . . ," *WF* 10.

141. Mae Tinée, "'Jewel' Based on Healing through Faith," *Chic Trib*, 6 Sept 1923, 19.

142. "And a Little Child Shall Lead Them," *WF* 10.

143. "A Chapter in Her Life," *Var*, 24.

144. *LAT*, 4 May 1924, 25. See also the cover of *FD*, 19 Aug 1923.

145. "Great Story; Famous Novel Is Brought to Rialto Screen," *Chicago Defender*, 16 Feb 1924, 6.

146. W. R. Wilkerson, "Opinions," *FD*, 21 Nov 1928, 4; Grace Kingsley, "Oh Joy," *LAT*, 16 Mar 1930, I4; Kingsley, "The Evolution of the Wild Party," *LAT*, 20 Apr 1930, K18; "Woman Made Film Director," *LAT*, 24 July 1933, A2. Quote from Kingsley, "Evolution."

147. Grace Kingsley, "On Bebe's Beach," *Screenland*, Dec 1927, 96–97.

148. "Park Lane Apartments in Transfer," *LAT*, 20 Oct 1929, D3. The estimate of Weber's fortune comes from Dunning, "The Gate Women Don't Crash," 29. For information on incomes and investments of other Hollywood notables in the early 1930s, see Myrtle Gebhart, "Money Shrieks in Hollywood," *LAT*, 22 Nov 1931, K3.

149. "Guild to Give Fiesta," *LAT*, 25 May 1930, B17; "Guild Planning Exhibit," *LAT*, 15 Mar 1931, 28. See also Duncan, "He Has Made His Garden Blossom," K2; and "Captain Harry Gantz Has Developed an 'El Dorado,'" D27.

150. Grace Kingsley, "Hobnobbing in Hollywood," *LAT*, 6 Dec 1933, 13; "State and Nation Representatives for Beaux Arts New Year Frolic Revealed," *LAT*, 24 Nov 1935, D2; Tip Poff, "That Certain Party," *LAT*, 19 May 1935, A1; "Bridge, Lunch and Show for Dakotans," *LAT*, 14 May 1932, A16; "Olympic Games Note," *LAT*, 16 May 1921, A8; "Stars Grace Olympic Luncheon," *LAT*, 26 May 1932, A10; "Heard on the Boulevard," *LAT*, 26 May 1932, A9; Julia Neal Levy, "Society," *LAT*, 9 June 1932, A6.

151. "Film Notables Plan Dwellings," *LAT*, 30 Oct 1927, E5.

152. *LAT*, 2 Feb 1930, B28.

153. "Duplicate City, Plan of Company," *LAT*, 29 Nov 1925, E6; Alma Whitaker, "Sugar and Spice," *LAT*, 6 Mar 1927, C13; *Palisades Post*, http://www.palisadespost.com/content/index.cfm?Story_ID=7370 (accessed 15 Feb 2013).

154. "Park Lane Apartments in Transfer," D3; "Apartment Deal Rued by Writer," *LAT,* 19 Dec 1929, A14; "Fight on Realty Deal Started by Lois Weber," *LAT,* 19 June 1930, A2; "Lois Weber Buys Hotel," *LAX,* 17 Oct 1929, n.p., LAXC; "Lois Weber Wins Injunction in Suit," *LAX,* 19 Dec 1929, n.p., LAXC; "Lois Weber Suit Testimony Today," *LAX,* 19 June 1930, n.p., LAXC; "Writ Denied Lois Weber," *LAX,* 20 June 1930, n.p., LAXC; "Lois Weber Loses First Tilt in Suit over Apartments," *LAX,* 20 June 1930, n.p., LAXC.

155. "$25,000 Robbery at Weber Home," *LAX,* 20 May 1930, n.p., LAXC; "Lois Weber's Home Robbed," *LAT,* 20 May 1930, A10; "Stolen Goods Identified as Lois Fuller's [sic]," *LAT,* 25 May, 1930, C8.

156. "Famous Ranch Changes Hands," *LAT,* 4 Aug 1931, 14. The property is now owned by California State University, Fullerton, thanks to a donation from the Chapman family, which purchased the property from Gantz in 1931. The house serves as the official residence for the university's president. See http://fullerton-web.civicasoft.com/depts/dev_serv/planning_/historic_fullerton/1918_1925_residential/stanley_chapman_house.asp (accessed 12 May 2010).

157. "Colman in 'Cynara'; Goldwyn's First in '32," *FD,* 6 Jan 1932, 1, 8; "Colman in 'Karamazov,'" *FD,* 11 Feb 1932, 2.

158. "Lois Weber Returns to Screen Work," *New York Telegraph,* 14 May 1932, n.p., MoMA; Kingsley, "Lloyd Debates Next Picture," *LAT,* 10 May 1932, 11; Beauchamp, *Without Lying Down,* 281, 283.

159. "'Min and Bill' Promises to Score for Writer," *LAT,* 16 Nov 1930, B13.

160. "Colman in 'Karamazov,'" 2.

161. Undated press release from United Artists Corporation, MoMA.

162. "Lois Weber Returns to Screen Work," n.p.; Kingsley, "Lloyd Debates Next Picture," 11.

163. Edwin Schallert, "'Cynara' Wins Preview Favor," *LAT,* 27 Oct 1932, 11; Mae Tinée, "Cynara, in Film, Is Warning to Blithe Ladies," *Chic Trib,* 26 Dec 1932, 23; Mordaunt Hall, "Ronald Colman, Kay Francis and Henry Stephenson in the Pictorial Translation of 'Cynara,'" *NYT,* 26 Dec 1932, 26; "Ronald Colman in Quiet, Human Play of Broken Pledge," *Wash Post,* 25 Dec 1932, A1.

164. "Macpherson, Weber Signed," *FD,* 26 July 1932, 2; "Jules Bernstein Sees Idealistic Film Trend," *FD,* 9 Aug 1932, 10.

165. "Lois Weber Engaged to Scout Talent for Universal," undated press release from Universal Pictures Corp., MoMA; "Contracts Given Two Newcomers in Screen Work," *LAT,* Apr 2, 1933, B6. On Carl Laemmle, Jr.'s tenure at Universal, see Bernard F. Dick, *City of Dreams: The Making and Remaking of Universal Pictures* (Lexington, KY: University of Kentucky Press, 1997), 73–94.

166. "Lois Weber at 'U,'" *Hollywood Reporter,* 28 Jan 1933, 1.

167. Unident. clipping, *(New York?) Daily News,* February 3, 1933, n.p., env. 2518, BRTC.

168. "Voice Halts Careers," *LAT,* 19 Feb 1933, B7.

169. See Constance Welch, "Toning Voices and Dialects in a School of Drama," *American Speech* 8, no. 2 (1933): 19–22.

170. Edna Ferber, "Glamour: 24 Hours in the Life of a Great Actress," *Hearst's International Cosmopolitan Magazine* 92, no. 3 (March 1932), 18–27; Edna Ferber, "Glamour," in *They Brought Their Women: A Book of Short Stories* (New York: Doubleday, Doran and Co., 1933), 5–39.

171. J.E. Smyth, *Edna Ferber's Hollywood: American Fictions of Gender, Race, and History* (Austin: University of Texas Press, 2010), 5. Later novels, including *Come and Get It* (1935) and *Giant* (1952), were also adapted into successful films.

172. "Projection Jottings," *NYT*, 2 July 1933, X3; Nelson B. Bell, "Universal Expands Output," *Wash Post*, 6 July 1933, 14; "Six Months to Come Expected to Excel Past," *Wash Post*, 15 Dec 1933, 17.

173. "Mason on Original," *Hollywood Reporter*, 10 Apr 1933, 3; Grace Kingsley, "Hobnobbing in Hollywood," *LAT*, 22 Apr 1933, A7.

174. Kingsley, "Hobnobbing in Hollywood," A7.

175. "Mason on Original," 3; "Lois Weber Writing 'Footlights' for 'U,'" *Hollywood Reporter*, 6 May 1933, 3; "Weber to Direct 'Glamour,'" *Hollywood Reporter*, 22 May 1933, 3.

176. Jan Herman, *A Talent for Trouble: The Life of Hollywood's Most Acclaimed Director, William Wyler* (New York: Da Capo, 1997), 120–21.

177. Ferber, "Glamour," 5.

178. Ibid., 7.

179. Weber's three draft continuity scripts for *Glamour* are held in the William Wyler Collection, AMPAS. See also "Weber Writing 'Footlights' for 'U,'" 3.

180. "Screen Notes," *NYT*, 31 Jan 1934, 21. *Glamour* was Doris Anderson's first script for Universal. She had been under contract at Paramount from 1927 to 1931, where she had written scripts directed by directors including Victor Fleming, Dorothy Arzner, and George Cukor. Gladys Unger, another experienced screenwriter, would co-write the adaptation of *Sylvia Scarlett* in 1936.

181. "Rialto," *Wash Post*, 14 Apr 1934, 14; "Glamour," *Var*, 15 May 1934, n.p., reprinted in *Variety Film Reviews*.

182. Quoted in Herman, *A Talent for Trouble*, 121.

183. *Hollywood Spectator*, 23 Dec 1933, n.p., quoted in Slide, *Lois Weber*, 149.

184. Although *White Heat* was the first picture shot on Kaua'i, Hawai'i was being used more often as a destination for location shooting in the 1930s, as well as a vacation destination for Hollywood celebrities. Projects shot on the island of Oahu, in and around Honolulu, include Harold Lloyd's *Feet First* (1930); *The Black Camel* (1931), one of Warner Oland's Charlie Chan films; and others in which Hawai'ian locations stand in for unspecified South Seas locales, such as *Bird of Paradise* (1932) with Dolores del Rio and Joel McCrea and *Jungle Princess* (1936), starring Dorothy Lamour and Ray Milland. For more detailed information, see the website *Hawaiiwood*, http://www.Hawaiiwood .com/Movies_and_TV/1930's_Movies/index.html. At the time Weber was

shooting on Kaua'i, Cecil B. DeMille was shooting *Four Frightened People* in and around Honolulu. The two directors sailed over to the Hawai'ian islands together in late August 1933. See Waldo Drake, "Filmmakers Turn Again to Hawaiians," *LAT,* 19 Aug 1933, 11. Weber apparently contacted DeMille again during their respective shoots, introducing a former employee whom she thought he might hire. See Robert S. Birchard, *Cecil B. DeMille's Hollywood* (Lexington: University of Kentucky Press, 2004) 268–69.

185. Brian Taves, "The B Film: Hollywood's Other Half," in *Grand Design: Hollywood as a Modern Business Enterprise, 1930–39,* ed. Tino Balio (Berkeley: University of California Press, 1993), 313–30; quotes on 313 and 330.

186. Quoted in Taves, "The B Film," 337.

187. "Island Film Ready for Cutting," n.p.; "Fame Parts Fairbanks Pair," *LAT,* 11 May 1933, A1. Pickford and Fairbanks evidently separated shortly after this; Pickford filed for divorce in December 1933. For additional background on Seven Seas, see "'Seven Seas' Will Also Make Studio Pictures," *Hollywood Reporter,* 25 Jan 1934, 3; and "Seven Seas Corp. Head Here for Production," *Hollywood Reporter,* 19 May 1934, 4.

188. Milton Gray, "James Bodrero," Michael Barrier.com, http://www .michaelbarrier.com/Interviews/Bodrero/Bodrero_interview.html (accessed 4 Jan 2010). James Bodrero's surname is misspelled "Bordrero" in some sources, including the AFI Catalogue.

189. Drake, "Filmmakers Turn Again to Hawaiians," 11; Waldo Drake, "Shipping News and Activities at Los Angeles Harbor," *LAT,* 25 Aug 1933, 13; "Backer of Film Thriller Sails," *LAT,* 26 Aug, 1933, A5; "All Work—No Play," *LAT,* 5 Sept 1933, 9; "Filming of Motion Picture 'Cane Fire' to Begin Next Friday Says Miss Weber," *Garden Island,* 29 August 1933, n.p.; "'Cane Fire' Players Arrive and Actual Filming of Movie Starts at Waimea," *Garden Island,* 5 Sept 1933, n.p. Articles from *Garden Island* courtesy of Hank Soboleski. See also Hank Soboleski, "'Cane Fire,'" *Garden Island,* 4 Sept 2009, http://www.kauaiworld .com/articles/2009/09/04/news/kauai_news/doc4aa0d0e6c49c4136898456 .txt (accessed 4 Jan 2010).

190. "'Cane Fire' Players Arrive," n.p.

191. "In the Islands," *NYT,* 16 June 1934, 20; *FD,* 15 June 1934, 16; "White Heat," *Billboard,* 30 June 1934, 21.

192. Birchard, *Cecil B. DeMille's Hollywood,* 130.

193. Charles Higham and Roy Moseley, *Cary Grant: The Lonely Heart* (San Diego: Harcourt Brace Jovanovich, 1989), 64. Cherrill was married to Cary Grant at the time.

194. Peter Hyun, *In the New World: The Making of a Korean American* (Honolulu: University of Hawai'i Press, 1995), 138.

195. "Two Features Planned by Seven Seas Corp.," *FD,* 28 July 1934, 1.

196. A print of *White Heat* has not been located, so my analysis is based entirely on plot elements drawn from reviews, as well as surviving production stills and publicity materials. See "In the Islands," 20; "White Heat," *Var,* 19 June 1934, 27; "White Heat," *Billboard,* 30 June 1934, 21; and *FD,* 15 June 1934, 16.

197. The title change apparently came quite late, since *Variety* reviewed the film as "Cane Fire" upon its opening in New York.

198. Susan Courtney, *Hollywood Fantasies of Miscegenation: Spectacular Narratives of Gender and Race* (Princeton: Princeton University Press, 2005), 133–41; quote on 136. For additional information on interracial romance films of the 1930s, see Roger Dooley, "Going Native: Seldom the Twain Shall Meet," in *From Scarface to Scarlett: American Films of the 1930s* (New York: Harcourt, Brace, Jovanovich, 1979), 205–16; and Thomas Doherty, "Primitive Mating Rituals: The Color Wheel of the Racial Adventure Film," in *Pre-Code Hollywood: Sex, Immorality, and Insurrection in American Cinema* (New York: Columbia University Press, 1999), 253–94. For information on Hollywood's depiction of the Pacific Islands, see Glenn K.S. Man, "Hollywood Images of the Pacific," *East-West Film Journal* 5, no. 2 (1991): 16–29; and Houston Wood, "Safe Savagery: Hollywood's Hawai'i," in *Displacing Natives: The Rhetorical Production of Hawai'i* (Lanham, MD: Rowman and Littlefield, 1999), 103–22.

199. Courtney discusses other "South Seas" interracial romances of this period. In *Aloha* (1931) the native woman similarly throws herself into a volcano in the end, but in pictures made after *White Heat*, such as *Jungle Princess* (1936), *Paradise Isle* (1937), and *Her Jungle Love* (1938), white men remain with native women in the end, though, significantly, none return to the United States, choosing to remain instead in their (frequently unspecified) tropical locales. See Courtney, *Hollywood Fantasies of Miscegenation*, 133–41.

200. Hyun, *In the New World*, 136.

201. *Photoplay*, Sept 1934, 98.

202. Slide, *Lois Weber*, 149.

203. Edwin Schallert, "The Pageant of the Film World," *LAT*, 23 Sept 1935, A15.

204. Aydelotte, "The Little Red Schoolhouse," 88.

205. Frank J. Wilstach, "Hollywood Rhetoric in Title," *NYT*, 2 Oct 1927, X7. See also Florey, "The Screen's First Woman Director," 61.

206. Aydelotte, "The Little Red Schoolhouse," 85.

207. Mlle. Chic, "The Greatest Woman Director," 25.

208. Aydelotte, "The Little Red Schoolhouse," 85.

209. "Lois Weber Denied Patent on Aladdin Lamp Trade Mark," *Billboard*, 8 Jan 1927, 6.

210. "Daily Talks by Mary Pickford; Personalities I Have Met: Lois Weber," n.p.

211. Weber, "How I Became A Motion Picture Director," 12. See also Larkin, "Price of Success," n.p.

212. Lois Weber, "Let the Church Help Make Pictures Better," *LAT*, 18 Apr 1921, II, 1; "Chicago Film Flickers," *Billboard*, 7 Apr 1917, 64.

213. "Daily Talks by Mary Pickford; Personalities I Have Met: Lois Weber," n.p.

214. Mlle. Chic, "The Greatest Woman Director," 25.

215. Ibid.

216. Aydelotte, "The Little Red Schoolhouse," 85.

217. Jennifer Peterson, "Glimpses of Animal Life: Nature Films and the Emergence of Classroom Cinema," in *Learning with the Lights Off,* ed. Devin Orgeron, Marsha Orgeron, and Dan Streible (New York: Oxford University Press, 212), 145. Peterson expands this article in her chapter "'The Five-Cent University': Educational Films and the Drive to Uplift the Cinema," in *Education in the School of Dreams: Travelogues and Early Non-fiction Film* (Durham, NC: Duke University Press, 2013), 101–36.

218. Devin Orgeron, Marsha Orgeron, and Dan Streible, "A History of Learning with the Lights Off," in Orgeron, Orgeron, and Streible, *Learning with the Lights Off,* 15–66; Oliver Gaycken, "The Cinema of the Future: Visions of the Medium as Modern Educator, 1895–1910," in Orgeron, Orgeron, and Streible, *Learning with the Lights Off,* 67–89; and Peterson, "Glimpses of Animal Life," 145–67.

219. Peterson, "Glimpses of Animal Life," 145.

220. See Jennifer Horne, "A History Long Overdue: The Public Library and Motion Pictures," in *Useful Cinema,* ed. Charles R. Acland and Haidee Wasson (Durham, NC: Duke University Press, 2011), 149–77.

221. Peak, "Only Woman Movie Director," C11; "Lois Weber Signed by DeMille," 98; "Third Woman Invades Realm of Pictures," *LAT,* 13 Aug 1933, A3; "Woman Makes Bow as Producer," *LAT,* 16 May 1937, C1; Edwin Schallert, "Movieland Jottings and Castings," *LAT,* 22 Aug 1939, I3. Emphasis added.

222. Philip K. Scheuer, "Why Can't Women Be Good Directors?" *LAT,* 14 Oct 1934, A1.

223. E. V. Durling, "On the Side," *LAT,* 9 Apr 1936, A1.

224. "Third Woman Invades Man's Realm," A3.

225. Edwin Schallert, "The Eternal Masculine," *LAT,* 22 June 1932, 11; Scheuer, "Why Can't Women Be Good Directors?" A1; "Mary Pickford Will Deny Old Filmdom Jinx," *Miami News,* 8 July 1935, 15.

226. Ivan St. Johns, "Good-Bye to Another Tradition," *Photoplay,* Mar 1927, 41; "Activities on the West Coast," *NYT,* 17 June 1934, X3; Dunning, "The Gate Women Don't Crash," 35; Edwin Schallert, "Leontine Sagan, Woman Film Director from Germany, Signed for Work in Hollywood," *LAT,* 14 June 1934, 11; Harry Alan Potamkin, "The Woman as Film-Director," *American Cinematographer,* Jan 1932, 10, 45.

227. Peak, "Only Woman Movie Director," C11; Dunning, "The Gate Women Don't Crash," 29. Another in this series of publicity pieces was Florey, "The Screen's First Woman Director," 60–61.

228. Weber, "Many Women Well Fitted," 3; Weber, "Hostility of Men Drawback to Women," 13.

229. *Film Mercury,* 6 July 1928, n.p., quoted in Slide, *Lois Weber,* 142.

230. Capt. Harry Gantz, "Letter to the Editor," *LAX,* 26 Dec 1928, n.p. LAXC; Louella Parsons, "Pathe, F.B.O., Radio Victor Merger Stirs Movieland," *Rochester Evening Journal and Post Express,* 27 Dec 1928, 22.

231. Schallert, "Movieland Jottings and Castings," 13.

232. Linda Arvidson Griffith, *When the Movies Were Young* (1925; repr., New York: Arno, 1977); Gene Gauntier, "Blazing the Trail," *Woman's Home Companion*, Nov 1928, 15–16, 132, 134. Shipman's serialized articles became the basis for her later book *The Silent Screen and My Talking Heart: An Autobiography* (Boise, ID: Boise State University, 1987). See also Christel Schmidt, "Preserving Pickford: The Mary Pickford Collection and the Library of Congress," *Moving Image* 3, no. 1 (Spring 2003): 64; and Amelie Hastie, *Cupboards of Curiosity: Women, Recollection, and Film History* (Durham, NC: Duke University Press, 2007), 39–71.

233. "Employees to Fete Producer," *LAT*, 5 Dec 1926, I9; "'Pioneers' Will Honor Carl Laemmle," *LAT*, 5 Dec 1926, I9; Lee Shippey, "The Lee Side o'L.A.," *LAT*, 12 Mar 1935, A4; Read Kendall, "Around and About in Hollywood," *LAT*, 11 May 1935, I7; Grace Kingsley, "Prehistoric Hi-Jinks in Hollywood," *LAT*, 19 Aug 1934, H3, H6.

234. Terry Ramsaye, *A Million and One Nights: A History of the Motion Picture through 1925* (1926; repr., New York: Simon and Schuster, 1986); Hampton, *A History of the Movies.*

235. "Now They Do the Bossing!" *LAT*, 18 Dec 1927, H4.

236. Julian appeared in more than twenty shorts written and directed by Weber and five of her features, including *The Merchant of Venice* (1914) and *The Dumb Girl of Portici* (1916).

237. Birchard, *Early Universal City*, 111.

238. See A.H. Giebler, "The Power behind the Picture," *St. Louis Daily Globe-Democrat*, 5 Aug 1917, n.p., author's collection. Griffith, DeMille, and Weber are profiled in the full-page story as "directors of brains and vision."

239. *The Unshod Maiden* survives at the Library of Congress. Ironically—and fittingly—pristine footage from the parody was used in the 2010 restoration of *Shoes* by EYE Film Institute Netherlands.

240. William M. Drew, *The Last Silent Picture Show: Silent Films on American Screens in the 1930s* (Lanham, MD: Scarecrow Press, 2010), 92–93; quote on 93.

241. "Reviews of Sound Shorts," *FD*, 20 Mar 1932, 9; Edwin Schallert, "Wife Who Fled Seen in Film," *LAT*, 8 Feb 1932, 7; *Hollywood Herald*, 8 Feb 1932, n.p., quoted in Slide, *Lois Weber*, 146.

242. See David J. Skal, *Hollywood Gothic: The Tangled Web of Dracula from Novel to Stage to Screen* (New York: Macmillan, 2004), 300; Tom Weaver, Michael Brunas, and John Brunas, *Universal Horrors: The Studio's Classic Films, 1931–1946* (New York: McFarland, 2007), 567.

243. "Mason on Original," 3.

244. "Island Film Ready for Cutting," n.p.

245. Weber to DeMille, 24 June 1939, quoted in Slide, *Lois Weber*, 149.

246. Nelson B. Bell, "Many Films Typical of Their Day Are Donated to Museum of Film Art's Library," *Wash Post*, 20 Nov 1935, 16.

247. Schallert, "Movieland Jottings and Castings," 13. Slide reports that Weber's sister Ethel tried for years to have it published without success, before it was eventually lost or stolen toward the end of her life. See Slide, *Lois Weber*, 151.

248. Myra Nye, "Society of Cinemaland," *LAT*, 16 Sept 1928, C29; Myra Nye, "Society of Cinemaland," *LAT*, 21 Dec 1930, B20; Grace Kingsley, "Hither and Thither with Stella," *LAT*, 23 Mar 1930, H6; "Campus Folk Fete Visitors," *LAT*, 25 July 1936, A5; Edwin Schallert, "The Pageant of the Film World," *LAT*, 23 Sept 1935, A15.

249. Slide, *Lois Weber*, 149.

250. Philip K. Scheuer, "Stars Become Spear-Bearers," *LAT*, 7 Feb 1932, B9.

251. "Two Veteran Directors Appear in 'True Heaven,'" *FD*, 11 Dec 1928, 7; "Actor's Funeral Will Be Today," *LAT*, 5 May 1939, I 7.

252. "Hedda Hopper's Hollywood," *LAT*, 30 Sept 1939, A7.

253. Hedda Hopper, "Lois Weber Critically Ill," *LAT*, 6 Nov 1929, A1; Hedda Hopper," Death Takes Lois Weber," *LAT*, 14 Nov 1939, A1; "Lois Weber Funeral Services Conducted," *LAT*, 18 Nov 1939, A10.

254. "Lois Weber, Director of Moving Pictures," *NYT*, 14 Nov 1939, 23; *Var*, 15 Nov 1939, 62; "Lois Weber, First Women Director, Dies," *LAX*, 14 Nov 1939, n.p., LAXC; "Lois Weber, Movie Star-Maker," n.d., n.p., env. 2518, RLC.

255. Hopper," Death Takes Lois Weber," A1, A2.

256. Koszarski, "The Years Have Not Been Kind to Lois Weber," 147.

CONCLUSION

Epigraph: *Los Angeles Herald*, 21 Feb 1921, n.p., quoted in Slide, *Early American Cinema*, 161–62.

1. Koszarski, "The Years Have Not Been Kind to Lois Weber.". The subtitle of Slide's 1996 book on Weber is *The Director Who Lost Her Way in History*.

2. McMahan, *Alice Guy Blaché; The Lost Garden: The Life and Cinema of Alice Guy Blaché*, dir. Marquise Lepage (National Film Board of Canada, 1995); Peter Flynn, "Gene Gauntier: Cinema's Forgotten Pioneer," unpublished paper presented at the University Film and Video Association Conference, 2011; "Nell Shipman: Canada's Forgotten Star," Toronto International Film Festival program, 2003; Giuliana Bruno, *Streetwalking on a Ruined Map: Cultural Theory and the City Films of Elvira Notari* (Princeton: Princeton University Press, 1993), 4.

3. Ramsaye, *A Million and One Nights*; Hampton, *A History of the American Film*; and Lewis Jacobs, *The Rise of American Film: A Critical History* (New York: Harcourt Brace, 1939).

4. See George C. Pratt, *Spellbound in Darkness: A History of the Silent Film*, rev. ed. (New York: Graphic Society, 1973); William Everson, *American Silent Film* (New York: Oxford University Press, 1978); Brownlow, *The Parade's Gone By . . .* ; Robinson, *From Peepshow to Palace*; and Richard Abel, ed. *The Encyclopedia of Early Cinema* (New York: Taylor and Francis, 2004). The work of Anthony Slide and Richard Koszarski marks a major exception in this regard.

5. See, for example, Robert Sklar, *Movie-Made America* (New York: Vintage, 1976); and Jon Lewis, *American Film: A History* (New York: W.W. Norton, 2007).

6. Cooper, *Universal Women*; Edmonds, *Big U*; Dick, *City of Dreams*; Birchard, *Early Universal City*.

7. Louis D. Giannetti and Scott Eyman, *Flashback: A Brief Film History*, 6th ed. (Boston: Allyn and Bacon, 2009), 45.

8. See, for example, Louise Heck-Rabi, *Women Filmmakers: A Critical Reception* (Lanham, MD: Scarecrow Press, 1984); Quart, *Women Directors*; Acker, *Reel Women*; and Gwendolyn Audrey Foster, *Women Film Directors: An International Bio-critical Dictionary* (Westport, CT: Greenwood, 1995).

Filmography

WITH MARTIN F. NORDEN

This filmography is necessarily incomplete. It relies on early detective work by Richard Braff, Anthony Slide, and American Film Institute catalog researchers, with additional information compiled and incorporated with the help of Martin F. Norden from trade periodicals, newspapers, and extant prints. While Weber reported working at outfits such as American Gaumont and Reliance early in her career, with a couple of exceptions her motion picture work only becomes legible after she joins Rex in late 1910. In the absence of formal credits for these early one- and two-reel shorts, I have assigned Weber credit for writing the scenarios, since most contemporary accounts indicate that she penned all of these early titles. Similarly, contemporary observers generally agree that Weber and her husband Phillips Smalley shared credit for directing or "producing" these shorts; so, like other historians, I have assigned the two equal credit on their Rex productions. Ascertaining directing credit on their early features has been more difficult. By 1916 most contemporary accounts give Weber sole credit for directing; when in doubt, prior to that I have elected to credit both Weber and Smalley with directing. Errors and omissions almost certainly remain.

ABBREVIATIONS

Where film prints are known to be extant, I have indicated their location using the following abbreviations. Prints that are incomplete are noted as "inc."

AUS   National Film and Sound Archive, Australia
BFI   British Film Institute, National Film and Television Archive
CF   Cinémathèque Française

CNC   National Centre for Cinema and the Moving Image, France

EYE   EYE Film Institute Netherlands

ITG   Cineteca del Friuli, Gemona, Italy

LOC   Library of Congress, Motion Picture, Broadcasting, and Recorded Sound Division

MoMA   Museum of Modern Art, New York

NFC   National Film Center, Tokyo

NILES   Niles Essanay Silent Film Museum

NZ   New Zealand Film Archive

UCLA   UCLA Film and Television Archive

WISC   Wisconsin Center for Film and Theater Research

FILMS

[*] Titles where Weber's involvement cannot be verified with certainty.

A Heroine of '76 (Rex, 1911). Dir.: Lois Weber and Phillips Smalley. Scr.: Lois Weber. Cast: Lois Weber, Gordon Sackville. 1 reel. Released 16 Feb 1911.

The Story of a Prayer Rug (Rex, 1911). Dir.: Lois Weber and Phillips Smalley. Scr.: Lois Weber. Cast: Lois Weber, Phillips Smalley. 1 reel. Released 23 Feb 1911.

By the Light of the Moon (Rex, 1911). Dir.: Lois Weber and Phillips Smalley. Scr.: Lois Weber. Cast: Lois Weber, Phillips Smalley. 1 reel. Released 2 Mar 1911.

The Fall of a Knight (Rex, 1911). Dir.: Lois Weber and Phillips Smalley. Scr.: Lois Weber. Cast: Lois Weber, Phillips Smalley. 1 reel. Released 9 Mar 1911.

Where the Shamrock Grows (Rex, 1911). Dir.: Lois Weber and Phillips Smalley. Scr.: Lois Weber. Cast: Lois Weber, Phillips Smalley. 1 reel. Released 16 Mar 1911.

Five Hours (Rex, 1911). Dir.: Lois Weber and Phillips Smalley. Scr.: Lois Weber. Cast: Lois Weber, Phillips Smalley. 1 reel. Released 23 Mar 1911.

As Ye Sow (Rex, 1911). Dir.: Lois Weber and Phillips Smalley. Scr.: Lois Weber. Cast: Lois Weber, Phillips Smalley. 1 reel. Released 30 March 1911.

The Heiress (Rex, 1911). Dir.: Lois Weber and Phillips Smalley. Scr.: Lois Weber. Cast: Lois Weber, Phillips Smalley. 1 reel. Released 6 Apr 1911.

The Little Major (Rex, 1911). Dir.: Lois Weber and Phillips Smalley. Scr.: Lois Weber, Cast: Lois Weber, Phillips Smalley. 1 reel. Released 13 Apr 1911. Archive: BFI [inc.].

A Daughter of the Revolution (Rex, 1911). Dir.: Lois Weber and Phillips Smalley. Scr.: Lois Weber. Cast: Lois Weber, Phillips Smalley. 1 reel. Released 20 Apr 1911.

The Realization (Rex, 1911). Dir.: Lois Weber and Phillips Smalley. Scr.: Lois Weber. Cast: Phillips Smalley. 1 reel. Released 27 Apr 1911.

The Ultimate Sacrifice (Rex, 1911). Dir.: Lois Weber and Phillips Smalley. Scr.: Lois Weber. Cast: Lois Weber, Phillips Smalley. 1 reel. Released 4 May 1911.

The Guardsman (Rex, 1911). Dir.: Lois Weber and Phillips Smalley. Scr.: Lois Weber. Cast: Lois Weber, Phillips Smalley. 1 reel. Released 11 May 1911.

An Exception to the Rule (Rex, 1911). Dir.: Lois Weber and Phillips Smalley. Scr.: Lois Weber. Cast: Lois Weber, Phillips Smalley. 1 reel. Released 18 May 1911.

Called Back (Rex, 1911). Dir.: Lois Weber and Phillips Smalley. Scr.: Lois Weber. Cast: Lois Weber, Phillips Smalley. 1 reel. Released 25 May 1911.

The Monogram "J.O." (Rex, 1911). Dir.: Lois Weber and Phillips Smalley. Scr.: Lois Weber. Cast: Lois Weber, Phillips Smalley. 1 reel. Released 1 Jun 1911.

From Death to Life (Rex, 1911). Dir.: Lois Weber and Phillips Smalley. Scr.: Lois Weber. Cast: Lois Weber and Phillips Smalley. 1 reel. Released 8 Jun 1911. Archive: LOC.

The Broken Coin (Reliance/NYMP 1911). Dir.: Lois Weber and Phillips Smalley. Scr.: Lois Weber. Cast: Lois Weber, Phillips Smalley. 1 reel. Released 10 Jun 1911.

The Twins (Rex, 1911). Dir.: Lois Weber and Phillips Smalley. Scr.: Lois Weber. Cast: Lois Weber. 1 reel. Released 15 Jun 1911.

On the Brink (Rex, 1911). Dir.: Lois Weber and Phillips Smalley. Scr.: Lois Weber. Cast: Lois Weber, Phillips Smalley, Charles DeForest. 1 reel. Released 24 Jun 1911. Archive: LOC.

What the Tide Told (Reliance/NYMP, 1911). Dir.: Lois Weber and Phillips Smalley. Scr.: Lois Weber. Cast: Lois Weber, Phillips Smalley. 1 reel. Released 24 Jun 1911.

Securing Evidence (Rex, 1911). Dir.: Lois Weber and Phillips Smalley. Scr.: Lois Weber. Cast: Lois Weber, Phillips Smalley. 1 reel. Released 29 Jun 1911.

Fate (Rex, 1911). Dir.: Lois Weber and Phillips Smalley. Scr.: Lois Weber. Cast: Lois Weber, Phillips Smalley. 1 reel. Released 6 Jul 1911.

The Vagabond (Rex, 1911). Dir.: Lois Weber and Phillips Smalley. Scr.: Lois Weber. Cast: Lois Weber, Phillips Smalley. 1 reel. Released 13 Jul 1911.

Sherlock Holmes, Jr. (Rex, 1911). Dir.: Lois Weber and Phillips Smalley. Scr.: Lois Weber. Cast: Lois Weber, Phillips Smalley. 1 reel. Released 20 Jul 1911.

The Artist Financier (Rex, 1911). Dir.: Lois Weber and Phillips Smalley. Scr.: Lois Weber. Cast: Lois Weber, Phillips Smalley. 1 reel. Released 3 Aug 1911.

The White Red Man (Rex, 1911). Dir.: Lois Weber and Phillips Smalley. Scr.: Lois Weber. Cast: Lois Weber, Phillips Smalley. 1 reel. Released 10 Aug 1911.

The Colonel's Daughter (Rex, 1911). Dir.: Lois Weber and Phillips Smalley. Scr.: Lois Weber. Cast: Lois Weber, Phillips Smalley. 1 reel. Released 17 Aug 1911. Archive: BFI.

Castles in the Air (Rex, 1911). Dir.: Lois Weber and Phillips Smalley. Scr.: Lois Weber. Cast: Lois Weber, Phillips Smalley. 1 reel. Released 24 Aug 1911.

The Torn Scarf (Rex, 1911). Dir.: Lois Weber and Phillips Smalley. Scr.: Lois Weber. Cast: Lois Weber, Phillips Smalley. 1 reel. Released 31 Aug 1911.

Faith (Rex, 1911). Dir.: Lois Weber and Phillips Smalley. Scr.: Lois Weber. Cast: Lois Weber, Phillips Smalley. 1 reel. Released 14 Sept 1911.

The Rose and the Dagger (Rex, 1911). Dir.: Lois Weber and Phillips Smalley. Scr.: Lois Weber. Cast: Lois Weber, Phillips Smalley. 1 reel. Released 21 Sept 1911.

The Derelict (Rex, 1911). Dir.: Lois Weber and Phillips Smalley. Scr.: Lois Weber. Cast: Lois Weber, Phillips Smalley. 1 reel. Released 28 Sept 1911.

Lost Illusions (Rex, 1911). Dir.: Lois Weber and Phillips Smalley. Scr.: Lois Weber. Cast: Lois Weber, Phillips Smalley, Harold Lockwood. 1 reel. Released 5 Oct 1911. Archive: EYE.

Chasing the Rainbow (Rex, 1911). Dir.: Lois Weber and Phillips Smalley. Scr.: Lois Weber. Cast: Helen Anderson. 1 reel. Released 12 Oct 1911.

Her Sister (Rex, 1911). Dir.: Lois Weber and Phillips Smalley. Scr.: Lois Weber. Cast: Lois Weber, Phillips Smalley. 1 reel. Released 19 Oct 1911.

A Breach of Faith (Rex, 1911). Dir.: Lois Weber and Phillips Smalley. Scr.: Lois Weber. 1 reel. Released 26 Oct 1911.

The Tale of a Cat (Rex, 1911). Dir.: Lois Weber and Phillips Smalley. Scr.: Lois Weber. Cast: Lois Weber, Helen Anderson. 1 reel. Released 2 Nov 1911.

Saints and Sinners (Rex, 1911). Dir.: Lois Weber and Phillips Smalley. Scr.: Lois Weber. Cast: Lois Weber, Phillips Smalley. 1 reel. Released 9 Nov 1911.

The Return (Rex, 1911). Dir.: Lois Weber and Phillips Smalley. Scr.: Lois Weber. 1 reel. Released 16 Nov 1911.

The Price (Rex, 1911). Dir.: Lois Weber and Phillips Smalley. Adapt.: Lois Weber. Cast: Lois Weber, Phillips Smalley. 1 reel. Released 23 Nov 1911. Archive: EYE.

The Stranger (Rex, 1911). Dir.: Lois Weber and Phillips Smalley. Scr.: Lois Weber. Cast: Lois Weber, Phillips Smalley. 1 reel. Released 30 Nov 1911.

The Measure of a Man (Rex, 1911). Dir.: Lois Weber and Phillips Smalley. Scr.: Lois Weber. Cast: Lois Weber, Phillips Smalley. 1 reel. Released 6 Dec 1911.

The Martyr (Rex, 1911). Dir.: Lois Weber and Phillips Smalley. Scr.: Lois Weber. Cast: Lois Weber. 1 reel. Released 21 Dec 1911.

An Unwelcome Santa Claus (Rex, 1911). Dir.: Lois Weber and Phillips Smalley. Scr.: Lois Weber. Cast: Lois Weber, Phillips Smalley. 1 reel. Released 28 Dec 1911.

The Parting of the Ways (Rex, 1912). Dir.: Lois Weber and Phillips Smalley. Scr.: Lois Weber. 1 reel. Released 4 Jan 1912.

Angels Unaware (Rex, 1912). Dir.: Lois Weber and Phillips Smalley. Scr.: Lois Weber. Cast: Lois Weber. 1 reel. Released 18 Jan 1912.

A Sane Asylum (Rex, 1912). Dir.: Lois Weber and Phillips Smalley. Scr.: Lois Weber. Cast: Phillips Smalley. 1 reel. Released 25 Jan 1912.

Fine Feathers (Rex, 1912). Dir.: Lois Weber and Phillips Smalley. Scr.: Lois Weber. Cast: Lois Weber, Phillips Smalley. 1 reel. Released 1 Feb 1912. Archive: LOC.

The Bargain (Rex, 1912). Dir.: Lois Weber and Phillips Smalley. Scr.: Lois Weber. Cast: Lois Weber. 1 reel. Released 8 Feb 1912.

Taming Mrs. Shrew (Rex, 1912). Dir.: Lois Weber and Phillips Smalley. Scr.: Lois Weber. Cast: Lois Weber, Phillips Smalley. 1 reel. Released 15 Feb 1912.

The Final Pardon (Rex, 1912). Dir.: Lois Weber and Phillips Smalley. Scr.: Lois Weber. Cast: Lois Weber, Phillips Smalley. 1 reel. Released 29 Feb 1912.

Eyes That See Not (Rex, 1912). Dir.: Lois Weber and Phillips Smalley. Scr.: Lois Weber. Cast: Lois Weber, Phillips Smalley. 1 reel. Released 14 Mar 1912.

The Price of Money (Rex, 1912). Dir.: Lois Weber and Phillips Smalley. Scr.: Lois Weber. Cast: Lois Weber, Phillips Smalley. 1 reel. Released 21 Mar 1912.

Love's Four Stone Walls (Rex, 1912). Dir.: Lois Weber and Phillips Smalley. Scr.: Lois Weber. 1 reel. Released 28 Mar 1912.

Modern Slaves (Rex, 1912). Dir.: Lois Weber and Phillips Smalley. Scr.: Lois Weber. Cast: Lois Weber, Phillips Smalley. 1 reel. Released 4 Apr 1912.

A Tangled Web (Rex, 1912). Dir.: Lois Weber and Phillips Smalley. Scr.: Lois Weber. Cast: Lois Weber, Phillips Smalley. 1 reel. Released 11 Apr 1912.

Beauty and the Beast (Rex, 1912). Dir.: Lois Weber and Phillips Smalley. Scr.: Lois Weber. Cast: Cleo Madison, Phillips Smalley. 1 reel. Released 18 Apr 1912.

Fate's Warning (Rex, 1912). Dir.: Lois Weber and Phillips Smalley. Scr.: Lois Weber. Cast: Lois Weber and Phillips Smalley. 1 reel. Released 2 May 1912.

Drawing the Line (Rex, 1912). Dir.: Lois Weber and Phillips Smalley. Scr.: Lois Weber. Cast: Lois Weber, Phillips Smalley. 1 reel. Released 9 May 1912.

Lost Years (Rex, 1912). Dir.: Lois Weber and Phillips Smalley. Scr.: Lois Weber. Cast: Lois Weber. 1 reel. Released 16 May 1912.

Grandfather's Clock (Rex, 1912). Dir.: Lois Weber and Phillips Smalley. Scr.: Lois Weber. Cast: Phillips Smalley. 1 reel. Released 30 May 1912.

The Price of Peace (Rex, 1912). Dir.: Lois Weber and Phillips Smalley. Scr.: Lois Weber. Cast: Lois Weber, Phillips Smalley. 1 reel. Released 6 Jun 1912.

The Flirt (Rex, 1912). Dir.: Lois Weber and Phillips Smalley. Scr.: Lois Weber. 1reel. Released 13 Jun 1912.

The Power of Thought (Rex, 1912). Dir.: Lois Weber and Phillips Smalley. Scr.: Lois Weber. Cast: Lois Weber, Phillips Smalley, Cleo Ridgley, W. H. Tooker, W. J. Sorelle. 1 reel. Released 20 Jun 1912.

The Weight of a Feather (Rex, 1912). Dir.: Lois Weber and Phillips Smalley. Scr.: Lois Weber. Cast: Cleo Madison. 1 reel. Released 27 Jun 1912.

A Prophet Without Honor (Rex/Universal, 1912). Dir.: Lois Weber and Phillips Smalley. Scr.: Lois Weber. Cast: Phillips Smalley. 1 reel. Released 4 Jul 1912. Archive: LOC.

The Greater Love (Rex/Universal, 1912). Dir.: Lois Weber and Phillips Smalley. Scr.: Lois Weber. Cast: Lois Weber, Phillips Smalley. 1 reel. Released 11 Jul 1912.

The Hidden Light (Rex/Universal, 1912). Dir.: Lois Weber and Phillips Smalley. Scr.: Lois Weber. Cast: Phillips Smalley. 1 reel. Released 18 Jul 1912.

The Hand of Mystery (Rex/Universal, 1912). Dir.: Lois Weber and Phillips Smalley. Scr.: Lois Weber. Cast: Cleo Madison. 1 reel. Released 25 Jul 1912.

The Lash of Fate (Rex/Universal, 1912). Dir.: Lois Weber and Phillips Smalley. Scr.: Lois Weber. 1 reel. Released 1 Aug 1912.

The Troubadour's Triumph (Rex/Universal, 1912). Dir.: Lois Weber and Phillips Smalley. Scr.: Lois Weber. Cast: Lois Weber, Phillips Smalley. 1 reel. Released 8 Aug 1912.

The Greater Christian (Rex/Universal, 1912). Dir.: Lois Weber and Phillips Smalley. Scr.: Lois Weber. Cast: Lois Weber, Phillips Smalley. 1 reel. Released 15 Aug 1912.

An Old-Fashioned Girl (Rex/Universal, 1912). Dir.: Lois Weber and Phillips Smalley. Scr.: Lois Weber. Cast: Lois Weber, Phillips Smalley. 1 reel. Released 22 Aug 1912.

A Japanese Idyll (Rex/Universal, 1912). Dir.: Lois Weber and Phillips Smalley. Scr.: Lois Weber. 1 reel. Released 29 Aug 1912. Archives: LOC, ITG.

From the Wilds (Rex/Universal, 1912). Dir.: Lois Weber and Phillips Smalley. Scr.: Lois Weber. 1 reel. Released 5 Sept 1912.

The Squatter's Rights (Rex/Universal, 1912). Dir.: Lois Weber and Phillips Smalley. Scr.: Lois Weber. 1 reel. Released 12 Sept 1912.

Far Away Fields (Rex/Universal, 1912). Dir.: Lois Weber and Phillips Smalley. Scr.: Lois Weber. Cast: Lois Weber, Phillips Smalley, Cleo Ridgley. 1 reel. Released 19 Sept 1912.

Leaves in the Storm (Rex/Universal 1912). Dir.: Lois Weber and Phillips Smalley. Scr.: Lois Weber. Cast: Lois Weber, Phillips Smalley. 1 reel. Released 20 Oct 1912.

The Flower Girl (Rex/Universal, 1913). Dir.: Lois Weber and Phillips Smalley. Scr.: Lois Weber. Cast: Lois Weber, Phillips Smalley. 1 reel. Released 16 Jan 1913.

He Never Knew (Rex/Universal, 1913). Dir.: Lois Weber and Phillips Smalley. Scr.: Lois Weber. Cast: Lois Weber, Phillips Smalley. 1 reel. Released 19 Jan 1913.

The Angelus (Rex/Universal, 1913). Dir.: Lois Weber and Phillips Smalley. Scr.: Lois Weber. Cast: Lois Weber, Phillips Smalley. 1 reel. Released 30 Jan 1913.

His Sister (Rex/Universal, 1913). Dir.: Lois Weber and Phillips Smalley. Scr.: Lois Weber. Cast: Lois Weber, Phillips Smalley. 1 reel. Released 9 Feb 1913.

Billy's Double Capture (Rex/Universal, 1913). Dir.: Lois Weber and Phillips Smalley. Scr.: Lois Weber. Cast: Lois Weber. 1 reel. Released 16 Feb 1913.

Two Thieves (Rex/Universal, 1913). Dir.: Lois Weber and Phillips Smalley. Scr.: Lois Weber. Cast: Lois Weber, Phillips Smalley. 1 reel. Released 23 Feb 1913.

In the Blood (Rex/Universal, 1913). Dir.: Lois Weber and Phillips Smalley. Scr.: Lois Weber. Cast: Lois Weber, Phillips Smalley. 1 reel. Released 2 Mar 1913.

Troubled Waters (Rex/Universal, 1913). Dir.: Lois Weber and Phillips Smalley. Scr.: Lois Weber. Cast: Lois Weber, Phillips Smalley. 1 reel. Released 9 Mar 1913.

Thou Shalt Not Steal (Rex/Universal, 1913). Dir.: Lois Weber and Phillips Smalley. Scr.: Lois Weber. Cast: Lois Weber, Phillips Smalley. 1 reel. Released 13 Mar 1913.

The Empty Box (Rex/Universal, 1913). Dir.: Lois Weber and Phillips Smalley. Scr.: Lois Weber. Cast: Lois Weber, Phillips Smalley. 1 reel. Released 16 Mar 1913.

Was She to Blame? (Rex/Universal, 1913). Dir.: Lois Weber and Phillips Smalley. Scr.: Lois Weber. 1 reel. Released 20 Mar 1913.

The Peacemaker (Rex/Universal, 1913). Dir.: Lois Weber and Phillips Smalley. Scr.: Lois Weber. Cast: Phillips Smalley. 1 reel. Released 23 Mar 1913.

Bobby's Baby (Rex/Universal, 1913). Dir.: Lois Weber and Phillips Smalley. Scr.: Lois Weber. Cast: Lois Weber, Phillips Smalley, Antrim Short. 1 reel. Released 6 Apr 1913.

Until Death (Rex/Universal, 1913). Dir.: Lois Weber and Phillips Smalley. Scr.: Lois Weber. Cast: Lois Weber, Phillips Smalley, Harry Pollard. 1 reel. Released 10 Apr 1913.

A Book of Verses (Rex/Universal, 1913). Dir.: Lois Weber and Phillips Smalley. Scr.: Lois Weber. Cast: Lois Weber, Phillips Smalley. 1 reel. Released 20 Apr 1913.

The Dragon's Breath (Rex/Universal, 1913). Dir.: Lois Weber and Phillips Smalley. Scr.: Lois Weber. Cast: Lois Weber, Phillips Smalley. 1 reel. Released 24 Apr 1913.

The Rosary (Rex/Universal, 1913). Dir.: Lois Weber and Phillips Smalley. Scr.: Lois Weber. Cast: Phillips Smalley, Margarita Fischer. 1 reel. Released 4 May 1913. Archive: BFI.

The Poverty of Riches (Rex/Universal, 1913). Dir.: Lois Weber and Phillips Smalley. Scr.: Lois Weber. Cast: Lois Weber, Phillips Smalley. 1 reel. Released 11 May 1913.

The Cap of Destiny (Rex/Universal, 1913). Dir.: Lois Weber and Phillips Smalley. Scr.: Lois Weber. Cast: Lois Weber, Phillips Smalley. 1 reel. Released 15 May 1913.

Gold and Two Men (Rex/Universal 1913). Dir.: Lois Weber and Phillips Smalley. Scr.: Lois Weber. Cast: Lois Weber, Phillips Smalley. 1 reel. Released 18 May 1913.

The Trifler (Rex/Universal 1913). Dir.: Lois Weber and Phillips Smalley. Scr.: Lois Weber. Cast: Lois Weber, Phillips Smalley. 1 reel. Released 25 May 1913.

*The Tourist and the Flower Girl (Rex/Universal, 1913). Dir.: Lois Weber and Phillips Smalley. Scr.: Lois Weber. Cast: Lois Weber. 1 reel. Released May 29, 1913.

The King Can Do No Wrong (Rex/Universal, 1913). Dir.: Lois Weber and Phillips Smalley. Scr.: Lois Weber. Cast: Lois Weber, Phillips Smalley. 3 reels. Released 12 Jun 1913.

The Pretender (Rex/Universal, 1913). Dir.: Lois Weber and Phillips Smalley. Scr.: Lois Weber. Cast: Lois Weber, Phillips Smalley, Lule Warrenton. 1 reel. Released 15 Jun 1913.

The Burden Bearer (Rex/Universal, 1913). Dir.: Lois Weber and Phillips Smalley. Scr.: Lois Weber. Cast: Lois Weber, Phillips Smalley. 1 reel. Released 26 Jun 1913.

Suspense (Rex/Universal, 1913). Dir.: Lois Weber and Phillips Smalley. Scr.: Lois Weber. Cast: Lois Weber, Valentine Paul, Douglas Gerrard, Sam

Kaufman. 1 reel. Released 6 Jul 1913. Archives: MoMA, BFI, ITG, UCLA, AUS.

Through Strife (Rex/Universal, 1913). Dir.: Lois Weber and Phillips Smalley. Scr.: Lois Weber. Cast: Lois Weber, Phillips Smalley. 1 reel. Released 10 Jul 1913.

Fallen Angel (Rex/Universal, 1913). Dir.: Lois Weber and Phillips Smalley. Scr.: Lois Weber. Cast: Lois Weber, Phillips Smalley. 2 reels. Released 24 Jul 1913.

Civilized and Savage (Rex/Universal, 1913). Dir.: Lois Weber and Phillips Smalley. Scr.: Lois Weber. Cast: Lois Weber, Phillips Smalley. 1 reel. Released 3 Aug 1913. Archive: BFI.

Just in Time (Rex/Universal, 1913). Dir.: Lois Weber and Phillips Smalley. Scr.: Lois Weber. Cast: Lois Weber, Phillips Smalley. 1 reel. Released 24 Aug 1913.

The Call (Rex/Universal, 1913). Dir.: Lois Weber and Phillips Smalley. Scr.: Lois Weber. Cast: Lois Weber, Phillips Smalley. 1 reel. Released 31 Aug 1913.

The Light Woman (Rex/Universal, 1913). Dir.: Lois Weber and Phillips Smalley. Scr.: Lois Weber. Cast: Lois Weber, Phillips Smalley. 1 reel. Released 7 Sept 1913.

Genesis IV: 9 (Rex/Universal, 1913). Dir.: Lois Weber and Phillips Smalley. Scr.: Lois Weber. Cast: Phillips Smalley, Rupert Julian, Grace Carlyle, Lule Warrenton. 2 reels. Released 14 Sept 1913.

Never Again (Rex/Universal 1913). Dir.: Lois Weber and Phillips Smalley. Scr.: Lois Weber. Cast: Lois Weber, Phillips Smalley. 1 reel. Released 18 Sept 1913.

His Brand (Rex/Universal, 1913). Dir.: Lois Weber and Phillips Smalley. Scr.: Lois Weber. Cast: Lois Weber, Phillips Smalley, Antrim Short, Rupert Julian, Lule Warrenton, Billy Gettinger. 1 reel. Released 2 Oct 1913.

Shadows of Life (Rex/Universal, 1913). Dir.: Lois Weber and Phillips Smalley. Scr.: Lois Weber and Elliott J. Clawson. Cast: Lois Weber, Phillips Smalley, Rupert Julian, Cleo Madison, Frank Lloyd. 2 reels. Released 9 Oct 1913.

Memories (Rex/Universal, 1913). Dir.: Lois Weber and Phillips Smalley. Scr.: Lois Weber. Cast: Lois Weber, Phillips Smalley, Ella Hall, Rupert Julian, Marie Walcamp, Lule Warrenton, Laura Oakley. 1 reel. Released 16 Oct 1913.

The Clue (Rex/Universal, 1913). Dir.: Lois Weber and Phillips Smalley. Scr.: Lois Weber. Cast: Phillips Smalley, Rupert Julian. 1 reel. Released 30 Oct 1913.

*The Thumb Print (Rex/Universal, 1913). Dir.: Lois Weber and Phillips Smalley. Scr.: Lois Weber. Cast: Robert Z. Leonard, Margarita Fischer, John Burton, Harry Tenbrook, Malcolm J. MacQuarrie. 2 reels. Released 23 Oct 1913.

The Haunted Bride (Rex/Universal, 1913). Dir.: Lois Weber and Phillips Smalley. Scr.: Lois Weber. Cast: Lois Weber, Phillips Smalley, Rupert Julian, W. R. Walters, Ella Hall. 1 reel. Released 9 Nov 1913.

The Blood Brotherhood (Rex/Universal, 1913). Dir.: Lois Weber and Phillips Smalley. Scr.: Lois Weber. Cast: Lois Weber, Phillips Smalley, Rupert Julian, W. R. Walters, Ella Hall. 1 reel. Released 16 Nov 1913.

Thieves and the Cross (Rex/Universal, 1913). Dir.: Lois Weber and Phillips Smalley. Scr.: Lois Weber. Cast: Lois Weber, Phillips Smalley, Rupert Julian, Agnes Gordon. 2 reels. Released 4 Dec 1913.

James Lee's Wife (Rex/Universal, 1913). Dir.: Lois Weber and Phillips Smalley. Adapt.: Lois Weber. Cast: Lois Weber, Phillips Smalley, Ella Hall, P. E. Peters. 1 reel. Released 7 Dec 1913.

The Mask (Rex/Universal, 1913). Dir.: Lois Weber and Phillips Smalley. Scr.: Lois Weber. Cast: Lois Weber, Phillips Smalley, Ella Hall, Lule Warrenton. 1 reel. Released 14 Dec 1913.

A Jew's Christmas (Rex/Universal, 1913). Dir.: Lois Weber and Phillips Smalley. Scr.: Lois Weber. Cast: Lois Weber, Phillips Smalley, Lule Warrenton, Ella Hall. 3 reels. Released 18 Dec 1913.

A Wife's Deceit (Rex/Universal, 1913). Dir.: Lois Weber and Phillips Smalley. Scr.: Lois Weber. Cast: Lois Weber, Phillips Smalley, Raymond Russell. 1 reel. Released 21 Dec 1913.

The Female of the Species (Rex/Universal, 1914). Dir.: Lois Weber and Phillips Smalley. Scr.: Lois Weber. Cast: Lois Weber, Phillips Smalley, Rupert Julian, Ella Hall, J. H. MacFarland, Mr. Brown. 1 reel. Released 1 Jan 1914.

A Fool and His Money (Rex/Universal, 1914). Dir.: Lois Weber and Phillips Smalley. Scr.: Lois Weber. Cast: Lois Weber, Phillips Smalley, Rupert Julian, Ella Hall, H. Browne. 1 reel. Released 4 Jan 1914.

The Option (Rex/Universal 1914). Dir.: Lois Weber and Phillips Smalley. Scr.: Lois Weber. Cast: Lois Weber, Phillips Smalley. 1 reel. Released 18 Jan 1914.

The Leper's Coat (Rex/Universal, 1914). Dir.: Lois Weber and Phillips Smalley. Scr.: Lois Weber. Cast: Lois Weber, Phillips Smalley, Rupert Julian, Jeanie Macpherson. 1 reel. 25 Jan 1914.

The Merchant of Venice (Universal, 1914). Dir.: Lois Weber and Phillips Smalley. Adapt.: Lois Weber. Cast: Lois Weber, Phillips Smalley, Douglas Gerrard, Rupert Julian, Edna Maison, Jeanie Macpherson. 4 reels. Released 1 Feb 1914.

The Coward Hater (Rex/Universal, 1914). Dir.: Lois Weber and Phillips Smalley. Scr.: Lois Weber. Cast: Lois Weber, Phillips Smalley, Rupert Julian, Theo Carew, Ella Hall, Fred Wilson. 1 reel. Released 8 Feb 1914.

The Man Who Slept (Victor, 1914). Scr.: Lois Weber. Cast: Eddie Lyons, Ella Hall, Lule Warrenton, R. W. Wallace. 1 reel. Released 9 Feb 1914.

An Old Locket (Rex/Universal, 1914). Dir.: Lois Weber and Phillips Smalley. Scr.: Lois Weber. Cast: Lois Weber, Phillips Smalley, Rupert Julian. 1 reel. Released 15 Feb 1914.

Woman's Burden (Rex/Universal, 1914). Dir.: Lois Weber and Phillips Smalley. Scr.: Lois Weber. Cast: Lois Weber, Ella Hall, Rupert Julian, Theo Carew, W. C. Browne. 2 reels. Released 22 Feb 1914.

The Weaker Sister (Rex/Universal, 1914). Dir.: Lois Weber and Phillips Smalley. Scr.: Lois Weber. Cast: Lois Weber, Phillips Smalley, Rupert Julian, Ella Hall, Theo Carew, Mrs. Short. 1 reel. Released 1 Mar 1914.

A Modern Fairy Tale (Rex/Universal, 1914). Dir.: Lois Weber and Phillips Smalley. Scr.: Lois Weber. Cast: Rupert Julian, Ella Hall, Phillips Smalley, Theo Carew. 1 reel. Released 8 Mar 1914.

The Spider and Her Web (Rex/Universal, 1914). Dir.: Lois Weber and Phillips Smalley. Scr.: Lois Weber. Cast: Lois Weber, Phillips Smalley, Wallace Reid,

Dorothy Davenport, Rupert Julian, William Wolbert. 2 reels. Released 26 Mar 1914.

In the Days of His Youth (Rex/Universal, 1914). Dir.: Lois Weber and Phillips Smalley. Scr.: Lois Weber. Cast: Phillips Smalley, Rupert Julian, A. McNair, A. Graham. 1 reel. Released 29 Mar 1914.

The Babies' Doll (Rex/Universal, 1914). Dir.: Lois Weber and Phillips Smalley. Scr.: Lois Weber. Cast: Lois Weber, Phillips Smalley, Irma Shorter, Doris Baker, H. Browne. 1 reel. Released 5 Apr 1914.

On Suspicion (Rex/Universal, 1914). Dir.: Lois Weber and Phillips Smalley. Scr.: Lois Weber. Cast: Lois Weber, Phillips Smalley, Henry A. Barrows, Frank Lloyd. 1 reel. Released 19 Apr 1914.

Risen from the Ashes (Rex/Universal 1914). Dir.: Lois Weber and Phillips Smalley. Scr.: Lois Weber. Cast: Lois Weber, Phillips Smalley. 1 reel. Released 23 Apr 1914.

An Episode (Rex/Universal, 1914). Dir.: Lois Weber and Phillips Smalley. Scr.: Lois Weber. Cast: Phillips Smalley, Rupert Julian, Ella Hall, H. Browne, Carmen De Fellippe, P. Emmons. 1 reel. Released 30 Apr 1914.

The Career of Waterloo Peterson (Rex/Universal, 1914). Dir.: Lois Weber and Phillips Smalley. Scr.: Lois Weber. Cast: Rupert Julian, Agnes Gordon, Ella Hall, Richard Rosson, Isidore Bernstein, William Foster, Dal Clawson. Split reel. Released 10 May 1914.

The Triumph of Mind (Bison/Universal, 1914). Dir.: Lois Weber and Phillips Smalley. Scr.: Lois Weber. Cast: Lois Weber, Phillips Smalley, Ella Hall, Rupert Julian, William H. Browne, Elsie Jane Wilson, Agnes Vernon, Philip Rossen. 3 reels. Released 23 May 1914.

Avenged (Rex/Universal, 1914). Dir.: Lois Weber and Phillips Smalley. Scr.: Lois Weber. Cast: Lois Weber, Phillips Smalley, Rupert Julian, Agnes Vernon. 1 reel. Released 24 May 1914.

The Stone in the Road (Rex/Universal, 1914). Dir.: Lois Weber and Phillips Smalley. Scr.: Lois Weber. Cast: Lois Weber, Phillips Smalley. 2 reels. Released 31 May 1914.

Closed Gates (Rex/Universal, 1914). Dir.: Lois Weber and Phillips Smalley. Scr.: Lois Weber. Cast: Lois Weber, Phillips Smalley. 1 reel. Released 7 Jun 1914.

The Pursuit of Hate (Rex/Universal, 1914). Dir.: Lois Weber and Phillips Smalley. Scr.: Lois Weber. Cast: Lois Weber, Phillips Smalley, Rupert Julian, Ella Hall. 1 reel. Released 14 Jun 1914.

Lost by A Hair (Rex/Universal, 1914). Dir.: Lois Weber and Phillips Smalley. Scr.: Lois Weber. Cast: Lois Weber, Phillips Smalley, Joe King, Ella Hall, Berry Schade, Beatrice Van, Phil Carr. 1 reel. Released 28 Jun 1914. Archive: LOC.

The Great Universal Mystery (Universal, 1914). Dir.: Allan Dwan. Cast: King Baggot, Pauline Bush, Ford Sterling, Lois Weber, Ella Hall, Hobart Henley, Francis Ford, Robert Z. Leonard, Cleo Madison, Rupert Julian, J. Warren Kerrigan, Grace Cunard, Phillips Smalley, Herbert Brenon, Carl Laemmle, Ethel Grandin, Matt Moore, Florence Lawrence, William Clifford, William Welsh, Betty Schade, Leah Baird, Al E. Christie, Victoria Forde, Murdock

MacQuarrie, Edna Maison, Frank Crane, Wilfred Lucas, Herbert Rawlinson, Eddie Lyons, Otis Turner. 1 reel. Released 10 Jul 1914.

Plain Mary (Rex/Universal, 1914). Dir.: Lois Weber and Phillips Smalley. Scr.: Lois Weber. Cast: Lois Weber. 1 reel. Released 12 Jul 1914.

Behind the Veil (Rex/Universal, 1914). Dir.: Lois Weber and Phillips Smalley. Scr.: Lois Weber. Cast: Lois Weber, Phillips Smalley. 1 reel. Released 2 Aug 1914.

Daisies (Rex/Universal, 1914). Dir.: Lois Weber and Phillips Smalley. Scr.: Lois Weber. Cast: Lois Weber, Phillips Smalley, Rupert Julian. 1 reel. Released 3 Sept 1914.

Helping Mother (Rex/Universal, 1914). Dir.: Lois Weber and Phillips Smalley. Scr.: Lois Weber. Cast: Lois Weber, Phillips Smalley, Beatrice Van, Joe Young. 3 reels. Released 10 Sept 1914.

The Opened Shutters (Universal, 1914). Dir.: Otis Turner. Adapt.: Lois Weber. Cast: William Worthington, Frank Lloyd, Herbert Rawlinson, Anna Little, Berry Schade, Cora Drew. 4 reels. Released 17 Nov 1914.

*The Traitor (Bosworth/Paramount, 1914). Dir.: Lois Weber and Phillips Smalley. 1 reel. Released Nov 1914.

False Colours (Bosworth/Paramount, 1914). Dir.: Lois Weber and Phillips Smalley. Scr.: Lois Weber. Cast: Lois Weber, Phillips Smalley, Dixie Carr, Adele Farrington, Herbert Standing, Courtenay Foote, Charles Marriott. 5 reels. Released 17 Dec 1914. Archives: LOC, UCLA [inc.].

It's No Laughing Matter (Bosworth/Paramount 1915). Dir. and scr.: Lois Weber. Cam.: Dal Clawson. Cast: Maclyn Arbuckle, Cora Drew, Myrtle Stedman, Charles Marriott, Adele Farrington, Frank Elliot. 4–5 reels. Released 14 Jan 1915. Archive: LOC [inc.].

Hypocrites (Bosworth/Paramount, 1915). Dir. and scr.: Lois Weber. Cam.: Dal Clawson and George W. Hill. Cast: Courtenay Foote, Herbert Standing, Myrtle Steadman, Adele Farrington, Margaret Edwards, Dixie Carr, Nigel de Brullier, Matty Roubert. 4 reels. Released 20 Jan 1915. Archives: AUS, LOC, UCLA.

Sunshine Molly (Bosworth/Paramount, 1915). Dir.: Lois Weber and Phillips Smalley. Scr.: Lois Weber. Story: Alice von Saxmar. Cam.: Dal Clawson. Cast.: Lois Weber, Phillips Smalley, Adele Farrington, Margaret Edwards, Herbert Standing, Vera Lewis, Roberta Hickman, Charles Marriot. 5 reels. Released 11 Mar 1915. Archive: LOC [inc.].

Captain Courtesy (Bosworth/Paramount, 1915). Dir.: Lois Weber. Cam.: Dal Clawson. Cast: Dustin Farnum, Courtenay Foote, Winifred Kingston, Herbert Standing, Jack Hoxie. 5 reels. Released 19 Apr 1915.

*Betty in Search of a Thrill (Bosworth/Paramount, 1915). Dir.: Phillips Smalley and Lois Weber? Scr.: Elsie Janis. Cast: Elsie Janis, Owen Moore, Juanita Hansen, Herbert Standing, Vera Lewis. 5 reels. Released 17 May 1915.

Scandal (Universal, 1915). Dir.: Lois Weber and Phillips Smalley. Scr.: Lois Weber. Cam.: Dal Clawson. Cast: Lois Weber, Phillips Smalley, Rupert Julian, Adele Farrington, Abe Mundon, Alice Thomson, Grace Johnson, Jim Mason,

Sis Matthews. 5 reels. Released 10 Jul 1915. Archive: LOC. (Note: archive print is 1918 reissue version.)

A Cigarette—That's All (Universal, 1915). Dir.: Lois Weber and Phillips Smalley. Scr.: Lois Weber. Story: Helena Evans. Cast: Jack Holt, Phillips Smalley, Maude George, Rupert Julian, H. Scott Leslie. 2 reels. Released 10 Aug 1915. Archive: BFI.

Jewel (Universal, 1915). Dir.: Lois Weber and Phillips Smalley. Adapt.: Lois Weber. Cast: Ella Hall, Rupert Julian, Frank Elliot, Hilda Hollis Sloman, Miss Brownell, T.D. Crittenden, Dixie Carr, T.W. Gowland, Abe Mundon, Jack Holt, Lule Warrenton. 5 reels. Released 30 Aug 1915.

Discontent (Universal, 1916). Dir.: Allen Siegler or Lois Weber. Scr.: Lois Weber. Cast: J. Edward Brown, Charles Hammond, Katherine Griffith, Marie Walcamp. 1 reel. Released 25 Jan 1916. Archive: LOC.

Hop, the Devil's Brew (Bluebird/Universal, 1916). Dir.: Lois Weber and Phillips Smalley. Scr.: Lois Weber. Cam.: Allen Siegler and Frank Williams. Cast: Lois Weber, Phillips Smalley, Marie Walcamp, Charles Hammond, Juan De La Cruz, Ethel Weber. 5 reels. Released 14 Feb 1916.

The Flirt (Bluebird/Universal, 1916). Dir.: Lois Weber and Phillips Smalley. Scr.: Lois Weber. Cast: Marie Walcamp, Grace Benham, Antrim Short, Ogden Crane, Nannine Wright, Juan De La Cruz, Paul Byron, Fred Church, Robert Lawlor, Robert M. Dunbar. 5 reels. Released 26 Mar 1916.

There Is No Place like Home (Rex/Universal, 1916). Dir. and scr.: Lois Weber. Cast: Antrim Short, Lou Short, Mrs. Short. 1 reel. Released 28 Mar 1916.

The Dumb Girl of Portici (Universal, 1916). Dir.: Lois Weber and Phillips Smalley. Adapt.: Lois Weber. Cam.: Dal Clawson, Allen Siegler, and R.W. Walter. Cast: Anna Pavlova, Rupert Julian, Laura Oakley, Wadsworth Harris, Douglas Gerrard, John Holt, Berry Schade, Edna Maison, Hart Hoxie, William Wolbert, N. De Brouillet, George A. Williams. 7–11 reels. Released 3 Apr 1916. Archives: BFI, LOC.

John Needham's Double (Bluebird/Universal, 1916). Dir.: Lois Weber and Phillips Smalley. Adapt.: Olga Printzlau. Cam.: Stephen S. Norton and Allen Siegler. Cast: Tyrone Power, Agnes Emerson, Frank Elliot, Walter Belasco, Frank Lanning, Buster Emmons, Marie Walcamp. 5 reels. Released 10 Apr 1916.

The Toll of the Angelus (Universal, 1916). Dir.: Lois Weber and Phillips Smalley. Scr.: Lois Weber. Cast: Lois Weber, Phillips Smalley. 1 reel. Released 14 Apr 1916. (Note: a rerelease of 1913's *The Angelus*.)

Where Are My Children? (Universal, 1916). Dir.: Lois Weber and Phillips Smalley. Scr.: Lois Weber. Story: Lucy Payton and Franklin Hall. Cam.: Allen Sieger and Stephen S. Norton. Cast: Tyrone Power, Helen Riaume, Marie Walcamp, Cora Drew, Juan De La Cruz, Rene Rogers, A.D. Blake, Mary MacLaren. 5 reels. Released May 1916. Archive: LOC.

The Eye of God (Bluebird/Universal, 1916). Dir.: Lois Weber and Phillips Smalley. Scr.: Lois Weber. Cam.: Stephen S. Norton and Allen Siegler. Cast: Tyrone Power, Ethel Weber, Lois Weber, Charles Gunn. 5 reels. Released 5 Jun 1916.

Shoes (Bluebird/Universal, 1916). Dir. and scr.: Lois Weber. Cam.: Stephen S. Norton, King D. Gray, and Allen Siegler. Cast: Mary MacLaren, Harry Griffith, Mrs. Witting, Jessie Arnold, William Mong. 5 reels. Released 26 Jun 1916. Archives: EYE, LOC, NFC. (Note: LOC footage is contained in reedited 1932 parody of the film entitled *The Unshod Maiden*.)

Saving the Family Name (Bluebird/Universal, 1916). Dir.: Lois Weber and Phillips Smalley. Scr.: Lois Weber. Cam.: Allen Siegler. Cast: Mary MacLaren, Girrard Alexander, Carl von Schiller, Jack Holt, Phillips Smalley, Harry Depp. 5 reels. Released 11 Sept 1916. Archives: LOC, CNC [inc.].

Idle Wives (Universal, 1916). Dir.: Lois Weber and Phillips Smalley. Scr.: Lois Weber. Cam.: Allen Siegler. Cast: Lois Weber, Phillips Smalley, Mary MacLaren, Edwin Hearn, Seymour Hastings, Countess Du Cello Pauline Aster, Cecilia Matthews, Ben Wilson, Maude George, Never Gerber. 7 reels. Released 18 Sept 1916. Archives: LOC, NZ [inc.].

Under the Spell (Rex/Universal, 1916). Dir.: Lois Weber and Phillips Smalley. Cast: Lois Weber, Phillips Smalley, Douglas Gerrard, Lule Warenton. 1 reel. Released 24 Sept 1916. (Note: a rerelease of 1913's *The Dragon's Breath*.)

The Halting Hand (Rex/Universal, 1916). Dir.: Lois Weber and Phillips Smalley. Cast: Lois Weber, Phillips Smalley, Douglas Gerrard, Lule Warenton. 1 reel. Released 25 Sept 1916. (Note: a rerelease of 1913's *Until*.)

Wanted—A Home (Universal, 1916). Dir.: Phillips Smalley. Scr.: Lois Weber. Cam.: Allen Siegler. Cast: Mary MacLaren, Jack Mulhall, Charles Marriott, Grace Johnson, Horace Morgan, Marian Sigler. 5 reels. Released 2 Oct 1916.

The Children Shall Pay (Universal, 1916). Dir.: Lois Weber and Phillips Smalley. Scr.: Lois Weber. Cast: Lois Weber, Phillips Smalley. 1 reel. Released 6 Dec 1916. (Note: a rerelease of 1914's *Behind the Veil*.)

The People vs. John Doe (Universal, 1916). Dir. and scr.: Lois Weber. Cam.: Allen Siegler. Cast: Harry De More, Evelyn Selbie, Willis Marks, Leah Baird, Maude George, Charles Hill Mailes, Robert Smith. 6 reels. Released 10 Dec 1916. Archive: LOC [inc.].

The Rock of Riches (Rex/Universal, 1916). Dir.: Lois Weber and Phillips Smalley. Scr.: Lois Weber. Cast: Lois Weber, Phillips Smalley. 1 reel. Released 23 Dec 1916. (Note: a rerelease of 1914's *The Stone in the Road*.)

The Gilded Life (Rex/Universal, 1916). Dir.: Lois Weber and Phillips Smalley. Scr.: Lois Weber. Cast: Lois Weber and Phillips Smalley. 2 reels. Released 29 Dec 1916. (Note: a rerelease 1913's *The Fallen Angel*.)

Alone in the World (Rex/Universal, 1916). Dir.: Lois Weber and Phillips Smalley. Scr.: Lois Weber. Cast: Lois Weber, Phillips Smalley, Antrim Short. 1 reel. Released 3 Jan 1917. (Note: a rerelease of 1913's *Bobby's Baby*.)

The Face Downstairs (Rex/Universal, 1917). Dir.: Lois Weber and Phillips Smalley. Scr.: Lois Weber. Cast: Lois Weber, Valentine Paul, Douglas Gerrard, Sam Kaufman. 1 reel. Released 10 Jan 1917. (Note: a rerelease of 1913's *Suspense*.)

The Mysterious Mrs. M. (Bluebird/Universal, 1917). Dir. and scr.: Lois Weber. Cam.: Allen Siegler. Cast: Harrison Ford, Mary MacLaren, Evelyn Selbie,

Willis Marks, Frank Brownlee, Bertram Grassby, Charles Mailes. 5 reels. Released 5 Feb 1917. Archive: LOC [inc.].

The Boyhood He Forgot (Rex/Universal, 1917). Dir.: Lois Weber and Phillips Smalley. Scr.: Lois Weber. Cast: Phillips Smalley, Rupert Julian, A. McNair, A. Graham. 1 reel. Released 24 Mar 1917. Note: a rerelease of *In the Days of His Youth.*)

Even as You and I (Universal, 1917). Dir.: Lois Weber. Scr.: Maude Grange. Story: Willis Woods. Cam.: Allen Siegler. Cast: Mignon Anderson, Ben Wilson, Bertram Grassby, Priscilla Dean, Harry Carter, Maude George, Hayward Mack, Earle Page, E. N. Wallock, Seymour Hastings, W. Mitchell. 7 reels. Released Apr 1917.

The Hand That Rocks the Cradle (Universal, 1917). Dir. and scr.: Lois Weber. Cam.: Allen Siegler. Cast: Lois Weber, Phillips Smalley, Priscilla Dean, Wedgewood Nowell, Evelyn Selbie, Harry De More. 6 reels. Released 13 May 1917.

The Price of a Good Time (Lois Weber Productions/Universal Jewel, 1917). Prod., dir., and scr.: Lois Weber. Story: Marion Orth. Cam: Allen Siegler. Cast: Mildred Harris, Ann Schaefer, Helene Rosson, Kenneth Harlan, Alfred Allen, Adele Farrington, Gertrude Astor. 6 reels. Released 4 Nov 1917.

The Doctor and the Woman (Lois Weber Productions/Universal Jewel, 1918). Prod., dir., and scr.: Lois Weber. Cam: Allen Siegler. Cast: Mildred Harris, True Boardman, Albert Roscoe, Zella Caull, Carl Miller. 6 reels. Released 4 Mar 1918.

For Husbands Only (Lois Weber Productions/Universal Jewel, 1918). Prod., dir., and adapt.: Lois Weber. Story: G. B. Stern. Cam.: Dal Clawson. Cast: Mildred Harris, Lew Cody, Fred Goodwins, Kathleen Kirkham, Henry A. Barrows. 6 reels. Released Aug 1918.

Borrowed Clothes (Lois Weber Productions/Universal Jewel, 1918). Prod., dir., and scr.: Lois Weber. Story: Marion Orth. Cam.: Roy Klaffki. Cast: Mildred Harris, Lew Cody, Edward J. Peel, Helen Rosson, George Nichols, Edythe Chapman, Fantine La Rue. 6 reels. Released 4 Nov 1918.

When a Girl Loves (Lois Weber Productions/Universal Jewel, 1919). Prod., dir., and scr.: Lois Weber. Cam.: Dal Clawson. Cast: Mildred Harris, William Stowell, Wharton Jones, Alfred Paget, Willis Marks. 6 reels. Released 15 Feb, 1919.

A Midnight Romance (Anita Stewart Productions/First National, 1919). Prod.: Louis B. Mayer. Dir. and scr.: Lois Weber. Cam.: Dal Clawson. Cast: Anita Stewart, Jack Holt, Edward Tilton, Elinor Hancock, Helen Yoder, Juanita Hansen, Montague Dumont. 6 reels. Released March 10, 1919. Archive: LOC [inc.].

Mary Regan (Anita Stewart Productions/First National, 1919). Prod.: Louis B. Mayer. Dir. and adapt.: Lois Weber. Cam.: Dal Clawson. Cast: Anita Stewart, Frank Mayo, Carl Miller, Barney Sherry, Brinsley Shaw, George Hernandez, L. W. Steers, Hedda Nova, Syn De Cona. 7 reels. Released 18 May 1919. Archive: CF.

Home (Lois Weber Productions/Universal, 1919). Prod., dir., and scr.: Lois Weber. Cast: Mildred Harris, Frank Elliott, John Cossar, Clarissa Selwynne, Dwight Crittenden, Lydia Knott. 6 reels. Released 31 Aug 1919.

Forbidden (Lois Weber Productions/Universal, 1919). Prod., dir., and scr.: Lois Weber. Story: E. V. Durling. Cam.: Roy Klaffki and Dal Clawson. Cast: Mildred Harris, Henry Woodward, Fred Goodwins, Priscilla Dean. 6 reels. Released 8 Sept 1919.

To Please One Woman (Lois Weber Productions/Paramount, 1921). Prod., dir., and scr.: Lois Weber. Cast: Claire Windsor, Edith Kessler, George Hackathorne, Edward Burns, Mona Lisa, Howard Gaye, L. C. Shumway, Gordon Griffith. 7 reels. Released 19 Dec 1920. Archive: WISC [inc.].

What's Worth While? (Lois Weber Productions/Paramount, 1921). Prod., dir., and scr.: Lois Weber. Cam.: William C. Foster. Cast: Claire Windsor, Arthur Stuart Hull, Mona Lisa, Louis Calhern. 6 reels. Released 27 Feb 1921. Archive: LOC [inc.].

Too Wise Wives (Lois Weber Productions/Paramount, 1921). Prod., dir., and scr.: Lois Weber. Story: Lois Weber and Marion Orth. Cam.: William C. Foster. Cast: Claire Windsor, Louis Calhern, Phillips Smalley, Mona Lisa. 6 reels. Released 22 May 1921. Archives: LOC, UCLA, ITG.

The Blot (Lois Weber Productions/F. B. Warren Corp., 1921). Prod., dir., and scr.: Lois Weber. Cam.: Philip R. Du Bois and Gordon Jennings. Cast: Claire Windsor, Louis Calhern, Margaret McWade, Marie Walcamp, Philip Hubbard. 7 reels. Released 4 Sept 1921. Archives: LOC, MOMA, UCLA, BFI.

What Do Men Want? (Lois Weber Productions/Wid Gunning Inc., 1921). Prod., dir., and scr.: Lois Weber. Cam.: Dal Clawson. Cast: Claire Windsor, J. Frank Glendon, George Jackathorne, Hallam Cooley, Edith Kessler. 7 reels. Released 3 Nov 1921. Archives: LOC, UCLA [inc.].

A Chapter in Her Life (Universal, 1923). Dir.: Lois Weber. Adapt.: Lois Weber and Doris Schroeder. Cam.: Ben Kline. Cast: Jane Mercer, Claude Gillingswater, Jacqueline Gadsden, Frances Raymond, Robert Frazer, Fred Thomson. 6 reels. Released 17 Sept 1923. Archives: LOC, UCLA, BFI, NILES.

The Marriage Clause (Universal, 1926). Dir. and adapt.: Lois Weber. Cam.: Hal Mohr. Cast: Billie Dove, Francis X. Bushman, Warner Oland, Henri La Garde, Grace Darmond. 8 reels. Released 12 Sept 1926. Archive: LOC [inc.].

Sensation Seekers (Universal, 1926). Dir. and scr.: Lois Weber. Cam.: Ben Kline. Cast: Billie Dove, Huntley Gordon, Raymond Bloomer, Phillips Smalley, Peggy Montgomery, Will Gregory, Helen Gilmore, Edith Yorke, Cora Williams, Sidney Arundel. 7 reels. Released 20 Mar 1927. Archive: UCLA.

Topsy and Eva (Feature Productions/United Artists, 1927). Dir.: Del Lord. Scr.: Scott Darling. Adapt.: Lois Weber [uncredited]. Cam.: John W. Boyle. Cast: Rosetta Duncan, Vivian Duncan, Gibson Gowland, Noble Johnson, Nils Asther, Marjorie Daw, Myrtle Ferguson, Henry Victor. 8 reels. Released 16 Jun 1927. Archives: LOC, UCLA [inc.].

The Angel of Broadway (DeMille Pictures/Pathé Exchange, 1927). Dir.: Lois Weber. Scr.: Lenore Coffee. Cam.: Arthur Miller. Cast: Leatrice Joy, Victor

Varconi, May Robson, Alice Lake, Elsie Bartlett, Ivan Lebedeff. 7 reels. Released 3 Oct 1927.

White Heat (Seven Seas Corp./Pinnacle Productions, 1934). Dir. and scr.: Lois Weber. Story: James Bodrero. Cam.: Alvin Wyckoff and Frank Titus. Cast: Virginia Cherrill, Mona Maris, Hardie Albright, David Newell. 6 reels. Released 15 Jul 1934.

Index

CPSIA information can be obtained
at www.ICGtesting.com
Printed in the USA
LVHW111548200220
647643LV00003B/644